WEBSTER'S
INSTANT WORD GUIDE

Webster's

INSTANT
WORD
GUIDE

A Merriam-Webster®

G. & C. MERRIAM COMPANY

Springfield, Massachusetts

Library of Congress Cataloging in Publication Data

Main entry under title:

Webster's instant word guide.

"A Merriam-Webster"

Based on Webster's seventh new collegiate dictionary.

1. Spellers.

PE1146.W37   428'.1   72-1947

ISBN 0-87779-173-2

MADE IN THE U.S.A.

91011KP7675

CONTENTS

PREFACE

Webster's Instant Word Guide is a convenient, quick-reference aid to word division, spelling, and often-confused words. Word division is based on the world-famous *Webster's Seventh New Collegiate Dictionary* and is indicated by a centered dot (*e.g.*, dis·cern·ible). The main stress, or emphasis in pronunciation, is indicated by a heavy mark following the stressed element (*e.g.*, em′pha·sis). In some words the stressed element is not suggested as a division point and the stress mark appears alone, without a centered dot (*e.g.*, a′bly). In some words of two syllables, the stress is equal and no stress mark is shown.

All who use words professionally—secretaries, students, writers—are continually faced with problems of where to divide a word at the end of a line, whether it is one *l* or two, is it *−er* or *−or*. *Webster's Instant Word Guide* is designed to provide fast help. In addition to indicating word division and spelling for more than 35,000 words, the handy guide gives hundreds of irregular forms and differentiates often-confused words by providing brief indicators of sense or short definitions. Included in the A−Z word list are the names of the U.S. states and major U.S. cities, the names of the world's countries, and adjectives of nationality. The names of foreign currency units are also listed.

Webster's Instant Word Guide offers a brief review of punctuation to aid the user faced with a problem such as *comma* or *semicolon*. The guide also includes a handy table of weights and measures, which indicates the metric system equivalents of standard U.S. measures. In addition, the guide contains a listing of some 1500 abbreviations and an easy-to-use table showing proofreaders' marks and symbols.

Although there are few hard-and-fast rules for end-of-line division of words, current practice provides some guidance. A single letter is not broken off, and many prefer to avoid breaking off a final unit of only two letters. The word guide indicates breaking points with a centered dot in cases of two letters, however, for those situations where it may be necessary. Other breaking points that are generally avoided include compound words joined by a hyphen. Most people avoid breaking such words at any point other than at the hyphen (e.g., *long-distance*). Dividing words at the end of consecutive lines is also generally avoided, and few would have more than two consecutive lines with end-of-line divisions. Abbreviations, contractions, and numbers are not divided, nor is the last word of a paragraph or of a page.

A

aard'vark
ab'a·cus
  pl ab'a·ci *or*
    ab'a·cus·es
ab·a·lo'ne
aban'don
aban'doned
aban'don·ment
abase'
abase'ment
abash'
abate'
abate'ment
ab'a·tis
  pl ab'a·tis *or*
    ab'a·tis·es
ab'at·toir
ab·ax'i·al
ab'ba·cy
ab·bé'
ab'bess
ab'bey
ab'bot
ab·bre'vi·ate
ab·bre'vi·at·ing
ab·bre·vi·a'tion
ab'di·cate
ab·di·ca'tion
ab'do·men
ab·dom'i·nal
ab·duct'
ab·duc'tion
ab·duc'tor
abe·ce·dar'i·an
ab·er'rant

ab·er·ra'tion
abet'
  abet'ted
  abet'ting
abet'tor
  or abet'ter
abey'ance
ab·hor'
ab·horred'
ab·hor'rence
ab·hor'rent
ab·hor'ring
abide
abil'i·ties
abil'i·ty
ab'ject
ab·jec'tion
ab'ject·ly
ab'ject·ness
ab·ju·ra'tion
ab·jure'
ab·late'
ab·la'tion
ab·la'tive
ab·la'tor
ablaze'
a'ble
able-bod'ied
ab·lu'tion
ab'ne·gate
ab·ne·ga'tion
ab·nor'mal
ab·nor·mal'i·ty
ab·nor'mal·ly
aboard'

abode'
abol'ish
ab·o·li'tion
ab·o·li'tion·ist
A'-bomb
abom'i·na·ble
abom'i·nate
abom·i·na'tion
ab·orig'i·nal
ab·orig'i·ne
aborn'ing
abort'
abor'tion
abor'tion·ist
abor'tive
abound'
about'
about-face'
above'
above'board
ab·ra·ca·dab'ra
abrade'
abra'sion
abra'sive
ab·re·act'
abreast'
abridge'
abridg'ment
  or abridge'ment
abroad'
ab'ro·gate
ab·ro·ga'tion
abrupt'
ab'scess
ab·scis'sa

1

ab·scis'sion
ab·scond'
ab'sence
ab'sent
ab'sen·tee
ab·sen·tee'ism
ab·sent·mind'ed
ab'sinthe
ab'so·lute
ab'so·lute·ly
ab·so·lu'tion
ab'so·lut·ism
ab·solve'
ab·sorb'
ab·sor'ben·cy
ab·sor'bent
ab·sorp'tion
ab·sorp'tive
ab·stain'
ab·ste'mi·ous
ab·sten'tion
ab'sti·nence
ab·stract'
ab·strac'tion
ab·struse'
ab·surd'
ab·sur'di·ty
abun'dance
abun'dant
abuse'
abu'sive
abut'
abut'ment
abut'tals
abut'ted
abut'ting

abys'mal
abys'mal·ly
abyss'
abys'sal
aca'cia
ac'a·deme
ac·a·dem'ic
ac·a·dem'i·cal·ly
ac·a·de·mi'cian
ac·a·dem'i·cism
acad'e·my
acan'thus
a cap·pel'la
ac·cede'
   *to agree (see
    exceed)*
ac·ce·le·ran'do
ac·cel'er·ate
ac·cel·er·a'tion
ac·cel'er·a·tor
ac'cent
ac·cen'tu·al
ac·cen'tu·ate
ac·cen·tu·a'tion
ac·cept'
   *to receive (see
    except)*
ac·cept·abil'i·ty
ac·cept'able
ac·cep'tance
ac·cep·ta'tion
ac'cess
   *approach (see
    excess)*
ac·ces'si·ble
ac·ces·si·bil'i·ty

ac·ces'sion
ac·ces'so·ry
ac'ci·dence
ac'ci·dent
ac·ci·den'tal
ac·ci·den'tal·ly
ac·claim'
ac·cla·ma'tion
ac·cli'mate
ac·cli·ma·ti·za'
   tion
ac·cli'ma·tize
ac·cliv'i·ty
ac'co·lade
ac·com'mo·date
ac·com'mo·dat·
   ing
ac·com·mo·da'
   tion
ac·com'pa·ni·
   ment
ac·com'pa·nist
ac·com'pa·ny
ac·com'plice
ac·com'plish
ac·com'plished
ac·com'plish·
   ment
ac·cord'
ac·cor'dance
ac·cor'dant
ac·cord'ing·ly
ac·cor'di·on
ac·cost'
ac·count'
ac·count·abil'i·ty

ac·count'a·ble

ac·coun'tan·cy

ac·coun'tant

ac·count'ing

ac·cou'ter

ac·cou'ter·ment

ac·cred'it

ac·cred·i·ta'tion

ac·cre'tion

ac·cru'al

ac·crue'

ac·cru'ing

ac·cul'tur·ate

ac·cul·tur·a'tion

ac·cu'mu·late

ac·cu·mu·la'tion

ac·cu'mu·la·tor

ac'cu·ra·cy

ac'cu·rate

ac'cu·rate·ly

ac'cu·rate·ness

ac·cursed'

ac·cus'al

ac·cu·sa'tion

ac·cu'sa·tive

ac·cuse'

ac·cus'er

ac·cus'tom

ac·cus'tomed

acer'bi·ty

ac·et·al'de·hyde

ac·et·an'i·lide

ac'e·tate

ace'tic
   chem (*see* ascetic)

ac'e·tone

acet'y·lene

ache

achieve'

achieve'ment

ach'ing

ach·ro·mat'ic

ac'id

acid'ic

acid·i·fi·ca'tion

acid'i·fy

acid'i·ty

ac·i·do'sis

acid'u·late

acid'u·lous

ack'ack

ac·knowl'edge

ac·knowl'edg·
   ment
   also ac·knowl'edge·
   ment

ac'me

ac'ne

ac'o·lyte

ac'o·nite

a'corn

acous'tic

acous'ti·cal

acous'ti·cal·ly

acous'tics

ac·quaint'

ac·quaint'ance

ac·quaint'ance-
   ship

ac·qui·esce'

ac·qui·es'cence

ac·qui·es'cent

ac·quire'

ac·quire'ment

ac·qui·si'tion

ac·quis'i·tive

ac·quis'i·tive·ness

ac·quit'

ac·quit'tal

ac·quit'ted

ac·quit'ting

a'cre

a'cre·age

ac'rid

acrid'i·ty

ac·ri·mo'ni·ous

ac'ri·mo·ny

ac'ro·bat

ac·ro·bat'ic

ac'ro·nym

ac·ro·pho'bia

acrop'o·lis

across'

across-the-board

acros'tic

ac'ry·late

acryl'ic

act'ing

ac·tin'ic

ac·tin'i·um

ac'tion

ac'tion·a·ble

ac'ti·vate

ac·ti·va'tion

ac'tive

ac'tive·ly

ac'tiv·ism

ac'tiv·ist

ac·tiv'i·ty
ac'tor
ac'tress
ac'tu·al
ac·tu·al'i·ty
ac'tu·al·ly
ac·tu·ar'i·al
ac'tu·ary
ac'tu·ate
ac'tu·a·tor
acu'i·ty
acu'men
ac'u·punc·ture
acute'
acute'ly
acute'ness
ad'age
ada'gio
ad'a·mant
ad·a·man'tine
ad'a·mant·ly
adapt'
  to fit (see adept;
  adopt)
adapt·abil'i·ty
adapt'able
ad·ap·ta'tion
adapt'er
ad'dend
ad·den'dum
  pl ad·den'da
ad'der
  snake
add'er
  one that adds
ad·dict'
  verb

ad'dict
  noun
ad·dic'tion
ad·dic'tive
ad·di'tion
ad·di'tion·al
ad·di'tion·al·ly
ad'di·tive
ad'dle
ad·dress'
ad·dress·ee'
ad·duce'
ad'e·noid
ad·e·noi'dal
ad'ept
  expert
adept'
  skilled (see adapt;
  adopt)
adept'ly
adept'ness
ad'e·qua·cy
ad'e·quate
ad'e·quate·ly
ad·here'
ad·her'ence
ad·her'ent
ad·he'sion
ad·he'sive
ad·he'sive·ness
ad hoc'
ad·i·a·bat'ic
adieu'
  pl adieus *or* adieux
ad in·fi·ni'tum
ad in'ter·im
adi·os'

ad'i·pose
ad·i·pos'i·ty
ad·ja'cent
ad·jec·ti'val
ad·jec·ti'val·ly
ad'jec·tive
ad·join'
ad·join'ing
ad·journ'
ad·journ'ment
ad·judge'
ad·ju'di·cate
ad·ju'di·ca·tion
ad'junct
ad·ju·ra'tion
ad·jure'
ad·just'
ad·just'able
ad·just'er
  or ad·jus'tor
ad·just'ment
ad'ju·tant
ad'ju·vant
ad lib'
  adverb
ad-lib'
  ad-libbed'
  ad-lib'bing
ad lib'i·tum
ad'man
ad·min'is·ter
ad·min'is·tra·ble
ad·min'is·trant
ad·min'is·trate
ad·min'is·tra'tion
ad·min'is·tra·tive
ad·min'is·tra·tor

ad′mi·ra·ble
ad′mi·ra·bly
ad′mi·ral
ad′mi·ral·ty
ad·mi·ra′tion
ad·mire′
ad·mir′er
ad·mis·si·bil′i·ty
ad·mis′si·ble
ad·mis′si·bly
ad·mis′sion
ad·mit′
ad·mit′tance
ad·mit′ted
ad·mit′ted·ly
ad·mit′ting
ad·mix′
ad·mix′ture
ad·mon′ish
ad·mo·ni′tion
ad·mon′i·to·ry
ad nau′se·am
ado′
ado′be
ad·o·les′cence
ad·o·les′cent
adopt′
  to accept (see adapt, adept)

adop′tion
adop′tive
ador′able
ad·o·ra′tion
adore′
adorn′
adorn′ment
adre′nal

adren′a·line
adre′nin
adrift′
adroit′
adroit′ly
adroit′ness
ad·sorb′
ad·sor′bent
ad·sorp′tion
ad·sorp′tive
ad′u·late
ad·u·la′tion
adult′
adul′ter·ant
adul′ter·ate
adul·ter·a′tion
adul′ter·er
adul′ter·ess
adul′ter·ous
adul′tery
adult′hood
ad′um·brate
ad·um·bra′tion
ad va·lo′rem
ad·vance′
ad·vance′ment
ad·van′tage
ad·van·ta′geous
ad′vent
ad·ven·ti′tious
ad·ven′ture
ad·ven′tur·er
ad·ven′ture·some
ad·ven′tur·ess
ad·ven′tur·ous
ad′verb
ad·ver′bi·al

ad·ver′bi·al·ly
ad′ver·sary
ad·ver′sa·tive
ad·ver′sa·tive·ly
ad·verse′
  against (see averse)

ad·verse′ly
ad·ver′si·ty
ad·vert′
ad′ver·tise
ad·ver·tise′ment
ad′ver·tis·er
ad′ver·tis·ing
ad·vice′
  noun, counsel (see advise)

ad·vis·abil′i·ty
ad·vis′able
ad·vise′
  verb, to give advice (see advice)

ad·vis′er
  or ad·vi′sor

ad·vise′ment
ad·vi′so·ry
ad′vo·ca·cy
ad′vo·cate
ae′gis
ae·o′li·an
ae′on
aer′ate
aer·a′tion
aer′i·al
aer′i·al·ist
aer′ie
a′ero
aer·o·bat′ics

aer'obe
aer·o'bic
aer'o·drome
aero·dy·nam'i·cal·ly
aero·dy·nam'ics
aer·o·log'i·cal
aer·ol'o·gist
aer·ol'o·gy
aer'o·naut
aer·o·nau'ti·cal
aer·o·nau'tics
aer·o·nom'i·cal
aer·on'o·mist
aer·on'o·my
aer'o·pause
aer'o·sol
ae'ro·space
a'ery
aes'thete
aes·thet'ic
aes·thet'i·cal·ly
aes·thet'i·cism
aes·thet'ics
aes'ti·vate
aes·ti·va'tion
af·fa·bil'i·ty
af'fa·ble
af'fa·bly
af·fair'
af·fect'
    to influence (see effect)
af·fec·ta'tion
af·fect'ed
af·fect'ing
af·fec'tion

af·fec'tion·ate
af'fer·ent
af·fi'ance
af·fi·da'vit
af·fil'i·ate
af·fil·i·a'tion
af·fin'i·ty
af·firm'
af·fir·ma'tion
af·fir'ma·tive
af·fix'
af·fla'tus
af·flict'
af·flic'tion
af·flic'tive
af'flu·ence
af'flu·ent
af·ford'
af·fray'
af·fright'
af·front'
af'ghan
af·ghan'i
Af·ghan'i·stan
afi·cio·na'do
afield'
afire'
aflame'
afloat'
aflut'ter
afoot'
afore'men·tioned
afore'said
afore'thought
afore'time
a for·ti·o'ri
afoul'

afraid'
afresh'
Af'ri·can
Af·ri·kaans'
Af'ro
af'ter
af'ter·birth
af'ter·burn·er
af'ter·care
af'ter·deck
af'ter·ef·fect
af'ter·glow
af'ter·life
af'ter·math
af·ter·noon'
af'ter·taste
af'ter·tax'
af'ter·thought
af'ter·ward
again'
against'
Aga'na
agape'
    adjective, gaping
aga'pe
    noun, self-giving concern
ag'ate
ag'ate·ware
aga've
age'less
a'gen·cy
agen'da
a'gent
age'-old
ag·gior·na·men'to
ag·glom'er·ate

ag·glom·er·a′tion
ag·glu′ti·nate
ag·glu·ti·na′tion
ag·gran′dize
ag·gran′dize·
  ment
ag′gra·vate
ag·gra·va′tion
ag′gre·gate
ag·gre·ga′tion
ag·gres′sion
ag·gres′sive
ag·gres′sive·ness
ag·gres′sor
ag·grieve′
aghast′
ag′ile
agil′i·ty
ag′i·tate
ag·i·ta′tion
ag′i·ta·tor
agleam′
aglit′ter
aglow′
ag·nos′tic
ag·nos′ti·cism
agog′
ag′o·nize
ag′o·niz·ing·ly
ag′o·ny
ago·ra′
  pl ago·rot′
ag·o·ra·pho′bia
ag·o·ra·pho′bic
agrar′i·an
agrav′ic
agree′

agree·abil′i·ty
agree′able
agree′able·ness
agree′ably
agree′ment
ag·ri·cul′tur·al
ag′ri·cul·ture
ag′ri·cul′tur·ist
ag·ro·nom′ic
ag·ro·nom′i·cal·ly
agron′o·mist
agron′o·my
aground′
a′gue
ahead′
ahoy′
aid
  help
aide
  assistant
aide-de-camp′
  pl aides-de-camp′
ai·grette′
ail
  ill (see ale)
ai′le·ron
ail′ment
aim′less
air
  chem (see heir)
air′borne
air′brush
air′bus
air-con·di′tioned
air·con·di′tion·er
air′con·di·tion·ing
air-cool

air′craft
air′crew
air′drome
air′drop
air-dry
air′field
air′flow
air′foil
air′frame
air′glow
air′lift
air′line
air′lin·er
air′mail
air′man
air mile
air-mind′ed
air′mo·bile
air′plane
air′port
air′post
air′ship
air′sick
air′-sick·ness
air′space
air′speed
air′stream
air′strip
air′tight
air-to-air′
air′wave
air′way
air′wor·thy
air′wor·thi·ness
air′y
aisle
  passage (see isle)

ajar′
akim′bo
Ak′ron
Al·a·bam′a
al′a·bas·ter
a la carte′
alac′ri·ty
a la mode′
alarm′
alarm′ist
Alas′ka
al′ba·core
Al·ba′nia
Al·ba′nian
Al′ba·ny
al′ba·tross
al·be′it
Al·ber′ta
al′bi·nism
al·bi′no
al′bum
al·bu′men
 egg white
al·bu′min
 protein
al·bu′min·
 ous
Al′bu·quer·
 que
al·cal′de
al·ca′zar
al′che·mist
al′che·my
al′co·hol
al·co·hol′ic
al′co·hol·ism

al′cove
al′der
al′der·man
ale
 beverage (see ail)
ale·a·tor′ic
ale′house
ale′wife
alert′
alert′ness
Al·ex·an′dria
al·ex·an′drine
al·fal′fa
al·fres′co
al′ga
 pl al·gae
al′ge·bra
al·ge·bra′ic
al′ge·ny
Al·ge′ria
Al·ge′ri·an
al′go·rithm
a′li·as
a′li·bi
a′lien
a′lien·able
a′lien·ate
alien·a′tion
a′lien·ist
alight′
align′
 also aline′
align′ment
 also aline′ment
alike′
al′i·ment

al·i·men′ta·ry
al′i·mo·ny
al′i·quot
alive′
al′ka·li
al′ka·line
al·ka·lin′i·ty
al′ka·lin·ize
al′ka·lize
al′ka·loid
al′kyd
all
 the whole (see awl)
Al′lah
all-Ameri′i·can
all-around′
al·lay′
al·le·ga′tion
al·lege′
al·leg′ed·ly
Al·le·ghe′ny
al·le′giance
al·le·gor′i·cal
al′le·go·ry
al·le′gro
al·le·lu′ia
Al′len·town
al′ler·gen
al·ler·gen′ic
al·ler′gic
al′ler·gist
al′ler·gy
al·le′vi·ate
al·le·vi·a′tion
al′ley
 passage (see ally)

al'ley·way
All·hal'lows
al·li'ance
al·lied'
al'li·ga·tor
al·lit'er·ate
al·lit·er·a'tion
al·lit'er·a·tive
al'lo·cate
al·lo·ca'tion
al·lo·ge·ne'ic
　　also al·lo·gen'ic

al·lot'
al·lot'ment
al·lot'ted
al·lot·tee'
al·lot'ting
all-out
all'over
al·low'
al·low'able
al·low'ance
al'loy
all-round
All Saints' Day
All Souls' Day
all'spice
al·lude'
　to refer (see elude)

al·lure'
al·lu'sion
　suggestion (see
　　illusion)

al·lu'sive
　suggestive (see
　　elusive; illusive)

al·lu'sive·ness
al·lure'
al·lure'ment
al·lu'vi·al
al·lu'vi·um
al·ly'
　verb; to unite (see
　　alley)

al'ly
　noun; friend (see
　　alley)

al·ma ma'ter
al'ma·nac
al·mi'ghty
al'mond
al'mo·ner
al'most
alms
alms'house
al'ni·co
al'oe
aloft'
alo'ha
alone'
along'
along'shore'
along'side
aloof'
aloof'ness
aloud'
al·pac'a
al'pen·horn
al'pen·stock
al'pha
al'pha·bet
al·pha·bet'ic

al·pha·bet'i·cal
al'pha·bet·ize
al·pha·met'ic
Al'pine
al·read'y
al'so
al'so-ran
al'tar
　noun; religion (see
　　alter)

al'tar·piece
al'ter
　verb; change (see
　　altar)

al·ter·a'tion
al'ter·cate
al·ter·ca'tion
al·ter e'go
al'ter·nate
al'ter·nate·ly
al'ter·nat·ing
al·ter·na'tion
al·ter'na·tive
al'ter·na·tor
al·though'
　also al·tho'

al·tim'e·ter
al'ti·tude
al'to
al·to·geth'er
al'tru·ism
al'tru·ist
al·tru·is'tic
al'um
alu'mi·na
alu'mi·num

alum'na
 pl alum'nae

alum'nus
 pl alum'ni

al'ways

amal'gam

amal'ga·mate

amal·ga·ma'tion

aman·u·en'sis
 pl aman·u·en'ses

am'a·ranth

am·a·ran'thine

Am·a·ril'lo

am·a·ryl'lis

amass'

am'a·teur

am'a·to·ry

amaze'

amaze'ment

amaz'ing·ly

am'a·zon

am·a·zo'ni·an

am·bas'sa·dor

am·bas·sa·do'ri·al

am·bas'sa·dress

am'ber

am'ber·gris

am·bi·dex'trous

am'bi·ence

am'bi·ent

am·bi·gu'i·ty

am·big'u·ous

am·bi'tion

am·bi'tious

am·biv'a·lence

am·biv'a·lent

am'ble

am·bro'sia

am·bro'sial

am'bu·lance

am'bu·lant

am'bu·la·to·ry

am'bus·cade

am'bush

ame'ba

ame'bic

ame'lio·rate

ame·lio·ra'tion

ame'na·ble

amend'
 to change (see emend)

amend'ment

amen'i·ty

amerce'

amerce'ment

Amer'i·can

Amer·i·ca'na

Amer'i·can·ism

Amer·i·can·iza'tion

Amer'i·can·ize

am·er·i'ci·um

Am'er·ind

Am·er·in'di·an

am'e·thyst

ami·a·bil'i·ty

a'mi·a·ble

a'mi·a·bly

am·i·ca·bil'i·ty

am'i·ca·ble

am'i·ca·bly

amid'
 or amidst'

amid'ships

ami'no

amiss'

am'i·ty

am'me·ter

am'mo

am·mo'nia

am'mo·nite

am·mo'ni·um

am·mu·ni'tion

am·ne'sia

am·ne'si·ac
 or am·ne'sic

am'nes·ty

amoe'ba
 pl amoe'bas or amoe'bae

amoe'bic

amoe'boid

amok'

among'
 also amongst'

amon·til·la'do

amor'al

amor'al·ly

am'o·rous

amor'phous

amor·ti·za'tion

am'or·tize

amount'

amour'

amour pro'pre

am'per·age

am'pere

am'per·sand
am·phet'a·mine
am·phib'i·an
am·phib'i·ous
am'phi·the·ater
am'pho·ra
  pl am'pho·rae *or*
    am'pho·ras

am'ple
am'pli·fi·ca'tion
am'pli·fi·er
am'pli·fy
am'pli·tude
am'ply
am'pul
  or am·poule

am·pul'la
  pl am·pul'ae

am'pu·tate
am·pu·ta'tion
am·pu·tee'
am'u·let
amuse'
amuse'ment
anach'ro·nism
anach·ro·nis'tic
an·a·con'da
an'a·dem
anae'mia
anae'mic
an·aer·o'bic
an·aes·the'sia
an·aes·thet'ic
a'na·gram
An'a·heim
a'nal

an·al·ge'sia
an·al·ge'sic
an'a·log
  or an'a·logue
anal'o·gous
an'a·logue
  or an'a·log
anal'o·gy
anal'y·sis
  pl anal'y·ses
an'a·lyst
  one who analyses
   (*see* annalist)
an·a·lyt'ic
  or an·a·lyt'i·cal
an'a·lyze
an'a·pest
an·a·pes'tic
an·ar'chic
  also an·ar'chi·cal
an'ar·chism
an'ar·chist
an·ar·chis'tic
an'ar·chy
an·astig·mat'ic
anath'e·ma
anath'e·ma·tize
an·a·tom'ic
  or an·a·tom'i·cal
anat'o·mist
anat'o·mize
anat'o·my
an'ces·tor
an·ces'tral
an'ces·try
an'chor

an'chor·age
an'cho·ress
an'cho·rite
an'cho·vy
an·cien ré·gime
an'cient
an'cil·lary
an·dan'te
and'iron
and/or
An·dor'ra
An·dor'ran
an'dro·gen
an'ec·dote
ane'mia
ane'mic
an·e·mom'e·ter
anem'o·ne
an'er·oid
an·es·the'sia
an·es·the·si·ol'o·
  gist
an·es·the·si·ol'·
  o·gy
an·es·thet'ic
anes'the·tist
anes'the·tize
an'gel
  spiritual being (*see*
   angle)
an·gel'ic
  or an·gel'i·cal
an·gel'i·cal·ly
An'ge·lus
an'ger
an·gi'na

an'gle
   math. (see angel*)*
an'gler
an'gle·worm
An'gli·can
an'gli·cism
an·gli·ci·za'tion
an'gli·cize
an'gling
an'glo·phile
an'glo·phobe
An·glo-Sax'on
an·go'ra
an'gri·ly
an'gry
angst
ang'strom
an'guish
an'gu·lar
an·gu·lar'i·ty
an·hy'drous
an'i·line
an·i·mad·ver'sion
an·i·mad·vert'
an'i·mal
an·i·mal'cule
an'i·mal·ism
an'i·mate
an'i·mat·ed
an·i·ma'tion
an'i·mism
an'i·mist
an·i·mis'tic
an·i·mos'i·ty
an'i·mus
an'ion

an'ise
an·is·ette'
ankh
an'kle
an'klet
an'nal·ist
   recorder of events
   (*see* analyst)
An·nap'o·lis
an·neal'
an·nex'
   verb
an'nex
   noun
an·nex·a'tion
an·ni'hi·late
an·ni·hi·la'tion
an·ni·ver'sa·ry
an·no Do'mi·ni
an'no·tate
an·no·ta'tion
an'no·ta·tor
an·nounce'
an·nounce'ment
an·nounc'er
an·noy'
an·noy'ance
an·nu·al
an'nu·al·ly
an·nu'i·tant
an·nu'i·ty
an·nul'
an'nu·lar
an·nul'ment
an·nun'ci·ate
an·nun·ci·a'tion

an·nun'ci·a·tor
an'ode
an'od·ize
an'o·dyne
anoint'
anom'a·lous
anom'a·ly
an·o·nym'i·ty
anon'y·mous
anoph'e·les
an·oth'er
an·ov'u·lant
an·ov'u·la·to·ry
an'swer
an'swer·able
ant·ac'id
an·tag'o·nism
an·tag'o·nist
an·tag·o·nis'tic
an·tag'o·nize
ant·arc'tic
Ant·arc'ti·ca
an'te
an·te·bel'lum
an·te·ced'ent
an'te·cham·ber
an'te·date
an·te·di·lu'vi·an
an'te·lope
an·te me·ri'di·em
an·te·mor'tem
an·te·na'tal
an·ten'na
an·te·pe'nult
an·te·pen·ul'ti·
   mate

an·te′ri·or
an′te·room
an′them
an′ther
ant′hill
an·thol′o·gy
an′thra·cite
an′thrax
an·thro·po·cen′tric
an′thro·poid
an·thro·po·log′i·cal
an·thro·pol′o·gist
an·thro·pol′o·gy
an·thro·po·mor′phic
an·thro·po·mor′phism
an′ti
an·ti·air′craft
an·ti·Amer′i·can
an·ti·bac·te′ri·al
an·ti·bal·lis′tic mis·sile
an·ti·bi·ot′ic
an′ti·body
an′tic
an′ti·christ
an·tic′i·pate
an·tic·i·pa′tion
an·tic′i·pa·to·ry
an·ti·cli·mac′tic
an·ti·cli′max
an·ti·de·pres′sant
an′ti·dote

an′ti·freeze
an′ti·gen
an·ti·grav′i·ty
an·ti·his′ta·mine
an·ti·in·tel·lec′tu·al·ism
an·ti·knock′
an·ti·log′a·rithm
an·ti·ma·cas′sar
an·ti·mag·net′ic
an·ti·mis·sile
an′ti·mo·ny
an·ti·pas′to
an·tip·a·thet′ic
an·tip′a·thy
an·ti·per·son·nel′
an·tiph′o·nal
an·tiph′o·nal·ly
an·tip′o·dal
an·tip′o·des
an·ti·pov′er·ty
an·ti·quar′i·an
an′ti·quary
an′ti·quat·ed
an·tique′
an·tiq′ui·ty
an·ti·se·mit′ic
an·ti-Sem′i·tism
an·ti·sep′sis
an·ti·sep′tic
an·ti·sep′ti·cal·ly
an·ti·so′cial
an·tith′e·sis
   pl an·tith′e·ses
an·ti·thet′i·cal
an·ti·thet′i·cal·ly

an·ti·tox′in
an·ti·trust′
an·ti·viv·i·sec′tion·ist
ant′ler
ant′lered
ant′onym
an′trum
a′nus
an′vil
anx·i′ety
anx′ious
any′body
any′how
any·more′
any′one
any′place
any′thing
any′way
any′where
any′wise
aor′ta
aor′tic
apace′
apart′
apart′heid
apart′ment
ap·a·thet′ic
ap·a·thet′i·cal·ly
ap′a·thy
aper·i·tif′
ap′er·ture
a′pex
   pl a′pex·es *or* a′pi·ces
apha′sia

aph·e′lion
   pl aph·e′lia
a′phid
a′phis
   pl a′phi·des
aph′o·rism
aph′o·ris·tic
aph·ro·dis′i·ac
a′pi·a·rist
a′pi·ary
ap′i·cal
apiece′
aplomb′
apoc′a·lypse
apoc·a·lyp′tic
apoc′ry·pha
apoc′ry·phal
ap′o·gee
apo·lit′i·cal
apol·o·get′ic
apol·o·get′i·cal·ly
apo·lo′gia
apol′o·gist
apol′o·gize
ap′o·logue
apol′o·gy
ap·o·plec′tic
ap′o·plexy
apos′ta·sy
apos′tate
a·pos·te·ri·o′ri
apos′tle
apos′to·late
ap·os·tol′ic
apos′tro·phe
apos′tro·phize

apoth′e·cary
ap′o·thegm
apoth·e·o′sis
Ap·pa·la′chian
ap·pall′
   also ap·pal′
ap′pa·nage
ap·pa·rat′us
   pl ap·pa·rat′us *or*
    ap·pa·rat′us·es
ap·par′el
ap·par′ent
ap·pa·ri′tion
ap·peal′
ap·pear′
ap·pear′ance
ap·pease′
ap·pease′ment
ap·pel′lant
ap·pel′late
ap·pel·la′tion
ap·pel·lee′
ap·pend′
ap·pend′age
ap·pen·dec′to·my
ap·pen·di·ci′tis
ap·pen′dix
   pl ap·pen′dix·es *or*
    ap·pen′di·ces
ap·per·cep′tion
ap·per·tain′
ap′pe·tite
ap′pe·tiz·er
ap′pe·tiz·ing
ap·plaud′
ap·plause′

ap′ple
ap′ple·jack
ap·pli′ance
ap·pli·ca·bil′i·ty
ap′pli·ca·ble
ap′pli·cant
ap·pli·ca′tion
ap′pli·ca·tor
ap·plied′
ap·pli·qué′
ap·ply′
ap·point′
ap·poin·tee′
ap·point′ive
ap·point′ment
ap·por′tion
ap·por′tion·ment
ap′po·site
ap·po·si′tion
ap·pos′i·tive
ap·prais′al
ap·praise′
   value (see apprise)
ap·prais′er
ap·pre′cia·ble
ap·pre′ci·ate
ap·pre·ci·a′tion
ap·pre′cia·tive
ap·pre·hend′
ap·pre·hen′sion
ap·pre·hen′sive
ap·pren′tice
ap·pren′tice·ship
ap·prise′

   inform (see
   appraise)

ap·proach'
ap·proach'able
ap·pro·ba'tion
ap·pro'pri·ate
ap·pro'pri·ate·ly
   ness
ap·pro·pri·a'tion
ap·prov'al
ap·prove'
ap·prox'i·mate
ap·prox'i·mate·ly
ap·prox·i·ma'tion
ap·pur'te·nance
ap·pur'te·nant
ap'ri·cot
A'pril
a pri·o'ri
a'pron
ap·ro·pos'
ap'ti·tude
apt'ly
apt'ness
aq'ua·cade
aq'ua·lung
aq·ua·ma·rine'
aq'ua·naut
aq'ua·plane
aquar'i·um
   pl aquar'i·ums *or*
    aquar'ia
aquat'ic
aq'ue·duct
a'que·ous
aq'ui·line
ar·a·besque'

Ara'bi·an
Ar'a·bic
ar'a·ble
ar'ba·lest
   or ar'ba·list
ar'bi·ter
ar·bit'ra·ment
ar'bi·trar'i·ly
ar'bi·trar·i·ness
ar'bi·trary
ar'bi·trate
ar·bi·tra'tion
ar'bi·tra·tor
ar'bor
ar·bo·re'al
ar·bo·re'tum
   pl ar·bo·re'tums *or*
    ar·bor·re'ta
ar·bor·vi'tae
ar·bu'tus
arc
   curve (see ark)
ar·cade'
ar·cane'
ar·chae·o·log'i·cal
ar·chae·ol'o·gist
ar·chae·ol'o·gy
ar·cha'ic
ar·cha'i·cal·ly
arch'an·gel
arch·bish'op
arch·bish'op·ric
arch·dea'con
arch·di'o·cese
arch·duch'ess
arch·duke'

arch·en'e·my
ar'cher
ar'cher·y
ar'che·type
arch·fiend'
ar·chi·epis'co·pal
ar·chi·pel'a·go
   pl ar·chi·pel'a·goes
    or ar·chi·pel'a·gos
ar'chi·tect
ar·chi·tec·ton'ics
ar·chi·tec'tur·al
ar'chi·tec·ture
ar'chi·trave
ar'chive
ar'chi·vist
arch'ly
arch'ness
arch'way
arc'tic
ar'dent
ar'dor
ar'du·ous
ar'ea
   space (see aria)
ar'ea·way
are'na
Ar·gen·ti'na
Ar'gen·tine
ar'gon
ar'go·sy
ar'got
ar'gu·able
ar'gue
ar'gu·ment
ar·gu·men·ta'tion

ar·gu·men'ta·tive
ar'gyle
a'ria
   song (see area)
ar'id
arid'i·ty
arise'
  arose'
  aris'en
  aris'ing
ar·is·toc'ra·cy
aris'to·crat
aris·to·crat'ic
arith'me·tic
ar·ith·met'i·cal
arith·me·ti'cian
Ar·i·zo'na
ark
  boat (see arc)
Ar'kan·sas
ar·ma'da
ar·ma·dil'lo
Ar·ma·ged'don
ar'ma·ment
ar'ma·ture
arm'chair
Ar·me'nian
arm'hole
ar'mi·stice
arm'let
ar'mor
ar'mored
ar'mor·er
ar·mo'ri·al
ar'mo·ry
arm'pit

arm'rest
ar'my
ar'ni·ca
aro'ma
ar·o·mat'ic
ar·o·mat'i·cal·ly
around'
arous'al
arouse'
ar·peg'gio
ar·raign'
ar·raign'ment
ar·range'
ar·range'ment
ar'rant
ar'ras
  pl ar'ras
ar·ray'
ar·rears'
ar·rest'
ar·ri·ère-pen·sée'
ar·riv'al
ar·rive'
ar'ro·gance
ar'ro·gant
ar'ro·gate
ar'row
ar'row·head
ar'row·root
ar·ro'yo
ar'se·nal
ar'se·nic
ar'son
ar·te'ri·al
ar·te'ri·ole
ar·te·rio·scle·ro'sis

ar·te·rio·scle·rot'ic
ar'te·ry
ar·te'sian
art'ful
art'ful·ly
ar·thrit'ic
ar·thri'tis
ar'thro·pod
ar'ti·choke
ar'ti·cle
ar·tic'u·lar
ar·tic'u·late
ar·tic'u·late·ly
ar·tic·u·la'tion
ar'ti·fact
  or ar'te·fact
ar'ti·fice
ar·tif'i·cer
ar·ti·fi'cial
ar·ti·fi·ci·al'i·ty
ar·ti·fi'cial·ly
ar·til'lery
art'i·ly
art'i·ness
ar'ti·san
art'ist
ar·tiste'
ar·tis'tic
ar·tis'ti·cal·ly
art'ist·ry
art'less
art'y
ar'um
Ar'y·an
as·bes'tos
  also as·bes'tus

as·cend'

as·cen'dan·cy
or as·cen'den·cy

as·cen'dant
or as·cen'dent

as·cen'sion

as·cent'
upward slope (see assent)

as·cer·tain'

as·cet'ic
austere (see acetic)

as·cet'i·cism

ascor'bic

as'cot

as·crib'able

as·cribe'

as·crip'tion

asep'tic

asex'u·al

ashamed'

ash'en

ash'lar

ashore'

a'shy

A'sian

aside'

as'i·nine

as·i·nin'i·ty

askance'

askew'

aslant'

asleep'

aso'cial

as·par'a·gus

as'pect

as'pen

as·per'i·ty

as·per'sion

as'phalt

as·phyx'ia

as·phyx'i·ate

as·phyx·i·a'tion

as'pic

as·pi·dis'tra

as'pi·rant

as'pi·rate

as·pi·ra'tion

as·pire'

as'pi·rin

as·sail'

as·sail'ant

as·sas'sin

as·sas'si·nate

as·sas·si·na'tion

as·sault'

as·say'
to try (see essay)

as·sem'blage

as·sem'ble

as·sem'bly

as·sem'bly·man

as·sent'
agree (see ascent)

as·sert'

as·ser'tion

as·sert'ive

as·sess'

as·sess'ment

as·ses'sor

as'set

as·sev'er·ate

as·sev·er·a'tion

as·si·du'i·ty

as·sid'u·ous

as·sign'

as·sign'able

as·sig·na'tion

as·sign'ment

as·sim'i·late

as·sim·i·la'tion

as·sist'

as·sis'tance

as·sis'tant

as·size'

as·so'ci·ate

as·so·ci·a'tion

as·so'cia·tive

as·so'nance

as'so·nant

as·sort'

as·sort'ed

as·sort'ment

as·suage'

as·sume'

as·sump'tion

as·sur'ance

as·sure'

as·sured'
pl as·sured' *or* as·sureds'

as'ta·tine

as'ter

as'ter·isk

as'ter·oid

asth'ma

asth·mat'ic

as·tig·mat'ic

as·tig·mat′i·cal·ly
astig′ma·tism
as·ton′ish
as·ton′ish·ment
as·tound′
astrad′dle
as′tra·khan
as′tral
astride′
as·trin′gen·cy
as·trin′gent
as·tro·bi·ol′o·gist
as·tro·bi·ol′o·gy
as·tro·dy·nam′ics
as′tro·labe
as·trol′o·ger
as·tro·log′i·cal
as·trol′o·gy
as′tro·naut
as·tro·nau′ti·cal
as·tro·nau′tics
as·tron′o·mer
as·tro·nom′i·cal
  or as·tro·nom′ic
as·tron′o·my
as·tro·phys′i·cist
as·tro·phys′ics
as·tute′
asun′der
asy′lum
asym·met′ric
  or asym·met′ri·cal
at′a·vism
at·a·vis′tic
ate·lier′
a′the·ism

a′the·ist
athe·is′tic
ath·e·nae′um
  or ath·e·ne′um
ath′lete
ath·let′ic
ath·let′i·cal·ly
ath·let′ics
athwart′
at′las
At·lan′ta
At·lan′tic
at′mo·sphere
at·mo·spher′ic
at·mo·sphe′rics
a′toll
at′om
atom′ic
atom′ics
at′om·ize
at′om·iz·er
aton′al
ato·nal′i·ty
aton′al·ly
atone′
atone′ment
a′tri·um
  pl a′tria *also*
   a′tri·ums
atro′cious
atroc′i·ty
at′ro·phy
at′ro·pine
at·tach′
at·ta·ché′
at·ta′ché case

at·tach′ment
at·tack′
at·tain′
at·tain·abil′i·ty
at·tain·able
at·tain′der
at·tain′ment
at·taint′
at′tar
at·tempt′
at·tend′
at·ten′dance
at·ten′dant
at·ten′tion
at·ten′tive
at·ten′u·ate
at·ten·u·a′tion
at·test′
at·tes·ta′tion
at′tic
at·tire′
at′ti·tude
at·ti·tu′di·nize
at·tor′ney
at·tract′
at·trac′tion
at·trac′tive
at·trib′ut·able
at′tri·bute
  noun
at·trib′ute
  verb
at·tri·bu′tion
at·trib′u·tive
at·tri′tion
at·tune′

atyp'i·cal
au'burn
au cou·rant
auc'tion
auc·tion·eer'
auc·to'ri·al
au·da'cious
au·dac'i·ty
au·di·bil'i·ty
au'di·ble
au'di·bly
au'di·ence
au'dio
au'dio·phile
au·dio·vi'su·al
au'dit
au·di'tion
au'di·tor
au·di·to'ri·um
au'di·to·ry
auf Wie'der·
  seh·en
au'ger
  tool (see augur)
aught
  zero (see ought)
aug·ment'
aug·men·ta'tion
au gra'tin
au'gur
  foretell (see auger)
au'gu·ry
au·gust'
Au'gust
Au·gus'ta
auk

au'ra
au'ral
  hearing (see oral)
au're·ate
au're·ole
au re·voir'
au'ri·cle
au·ric'u·lar
au·rif'er·ous
au·ro'ra
  pl au·ro'rae *or*
  au·ro'ras
au·ro'ra aus·tra'
  lis
au·ro'ra bo·re·
  al'is
aus'form
aus'pice
aus·pi'cious
aus·tere'
aus·ter'i·ty
Aus'tin
aus'tral
Aus·tra'lia
Aus·tra'lian
Aus'tria
Aus'tri·an
au·then'tic
au·then'ti·cal·ly
au·then'ti·cate
au·then·ti·ca'tion
au·then·tic'i·ty
au'thor
au'thor·ess
au·thor·i·tar'i·an
au·thor'i·ta·tive

au·thor'i·ty
au·tho·ri·za'tion
au'tho·rize
au'thor·ship
au'to
au'to·bahn
au·to·bi·og'ra·
  pher
au·to·bi·o·graph'i·
  cal
au·to·bi·og'ra·phy
au·toch'tho·nous
au·toc'ra·cy
au'to·crat
au·to·crat'ic
au·to·crat'i·cal·ly
au'to·graph
au·to·in·tox·i·ca'tion
au'to·mate
au·to·mat'ic
au·to·mat'i·cal·ly
au·to·ma'tion
au·tom·a·ti·za'tion
au·tom'a·tize
au·tom'a·ton
au·to·mo·bile'
au·to·mo·bil'ist
au·to·mo'tive
au·ton'o·mous
au·ton'o·my
au'top·sy
au·to·stra'da
au'tumn
au·tum'nal
aux·il'ia·ry
aux'in

avail′
avail·abil′i·ty
avail′able
av′a·lanche
avant-garde′
av′a·rice
av·a·ri′cious
avenge′
aveng′er
av′e·nue
aver′
av′er·age
aver′red
aver′ring
averse′
  reluctant (see
    adverse)
aver′sion
avert′
a′vi·an
a′vi·ary
a′vi·a·tion
a′vi·a·tor
avi·a′trix
av′id
avid′i·ty
av′id·ly
av·o·ca′do
av·o·ca′tion
avoid′
avoid′able
avoid′ance
av·oir·du·pois′
avow′
avow′al
avun′cu·lar

await′
awake′
awak′en
award′
aware′
aware′ness
awash′
away′
aweigh′
awe′some
awe′strick·en
  or awe′struck
aw′ful
aw′ful·ly
awhile′
awhirl′
awk′ward
awk′ward·ness
awl
  tool (see all)
aw′ning
a′woke
awry′
ax
  or axe
ax′i·al
ax′i·om
ax·i·om·at′ic
ax′is
  pl ax′es
ax′le
axle′tree
aza′lea
az′i·muth
Az′tec
a′zure

B

bab′bitt
bab′ble
ba′bel
ba·boon′
ba·bush′ka
ba′by
ba′by-sit
ba′by-sit·ter
bac·ca·lau′re·ate
bac·ca·rat′
bac′cha·nal
bac·cha·na′lia
bac·cha·na′lian
bach′e·lor
ba·cil′lus
  pl ba·cil′li

back′ache
back-bench′er
back′bite
back′bit·er
back′board
back·bone′
back′drop
back′er
back′field
back′fire
back′gam·mon
back′ground
back′hand
back′hand·ed
back′ing
back′lash
back′log
back′rest

ban

back·side
back'slap
back'slap·per
back'slide
back'slid·er
back'spin
back'stage
back'stairs
back'stop
back'stretch
back'stroke
back talk
back'track
back'up *noun*
back'ward
  or back'wards
back'ward·ness
back'wash
back·woods'
ba'con
bac·te'ri·al
bac·te·ri·cid'al
bac·te·ri·o·log'i·cal
bac·te·ri·ol'o·gist
bac·te·ri·ol'o·gy
bac·te'ri·um
  pl bac·te'ria

badge
bad'ger
bad·i·nage'
bad'land
bad'min·ton
bad'ness
Bae'de·ker
baf'fle
bag

bagged
bag'ging
bag·a·telle'
ba'gel
bag'gage
bag'gy
ba'gnio
bag'pipe
ba·guette'
Ba·ha'ma
Ba·ha'mi·an
baht
  pl bahts *or* baht
bail
  security (see bale)
bai'liff
bai'li·wick
bails'man
bait
  lure (see bate)

baize
bak'er
bak·er's doz·en
bak'ery
bak'sheesh
bal·a·lai'ka
bal'ance
bal·bo'a
bal·brig'gan
bal'co·ny
bal'da·chin
  or bal·da·chi'no
bal'der·dash
bald'ness
bale
  bundle (see bail)

bal'er
bale'ful
balk
Bal'kan
balky
ball
  rounded body (see bawl)

bal'lad
bal'last
ball'car·ri·er
bal·le·ri'na
bal'let
bal·let'o·mane
bal·lis'tic
bal·lis'tics
bal·loon'
bal·loon'ist
bal'lot
ball-point
ball'room
bal'ly·hoo
balmy
bal'sa
bal'sam
Bal'tic
Bal'ti·more
bal'us·ter
bal'us·trade
bam·boo'
bam·boo'zle
ban
  banned
  ban'ning
ban
  pl ba'ni

ba·nal′
ba·nal′i·ty
ba·na′na
band
  strip (see ban)
ban′dage
ban·dan′na
  or ban·dan′a
band′box
ban′de·role
  or ban′de·rol
ban′dit
ban′dit·ry
band′mas·ter
ban·do·lier′
  or ban·do·leer′
band′stand
band′wag·on
ban′dy
bane′ful
ban′gle
bang′tail
bang′-up
ban′ish
ban′ish·ment
ban′is·ter
ban′jo
ban′jo·ist
bank′book
bank′er
bank′roll
bank′rupt
bank′rupt·cy
ban′ner
ban′nock
banns
  marriage

ban′quet
ban·quette′
ban′shee
ban′tam
ban′ter
Ban′tu
Ban′tu·stan
ban′yan
ban·zai′
bao′bab
bap′tism
bap·tis′mal
Bap′tist
bap′tis·tery
bap′tize
bar
  barred
bar′ring
Bar·ba′dos
Bar·ba′di·an
bar·bar′i·an
bar·bar′ic
bar′ba·rism
bar·bar′i·ty
bar′ba·rous
bar′be·cue
bar′bell
bar′ber
bar′ber·ry
bar′bi·tal
bar·bit′u·rate
bar′ca·role
  or bar′ca·rolle
bard
  poet (see barred*)*
bare
  naked (see bear*)*

bare′back
bare·faced
bare′foot
  or bare·foot′ed
bare-hand′ed
bare·head′ed
bare′ly
bar′gain
barge′man
bar′i·tone
bar′i·um
bar′keep·er
bark′er
bar′ley
bar′maid
bar′man
bar mitz′vah
  masc (see bas
  mitzvah*)*
bar′na·cle
barn′storm
barn′yard
ba′ro·graph
ba·rom′e·ter
baro·met′ric
bar′on
  a noble (see barren*)*
bar′on·age
bar′on·ess
bar′on·et
bar′on·et·cy
ba·ro′ni·al
bar′ony
ba·roque′
ba·rouche′
bar′racks
  sing or pl

bayberry

bar·ra·cu'da
bar·rage'
bar'ra·try
barred
    shut out (see bard)

bar'rel
bar'ren
    sterile (see baron)

bar'ren·ness
bar·rette'
bar'ri·cade
bar'ri·er
bar'ring
bar'ris·ter
bar'room
bar'row
bar'tend·er
bar'ter
bas'al
ba'salt
ba·sal'tic
base
    foundation (see bass)

base'ball
base'board
base·born
base'less
base'ly
base'ment
base'ness
base'run·ning
bash'ful
bash'ful·ness
ba'sic
ba'si·cal·ly
bas'il

ba·sil'i·ca
bas'i·lisk
ba'sin
ba'sis
    pl ba'ses

bask
bas'ket
bas'ket·work
bas'ket·ball
bas mitz'vah
    fem (see bar
    mitzvah)

Basque
bas-re·lief'
bass
    fish, deep voice (see
    base)

bas·si·net'
bas'so
bas·soon'
bass'wood
bas'tard
bas'tard·ize
baste
bas'tion
bas'tioned
bat
    bat'ted
    bat'ting

batch
bate
    moderate (see bait)

ba·teau'
    also bat·teau'
    pl ba·teaux'

bath
    pl baths

bathe
bath'er
ba·thet'ic
bath'house
ba'thos
bath'robe
bath'room
bath'tub
ba'thy·scaphe
bathy'sphere
ba·tik'
ba·tiste'
bat'man
ba·ton'
Bat·on Rouge'
bats'man
bat·tal'ion
bat'ten
bat'ter
bat'ter·ing ram
bat'tery
bat'ting
bat'tle
bat'tle-ax
bat'tle·dore
bat'tle·field
bat'tle·ment
bat'tle·ship
bau'ble
baux'ite
Ba·var'i·an
bawd'i·ly
bawd'i·ness
bawd'y
bawl
    bellow (see ball)

bay'ber·ry

bay'o·net
 bay'o·net·ed
  also bay'o·net·ted
 bay'o·net·ing
  also bay'o·net·ting
bay'ou
ba·zaar'
 marketplace (see bizarre)
ba·zoo'ka
beach
 shore (see beech)
beach'comb·er
beach'head
bea'con
bead
bead'ing
bea'dle
bead'y
bea'gle
bea'ker
bean'ie
bear
 animal (see bare)
bear
 carry (see bare)
 bore
 borne
  also born
bear'able
beard'less
bear'er
bear'ing
bear'ish
bear'skin
beast'ly

beat
 to strike (see beet)
beat
beat'en
 or beat
beat'ing
be·atif'ic
be·at·i·fi·ca'tion
be·at'i·fy
be·at'i·tude
beat'nik
beau
 pl beaux *or*
  beaus
 suitor (see bow)
Beau·jo·lais'
beau monde'
Beau'mont
beau'te·ous
beau·ti'cian
beau·ti·fi·ca'tion
beau'ti·fi·er
beau'ti·ful
beau'ti·ful·ly
beau'ti·fy
beau'ty
bea'ver
be·calm'
be·cause'
beck'on
be·cloud'
be·come'
be·com'ing
be·com'ing·ly
bed
 bed'ded
 bed'ding

be·daz'zle
be·daz'zle·ment
bed'bug
bed'clothes
bed'ding
be·deck'
be·dev'il
bed'fel·low
bed'lam
bed'ou·in
be·drag'gled
bed'rid·den
bed'rock
bed'roll
bed'room
bed'side
bed'sore
bed'spread
bed'stead
bed'time
beech
 tree (see beach)
beech'nut
beef
 pl beeves *or* beefs
beef'steak
beef'y
bee'hive
bee'keep·er
bee'keep·ing
bee'line
beer
 beverage (see bier)
beer'y
bees'wax
 vegetable (see beat)

benevolent

bee'tle
be·fall'
be·fit'
be·fog'
be·fore'
be·fore'hand
be·friend'
be·fud'dle
beg
  beg'ged
  beg'ging
be·get'
  be·got'
  be·got'ten
    or be·got'
  be·get'ting
beg'gar
beg'gar·ly
be·gin'
  be·gan'
  be·gun'
be·gin'ner
be·gone'
be·go'nia
be·grime'
be·grudge'
be·guile'
be·guine'
be'gum
be·half'
be·have'
be·hav'ior
be·hav'ior·al
be·hav'ior·ism
be·hav'ior·ist
be·head'

be·he'moth
be·hest'
be·hind'
be·hind'hand
be·hold'
be·hold'en
be·hold'er
be·hoove'
  or be·hove'
beige
be·in
be'ing
be·la'bor
be·lat'ed
be·lay'
belch
be·lea'guer
bel'fry
Bel'gian
Bel'gium
be·lie'
be·lief'
be·liev'able
be·lieve'
be·liev'er
be·lit'tle
bel·la·don'na
bell'boy
belles let·tres
bell'hop
bel'li·cose
bel·li·cos'i·ty
bel·lig'er·ence
bel·lig'er·en·cy
bel·lig'er·ent
bel'low

bel'lows
bell'weth·er
bel'ly
be·long'
be·long'ings
be·loved'
be·low'
belt'tight·en
belt'way
bem'e·gride
be·mire'
be·moan'
be·muse'
bend
  bent
  bend'ing
ben·day
be·neath'
ben'e·dict
ben·e·dic'tion
ben·e·fac'tion
ben'e·fac·tor
ben'e·fac·tress
ben'e·fice
be·nef'i·cence
be·nef'i·cent
ben·e·fi'cial
ben·e·fi'cial·ly
ben·e·fi'ciary
ben'e·fit
  ben'e·fit·ed
    or ben'e·fit·ted
  ben'e·fit·ing
    or ben'e·fit·ting
be·nev'o·lence
be·nev'o·lent

be·night'ed
be·nign'
be·nig'nant
be·nig'ni·ty
be·nign'ly
ben'i·son
ben'thic
  or ben'thal
ben'thos
be·numb'
ben'zene
ben'zine
ben·zo'ic
ben'zo·in
ben'zol
be·queath'
be·quest'
be·rate'
Ber'ber
ber·ceuse'
be·reave'
  be·reaved'
  bereft'
  be·reav'ing
be·reave'ment
be·ret'
beri·ber'i
Berke'ly
Ber·mu'da
Ber·mu'di·an
  or Ber·mu'dan
ber'ry
  fruit (see bury)
ber·serk'
berth
  position, bed (see birth)

ber'yl
be·ryl'li·um
be·seech'
  be·sought'
    or be·seeched'
be·seech'ing
be·set'
be·set'ting
be·side'
be·sides'
be·siege'
be·sieg'er
be·smirch'
be·sot'ted
be·span'gle
bes'tial
bes·ti·al'i·ty
bes'ti·ary
be·stir'
be·stow'
bet
  bet
    or bet'ted
  bet'ting
be'ta
bête noire
  pl bêtes noires
be·tray'
be·tray'al
be·tray'er
be·troth'
be·troth'al
be·trothed'
bet'ter
  comp. of good, well (see bettor)
bet'ter·ment

bet'tor
  or bet'ter
  one that bets (see better)
be·tween'
be·twixt'
bev'el
  bev'eled
    or bev'elled
  bev'el·ing
    or bev'el·ling
bev'er·age
bev'y
be·wail'
be·ware'
be·wil'der
be·wil'der·ment
be·witch'
be·yond'
bez'el
bi·an'nu·al
bi'as
  bi'ased
    or bi'assed
  bi'as·ing
    or bi'as·sing
bi·be·lot'
Bi'ble
bib'li·cal
bib·li·og'ra·pher
bib·li·o·graph'ic
bib·li·o·graph'i·cal
bib·li·og'ra·phy
bib'lio·phile
bib'u·lous
bi·cam'er·al
bi·car'bon·ate

bi·cen·ten′ary
bi·cen·ten′ni·al
bi′ceps
bi·chlo′ride
bick′er
bi·cus′pid
bi′cy·cle
bid
  bade
    or bid
  bid′den
    or bid *also* bade
  bid′ding
bid′da·ble
bid′der
bide
  bode
    or bid′ed
  bid′ed
  bid′ing
bi·en′ni·al
bi·en′ni·al·ly
bi·en′ni·um
  pl bi·en′ni·ums *or*
    bi·en′nia
bier
  coffin stand (*see*
    beer)
bi·fo′cals
bi′fur·cate
bi·fur·ca′tion
big′a·mist
big′a·mous
big′a·my
big′horn
bight
big′it

big′ness
big′ot
big′ot·ed
big′ot·ry
big′wig
bi′jou
  pl bi′joux
bikeway
bi·ki′ni
bi·lat′er·al
bi·lat′er·al·ly
bilge
bi·lin′gual
bil′ious
bill′board
bil′let
bil·let-doux′
  pl bil·lets-doux′
bill′fold
bill′head
bill′iards
bill′ing
bil′lings·gate
bil′lion
  pl billions *or* billion
bil′lionth
bil′low
bil′lowy
bil′ly
bil′ly goat
bi·met′al·lism
bi·month′ly
bi′na·ry
bin·au′ral
bind
  bound
  bind′ing

bind′er
bind′ing
binge
bin′na·cle
bin·oc′u·lar
bi·no′mi·al
bio·as·tro·nau′tics
bio·chem′i·cal
bio·chem′ist
bio·chem′is·try
bio·de·grad·
  abil′i·ty
bio·de·grad′able
bio·ge·og′ra·pher
bio·ge·o·graph′ic
bio·ge·og′ra·phy
bi·og′ra·pher
bi·o·graph′i·cal
bi·og′ra·phy
bi·o·log′i·cal
bi·ol′o·gist
bi·ol′o·gy
bio·med′i·cal
bio·med′i·cine
bi·on′ics
bio·phys′ics
bi′op·sy
bio′sphere
bio·syn·thet′ic
bio·syn·thet′i·
  cal·ly
bio·syn′the·sis
bi·ot′ic
bi′o·tin
bi·par′ti·san
bi·par′tite
bi′ped

bi'plane
bi·ra'cial
bird'bath
bird'house
bird'ie
bird'lime
bird'seed
bird's'-eye
bi·ret'ta
Bir'ming·ham
birth
   being born (see berth)
birth'day
birth'mark
birth'place
birth'rate
birth'right
birth'stone
bis'cuit
bi'sect
bi·sex'u·al
bish'op
bish'op·ric
Bis'marck
bis'muth
bi'son
   pl bi'son
bisque
bis'tro
bitch
bite
   bit
   bit'ten
     also bit
   bit'ing

bit'ter
bit'tern
bit'ter·ness
bit'ters
bit'ter·sweet
bi·tu'men
bi·tu'mi·nous
bi'valve
biv'ouac
   biv'ouacked
   biv'ouack·ing
bi·week'ly
bi·zarre'
   odd (see bazaar)
bi·zarre'ly
bi·zon'al
blab
   blabbed
   blab'bing
black'a·moor
black'ball
black'ber·ry
black'bird
black'board
black'en
black'guard
black'head
black'jack
black'list
black'mail
black'out
black'smith
black'thorn
black'top
blad'der
blame'less

blame'wor·thi·
   ness
blame'wor·thy
blanc·mange'
blan'dish·
   ment
blan'ket
blar'ney
bla·sé'
blas·pheme'
blas'phe·mous
blas'phe·my
blast off
bla'tan·cy
bla'tant
blath'er
blaz'er
bla'zon
bleach'ers
bleak'ly
bleed
bled
bleed·ing
blem'ish
bless'ed·ness
blight
blind'fold
blink'er
blin'tze
bliss'ful
bliss'ful·ly
blis'ter
blithe'ly
blithe'some
blitz
blitz'krieg

bliz'zard
bloat'er
bloc
  group
block
  solid piece
block·ade
block'bust·er
block'head
block'house
blond
  also blonde
blood'cur·dling
blood'hound
blood'less
blood'mo·bile
blood pressure
blood'shed
blood'shot
blood'stain
blood'stone
blood'stream
blood'suck·er
blood'thirst·i·ly
blood'thirsty
blood'y
bloop'er
blos'som
blot
  blot'ted
  blot'ting
blotch
blot'ter
blot'ting
blouse
blow-by-blow

blow'gun
blow'out
blow'pipe
blow'sy
blow'torch
blow'y
blub'ber
blu'cher
blud'geon
blue'bell
blue'ber·ry
blue'bird
blue'fish
blue'grass
blue'nose
blue'point
blue'print
blue'stock·ing
blu'et
bluff'er
blu'ing
  or blue'ing
blu'ish
blun'der
blun'der·buss
blunt'ly
blunt'ness
blur
  blurred
  blur'ring
blur'ry
blus'ter
blus'tery
bo'a
boar
  animal (see *bore*)

board'er
  lodger (see *border*)
board'ing·house
board'walk
boast'er
boast'ful
boast'ful·ly
boat hook
boat'house
boat'ing
boat'man
boat'swain
bob
  bobbed
  bob'bing
bob'bin
bob'ble
bob'by-sox·er
bob'cat
bob'o·link
bob'sled
bob·white'
boc'cie
bode
bod'ice
bodi'less
bodi'ly
bod'kin
bod'y·guard
Boer
bog
  bogged
  bog'ging
bo'gey
  or bo'gy *or* bo'gie
bo'gey·man

bo'gus
Bo·he'mi·an
boil'er
boil'er·mak·er
boil'er·plate
Boi'se
bois'ter·ous
bold'face
bold-faced
bold'ly
bold'ness
bo·le'ro
bo·li'var
  pl bo·li'vars *or*
  bo·li·va'res

Bo·liv'i·a
Bo·liv'i·an
bo'lo
bo·lo'gna
Bol'she·vik
Bol'she·vism
bol'ster
bo'lus
bom·bard'
bom'bar·dier'
bom·bard'ment
bom'bast
bom·bas'tic
bom·ba·zine'
bomb'er
bomb'proof
bomb'shell
bomb'sight
bo'na fide
bo·nan'za
bon'bon

bond'age
bond'hold·er
bonds'man
bone'less
bon'er
bon'fire
bon'go
bon·ho·mie'
bo·ni'to
bon mot'
  pl bons mots' *or*
  bon mots'

bon'net
bon'ny
  also bon'nie

bon·sai'
  pl bon·sai'
bo'nus
bon vi·vant'
  pl bons vi·vants' *or*
  bon vi·vants'

bon voy·age'
bo'ny
boo'by
boo'dle
book'case
book'end
book'ie
book'ish
book'keep·er
book'keep·ing
book'let
book'mak·er
book'mak·ing
book'mark
book'mo·bile

book'plate
book'sell·er
book'shelf
boo'mer·ang
boom'town
boon'dog·gle
boon'dog·gling
boor'ish
boost'er
boot'black
boo'tee
  or boo'tie
  baby's sock (see
  booty)

booth
  pl booths
boot'leg
boot'leg·ger
boo'ty
  loot (see bootee)
booze
booz'y
bo·rac'ic acid
bo'rax
bor'der
  edge (see boarder)
bor'der·land
bor'der·line
bore
  drill, tire (see boar)
bo're·al
bore'dom
bor'er
bo'ric
born
  produced

borne
carried

bo'ron

bor'ough
town (see burro,
burrow)

bor'row

borsch
or borscht

bos'om

boss'i·ness

boss'y

Bos'ton

Bos·to'ni·an

bo'sun

bo·tan'i·cal

bot'a·nist

bot'a·ny

botch

both'er

both'er·some

Bo·tswa'na

bot'tle

bot'tle·neck

bot'tom

bot'tom·less

bot'u·lism

bou'doir

bouf·fant'

bough
tree branch (see bow)

bought

bouil'lon
soup (see bullion)

boul'der

bou'le·vard

bounce

bounc'er

bound

bound'a·ry

bound'en

bound'less

boun'te·ous

boun'ti·ful

boun'ti·ful·ly

boun'ty

bou·quet'

bour'bon

bour'geois
pl bour'geois

bour·geoi·sie'

bourse

bou·tique'

bou·ton·niere'

bo'vine

bow
submit (see bough)

bow
knot (see beau)

bowd'ler·ize

bow'el

bow'er

bowl'ful

bow'leg·ged

bowl'er

bowl'ing

bow'man

bow'sprit

bow'string

box'car

box'er

box'ing

box'wood

boy
male child (see
buoy)

boy'cott

boy'hood

boy'ish

boy'sen·ber·ry

brace'let

brack'en

brack'et

brack'ish

brag

bragged

brag'ging

brag·ga·do'cio

brag'gart

Brah'min

braid

braille

brain'child

brain'less

brain'storm

brain'wash·ing

brain'y

braise
cook (see braze)

brake
slow (see break)

brake'man

bram'ble

bran'dish

brand'-new

bran'dy

bras·siere'

bras'sy
bra·va'do
brave'ly
brav'ery
bra'vo
bra·vu'ra
brawl
brawl'er
brawn'y
braze
  solder (see braise)
bra'zen
bra'zen·ness
bra'zier
Bra·zil'
Bra·zil'ian
breach
  break (see breech)
bread'bas·ket
bread'board
breadth
  width (see breath)
bread'win·ner
break
  rupture (see brake)
  broke
  bro'ken
  break'ing
break'able
break'age
break'down
break'er
break'fast
break'front
break'out
break'through

break'wa·ter
breast'bone
breast'plate
breast'stroke
breast'work
breath
  air (see breadth)
breathe
breath'er
breath'less
breath'tak·ing
breech
  trousers (see breach)
breed
bred
breed'ing
breed'er
breeze'way
bree'zy
breth'ren
bre·vet'
bre'via·ry
brev'i·ty
brew'ery
brib'ery
bric'-a-brac
brick'bat
brick'lay·er
brid'al
  wedding (see bridle)
bride'groom
brides'maid
bridge'head
Bridge'port
bridge'work

bri'dle
  restrain (see bridal)
brief'case
bri'er
  or bri'ar
bri·gade'
brig·a·dier'
brig'and
brig'an·tine
bright'en
bright'ly
bright'ness
bril'liance
bril'lian·cy
bril'liant
bril·lian·tine'
brim·ful
brim'stone
brin'dled
bring
  brought
  bring'ing
brin'y
bri·oche'
bri·quette'
  or bri·quet'
bris'ket
brisk'ly
bris'ling
  or bris'tling
bris'tle
bris'tly
Brit'ain
  country (see Briton)
Bri·tan'nic
Brit'ish

buggy

Brit′on
person (see Britain)

brit′tle

broach
open (see brooch)

broad′band

broad′cast

broad′cast
also broad′cast·ed

broad′cast·ing

broad′cloth

broad′en

broad′-mind·ed

broad′side

broad′sword

bro·cade′

broc′co·li

bro′chette′

bro·chure′

bro′gan

brogue

broil′er

bro′ken

bro·ken·heart′ed

bro′ker

bro′ker·age

bro′mide

bro·mid′ic

bro′mine

bron′chi·al

bron·chi′tis

bron′chus
pl bron′chi

bron′co

brooch
ornament (see broach)

brood′er

brook′let

Brook′lyn

broom′stick

broth′el

broth′er

broth′er·hood

broth′er-in-law
pl broth′ers-in-law

broth′er·li·ness

broth′er·ly

brougham

brought

brou·ha′ha

brow′beat

brown′ie

brown′stone

browse

bru′in

bruise

bruis′er

bru·net′
or bru·nette′

brush′-off

brush′wood

brusque

brusque′ly

brus·sels sprout′

bru′tal

bru·tal′i·ty

bru′tal·ly

brut′ish

bub′ble

bub′bly

bu·bon′ic

buc·ca·neer′

buck′board

buck′et

buck′et·ful

bucket seat

buck′le

buck′ler

buck′ram

buck′saw

buck′shot

buck′skin

buck′wheat

bu·col′ic

bud

bud′ded

bud′ding

Bud′dha

Bud′dhism

Bud′dhist

bud′dy

budge

bud′get

Buf′fa·lo
city

buf′fa·lo
pl buf′fa·lo *or*
buf′fa·loes
animal

buff′er

buf′fet
strike

buf·fet′
sideboard

buf·foon′

buf·foon′ery

bug′a·boo

bug′bear

bug′gy

bu′gle
bu′gler
build
  built
  build′ing
build′er
build′ing
built-in
bul′bous
Bul·gar′ia
Bul·gar′i·an
bulge
bulg′ing
bulk′head
bulk′i·ly
bulk′i·ness
bulk′y
bull′dog
bull′doze
bull′doz·er
bul′let
bul′le·tin
bul·let-proof′
bull′fight
bull′finch
bull′frog
bull·head′ed
bul′lion
  precious metal (see bouillon)
bull′ish
bul′lock
bul′ly
bul′rush
bul′wark
bum

bummed
bum′ming
bum′ble·bee
bump′er
bump′kin
bump′tious
bump′y
bun′co
  or bun′ko
bun′dle
bung
bun′ga·low
bung′hole
bun′gle
bun′gler
bun′ion
bun′ker
bun′kum
  or bun′combe
bun′ting
buoy
  float (see boy)
buoy′an·cy
buoy′ant
bur′den
bur′den·some
bur′dock
bu′reau
  pl bu′reaus *also*
  bu′reaux
bu·reau′cra·cy
bu·reau′crat
bu·reau·crat′ic
bur′geon
bur′gess
bur′gher

bur′glar
bur′glar·ize
bur′gla·ry
bur′go·mas·ter
Bur′gun·dy
bur′i·al
bur′lap
bur·lesque′
bur′ly
Bur′ma
Bur′man
Bur·mese′
burn
  burned
  or burnt
burn′ing
burn′er
bur′nish
bur·noose′
  or bur·nous′
burn′out
burr
bur′ro
  donkey (see burrow
  borough)
bur′row
  hole (see burro,
  borough)
bur′sar
bur·si′tis
burst
  burst
  or bursted
burst′ing
Bu·run′di
Bu·run′di·an

bury
inter (see berry)

bus
pl bus'es *or* bus'ses
vehicle (see buss)

bus'boy
bus'by
bush'el
bush'ing
bush'whack
bus'i·ly
busi'ness
busi'ness·man
bus'kin
buss
kiss (see bus)

bus'tle
bus'y
busy'body
but
conj, prep (see butt)

butch'er
butch'ery
but'ler
butt
strike (see but)

but'ter
but'ter·cup
but'ter·fat
but'ter·fin·gered
but'ter·fin·gers
but'ter·fly
but'ter·milk
but'ter·nut
but'ter·scotch
but'tery

but'tocks
but'ton
but'ton·hole
but'ton·hook
but'tress
bux'om
buy
bought
buy'ing
buy'er
buz'zard
buzz'er
by'gone
by'law
or bye'law

by'-line
by'pass
by'path
by'play
by'-prod·uct
by'stand·er
byte
by'way
by'word

C

ca·bal'
ca·bal'led
ca·bal'ling
ca·ba'na
cab·a·ret'
cab'bage
cab'by
or cab'bie

cab'in

cab'i·net
cab'i·net·mak·er
cab'i·net·mak·ing
cab'i·net·work
ca'ble
ca'ble·gram
cab'man
cab'o·chon
ca·boose'
cab·ri·o·let'
cab'stand
ca·cao'
cache
ca·chet'
cack'le
ca·coph'o·nous
ca·coph'o·ny
cac'tus
pl cac'ti *or*
cac'tus·es

cad'dish
cad'dish·ness
ca·dav'er
ca·dav'er·ous
cad'die
or cad'dy
golf (see caddy)

cad'dish
cad'dy
small box (see
caddie)

ca'dence
ca·den'za
ca·det'
cadge
cad'mi·um
cad're

ca·du'ce·us
  pl ca·du'cei
Cae'sar
cae·su'ra
ca·fé'
ca·fé au lait'
caf·e·te'ri·a
caf·feine'
caf·tan'
ca'gey
  also ca'gy
ca'gi·ly
cag'i·ness
ca·hoot'
cais'son
cai'tiff
ca·jole'
ca·jole'ment
ca·jol'ery
Ca'jun
cal'a·bash
cal'a·boose
cal'a·mine
ca·lam'i·tous
ca·lam'i·ty
cal·car'e·ous
cal·ci·fi·ca'tion
cal'ci·fy
cal'ci·mine
cal·ci·na'tion
cal·cine'
cal'ci·um
cal'cu·la·ble
cal'cu·late
cal'cu·lat·ing
cal·cu·la'tion

cal'cu·la·tor
cal'cu·lus
cal'dron
cal'en·dar
  time (see calender)
cal'en·der
  press (see calendar)
cal'ends
calf
  pl calves
calf'skin
Cal'ga·ry
cal'i·ber
  or cal'i·bre
cal'i·brate
cal·i·bra'tion
cal'i·co
Cal·i·for'nia
cal'i·per
  or cal'li·per
ca'liph
  or ca'lif

ca'liph·ate
cal·is·then'ics
calk
cal'la
call'back
call'-board
call'er
cal·lig'ra·pher
cal·lig'ra·phy
call'ing
cal·li'o·pe
cal'lous
  unfeeling (see
  callus)

cal'low
cal'lus
  tissue (see callous)
calm'ly
cal'o·mel
ca·lor'ic
cal'o·rie
cal·o·rim'e·ter
cal'u·met
ca·lum'ni·ate
ca·lum·ni·a'tion
ca·lum'ni·a·tor
ca·lum'ni·ous
cal'um·ny
calve
Cal'vin·ism
Cal·vin·is'tic
ca·lyp'so
ca'lyx
cam·a·rad'e·rie
cam'ber
cam'bi·um
Cam·bo'di·a
Cam·bo'di·an
cam'bric
Cam'bridge
Cam'den
cam'el
ca·mel'lia
  also ca·me'lia
Cam'em·bert
cam'eo
cam'era
Cam·er·oon'
Cam·er·oo'ni·an
cam'i·sole

cap

cam'o·mile
cam'ou·flage
cam·paign'
cam·pa·ni'le
camp'er
cam'phor
cam'phor·ate
cam·po·ree'
camp'stool
cam'pus
cam'shaft
can
  canned
  can'ning
Can'a·da
Ca·na'di·an
ca·naille'
ca·nal'
ca·nal·iza'tion
ca·nal'ize
can'a·pé
  food (see canopy)
ca·nard'
ca·nar'y
ca·nas'ta
can'can
can'cel
  can'celed
    or can'celled
  can'cel·ing
    or can'cel·ling
can·cel·la'tion
can'cel·lous
can'cer
can'cer·ous
can·de·la'bra

can·de·la'brum
  pl can·de·la'bra *also*
  can·de·la'brums

can·des'cence
can·des'cent
can'did
can'di·da·cy
can'di·date
can'died
can'dle
can'dle·light
Can'dle·mas
can'dle·pin
can'dle·stick
can'dle·wick
can'dor
can'dy
cane'brake
ca'nine
can'is·ter
can'ker
can'ker·ous
can'ker·worm
can'nel coal
can'nery
can'ni·bal
can'ni·balism
can·ni·bal·is'tic
can'ni·bal·ize
can'ni·ly
can'ni·ness
can'non
  gun (see canon)
can·non·ade'
can'non·ball
can·non·eer'

can'not
can'ny
ca·noe'
can'on
  principle (see
  cannon)

ca·non'i·cal
can·on·iza'tion
can'on·ize
can'o·py
  shelter (see canape)

can·ta'bi·le
can'ta·loupe
can·tan'ker·ous
can·ta'ta
can·teen'
can'ter
  gallop (see cantor)

can'ti·cle
can'ti·le·ver
can'to
Can'ton
can'ton
can'ton·al
can·ton'ment
can'tor
  singer (see canter)

can'vas
  cloth (see *canvass*)

can'vas·back
can'vass
  solicit (see canvas)

can'yon
caou·tchouc'
cap
  capped

cap′ping
ca·pa·bil′i·ty
ca′pa·ble
ca′pa·bly
ca·pa′cious
ca·pac′i·tance
ca·pac′i·tor
ca·pac′i·ty
ca·par′i·son
ca′per
cape′skin
cap·il·lar′i·ty
cap′il·lary
cap′i·tal
  city, wealth (*see* capitol)
cap′i·tal·ism
cap′i·tal·ist
cap·i·tal·is′tic
cap·i·tal·is′ti·cal·ly
cap·i·tal·iza′tion
cap′i·tal·ize
cap′i·tal·ly
cap·i·ta′tion
cap′i·tol
  building (*see* capital)
ca·pit′u·late
ca·pit·u·la′tion
ca′pon
ca·pric′cio
ca·price′
ca·pri′cious
cap′ri·ole
cap′size
cap′stan

cap′su·lar
cap′su·late
cap′sule
cap′tain
cap′tain·cy
cap′tion
cap′tious
cap′ti·vate
cap·ti·va′tion
cap′tive
cap·tiv′i·ty
cap′tor
cap′ture
Cap′u·chin
car·a·bao′
car′a·cole
ca·rafe′
car′a·mel
car′a·pace
car′at
  weight (*see* caret, carrot)
car′a·van
car·a·van′sa·ry
  or car·a·van′se·rai
car′a·vel
car′a·way
car′bide
car′bine
car·bo·hy′drate
car·bol′ic
car′bon
car′bon·ate
car·bon·a′tion
car′bon dat′ing
car·bon′ic

car·bon·if′er·ous
car·bon·iza′tion
car′bon·ize
car′boy
car′bun·cle
car′bu·re·tor
car′cass
car·cin′o·gen
car·cin·o·gen′ic
car·ci·no′ma
car′da·mom
card′board
card′-car′ry·ing
car′di·ac
car′di·gan
car′di·nal
car·di·nal′i·ty
car′dio·gram
car′dio·graph
car·di·og′ra·phy
car·di·ol′o·gy
car·dio·vas′cu·lar
ca·reen′
ca·reer′
care′free
care′ful
care′ful·ly
care′less
ca·ress′
car′et
  insert mark (*see* carat, carrot)
care′tak·er
care′worn
car′fare
car′go

car'hop
Ca·rib·be'an
car'i·bou
car·i·ca·ture
car·i·ca·tur'ist
car'ies
   tooth decay (see carries)

car'il·lon
car'load
car·min'a·tive
car'mine
car'nage
car'nal
car·nal'i·ty
car'nal·ly
car·na'tion
car·nau'ba
car·ne'lian
car'ni·val
car'ni·vore
car·niv'o·rous
car'ol
   song (see carrel)

car'om
car'o·tene
ca·rot'id
ca·rous'al
ca·rouse'
car'pel
car'pen·ter
car'pen·try
car'pet
car'pet·bag
car'pet·bag·ger
car'pet·ing

car'port
car'rel
   library study (see carol)

car'riage
car'ri·er
car'ries
   totes (see caries)

car'ri·on
car'rot
   vegetable (see carat, caret)

car·rou·sel'
   or car·ou·sel'

car'ry
car'ry·all
car'ry·on
car'ry-over
car'sick
Car'son City
cart'age
carte blanche
car·tel'
car'ti·lage
car·ti·lag'i·nous
car'to·gram
car·tog'ra·pher
car·to·graph'ic
car·tog'ra·phy
car'ton
car·toon'
cartoon'ist
car'tridge
cart'wheel
carv'er
carv'ing

car·y·at'id
   pl car·y·at'ids *or*
   car·y·at'i·des

ca·sa'ba
cas·cade'
cas·car'a
ca·sein'
case'ment
cash'ew
cash·ier'
cash'mere
cas'ing
ca·si'no
   gambling hall (see cassino)

cas'ket
cas·sa'va
cas'se·role
cas·sette'
cas'sia
cas·si'no
   card game (see casino)

cas'sock
cast
   throw (see caste)

cast
cast'ing
cas·ta·nets'
cast'away
caste
   class (see cast)

cas'tel·lat·ed
cast'er
   or cas'tor

cas'ti·gate

cas·ti·ga'tion
cast'ing
cast i'ron
cas'tle
cast'-off
   adj
cast'off
   noun
cas'tor
cas'trate
cas·tra'tion
ca'su·al
ca'su·al·ly
ca'su·al·ty
ca'su·ist
ca·su·is'tic
ca·su·is'ti·cal
ca'su·ist·ry
ca·sus bel'li
cat'a·clysm
cat·a·clys'mic
cat'a·comb
cat'a·falque
Cat'a·lan
cat'a·lep·sy
cat·a·lep'tic
cat'a·log
   or cat'a·logue
cat'a·log·er
   or cat'a·logu·er
ca·tal'pa
ca·tal'y·sis
cat'a·lyst
cat·a·ma·ran'
cat'a·pult
cat'a·ract

ca·tarrh'
ca·tarrh'al
ca·tas'tro·phe
cat·a·stroph'ic
cat'call
catch
   caught
   catch'ing
catch'all
catch'er
catch'ing
catch'ment
catch'pen·ny
catch'word
catch'y
cat'e·chism
cat'e·chist
cat'e·chize
cat·e·chu'men
cat·e·gor'i·cal
cat·e·go'ri·cal·ly
cat'e·go·rize
cat'e·go·ry
ca'ter
ca·ter·cor'ner
   or cat·er·cor'nered
cat'er·er
cat'er·pil·lar
cat'er·waul
cat'fish
cat'gut
ca·thar'sis
ca·thar'tic
ca·the'dral
cath'e·ter
cath'ode

ca·thod'ic
cath'o·lic
Ca·thol'i·cism
cath·o·lic'i·ty
cat'ion
cat'kin
cat'like
cat'nap
cat'nip
cat-o'-nine'-tails
   pl cat-o'-nine'-tails
cat's'-paw
cat'sup
cat'tail
cat'ti·ly
cat'ti·ness
cat'tle
   pl cat'tle
cat'ty
cat·ty-cor'ner
   or cat·ty-cor'nered
cat'walk
Cau·ca'sian
Cau'ca·soid
cau'cus
cau'dal
cau'li·flow·er
caulk
   make watertight
   (*see* cork)
caus'al
cau·sal'i·ty
caus'al·ly
cau·sa'tion
caus'ative
cause cé·lè'bre
   pl causes cé·lè'bres

centurion

cau·se·rie'
cause'way
caus'tic
caus'ti·cal·ly
cau·ter·i·za'tion
cau'ter·ize
cau'tion
cau'tion·ary
cau'tious
cav·al·cade'
cav·a·lier'
cav'al·ry
cav'al·ry·man
ca·ve·at emp'tor
cave'-in
cave'man
cav'ern
cav'ern·ous
cav'i·ar
cav'il

  cav'iled
    or cav'illed

  cav'il·ing
    or cav'il·ling

cav'i·ty
ca·vort'
ca'vy
cay·enne'
cay'use
cease-fire'
cease'less
ce'cum
  pl ce'ca *or* ce'cums

ce'dar
Ce'dar Rap'ids
ce'di

ce·dil'la
ceil'ing
cel'an·dine
cel'e·brant
cel'e·brate
cel'e·brat·ed
cel·e·bra'tion
ce·leb'ri·ty
ce·ler'i·ty
cel'ery
ce·les'ta
ce·les'tial
ce'li·ac
cel'i·ba·cy
cel'i·bate
cel'lar
cel'lar·age
cel·lar·ette'
  or cel·lar·et'
cel'list
cel'lo
cel'lo·phane
cel'lu·lar
cel'lu·loid
cel'lu·lose
Cel'si·us
Celt'ic
cem'ba·lo
ce·ment'
ce·men·ta'tion
cem'e·tery
cen'o·bite
cen·o·bit'ic
cen'o·taph
cen'ser
  vessel (see censor)

cen'sor
  suppressor (see censer)

cen·so'ri·al
cen·so'ri·ous
cen'sor·ship
cen'sur·able
cen'sure
cen'sur·er
cen'sus
cen'taur
cen·ta'vo
cen·te·nar'i·an
cen·ten'a·ry
cen·ten'ni·al
cen·ten'ni·al·ly
cen'ter
cen'ter·board
cen'ter·piece
cen·tes'i·mal
cen·tes'i·mo
  pl cen·tes'i·mi

cen'ti·grade
cen'ti·gram
cen'time
cen'ti·me·ter
cen'ti·mo
cen'ti·pede
cen'tral
cen·tral·iza'tion
cen'tral·ize
cen·trif'u·gal
cen'tri·fuge
cen·trip'e·tal
cen'trist
cen·tu'ri·on

cen'tu·ry
ce·phal'ic
ce·ram'ic
ce·ram'ist
  or ce·ram'i·cist
ce're·al
  grain (see serial)
cer·e·bel'lum
ce·re'bral
cer'e·brate
cer·e·bra'tion
ce·re'brum
cer·e·mo'ni·al
cer·e·mo'ni·al·ly
cer·e·mo'ni·ous
cer'e·mo·ny
ce·rise'
ce'ri·um
cer'met
cer'tain
cer'tain·ly
cer'tain·ty
cer·tif'i·cate
cer·ti·fi·ca'tion
cer'ti·fy
cer'ti·tude
ce·ru'le·an
cer'vi·cal
cer'vix
  pl cer'vi·ces
ce·sar'e·an
  or ce·sar'i·an
ce'si·um
ces·sa'tion
ces'sion
  yielding (see
  session)

cess'pool
Cey·lon'
Cey·lon·ese'
Cha'blis
cha'-cha
Chad
Chad'ian
chafe
  rub (see chaff)
chaff
  husks (see chafe)
chaf'finch
chaf'ing
cha·grin'
  cha·grined'
  cha·grin'ing
chain-re·act'
chair'man
chaise longue
chal·ced'o·ny
cha·let'
chal'ice
chalk'board
chalk'y
chal'lenge
chal'lis
  also chal'lie
cham'ber
cham'ber·lain
cham'ber·maid
cham'bray
cha·me'leon
cham'fer
cham'ois
cham'my
cham'o·mile

cham·pagne'
  wine (see
  champaign)

cham·paign'
  open country (see
  champagne)

cham'pi·on
cham'pi·on·ship
chan'cel
chan'cel·lery
  or chan·cel·lory
chan'cel·lor
chan'cery
chan'cre
chancy
chan·de·lier'
chan'dler
change'able
chang'er
change'ful
change'less
change'ling
chan'nel
  chan'neled
    or chan'nelled
  chan'nel·ing
    or chan·nel·ling
chan·nel·iza'tion
chan'nel·ize
chan·son
chan·teuse'
chan'tey
  or chan'ty
chan·ti·cleer'
chan'try
Cha'nu·kah

cha'os
cha·ot'ic
cha·ot'i·cal·ly
chap
  chapped
  chap'ping
chap'book
chap'el
chap'er·on
  or chap'er·one
chap'fall·en
chap'lain
chap'let
chap'ter
char
  charred
  char'ring
char'ac·ter
char·ac·ter·is'tic
char·ac·ter·is'ti·
  cal·ly
char·ac·ter·i·za'
  tion
char'ac·ter·ize
cha·rade'
char'coal
charge'able
charge'-a-plate
  or charge plate
char·gé d'af·
  faires'
  pl char·gés
  d'af·faires'
char'ger
char'i·ly
char'i·ness

char'i·ot
char·i·o·teer'
cha·ris'ma
char·is·mat'ic
char'i·ta·ble
char'i·ty
char'la·tan
Charles'ton
  S.C., W.Va.
char'ley horse
Char'lotte
charm'er
charm'ing
char'nel
char'ter
char·treuse'
char'wom·an
char'y
chased
  pursued (see chaste*)*
chas'er
chasm
chas'sis
chaste
  virtuous (see chased*)*
chas'ten
chas·tise'
chas·tise'ment
chas'ti·ty
chas'u·ble
châ·teau'
  pl châ·teaus' *or*
  châ·teaux'
chat'e·laine
Chat·ta·noo'ga

chat'tel
chat'ter
chat'ter·box
chat'ty
chauf'feur
chau'vin·ism
chau'vin·ist
chau·vin·is'tic
chau·vin·is'ti·
  cal·ly
cheap
  inexpensive (see
  cheep*)*
cheap'en
cheap'skate
cheat'er
check'book
check'er
check'er·board
check'ers
check'list
check'mate
check'off
check'out
check'point
check'room
check'up
ched'dar
cheek'bone
cheek'i·ly
cheek'i·ness
cheek'y
cheep
  peep (see cheap*)*
cheer'ful
cheer'ful·ly

cheer′i·ly
cheer′i·ness
cheer′lead·er
cheer′less
cheer′y
cheese′burg·er
cheese′cloth
chees′y
chef d′oeu·vre
  pl chefs d′oeu·vre
chem′i·cal
chem′i·cal·ly
che·mise′
chem′ist
chem′is·try
chemo·ther′a·py
chem′ur·gy
che·nille′
cher′ish
che·root′
cher′ry
cher′ub
  pl cher′ubs *or*
  cher′u·bim

ches′ter·field
chest′nut
che·val′
chev·a·lier′
chev′i·ot
chev′ron
chew′y
Chey·enne′
Chi·an′ti
chiao
  pl chiao

chiar·oscu′ro

chic
  stylish (*see* chick)
Chi·ca′go
chi·ca′nery
chi′chi
chick
  young bird (*see*
  chick)
chick′a·dee
chick′en
chick·en·heart′ed
chick′weed
chic′o·ry
chide
  chid
   or chid′ed
  chid
   or chid′den *or*
   chid′ed
  chid′ing
chief′ly
chief′tain
chif·fon′
chif·fo·nier′
chig′ger
chi′gnon
chil′blain
child′birth
child′hood
child′like
chil′dren
Chile
Chil′ean
chill′er
chill′i·ness
chill′y
chi·me′ra
  or chi·mae′ra

chi·mer′i·cal
chim′ney
chim·pan·zee′
chin
  chinned
  chin′ning
Chi′na
chi′na
chin·chil′la
Chi·nese′
chi′no
chintz
chip
chipped
chip′ping
chip′munk
chip′per
chi·rog′ra·pher
chi·ro·graph′ic
chi·rog′ra·phy
chi·ro·man·cy
chi·rop′o·dist
chi·rop′o·dy
chi·ro·prac′tic
chi·ro·prac′tor
chis′el
  chis′eled
   or chis′elled
  chis′el·ing
   or chis′el·ling
chis′el·er
chit′chat
chit′ter·lings
  or chit′lings *or*
  chit′lins

chi·val′ric

chiv′al·rous
chiv′al·ry
chlo′ral
chlor′dane
chlo′ric
chlo′ride
chlo′ri·nate
chlo·ri·na′tion
chlo′rine
chlo′ro·form
chlo′ro·phyll
chock′a·block
chock-full
choc′o·late
choir
  singers (see quire)
choir′boy
choir′mas·ter
chol′er
chol′era
chol′er·ic
cho·les′ter·ol
chon
  pl chon
choose
  chose
  cho·sen
choos′er
choos′y
  or choos′ey
chop
  chopped
  chop′ping
chop′house
chop′per
chop′pi·ly

chop′pi·ness
chop′py
chop′stick
chop su′ey
cho′ral
  of a choir or chorus
  (*see* chorale,
  coral)
cho·rale′
  hymn tune (*see*
  choral, coral)
cho′ral·ly
chord
  music (*see* cord)
chore
cho·re′a
cho·re·og′ra·pher
cho·reo·graph′ic
cho·reo·graph′i·
  cal·ly
cho·re·og′ra·phy
cho′ris·ter
chor′tle
cho′rus
cho′sen
chow′chow
chow′der
chow mein
chrism
chris′ten
chris′ten·ing
Chris′ten·dom
Chris′tian
chris·ti·an′ia
Chris·ti·an′i·ty
Chris′tian·ize

chris′tie
  or chris′ty
Christ′mas
Christ′mas·tide
chro·mat′ic
chro·ma·tic′i·ty
chro·mato·
  graph′ic
chro·mato·graph′
  i·cal·ly
chrome
chro′mic
chro′mite
chro′mi·um
chro′mo
chro·mo·som′al
chro′mo·some
chron′ic
chron′i·cal·ly
chron′i·cle
chron′i·cler
chron′o·graph
chron·o·log′i·cal
chro·nol′o·gist
chro·nol′o·gy
chro·nom′e·ter
chrys′a·lis
chry·san′the·
  mum
chrys′o·lite
chub′bi·ness
chub′by
chuck′hole
chuck′le
chug
  chugged

chug'ging
chuk'ka
  boot (see chukker)
chuk'ker
  or chuk·ka
  polo (see chukka)
chum
  chummed
  chum'ming
chum'mi·ness
chum'my
chunk'y
church'go·er
church'less
church'man
church'war·den
church'yard
churl
churl'ish
churn
chute
  slide (see shoot)
chut'ney
ci·ca'da
cic'a·trix
  pl cic'a·tri·ces
ci·ce·ro'ne
ci'der
ci·gar'
cig·a·rette'
cin·cho'na
Cin·cin·nat'i
cinc'ture
cin'der
cin'e·ma
cin·e·mat'ic

cin·e·mat'o·graph
cin·e·ma·tog'ra·pher
cin·e·mat·o·graph'ic
cin·e·ma·tog'ra·phy
cin·er·ar'i·um
  pl cin·er·ar'ia
cin'na·bar
cin'na·mon
ci'pher
cir'ca
cir'cle
cir'clet
cir'cuit
cir·cu'itous
cir'cuit·ry
cir·cu'ity
cir'cu·lar
cir'cular
cir·cu·lar'i·ty
cir·cu·lar·iza'tion
cir'cu·lar·ize
cir'cu·late
cir·cu·la'tion
cir'cu·la·to·ry
cir·cum·am'bu·late
cir'cum·cise
cir·cum·ci'sion
cir·cum'fer·ence
cir'cum·flex
cir·cum·lo·cu'tion
cir·cum·lu'nar

cir·cum·nav'i·gate
cir·cum·nav·i·ga'tion
cir·cum·po'lar
cir'cum·scribe
cir·cum·scrip'tion
cir'cum·spect
cir·cum·spec'tion
cir'cum·stance
cir·cum·stan'tial
cir·cum·stan'tial·ly
cir·cum·vent'
cir·cum·ven'tion
cir'cus
cir·rho'sis
cir·ro·cu'mu·lus
cir·ro·stra'tus
cir'rus
cis·lu'nar
cis'tern
cit'a·del
ci·ta'tion
cite
  quote (see sight)
cit'i·fy
cit'i·zen
cit'i·zen·ry
cit'i·zen·ship
ci'trate
cit'ric
cit'ron
cit·ro·nel'la
cit'rus
cit'y

cit'y-state
civ'et
civ'ic
civ'ics
civ'il
ci·vil'ian
ci·vil'i·ty
civ·i·li·za'tion
civ'i·lize
civ'il·ly
claim'ant
clair·voy'ance
clair·voy'ant
clam'bake
clam'ber
clam'mi·ness
clam'my
clam'or
clam'or·ous
clam'shell
clan·des'tine
clan'gor
clan'gor·ous
clan'nish
clap
  clapped
  clap'ping
clap'board
clap'per
clap'trap
claque
clar'et
clar·i·fi·ca'tion
clar'i·fy
clar·i·net'
clar·i·net'ist

clar'i·on
clar'i·ty
clas'sic
clas'si·cal
clas'si·cal·ly
clas'si·cism
clas'si·cist
clas·si·fi'able
clas·si·fi·ca'tion
clas'si·fied
clas'si·fy
class'mate
class'room
clat'ter
clause
claus·tro·pho'bia
clav'i·chord
clav'i·cle
cla·vier'
clay'ey
clay'more
clean-cut
clean'er
clean'li·ness
clean'ly
clean'ness
cleanse
cleans'er
clear'ance
clear-cut
clear·head'ed
clear'ing
clear'ing·house
cleav'age
cleave
  cling

cleaved
  or clove
cleav'ing
cleave
  split
cleaved
  also cleft *or*
  clove
cleaved
  also cleft *or*
  clo'ven
cleav'ing
cleav'er
clem'a·tis
clem'en·cy
clem'ent
clere'sto·ry
  or clear·sto·ry
cler'gy
cler'gy·man
cler'ic
cler'i·cal
cler'i·cal·ism
Cleve'land
clev'er
clev'er·ness
clew
cli·ché'
cli'ent
cli·en·tele'
cliff'-hang·er
cli·mac'tic
  of a climax (see
  climatic)
cli'mate
cli·mat'ic
  weather (see
  climactic)
cli·ma·to·log'i·cal

cli·ma·tol′o·gist
cli·ma·tol′o·gy
cli′max
climb′er
clinch′er
cling
  clung
  cling′ing
clin′ic
clin′i·cal
clin′i·cal·ly
cli·ni′cian
clin′ker
clip
  clipped
  clip′ping
clip′board
clip′per
clip′ping
clip′sheet
clique
clit′o·ral
  or cli·tor′ic
clit′o·ris
cloche
clock′wise
clock′work
clod′hop·per
clog
  clogged
  clog′ging
cloi·son·né′
clois′ter
closed-end
close′fist′ed
close′ly

close·mouthed
close′ness
clos′et
close′-up
clo′sure
clot
  clot′ted
  clot′ting
cloth
  fabric (see clothe)
clothe
  to dress (see cloth)
  clothed
    or clad
  cloth′ing
clothes′horse
clothes′pin
clothes′press
cloth′ier
cloth′ing
clo′ture
cloud′burst
cloud′i·ness
clo′ver
clo′ver·leaf
clown′ish
club
  clubbed
  club′bing
club·foot
club′house
clue
clum′si·ly
clum′si·ness
clum′sy
clus′ter

clut′ter
coach′er
coach′man
co·ad′ju·tor
co·ag′u·lant
co·ag′u·late
co·ag·u·la′tion
co·ag′u·lum
  pl co·ag′u·la
co·alesce′
co·ales′cence
coal′field
co·ali′tion
coarse
  rough (see course)
coarse′ness
coars′en
coarse′ness
coast′al
coast′er
coast guard
coast′line
coat′ing
co·au′thor
coax′er
co·ax′i·al
co′balt
cob′ble
cob′bler
cob′ble·stone
co′bra
cob′web
co′ca
co·caine′
coc′cus
  pl coc′ci

coc'cyx
  pl coc'cy·ges *also*
    coc'cyx·es

coch'i·neal
coch'lea
cock·ade'
cock'a·too
cock'crow
cock'er·el
cock'eyed
cock'fight
cock'i·ly
cock'i·ness
cock'le
cock'le·shell
cock'ney
cock'pit
cock'roach
cock·sure'
cock'tail
cock'y
co'coa
co'co·nut
co·coon'
co'da
cod'dle
co'deine
co'dex
  pl co'di·ces

cod'fish
cod'ger
cod'i·cil
cod·i·fi·ca'tion
cod'i·fy
co·ed·u·ca'tion
co·ed·u·ca'tion·al

co·ef·fi'cient
co·ef·fi'cient
co·e'qual
co·erce'
co·er'cion
co·er'cive
co·e'val
co·ex·ist'
co·ex·is'tence
co·ex·ten'sive
cof'fee
cof'fee·house
cof'fee·pot
cof'fer
cof'fer·dam
cof'fin
co'gen·cy
co'gent
cog'i·tate
cog·i·ta'tion
co'gnac
cog'nate
cog·ni'tion
cog'ni·tive
cog'ni·zance
cog'ni·zant
cog·no'men
cog'wheel
co·hab'it
co·hab·i·ta'tion
co'heir
co·here'
co·her'ence
co·her'ent
co·he'sion
co·he'sive

co'hort
coif·feur'
coin'age
co·in·cide'
co·in'ci·dence
co·in'ci·dent
co·in·ci·den'tal
co·ition'
co'itus
co'la
col'an·der
cold-blood'ed
cold'ly
cold'ness
cole'slaw
col'ic,
col·i·se'um
co·li'tis
col·lab'o·rate
col·lab·o·ra'tion
col·lab'o·ra·tor
col·lage'
col·lapse'
col·laps'ible
col'lar
col'lar·bone
col'lard
col·late'
col·lat'er·al
col·la'tion
col·la'tor
col'league
col·lect'
col·lect'ed
col·lect'ible
  or col·lect'able

col·lec'tion
col·lec'tive
col·lec'tive·ly
col·lec'tiv·ism
col·lec·tiv·is'tic
col·lec'tiv·ize
col·lec'tor
col'leen
col'lege
col·le·gi·al'i·ty
col·le'gian
col·le'giate
col·le'gium
col·lide'
col'lie
col'lier
col'liery
col·li'sion
col·lo·ca'tion
col·lo'di·on
col'loid
col·loi'dal
col·lo'qui·al
col·lo'qui·al·ism
col·lo'qui·um
col'lo·quy
col·lu'sion
col·lu'sive
co·logne'
Co·lom'bia
Co·lom'bi·an
co'lon
  biol; punctuation

co·lon'
  pl co·lo'nes
  currency

col'o·nel
  military (see kernal)

co·lo'ni·al
co·lo'ni·al·ism
col'o·nist
col·o·ni·za'tion
col'o·nize
col'o·niz·er
col·on·nade'
col'o·ny
col'o·phon
col'or
Col·o·ra'do
Col·o·ra'do
  Springs
col·or·a'tion
col·or·a·tu'ra
col'or-blind
col'or·cast
col'ored
col'or·fast
col·or·fast'ness
col'or·ful
col'or·less
co·los'sal
col·os·se'um
co·los'sus
Co·lum'bia
col'um·bine
Co·lum'bus
col'umn
co·lum'nar
col'um·nist
co'ma
  unconsciousness (see comma)

co'ma·tose
com·bat'
com·bat'ant
com·bat'ive
comb'er
com·bi·na'tion
com·bine'
comb'ings
com'bo
com·bus'ti·ble
com·bus'tion
come
  came
  come
  com'ing
come'back
co·me'di·an
co·me·di·enne'
come'down
com'e·dy
come'li·ness
come'ly
come'-on
co·mes'ti·ble
com'et
come·up'
  pance
com'fit
com'fort
com'fort·able
com'fort·ably
com'fort·er
com'ic
com'i·cal
com'ing
com'i·ty

com'ma
punctuation (see coma)

com·mand'
com'man·dant
com·man·deer'
com·mand'er
com·mand'ment
com·man'do
  pl com·man'dos *or* com·man'does

com·mem'o·rate
com·mem·o·ra'tion
com·mem'o·ra·tive
com·mence'
com·mence'ment
com·mend'
com·mend'able
com·men·da'tion
com·men·su·ra·bil'i·ty
com·men'su·ra·ble
com·men'su·rate
com'ment
com'men·tary
com'men·ta·tor
com'merce
com·mer'cial
com·mer'cial·ism
com·mer·cial·iza'tion
com·mer'cial·ize
com·mer'cial·ly
com·mi·na'tion

com'mi·na·to·ry
com·min'gle
com·mis'er·ate
com·mis·er·a'tion
com'mis·sar
com·mis·sar'i·at
com'mis·sary
com·mis'sion
com·mis'sion·er
com·mit'
  com·mit'ted
  com·mit'ting
com·mit'ment
com·mit'tal
com·mit'ted
com·mit'tee
com·mit'tee·man
com·mode'
com·mo'di·ous
com·mod'i·ty
com'mo·dore
com'mon
com'mon·al·ty
com'mon·er
com'mon·ly
com'mon·ness
com'mon·place
com'mon·weal
com'mon·wealth
com·mo'tion
com·mu'nal
com·mune'
com·mu'ni·ca·ble
com·mu'ni·cant
com·mu'ni·cate
com·mu·ni·ca'tion

com·mu'ni·ca·tive
com·mu'nion
com·mu'ni·qué
com'mu·nism
com'mu·nist
com·mu·nis'tic
com·mu·nis'ti·cal·ly
com·mu'ni·ty
com'mu·nize
com·mat'able
com·mu·ta'tion
com'mu·ta·tor
com·mute'
com·mut'er
com·pact'
com'pact·or
  or com'pact·er

com·pan'ion
com·pan'ion·able
com·pan'ion·ship
com·pan'ion·way
com'pa·ny
com'pa·ra·ble
com·par'a·tive
com·par'a·tive·ly
com·pare'
com·par'i·son
com·part'ment
com·part·men'tal·ize
com'pass
com·pas'sion
com·pas'sion·ate
com·pat·i·bil'i·ty
com·pat'i·ble

com·pa′tri·ot
com′peer
com·pel′
com·pen′di·um
  pl com·pen′di·ums
  or com·pen′dia
com′pen·sate
com·pen·sa′tion
com·pen′sa·to·ry
com·pete′
com′pe·tence
com′pe·ten·cy
com′pe·tent
com·pe·ti′tion
com·pet′i·tive
com·pet′i·tor
com·pi·la′tion
com·pile′
com·pil′er
com·pla′cence
com·pla′cen·cy
com·pla′cent
  self-satisfied (see
  complaisant)
com·plain′
com·plain′ant
com·plaint′
com·plai′sance
com·plai′sant
  affable (see
  complacent)
com·ple·ment
  full quantity (see
  compliment)
com·ple·men′
  ta·ry

com·plete′
com·plete′ness
com·ple′tion
com·plex′
com·plex′ion
com·plex′i·ty
com·pli′ance
com·pli′an·cy
com·pli′ant
com′pli·cate
com′pli·cat·ed
com·pli·ca′tion
com·plic′i·ty
com·pli′er
com′pli·ment
  flatter (see
  complement)
com·pli·men′ta·ry
com·ply′
com·po′nent
com·port′
com·port′ment
com·pose′
com·posed′
com·pos′er
com·pos′ite
com·po·si′tion
com·pos′i·tor
com′post
com·po′sure
com′pote
com·pound′
  verb
com′pound
  adj, noun
com·pre·hend′

com·pre·hen′si·
  ble
com·pre·hen′sion
com·pre·hen′sive
com·press′
  verb
com′press
  noun
com·pressed′
com·pres′sion
com·pres′sor
com·prise′
com′pro·mise
comp·trol′ler
com·pul′sion
com·pul′sive
com·pul′so·ry
com·punc′tion
com·pu·ta′tion
com·pute′
com·put′er
com·put·er·iz′
  able
com·put·er·iza′
  tion
com·put′er·ize
com′rade
com′sat
con
  conned
  con′ning
con bri′o
con·cat·e·na′tion
con·cave′
con·cav′i·ty
con·ceal′

confer

con·ceal'ment
con·cede'
con·ceit
con·ceit'ed
con·ceiv'able
con·ceiv'ably
con·ceive'
con·cel'e·brant
con'cen·trate
con·cen·tra'tion
con·cen'tric
con'cept
con·cep'tion
con·cep'tu·al
con·cep·tu·al·
  iza'tion
con·cep'tu·al·ize
con·cep'tu·al·ly
con·cern'
  con·cerned'
  con·cern'ing
con·cern'ment
con·cert'
  verb
con'cert
  noun
con·cert'ed
con·cer·ti'na
con'cert·mas·ter
con·cer'to
  pl con·cer'ti *or*
  con·cer'tos

con·ces'sion
con·ces·sion·
  aire'
con·ces'sive

conch
  pl conchs *or*
  conch'es

con·cierge'
con·cil'i·ate
con·cil·i·a'tion
con·cil'ia·to·ry
con·cise'
con·cise'ness
con'clave
con·clude'
con·clu'sion
con·clu'sive
con·coct'
con·coc'tion
con·com'i·tant
con'cord
con·cor'dance
con·cor'dant
con·cor'dat
con'course
con·cres'cence
con·cres'cent
con·crete'
con·cre'tion
con·cu'bi·nage
con'cu·bine
con·cu'pis·cence
con·cur'
  con·curred'
  con·cur'ing
con·cur'rence
con·cur'rent
con·cus'sion
con·demn'
con·dem·na'tion

con·dem'na·to·ry
con·den·sa'tion
con·dense'
con·dens'er
con·de·scend'
con·de·scend'ing·ly
con·de·scen'sion
con·dign'
con'di·ment
con·di'tion
con·di'tion·al
con·di'tioned
con·do'lence
con·do·min'i·um
con·do·na'tion
con·done'
con'dor
con·duce'
con·du'cive
con'duct
con·duc'tance
con·duc'tion
con·duc'tive
con·duc·tiv'i·ty
con·duc'tor
con'duit
Con·es·to'ga
co'ney
con·fab·u·la'tion
con·fec'tion
con·fec'tion·er
con·fec'tion·ery
con·fed'er·a·cy
con·fed'er·ate
con·fed·er·a'tion
con·fer'

con·ferred'
con·fer'ring
con·fer·ee'
con·fer·ence
con·fess'
con·fess'ed·ly
con·fes'sion
con·fes'sion·al
con·fes'sor
con·fet'ti
con'fi·dant
   friend (see
   confident)

con·fide'
con'fi·dence
con'fi·dent
   assured (see
   confidant)
con·fi·den'tial
con·fi·den'tial·ly
con·fid'ing
con·fig·u·ra'tion
con·fine'
con·fine'ment
con·fin'er
con·firm'
con·fir·ma'tion
con·fir'ma·to·ry
con·firmed'
con'fis·cate
con·fis·ca'tion
con·fis'ca·to·ry
con·fla·gra'tion
con'flict
con'flu·ence
con'flu·ent
con'flux

con·form'
con·form'able
con·for'mance
con·for·ma'tion
con·form'ist
con·for'mi·ty
con·found'
con·fra·ter'ni·ty
con'frere
con·front'
con·fron·ta'tion
Con·fu'cian·ism
con·fuse'
con·fus'ed·ly
con·fu'sion
con·fu·ta'tion
con·fute'
con'ga
con·geal'
con·ge'nial
con·gen'i·tal
con'ger
con'ge·ries
con·gest'
con·ges'tion
con·glom'er·ate
con·glom·er·a'tion
Con'go
Con·go·lese'
con·grat'u·late
con·grat·u·la'tion
con·grat'u·la·to·ry
con'gre·gate
con·gre·ga'tion
con·gre·ga'tion·al
Con·gre·ga'tion·
   al·ism

Con·gre·ga'tion·
   al·ist
con'gress
con·gres'sio·nal
con'gress·man
con·gru'ence
con·gru'en·cy
con·gru'ent
con·gru'i·ty
con'gru·ous
con'ic
con'i·cal
con'i·fer
co·nif'er·ous
con·jec'tur·al
con·jec'ture
con·join'
con·joint'
con'ju·gal
con'ju·gate
con·ju·ga'tion
con·junct'
con·junc'tion
con·junc'tive
con·junc·ti·vi'tis
con·junc'ture
con·ju·ra'tion
con'jure
con'jur·er
   or con'ju·ror
con·nect'
Con·nect'i·cut
con·nec'tion
con·nec'tive
con·nec'tor
con·nip'tion
con·niv'ance

- con·nive'
- con·nois·seur'
- con·no·ta'tion
- con·no·ta·tive
- con·note'
- con·nu'bi·al
- con'quer
- con'quer·or
- con'quest
- con·quis'ta·dor
  pl con·quis·ta·do'res
  or
  con·quis'ta·dors
- con·san·guin'e·ous
- con·san·guin'i·ty
- con'science
- con·sci·en'tious
- con'scious
- con'scious'ness
- con·script'
- con·scrip'tion
- con'se·crate
- con·se·cra'tion
- con·sec'u·tive
- con·sen'sus
- con·sent'
- con'se·quence
- con'se·quent
- con·se·quen'tial
- con'se·quent·ly
- con·ser·va'tion
- con·ser·va'tion·ist
- con·ser'va·tism
- con·ser'va·tive
- con·ser'va·tor
- con·ser'va·to·ry
- con·serve'

- con·sid'er
- con·sid'er·able
- con·sid'er·ably
- con·sid'er·ate
- con·sid·er·a'tion
- con·sid'ered
- con·sid'er·ing
- con·sign'
- con·sign·ee'
- con·sign'ment
- con·sign'or
- con·sist'
- con·sis'tence
- con·sis'ten·cy
- con·sis'tent
- con·sis'to·ry
- con·so·la'tion
- con·so'la·to·ry
- con·sole'
  verb
- con'sole
  noun
- con·sol'i·date
- con·sol·i·da'tion
- con·som·mé'
- con'so·nance
- con'so·nant
- con·so·nan'tal
- con'sort
  noun
- con·sort'
  verb
- con·sor'tium
- con·spec'tus
- con·spic'u·ous
- con·spir'a·cy
- con·spir'a·tor

- con·spire'
- con'sta·ble
- con·stab'u·lary
- con'stan·cy
- con'stant
- con·stel·la'tion
- con·ster·na'tion
- con'sti·pate
- con·sti·pa'tion
- con·stit'u·en·cy
- con·stit'u·ent
- con'sti·tute
- con·sti·tu'tion
- con·sti·tu'tion·al
- con·sti·tu·tion·al'i·ty
- con·sti·tu'tion·al·ly
- con'sti·tu·tive
- con·strain'
- con·straint'
- con·strict'
- con·stric'tion
- con·stric'tive
- con·struct'
- con·struc'tion
- con·struc'tive
- con·struc'tion·ist
- con·struc'tor
- con·strue'
- con·sub·stan·ti·a'tion
- con'sul
- con'sul·ar
- con'sul·ate
- con·sult'
- con·sul'tant

con·sul·ta'tion
con·sul'ta·tive
con·sume'
con·sum'er
con·sum'er·ism
con·sum'mate
adj
con'sum·mate
verb
con·sum·ma'tion
con·sump'tion
con·sump'tive
con'tact
con·ta'gion
con·ta'gious
con·tain'
con·tain'er
con·tain·er·iza'
tion
con·tain'er·ize
con·tain'ment
con·tam'i·nant
con·tam'i·nate
con·tam·i·na'tion
con·temn'
con'tem·plate
con·tem·pla'tion
con·tem'pla·tive
con·tem·po·ra'ne·
ous
con·tem'po·rary
con·tempt'
con·tempt'ible
con·temp'tu·ous
con·tend'
con·tend'er

con·tent'
adj, verb
con'tent
noun
con·tent'ed
con·ten'tion
con·ten'tious
con·tent'ment
con·ter'mi·nous
con·test'
verb
con'test
noun
con·tes'tant
con'text
con·tex'tu·al
con·ti·gu'i·ty
con·tig'u·ous
con'ti·nence
con'ti·nent
con·ti·nen'tal
con·tin'gen·cy
con·tin'gent
con·tin'u·al
con·tin'u·al·ly
con·tin'u·ance
con·tin·u·a'tion
con·tin'ue
con·ti·nu'i·ty
con·tin'u·ous
con·tin'u·um
pl con·tin'ua *or*
con·tin'u·ums

con·tort'
con·tor'tion
con·tor'tion·ist

con'tour
con'tra·band
con·tra·cep'tion
con·tra·cep'tive
con'tract
noun
con·tract'
verb
con·trac'tile
con·trac·til'i·ty
con·trac'tion
con·trac'tor
con·trac'tu·al
con·trac'tu·al·ly
con·tra·dict'
con·tra·dic'tion
con·tra·dic'to·ry
con·tra·dis·tinc'
tion
con'trail
con·tral'to
con·trap'tion
con·tra·pun'tal
con·tra·ri'e·ty
con'trar·i·ly
con'trar·i·wise
con'trary
con'trast
noun
con·trast'
verb
con·tra·vene'
con·tra·ven'tion
con'tre·temps
con·trib'ute
con·tri·bu'tion

con·trib'u·tor
con·trib'u·to·ry
con'trite
con'tri·tion
con·triv'ance
con·trive'
con·triv'er
con·trol'
　con·trolled'
　con·trol'ling
con·trol'ler
con'tro·ver·sial
con'tro·ver·sy
con'tro·vert
con·tro·vert'i·ble
con·tu·ma'cious
con·tu'ma·cy
con·tu·me'li·ous
con'tu·me·ly
con·tuse'
con·tu'sion
co·nun'drum
con·ur·ba'tion
con·va·lesce'
con·va·les'cence
con·va·les'cent
con·vec'tion
con·vene'
con·ve'nience
con·ve'nient
con'vent
con·ven'ti·cle
con·ven'tion
con·ven'tion·al
con·ven·tion·al'
　i·ty

con·ven'tion·al·
　ize
con·ven'tual
con·verge'
con·ver'gence
　or con·ver'gen·cy
con·ver'gent
con·ver'sant
con·ver·sa'tion
con·ver·sa'tion·al
con·verse'
　verb, adj
con'verse
　noun
con·verse'ly
con·ver'sion
con·vert'
　verb
con'vert
　noun
con·vert'er
　or con·ver'tor
con·vert'i·ble
con·vex'
con·vex'i·ty
con·vey'
con·vey'ance
con·vey'er
　or con·vey'or
con'vict
　noun
con·vict'
　verb
con·vic'tion
con·vince'
con·vinc'ing

con·viv'ial
con·viv·i·al'i·ty
con·viv'ial·ly
con·vo·ca'tion
con·voke'
con·vo·lut·ed
con·vo·lu'tion
con'voy
con·vulse'
con·vul'sion
con·vul'sive
cook'book
cook'ery
cook'ie
　or cook'y
cook'out
cook'stove
cool'ant
cool'er
coo'lie
　laborer (see coolly)
cool'ly
　chillily (see coolie)
cool'ness
co'-op
coo'per
coo'per·age
co·op'er·ate
co·op·er·a'tion
co·op'er·a·tive
co·op'er·a·tor
co-opt'
co·or'di·nate
co·or'di·nates
co·or·di·na'tion
co·or'di·na·tor

co·part'ner
cop'i·er
co'pi·lot
cop'ing
co'pi·ous
cop'per
cop'per·as
cop'per·head
cop'pice
co'pra
cop'u·la
cop'u·late
cop·u·la'tion
cop'u·la·tive
copy'book
copy'boy
copy'cat
copy'desk
copy'ist
copy'read·er
copy'right
co·quet'
   or co·quette'
   co·quet'ted
   co·quet'ting
co'quet·ry
co·quette'
co·quett'ish
cor'a·cle
cor'al
   marine skeleton
   (*see* choral,
   chorale)
cor'bel
cord
   string (*see* chord)
cord'age

cor'dial
cor·di·al'i·ty
cor'dial·ly
cor·dil·le'ra
cord'less
cor'do·ba
cor'don
cor'do·van
cor'du·roy
core
   center (*see* corps)
co·re·spon'dent
   law (*see*
   correspondent)
co'ri·an·der
cork
   stopper (*see* caulk)
cork'screw
cor'mo·rant
corn'cob
corn'crib
cor'nea
cor'ner
cor'ner·stone
cor·net'
corn'flow·er
cor'nice
corn'meal
corn'stalk
corn'starch
cor·nu·co'pi·a
corn'y
co·rol'la
cor'ol·lary
co·ro'na
cor'o·nary

cor·o·na'tion
cor'o·ner
cor·o·net'
cor'po·ral
cor'po·rate
cor·po·ra'tion
cor'po·ra·tive
cor·po're·al
corps
   group (*see* core,
   corpse)
corpse
   dead body (*see* corps)
cor'pu·lence
cor'pu·lent
cor'pus
cor'pus·cle
cor'pus de·lic'ti
Cor·pus Chris'ti
cor·ral'
cor·rect'
cor·rec'tion
cor·rec'tive
cor're·late
cor·re·la'tion
cor·rel'a·tive
cor·re·spond'
cor·re·spon'dence
cor·re·spon'dent
   writer (*see*
   corespondent)
cor'ri·dor
cor·ri·gen'dum
cor·rob'o·rate
cor·rob·o·ra'tion
cor·rob'o·ra·tive

cor·rob'o·ra·to·ry
cor·rode'
cor·ro'sion
cor·ro'sive
cor'ru·gate
cor·ru·ga'tion
cor·rupt'
cor·rupt'i·ble
cor·rup'tion
cor'sair
cor'set
cor'tege
cor'tex
   pl cor'ti·ces *or*
   cor'tex·es
cor'ti·cal
cor'ti·sone
co·run'dum
cor'us·cate
cor·us·ca'tion
cor·vette'
co·ry'za
co·sig'na·to·ry
cos·met'ic
cos·me·tol'o·gist
cos·me·tol'o·gy
cos'mic
cos·mog'o·ny
cos·mo·log'i·cal
cos·mol'o·gy
cos'mo·naut
cos·mo·pol'i·tan
cos·mop'o·lite
cos'mos
cos'sack
Cos·ta Ri'ca

Cos·ta Ri'can
cost'li·ness
cost'ly
cos'tume
cos'tum·er
cos·tu'mi·er
co'te·rie
co·ter'mi·nal
co·ter'mi·nous
co·til'lion
cot'tage
cot'ter
cot'ton
cot'ton·seed
cot'ton·tail
cot'ton·wood
cot·y·le'don
couch'ant
cou'gar
cough
cou'lomb
coun'cil
   assembly (see
   counsel)

coun'cil·lor
   or coun'cil·or
   council member
   (*see* counselor)

coun'cil·man
coun'sel
   advice (see council)

coun'sel
coun'seled
   or coun'selled

coun'sel·ing
   or coun'sel·ling

coun'sel·or
   or coun'sel·lor
   adviser
   (*see* councillor)

count'able
count'down
coun'te·nance
count'er
coun·ter·act'
coun·ter·ac'tive
coun'ter·at·tack
coun'ter·bal·ance
   noun

coun·ter·bal'ance
   verb

coun'ter·claim
coun·ter·clock'
   wise
coun·ter·es·pi·o·
   nage
coun'ter·feit
coun'ter·feit·er
coun·ter·in·tel'li·
   gence
coun·ter·in·sur'
   gen·cy
count'er·man
coun'ter·mand
coun'ter·mea·sure
coun·ter·of·fen·sive
coun'ter·pane
coun'ter·part
coun'ter·point
coun'ter·poise
coun·ter·rev·o·lu'
   tion

coun·ter·sig'na·ture

coun'ter·sign

coun'ter·sink

coun'ter·ten·or

coun'ter·weight

count'ess

count'less

coun'tri·fied
    or coun'try·fied

coun'try

coun'try·man

coun'try·side

coun'ty

coup de grace'

coup d'etat'

cou·pé'
    or coupe

cou'ple

cou'plet

cou'pling

cou'pon

cour'age

cou·ra'geous

cou'ri·er

course
    track (see coarse)

cours'er

cour'te·ous

cour'te·san

cour'te·sy

court'house

court'ier

court'li·ness

court'ly

court'-mar·tial
    pl courts'-martial

court'room

court'ship

court'yard

cous'in

cov'en

cov'e·nant

cov'er

cov'er·age

cov'er·all

cov'er·let

cov'ert

cov'et

cov'et·ous

cov'ey

cow'ard

cow'ard·ice

cow'ard·li·ness

cow'bell

cow'boy

cow'er

cow'hide

cow'lick

cowl'ing

co'-work·er

cow'poke

cow'punch·er

cow'slip

cox'comb

cox'swain

coy'ly

coy'ness

coy'ote

coz'en

co'zi·ly

co'zi·ness

co'zy

crab'bed

crab'by

crack'down

crack'er

crack'er·jack

crack'le

crack'pot

crack'-up

cra'dle

craft'i·ness

crafts'man

craft'y

crag'gy

cram

    crammed

    cram'ming

cran'ber·ry

cra'ni·al

cra'ni·um
    pl cra'ni·ums *or*
    cra'nia

crank'case

crank'i·ly

crank'i·ness

crank'shaft

crank'y

cran'ny

crap'shoot·er

crash'-land

crass'ly

cra'ter

cra·vat'

cra'ven

crav'ing

craw'fish

cray'fish

cray'on

cra'zi·ly

cra′zi·ness
cra′zy
creak
  squeak (see creek)
creak′y
cream′ery
cream′y
cre·ate′
cre·a′tion
cre·a′tive
cre·a·tiv′i·ty
cre·a′tor
crea′ture
crèche
cre′dence
cre·den′tial
cred·i·bil′i·ty
cred′i·ble
cred′it
cred′it·able
cred′it·ably
cred′i·tor
cre′do
cre·du′li·ty
cred′u·lous
creek
  stream (see creak)
creel
creep
  crept
  creep′ing
creep′er
creep′ing
creep′y
cre′mate
cre·ma′tion
cre′ma·to·ry

cren′el·late
  or cren′el·ate
cren·el·la′tion
Cre′ole
cre′o·sote
crepe
  or crêpe
cre·pus′cu·lar
cre·scen′do
cres′cent
crest′fall·en
cre·ta′ceous
cre′tin
cre′tonne
cre·vasse′
crev′ice
crib
  cribbed
  crib′bing
crib′bage
crick′et
cri′er
crim′i·nal
crim·i·nal′i·ty
crim′i·nal·ly
crim·i·no·log′i·cal
crim·i·nol′o·gist
crim·i·nol′o·gy
crim′son
cringe
crin′kle
crin′kly
crin′o·line
crip′ple
cri′sis
crisp′ly
crisp′ness

crisp′y
criss′cross
cri·te′ri·on
crit′ic
crit′i·cal
crit′i·cal·ly
crit′i·cism
crit′i·cize
cri·tique′
crit′ter
croak
cro·chet′
crock′ery
croc′o·dile
cro′cus
crois·sant′
cro′ny
crook′ed
croon′er
crop
  cropped
  crop′ping
crop′land
crop′per
cro·quet′
  game (see croquette)
cro·quette′
  food (see croquet)
cro′sier
cross′bar
cross′bow
cross′breed
cross′-coun·try
cross·cur′rent
cross′cut
cross-ex·am·i·na′
  tion

cross-ex·am′ine
cross′-eye
cross′-eyed
cross′hatch
cross′ing
cross′over
cross′piece
cross′-pol′li·nate
cross-pol·li·
  na′tion
cross′-pur′pose
cross′-ques′tion
cross-re·fer′
cross-ref′er·ence
cross′road
cross′walk
cross′wise
crotch
crotch′et
crotch′et·i·ness
crotch′ety
crou′pi·er
crou′ton
crow
  crowed
  crow′ing
crow′bar
crow′foot
cru′cial
cru′ci·ble
cru′ci·fix
cru·ci·fix′ion
cru′ci·form
cru′ci·fy
crude′ly
cru′el
cru·el·ly

cru′el·ty
cru′et
cruis′er
crul′ler
crum′ble
crum′bly
crum′pet
crum′ple
cru·sade′
cru·sad′er
crust′al
crust′y
crus·ta′cean
crutch
crux
cru·zei′ro
cry′ba·by
cryo·bi·o·log′i·cal
cryo·bi·ol′o·gist
cryo·bi·ol′o·gy
cry·o·gen′ic
cry·o·gen′i·cal·ly
cry·o·gen′ics
cry·o·sur′gery
crypt
cryp′tic
cryp′to·gram
cryp·tog′ra·pher
cryp·tog′ra·phy
crys′tal
crys′tal·line
crys·tal·li·za′tion
crys′tal·lize
Cu′ba
Cu′ban
cub′by·hole
cu′bic

cu′bi·cal
  like a cube (see
  cubicle)

cu′bi·cle
  compartment (see
  cubical)

cu′bit
cuck′old
cuck′oo
cu′cum·ber
cud′dle
cud′gel
cue
  signal (see que)

cui·sine′
cul-de-sac′
  pl culs-de-sac′ *also*
  cul-de-sacs′

cul′i·nary
cull
cul′mi·nate
cul·mi·na′tion
cul′pa·ble
cul′prit
cult′ist
cul·ti·va·ble
cul·ti·vat·able
cul′ti·vate
cul·ti·va′tion
cul′ti·va·tor
cul′tur·al
cul′tur·al·ly
cul′ture
cul′tured
cul′vert
cum′ber·some
cum′brous
cum′mer·bund

cu'mu·la·tive
cu'mu·lus
cu·ne'i·form
cun'ning
cup'bear·er
cup'board
cup'cake
cup'ful
cu'pid
cu·pid'i·ty
cu'po·la
cur'able
cu'rate
cu'ra·tive
cu·ra'tor
curb'ing
cur'dle
cu·ré
cure'-all
cur'few
cu'ria
cu'rio
cu·ri·os'i·ty
cu'ri·ous
cu'ri·ous·ly
cu'ri·um
curl'er
curl'i·cue
curl'y
cur'rant
  berry (see current)
cur'ren·cy
cur'rent
  present (see
  currant)
cur·ric'u·lum
  pl cur·ric'u·la or
  cur·ric'ulums

cur'ry
cur'ry·comb
cur'sive
cur'so·ri·ly
cur'so·ry
curt'ly
cur·tail'
cur'tain
curt'sy
  or curt'sey
cur'va·ture
curve
cush'ion
cus'pi·dor
cus'tard
cus·to'di·al
cus·to'di·an
cus'to·dy
cus'tom
cus·tom·ar'i·ly
cus'tom·ary
cus·tom-built'
cus'tom·er
cus'tom·house
cus·tom-made'
cut
  cut
  cut'ting
cut-and-dried'
cu·ta'ne·ous
cut'back
cu'ti·cle
cut'lass
cut'lery
cut'let
cut'off
cut'ter

cut'throat
cut'ting
cut'tle·bone
cut'tle·fish
cut'up
cut'worm
cy'a·nide
cy·ber·nat'ed
cy·ber·na'tion
cy·ber·net'ics
cy'cla·mate
cy'cla·men
cy'cle
cy'clic
cy'cli·cal
cy'clist
cy·clom'e·ter
cy'clone
cy·clon'ic
cy·clo·pe'dia
  or cy·clo·pae'dia

cy'clo·tron
cyg'net
cyl'in·der
cy·lin'dri·cal
cym'bal
  musical instrument
  (see symbol)

cyn'ic
cyn'i·cal
cyn'i·cism
cy·no·sure'
cy'press
Cy'prus
Cyp'ri·ot
  or Cyp'ri·ote

cyst

cys'tic
cy'to·plasm
czar
cza·ri'na
czar'ist
Czech
Czecho·slo'vak
  or Czecho·slo·va'
    ki·an

Czecho·slo·va'kia

D

dab
 dabbed
 dab'bing
dab'ble
dab'bler
dachs'hund
dac'tyl
dac·tyl'ic
dad'dy
daf'fo·dil
dag'ger
da·guerre'o·type
dahl'ia
Da·ho'man
  or Da·ho'me·an *or*
    Da·ho'mey·an

Da·ho'mey
dai'ly
dain'ti·ly
dain'ti·ness
dain'ty
dai'qui·ri
dair'y

dairy'maid
dairy'man
da'is
dai'sy
da·la'si
Dal'las
dal'li·ance
dal'ly
 dal'lied
 dal'ly·ing
dal·ma'tian
dam
  barrier (see damn)
 dammed
 dam'ming
dam'age
dam'a·scene
dam'ask
dammed
  *blocked (see
    damned)*

damn
  condemn (see dam)
dam'na·ble
dam'na·bly
dam·na'tion
damned
  condemned
damp'en
damp'en·er
damp'er
damp'ness
dam'sel
dam'son
danc'er
dan'de·li·on

dan'der
dan'di·fy
dan'dle
dan'druff
dan'dy
dan'dy·ish
dan'ger
dan'ger·ous
dan'gle
Dan'ish
dan·seuse'
dap'per
dap'ple
dare'dev·il
dar'ing
dark'en
dark'room
dar'ling
dash'board
dash'ing
das·tard'ly
da'ta
date'less
date'line
da'tive
da'tum
  pl da'ta
daugh'ter
daugh'ter-in-law
  pl daugh'ters-in-law
daunt'less
dau'phin
dav'en·port
da'vit
daw'dle
daw'dler

daw'dling
day'bed
day'book
day'break
day'dream
day'light
day'time
Day'ton
daz'zle
daz'zling·ly
dea'con
dea'con·ess
de·ac·ti·va'tion
de·ac'ti·vate
dead'beat
dead'en
dead'line
dead'li·ness
dead'lock
dead'ly
dead'pan
dead'weight
dead'wood
deaf'en
deaf'mute
deaf'ness
deal
  dealt
  deal'ing
deal'ing
Dear'born
dear'ly
dearth
death'bed
death'blow
death'less

death'like
death'ly
death's'-head
death'watch
de·ba'cle
de·bar'
de·bark'
de·bar·ka'tion
de·base'
de·bat'able
de·bate'
de·bat'er
de·bauch'
de·bauch'ery
de·ben'ture
de·bil'i·tate
de·bil·i·ta'tion
de·bil'i·ty
deb'it
deb·o·nair'
de·bouch'
de·brief'
de·bris'
  pl de·bris'

debt'or
de·bunk'
de'but
deb'u·tante
dec'ade
dec'a·dence
dec'a·dent
de'cal
de·cal·co·ma'nia
dec'a·logue
de·camp'
de·cant'

de·cant'er
de·cap'i·tate
de·cap·i·ta'tion
deca·syl·lab'ic
de·cath'lon
de·cay'
de·cease'
de·ceased'
de·ce'dent
de·ceit'
de·ceit'ful
de·ceit'ful·ly
de·ceive'
de·ceiv'er
de·cel'er·ate
de·cel·er·a'tion
de·cel'er·a·tor
De·cem'ber
de'cen·cy
de·cen'ni·al
de·cen'ni·al·ly
de'cent
  proper (see descent, dissent)

de·cen·tral·iza'-
  tion
de·cen'tral·ize
de·cep'tion
de·cep'tive·ly
dec'i·bel
de·cide'
de·cid'ed
de·cid'u·ous
dec'i·mal
dec'i·mal·ize
dec'i·mal·ly

dec'i·mate
de·ci'pher
de·ci'pher·able
de·ci'sion
de·ci'sive
de·ci'sive·ness
deck'hand
deck'le
de·claim'
dec·la·ma'tion
de·clam'a·to·ry
dec·la·ra'tion
de·clar'a·tive
de·clar'a·to·ry
de·clare'
de·clar'er
de·clas'si·fy
de·clen'sion
de·clin'able
dec'li·nate
dec'li·na'tion
de·cline'
de·cliv'i·ty
de·code'
dé·col·le·tage'
dé·col·le·té'
de·co·lo·ni·al·iza'
   tion
de·com·mis'sion
de·com·pose'
de·com·po·si'tion
de·com·press'
de·com·pres'sion
de·con·tam'i·nate
de·con·tam·i·na'
   tion
de·con·trol'

de·cor'
   or dé·cor'
dec'o·rate
dec·o·ra'tion
dec'o·ra·tive
dec'o·ra·tor
dec'o·rous
de·co'rum
de·coy'
de·crease'
de·cree'
dec're·ment
de·crep'it
de·crep'i·tate
de·crep'i·tude
de·cre·scen'do
de·cry'
ded'i·cate
ded·i·ca'tion
ded'i·ca·to·ry
de·duce'
de·duc'ible
de·duct'
de·duct'ible
de·duc'tion
de·duc'tive
deep'en
deep'ly
deep-root'ed
deep'sea
deep-seat'ed
deer'skin
de·es·ca·la'tion
de·es'ca·late
de·face'
de·face'ment
de fac'to

de·fal'cate
de·fal·ca'tion
de·fal'ca·tor
def·a·ma'tion
de·fam'a·to·ry
de·fame'
de·fault'
de·fault'er
de·feat'
de·feat'ism
de·feat'ist
def'e·cate
def·e·ca'tion
de'fect
   noun
de·fect'
   verb
de·fec'tion
de·fec'tive
de·fec'tor
de·fend'
de·fen'dant
de·fend'er
de·fense'
   or de·fence'
de·fense'less
de·fen'si·ble
de·fen'sive
de·fer'
de·ferred'
de·fer'ring
def'er·ence
   respect (see
   difference)
def·er·en'tial
de·fer'ment
de·fer'rable

de·fi′ance
de·fi′ant
de·fi′cien·cy
de·fi′cient
def′i·cit
de·file′
de·file′ment
de·fin′able
de·fine′
de·fin′er
def′i·nite
def·i·ni′tion
de·fin′i·tive
de·flate′
de·fla′tion
de·fla′tion·ary
de·flect′
de·flec′tion
de·flec′tor
de·fo′li·ant
de·fo′li·ate
de·fo·li·a′tion
de·form′
de·for·ma′tion
de·for′mi·ty
de·for·es·ta′tion
de·fraud′
de·fray′
de·fray′al
de·frost′
deft′ly
de·funct′
de·fy′
de·gen′er·a·cy
de·gen′er·ate
de·gen·er·a′tion
de·gen′er·a·tive

de·grad′able
deg·ra·da′tion
de·grade′
de·gree′
de·gree′-day
de·hu·man·iza′·
 tion
de·hu′man·ize
de·hu·mid′i·fy
de·hy′drate
de·hy·dra′tion
de·hy·drog′e·
 nate
de·hy·drog·e·na′·
 tion
de·ice′
de·ic′er
de·if·i·ca′tion
de′ify
deign
de′ism
de·is′tic
de′ity
de·ject′ed
de·jec′tion
de ju′re
Del′a·ware
de·lay′
de′le
de·lec′ta·ble
de·lec·ta′tion
del′e·gate
del·e·ga′tion
de·lete′
del·e·te′ri·ous
de·le′tion
delft′ware

de·lib′er·ate
de·lib′er·ate·
 ness
de·lib·er·a′tion
de·lib′er·a·tive
del′i·ca·cy
del′i·cate
del·i·cate′ly
del·i·ca·tes·sen′
de·li′cious
de·light′
de·light′ful·ly
de·light′ed
de·lim′it
de·lin′e·ate
de·lin·e·a′tion
de·lin′quen·cy
de·lin′quent
del·i·quesce′
del·i·ques′cent
de·lir′i·ous
de·lir′i·um
 tre′mens
de·liv′er
de·liv′er·ance
de·liv′er·er
de·liv′er·y
de·louse′
del·phin′i·um
del′ta
de·lude′
del′uge
de·lu′sion
de·lu′sive
de·luxe′
delve
de·mag′ne·tize

dem·a·gog'ic
dem'a·gogue
  or dem'a·gog
dem'a·gogu·ery
dem'a·gogy
de·mand'
de·mar'cate
de·mar·ca'tion
de·marche'
de·mean'
de·mea'nor
de·ment'ed
de·men'tia
de·mer'it
de·mesne'
demi'god
demi'john
de·mil·i·ta·ri·za'-
  tion
de·mil'i·ta·rize
de'mi·monde
de·mise'
demi'tasse
de·mo·bi·li·za'tion
de·mo'bi·lize
de·moc'ra·cy
dem'o·crat
dem·o·crat'ic
dem·o·crat'i·cal·ly
de·moc·ra·ti·za'-
  tion
de·moc'ra·tize
de·mog'ra·pher
de·mo·graph'ic
de·mo·graph'ic-
  al·ly

de·mog'ra·phy
de·mol'ish
dem·o·li'tion
de'mon
  or dae'mon
de·mon·e·ti·za'-
  tion
de·mon'e·tize
de·mo'ni·ac
de·mo·ni'a·cal·ly
de·mon'ic
de·mon'i·cal·ly
de·mon·ol'o·gy
de·mon'stra·ble
dem'on·strate
dem·on·stra'tion
de·mon·stra'tive
dem'on·stra·tor
de·mor·al·iza'-
  tion
de·mor'al·ize
de·mote'
de·mot'ic
de·mo'tion
de·mul'cent
de·mur'
  object (*see* demure)
de·murred',
de·mur'ing
de·mure'
  prim (*see* demur)
de·mur'rage
de·mur'rer
de·na·tion·al·iza'-
  tion
de·na'tion·al·ize

de·nat·u·ral·iza'-
  tion
de·nat'u·ral·ize
de·na'tur·ant
de·na'ture
den'dri·form
den·dro·chron·o·-
  log'i·cal·ly
den·dro·chro·nol'-
  o·gy
den·dro·log'ic
den·drol'o·gist
den·drol'o·gy
den'gue
de·ni'al
den'ier
den'i·grate
den'im
den'i·zen
Den'mark
de·nom'i·nate
de·nom·i·na'tion
de·nom'i·na·tor
de·no·ta'tion
de·no'ta·tive
de·note'
de·noue·ment'
de·nounce'
dense'ly
den'si·ty
den'tal
den'tal·ly
den'ti·frice
den'tin
  or den'tine
den'tist

den'tist·ry
den·ti'tion
den'ture
de·nu·da'tion
de·nude'
de·nun·ci·a'tion
Den'ver
de·ny'
de·o'dor·ant
de·o'dor·ize
de·o'dor·iz·er
de·ox'i·dize
de·ox'i·diz·er
de·oxy·ri'bo·nu·
  cle·ic
de·part'
de·part'ment
de·part·men'tal
de·part·men'tal·
  ize
de·par'ture
de·pend'
de·pend·abil'i·ty
de·pend'able
de·pen'dence
  also de·pen'dance
de·pen'den·cy
de·pen'dent
de·per·son·al·iza'
  tion
de·per'son·al·ize
de·pict'
de·pic'tion
de·pic'ture
de·pil'a·to·ry
de·plane'

de·plete'
de·ple'tion
de·plor'able
de·plore'
de·po·lar·iza'tion
de·po'lar·ize
de·ploy'
de·po'nent
de·pop'u·late
de·pop·u·la'tion
de·port'
de·por·ta'tion
de·por·tee'
de·port'ment
de·pose'
de·pos'it
de·pos'i·tor
dep·o·si'tion
de·pos'i·to·ry
de'pot
de·pra·va'tion
  corrupt (*see*
   depravation)
de·prave'
de·praved'
de·prav'i·ty
dep're·cate
dep·re·ca'tion
dep're·ca·to·ry
de·pre'ci·ate
de·pre·ci·a'tion
dep·re·da'tion
de·press'
de·pres'sant
de·pres'sion
de·pres'sur·ize

dep·ri·va'tion
de·prive'
  loss (*see*
   depravation)
depth
dep·u·ta'tion
de·pute'
dep'u·tize
dep'u·ty
de·rail'
de·range'
de·range'ment
der'by
der'e·lict
der·e·lic'tion
de·ride'
de ri·gueur'
de·ri'sion
de·ri'sive
der·i·va'tion
de·riv'a·tive
de·rive'
der·ma·ti'tis
der·ma·tol'o·gist
der·ma·tol'o·gy
der'mis
der'o·gate
der·o·ga'tion
de·rog·a·to'ri·ly
de·rog'a·to·ry
der'rick
der·ri·ere'
  or der·ri·ère'
der·ring-do'
der'rin·ger
der'vish

de·sal'i·nate
de·sal·i·na'tion
de·sal'i·nize
de·sal·i·ni·za'tion
de·salt'
des'cant
de·scend'
de·scen'dant
   or de·scen'dent
de·scent'
   decline (see decent,
   dissent)

de·scrib'able
de·scribe'
de·scrip'tion
de·scrip'tive
de·scrip'tor
de·scry'
des'e·crate
des·e·cra'tion
de·seg're·gate
de·seg·re·ga'tion
de·sen·si·ti·za'-
   tion
de·sen'si·tize
de·sen'si·tiz·er
des'ert
   barren area (see
   dessert)

de·sert'
   leave (see dessert)

de·sert'er
de·ser'tion
de·serve'
de·serv'ed·ly
de·serv'ing

des'ic·cant
des'ic·cate
des·ic·ca'tion
des'ic·ca·tor
de·sid·er·a'tum
   pl de·sid·er·a'ta
de·sign'
des'ig·nate
des·ig·na'tion
de·sign'er
de·sign'ing
de·sir·abil'i·ty
de·sir'able
de·sire'
de·sir'ous
de·sist'
Des Moines'
des'o·late
des'o·late·ly
des·o·la'tion
des·oxy·ri'bo·nu·
   cle·ic
de·spair'
de·spair'ing·ly
des·patch'
des·per·a'do
   pl des·per·a'does *or*
   des·per·a'dos

des'per·ate
   hopeless (see
   disparate)

des'per·ate·ly
des·per·a'tion
de·spic'a·ble
des·pi'ca·bly
de·spise'

de·spite'
de·spoil'
de·spoil'ment
de·spo·li·a'tion
de·spond'
de·spon'den·cy
de·spon'dent
des'pot
des·pot'ic
des·pot'i·cal·ly
des'po·tism
des·sert'
   sweet (see desert)

des·ti·na'tion
des'tine
des'ti·ny
des'ti·tute
des·ti·tu'tion
de·stroy'
de·stroy'er
de·struct'
de·struc·ti·bil'i·ty
de·struc'ti·ble
de·struc'tion
de·struc'tive
de·struc'tive·ness
de·struc'tor
des'ue·tude
des'ul·to·ry
de·tach'
de·tach'able
de·tached'
de·tach'ment
de·tail'
de·tain'
de·tect'

de·tect'able
de·tec'tion
de·tec'tive
de·tec'tor
dé·tente'
de·ten'tion
de·ter'
  de·terred'
  de·ter'ing
de·ter'gent
de·te'ri·o·rate
de·te·ri·o·ra'tion
de·ter'min·able
de·ter'min·ably
de·ter'mi·na·cy
de·ter'mi·nant
de·ter'mi·nate
de·ter·mi·na'tion
de·ter'mine
de·ter'mined
de·ter'mined·ly
de·ter'mined·ness
de·ter'min·ism
de·ter'min·ist
de·ter'rence
de·ter'rent
de·test'
de·test'able
de·test'ably
de·tes·ta'tion
de·throne'
de·throne'ment
det'o·nate
det·o·na'tion
det'o·na·tor
de'tour

de·tract'
de·trac'tion
de·trac'tor
de·train'
det'ri·ment
det·ri·men'tal·ly
de·tri'tus
De·troit'
deuce
deu·te'ri·um
deut·sche mark'
de·val·u·a'tion
de·val'ue
dev'as·tate
dev·as·ta'tion
de·vel'op
de·vel'op·er
de·vel'op·ment
de·vel·op·men'
  tal·ly
de'vi·ant
de'vi·ate
de·vi·a'tion
de·vice'
  mechanism (see
  devise)
dev'il
  dev'iled
   or dev'illed
  dev'il·ing
   or dev'il·ling
dev'il·ish
dev'il·ment
dev'il·ry
  or dev'il·try
de'vi·ous

de·vis'able
de·vise'
  invent (see device)
de·vi'tal·ize
de·vit'ri·fy
de·void'
dev·o·lu'tion
de·volve'
de·vote'
de·vot'ed
dev·o·tee'
de·vo'tion
de·vo'tion·al
de·vour'
de·vour'er
de·vout'
de·vout'ness
dew
dew'ber·ry
dew'drop
dew'lap
dew'y
dex·ter'i·ty
dex'ter·ous
dex'trose
dhow
di·a·be'tes
di·a·bet'ic
di·a·bol'ic
di·a·bol'i·cal·ly
di·a·crit'ic
di·a·crit'i·cal
di'a·dem
di·aer'e·sis
  pl di·aer'e·ses
di'ag·nose

di·ag·no′sis
  pl di·ag·no′ses
di·ag·nos′tic
di·ag·nos′ti·cal·ly
di·ag·nos·ti′cian
di·ag′o·nal
di·ag′o·nal·ly
di′a·gram
  di′a·gramed
    or di′a·grammed
  di′a·gram·ing
    or di′a·gram·ming
di·a·gram·mat′ic
di·a·gram·mat′i·
    cal·ly
di′al
  di′aled
    or di′alled
  di′al·ing
    or di′al·ling
di′a·lect
di·a·lec′tic
di′a·logue
  or di′a·log
di·am′e·ter
di·a·met′ri·cal·ly
di′a·mond
di′a·mond·back
di·a·pa′son
di′a·per
di·aph′a·nous
di′a·phragm
di·a·phrag·mat′ic
di′a·rist
di·ar·rhe′a
  or di·ar·rhoe′a

di′a·ry
di·as′to·le
di·a·stroph′ic
di·as′tro·phism
dia·ther·my
dia·ton′ic
dia·ton′i·cal·ly
di′a·tribe
dib′ble
dice
di·chot′o·my
dick′er
dick′ey
  or dick′y
di·cot·y·le′don
di·cot·y·le′don·ous
Dic′ta·phone
dic′tate
dic·ta′tion
dic·ta·tor
dic·ta·to′ri·al
dic·ta′tor·ship
dic′tion
dic′tio·nary
Dic′to·graph
dic′tum
  pl dic′ta *also*
    dic′tums
di·dac′tic
di·dac′ti·cal·ly
di·dac′ti·cism
die
  verb, expire (see
    dye)

died
dying

die
  pl dice *or* dies
  noun, cube (see dye)

die
  noun, stamp (see
    dye)

die′hard
di·elec′tric
di·er·e′sis
die′sel
di′et
di′etary
di·etet′ic
di·etet′ics
di·eti′tian
  or di·eti′cian
dif′fer
dif′fer·ence
  unlikeness (see
    deference)
dif′fer·ent
dif·fer·en′tial
dif·fer·en′ti·ate
dif·fer·en·ti·a′tion
dif′fi·cult
dif′fi·cul·ty
dif′fi·dence
dif′fi·dent
dif·frac′tion
dif·fuse′
dif·fu′sion
dig
  dug
  dig′ging
di′gest
  noun

disaffection

di·gest′
  verb
di·gest·ibil′i·ty
di·gest′ible
di·ges′tion
di·ges′tive
dig′ger
dig′it
dig′i·tal
dig′i·tal·ly
dig·i·tal′is
dig′ni·fied
dig′ni·fy
dig′ni·tary
dig′ni·ty
di·gress′
di·gres′sion
di·gres′sive
di·lap′i·dat·ed
di·lap·i·da′tion
dil·a·ta′tion
di·late′
di·la′tion
dil′a·to·ry
di·lem′ma
dil·et·tante′
  pl dil·et·tantes′ *or*
  dil·et·tan′ti
dil′i·gence
dil′i·gent
dil′ly·dal·ly
dil′u·ent
di·lute′
di·lu′tion
dim
  dimmed

dim′ming
di·men′sion
di·men′sion·al
di·min′ish
di·min·u·en′do
dim·i·nu′tion
di·min′u·tive
dim′i·ty
dim′ly
dim′mer
dim′out
dim′ple
di·nar′
din′er
  one that dines (see dinner)
di·nette′
din′ghy
  boat (see dingy)
din′gi·ness
din′gy
  dull (see dinghy)
din′ky
din′ner
  meal (see diner)
din′ner·ware
di′no·saur
di·oc′e·san
di′o·cese
di·o·ra′ma
di·ox′ide
dip
  dipped
  dip′ping
diph·the′ria
diph′thong

di·plo′ma
di·plo′ma·cy
dip′lo·mat
dip·lo·mat′ic
dip·lo·mat′i·cal·ly
di·plo′ma·tist
dip′per
dip·so·ma′nia
dip·so·ma′ni·ac
dip′stick
dip′ter·an
dip′ter·ous
di·rect′
di·rec′tion
di·rec′tion·al
di·rec′tive
di·rect′ly
di·rec′tor
di·rec′tor·ate
di·rec′tor·ship
di·rec′to·ry
dire′ful
dirge
dir·ham′
dir′i·gi·ble
dirndl
dirt′i·ness
dirt′y
dis·abil′i·ty
dis·a′ble
dis·abuse′
dis·ad·van′tage
dis·ad·van·ta′-
  geous
dis·af·fect′
dis·af·fec′tion

dis·agree'
dis·agree'able
dis·agree'ably
dis·agree'ment
dis·al·low'
dis·al·low'ance
dis·ap·pear'
dis·ap·pear'ance
dis·ap·point'
dis·ap·point'ment
dis·ap·pro·ba'tion
dis·ap·prov'al
dis·ap·prove'
dis·arm'
dis·ar'ma·ment
dis·ar·range'
dis·ar·range'ment
dis·ar·ray'
dis·as·sem'ble
dis·as·so'ci·ate
di·sas'ter
di·sas'trous
dis·avow'
dis·avow'al
dis·band'
dis·bar'
dis·bar'ment
dis·be·lief'
dis·be·lieve'
dis·be·liev'er
dis·bur'den
dis·burse'
   pay out (see
   disperse)

dis·burse'ment
disc

dis·card'
dis·cern'
dis·cern'ible
dis·cern'ing
dis·cern'ment
dis·charge'
   verb
dis'charge
   noun
dis·charge'able
dis·ci'ple
dis·ci·pli·nar'i·an
dis'ci·plin·ary
dis'ci·pline
dis·claim'
dis·claim'er
dis·close'
dis·clo'sure
dis·cog'ra·pher
dis·cog'ra·phy
dis·col'or
dis·col·or·a'tion
dis·com·bob'u·
   late
dis·com'fit
dis·com'fi·ture
dis·com'fort
dis·com·mode'
dis·com·pose'
dis·com·po'sure
dis·con·cert'
dis·con·nect'
dis·con·nect'ed
dis·con·nec'tion
dis·con'so·late
dis·con·tent'

dis·con·tin'u·ance
dis·con·tin'ue
dis·con·ti·nu'i·ty
dis·con·tin'u·ous
dis'co·phile
dis'cord
dis·cor'dant
dis·co·theque'
dis'count
dis·count'able
dis·coun'te·nance
dis·cour'age
dis·cour'age·ment
dis'course
   noun
dis·course'
   verb
dis·cour'te·ous
dis·cour'te·sy
dis·cov'er
dis·cov'er·er
dis·cov'ery
dis·cred'it
dis·cred'it·able
dis·creet'
   prudent (see
   discrete)

dis·crep'an·cy
dis·crep'ant
dis·crete'
   distinct (see
   discreet)

dis·cre'tion
dis·cre'tion·ary
dis·crim'i·nate
dis·crim·i·na'tion

dis·crim′i·nat·ing
dis·crim′i·na·to·ry
dis·cur′sive
dis′cus
  disk (see discuss)
dis·cuss′
  argue (see discus)
dis·cus′sant
dis·cus′sion
dis·dain′
dis·dain′ful·ly
dis·ease′
dis·em·bark′
dis·em·bar·ka′tion
dis·em·bod′y
dis·em·bow′el
dis·em·bow′el·
  ment
dis·en·chant′
dis·en·cum′ber
dis·en·gage′
dis·en·tan′gle
dis·es·tab′lish
dis·es·tab′lish·
  ment
dis·es·teem′
dis·fa′vor
dis·fig′ure
dis·fig′ure·ment
dis·fran′chise
dis·gorge′
dis·grace′
dis·grace′ful·ly
dis·grun′tle
dis·guise′
dis·gust′

dis·gust′ed·ly
dis·ha·bille′
dis·har′mo·ny
dish′cloth
dis·heart′en
di·shev′el
  di·shev′eled
  or di·shev′elled

di·shev′el·ing
  or di·shev′el·ling

dis·hon′est
dis·hon′es·ty
dis·hon′or
dis·hon′or·able
dis·hon′or·ably
dish′rag
dish′wash·er
dish′wa·ter
dis·il·lu′sion
dis·il·lu′sion·ment
dis·in·cli·na′tion
dis·in·cline′
dis·in·fect′
dis·in·fec′tant
dis·in·fec′tion
dis·in·gen′u·ous
dis·in·her′it
dis·in′te·grate
dis·in′te·gra′tion
dis·in·ter′
dis·in′ter·est·ed
dis·in′ter·est·ed·
  ness
dis·join′
dis·joint′
dis·joint′ed

disk
  or disc
dis·like′
dis·lo·cate
dis·lo·ca′tion
dis·lodge′
dis·loy′al
dis·loy′al·ty
dis′mal
dis′mal·ly
dis·man′tle
dis·may′
dis·mem′ber
dis·mem′ber·ment
dis·miss′
dis·miss′al
dis·mount′
dis·obe′di·ence
dis·o·be′di·ent
dis·obey′
dis·or′der
dis·or′der·ly
dis·or·ga·ni·za′·
  tion
dis·or′ga·nize
dis·own′
dis·par′age
dis·par′age·ment
dis·par′ag·ing·ly
dis·par′ate
  dissimilar (see
  desperate)

dis·par′i·ty
dis·pas′sion·ate
dis·pas′sion·ate·ly
dis·patch′

dis·patch′er
dis·pel′
  dis·pell′ed
  dis·pel′ling
dis·pens′able
dis·pen′sa·ry
dis·pen·sa′tion
dis·pense′
dis·pens′er
dis·per′sal
dis·perse′
  spread (*see* disburse)

dis·per′sion
dis·pir′it
dis·place′
dis·place′ment
dis·play′
dis·please′
dis·plea′sure
dis·port′
dis·pos′able
dis·pos′al
dis·pose′
dis·pos′er
dis·po·si′tion
dis·pos·sess′
dis·pos·ses′sion
dis·proof′
dis·pro·por′tion
dis·pro·por′tion·ate
dis·prove′
dis·put·abil′i·ty
dis·put′able
dis·pu′tant

dis·pu·ta′tion
dis·pu·ta′tious
dis·pute′
dis·put′er
dis·qual·i·fi·ca′tion
dis·qual′i·fy
dis·qui′et
dis·qui′etude
dis·qui·si′tion
dis·re·gard′
dis·re·gard′ful
dis·re·pair′
dis·rep′u·ta·ble
dis·rep′u·ta·bly
dis·re·pute′
dis·re·spect′
dis·re·spect′ful·ly
dis·robe′
dis·rupt′
dis·rup′tion
dis·rup′tive
dis·sat·is·fac′tion
dis·sat′is·fy
dis·sect′
dis·sect′ed
dis·sec′tion
dis·sem′ble
dis·sem′bler
dis·sem′i·nate
dis·sem·i·na′tion
dis·sen′sion
dis·sent′
  disagree (*see* decent, descent)

dis·sent′er

dis·sen′tient
dis·ser·ta′tion
dis·ser′vice
dis·sev′er
dis′si·dence
dis′si·dent
dis·sim′i·lar
dis·sim·i·lar′i·ty
dis·sim′u·late
dis·sim·u·la′tion
dis′si·pate
dis′si·pat·ed
dis·si·pa′tion
dis·so′ci·ate
dis·so·ci·a′tion
dis·sol′u·ble
dis′so·lute
dis′so·lute·ness
dis·so·lu′tion
dis·solve′
dis′so·nance
dis′so·nant
dis·suade′
dis·sua′sion
dis′taff
dis·sym′me·try
dis′tance
dis′tant
dis·taste′
dis·taste′ful
dis·tem′per
dis·tend′
dis·ten′sion
  or dis·ten′tion

dis′tich
dis·ti·chous

dis·till'
  also dis·til'

dis·til·ate

dis·til·la'tion

dis·till'er

dis·till'ery

dis·tinct'

dis·tinc'tion

dis·tinc'tive

dis·tin'guish

dis·tin'guish·able

dis·tin'guish·ably

dis·tort'

dis·tor'tion

dis·tract'

dis·trac'tion

dis·train'

dis·trait'

dis·traught'

dis·tress'

dis·tress'ful·ly

dis·trib'ute

dis·tri·bu'tion

dis·trib'u·tive

dis·trib'u·tor

dis'trict

Dis'trict of Co·
  lum'bia

dis·trust'

dis·trust'ful·ly

dis·turb'

dis·tur'bance

dis·turbed'

dis·u'nion

dis·unite'

dis·u'ni·ty

dis·use'

ditch

dith'er

dit'to

dit'ty

di·uret'ic

di·ur'nal

di'va
  pl di'vas *or* di've

di'va·gate

di·va·ga'tion

di'van

dive

  dived
    or dove

  dived

  div'ing

div'er

di·verge'

di·ver'gence

di·ver'gent

di'vers
  various (*see* diverse)

di·verse'
  unlike (*see* divers)

di·ver·si·fi·ca'tion

di·ver'si·fy

di·ver'sion

di·ver'sion·ary

di·ver'si·ty

di·vert'

di·vest'

di·vide'

div'i·dend

di·vid'ers

div·i·na'tion

di·vine'

di·vin'er

di·vin'i·ty

di·vis·i·bil'i·ty

di·vis'i·ble

di·vi'sion

di·vi'sion·al

di·vi'sive

di·vi'sor

di·vorce'

di·vor·cée'

div'ot

di·vulge'

diz'zi·ly

diz'zi·ness

diz'zy

do

  did

  done

  do'ing

  does

dob'bin

do'cent

doc'ile

do·cil'i·ty

dock'age

dock'et

dock'hand

dock'yard

doc'tor

doc'tor·al

doc'tor·ate

doc·tri·naire'

doc'tri·nal

doc'trine

doc'u·ment

doc·u·men'ta·ry
doc·u·men·ta'tion
dod'der
dodge
do'do
   pl do'does *or* do'dos
doe'skin
doff
dog
   dogged
   dog'ging
dog'cart
dog'catch·er
doge
dog'-ear
dog'fight
dog'fish
dog'ged
dog'ger·el
dog'house
dog'ma
dog·mat'ic
dog·mat'i·cal·ly
dog'ma·tism
dog'ma·tist
dog'trot
doi'ly
do'ings
do-it-your·self'
dol'drums
dole'ful
dole'ful·ly
dol'lar
dol'lop
dol'ly
dol'men

do'lor
do'lor·ous
dol'phin
dolt'ish
do·main'
do·mes'tic
do·mes'ti·cal·ly
do·mes'ti·cate
do·mes·ti·ca'tion
do·mes·tic'i·ty
dom'i·cile
dom·i·cil'i·ary
dom'i·nance
dom'i·nant
dom'i·nate
dom·i·na'tion
dom·i·neer'
Do·min'i·can Re-
   pub·lic
do·min'ion
dom'i·no
   pl dom'i·noes *or*
   dom'i·nos
don
   donned
   don'ning
do'nate
do·na'tion
don'key
don'ny·brook
do'nor
doo'dad
doo'dle
doo'dler
dooms'day
door'jamb

door'keep·er
door'knob
door'man
door'mat
door'plate
door'step
door'way
door'yard
dop'ant
dor'man·cy
dor'mant
dor'mer
dor'mi·to·ry
dor'mouse
   pl dor'mice
dor'sal
do'ry
dos'age
dos'sier
dot
   dot'ted
   dot'ting
dot'age
dot'ard
dot'ing
dou'ble
dou·ble-cross'
dou·ble-cross'er
dou·ble-deal'er
dou·ble-deal'ing
dou·ble-deck'er
dou·ble en·ten'dre
dou·ble-head'er
dou·ble-park'
dou'ble-quick
dou·ble-space'

dou'blet
dou'ble-talk
dou·ble·think
dou·bloon'
dou'bly
doubt
doubt'ful
doubt'ful·ly
doubt'less
douche
dough
dough'boy
dough'nut
dough'ty
dough'y
dour
douse
dove'cote
or dove'cot
Do'ver
dove'tail
dow'a·ger
dowd'i·ly
dowd'i·ness
dowd'y
dow'el
dow'er
down'beat
down'cast
down'fall
down'fal·len
down'grade
down·heart'ed
down·hill'
down'pour
down·range'

down'right
down·stage
down'stairs'
down'stream'
down'stroke
down'swing
down-to-earth
down'town
down·trod'den
down'turn
down'ward
also down'wards
down·wind
down'y
dow'ry
dox·ol'o·gy
doze
doz'en
doz'enth
drach'ma
dra·co'ni·an
draft·ee'
drafts'man
draft'y
drag
dragged
drag'ging
drag'net
drag'o·man
pl drag'o·mans or
drag'o·men
drag'on
drag'on·fly
dra·goon'
drain'age
drain'pipe

dra'ma
dra·mat'ic
dra·mat'i·cal·ly
dram'a·tist
dram·a·ti·za'tion
dram'a·tize
drap'er
drap'ery
dras'tic
dras'ti·cal·ly
draw
drew
drawn
draw'ing
draw'back
draw'bridge
draw'er
draw'ing
drawl
draw'string
dread'ful
dread'ful·ly
dread'nought
dream
dreamed
or dreamt
dream'ing
dream'er
dream'i·ly
dream'land
dream'like
dream'world
dream'y
drear'i·ly
drear'y
dredge

dredg′er
dress′mak·er
dress′mak·ing
dres·sage′
dress′er
dress′ing
dress′y
drib′ble
drib′let
dri′er
  also dry′er
drift′er
drift′wood
drill′er
drill′mas·ter
dri′ly
drink
  drank
  drunk
    or drank
  drink′ing
drink′able
drip
  dripped
    or dript
  drip′ping
drip-dry
drive
  drove
  driv′en
  driv′ing
drive′-in
driv′el
  driv′eled
    or driv′elled

driv′el·ing
  or driv′el·ling
driv′el·er
  or driv′el·ler
driv′er
drive′way
driz′zle
droll′ery
drol′ly
drom′e·dary
drop
  dropped
  drop′ping
drop′kick
drop′let
drop′out
drop′per
drop′sy
dross
drought
  or drouth
drov′er
drowse
drows′i·ly
drows′i·ness
drows′y
drub
  drubbed
  drub′bing
drudge
drudg′ery
drug
  drugged
  drug′ging
drug′gist

drug′store
dru′id
drum
  drummed
  drum′ming
drum′beat
drum′mer
drum′stick
drunk′ard
drunk′en·ness
dry′-clean
dry′er
dry′ly
dry′ness
dry-rot′
du′al
  double (*see* duel)
du′al·ism
du·al′i·ty
du′al·ly
dub
  dubbed
  dub′bing
du·bi′ety
du′bi·ous
du′bi·ous·ness
du′cal
duc′at
duch′ess
duch′y
duck′bill
duck′board
duck′ling
duck′pin
duc′tile

duc·til′i·ty
duct′less
dud′geon
du′el
   combat (see dual)
du′el·ist
  or du′el·list
du·et′
duf′fer
dug′out
duke′dom
dul′cet
dul′ci·mer
dull′ard
dull′ness
  or dul′ness
dul′ly
Du Luth′
du′ly
dumb′bell
dumb′found′
  or dum·found′
dumb′ly
dumb′wait′er
dum′dum
dum′my
dump′ling
dump′y
dun
  dunned
  dun′ning
dun′der·head
dun·ga·ree′
dun′geon
dung′hill

du·o·de′nal
du·o·de′num
du′plex
du′pli·cate
du·pli·ca′tion
du′pli·ca·tor
du·plic′i·ty
du·ra·bil′i·ty
du′ra·ble
du′rance
du·ra′tion
du·ress′
dur′ing
dusk′i·ly
dusk′i·ness
dusk′y
dust′er
dust′i·ly
dust′i·ness
dust′less
dust′off
dust′pan
dust′y
Dutch
du′te·ous
du′ti·able
du′ti·ful
du′ti·ful·ly
du′ty
dwarf
  pl dwarfs *or*
    dwarves
dwarf′ish
dwell
  dwelt
  or dwelled

dwell′ing
dwin′dle
dwin′dling
dyb′buk
dye
  color (see die)
dyed
dye′ing
dye′stuff
dy·nam′ic
dy·nam′i·cal·ly
dy′na·mism
dy′na·mite
dy′na·mo
dy′nast
dy·nas′tic
dy′nas·ty
dyne
dy′node
dys′en·tery
dys·pep′sia
dys·pep′tic
dys·pep′ti·cal·ly
dys·tro′phic
dys′tro·phy

E

ea′ger
ea′ger·ly
ea′ger·ness
ea′gle
ea′glet
ear′ache
ear′drum
ear′li·ness

ear'lobe
ear'ly
ear'mark
ear'muff
ear'nest
ear'nest·ly
ear'nest·ness
earn'ings
ear'phone
ear'ring
ear'shot
ear'split·ting
earth'en
earth'en·ware
earth'i·ness
earth'ling
earth'ly
earth'quake
earth'shak·ing
earth'work
earth'worm
earth'y
ear'wax
ea'sel
ease'ment
eas'i·ly
eas'i·ness
east'er·ly
east'ern
East'ern·er
east'ward
eas'y
easy·go'ing
eat
  ate
  eat'en

eat'ing
eat'able
eat'er
eau de co·logne'
  pl eaux de co·logne'
eaves
eaves'drop
eaves'drop·per
eb'o·ny
ebul'lience
ebul'lient
eb'ul·lism
eb·ul·li'tion
ec·cen'tric
ec·cen'tri·cal·ly
ec·cen·tric'i·ty
ec·cle·si·as'tic
ec·cle·si·as'ti·cal
ech'e·lon
ech'o
  pl ech'oes
echo·lo·ca'tion
éclair'
éclat'
eclec'tic
eclipse'
eclip'tic
ec'logue
ec·o·log'ic
  or ec·o·log'i·cal
ec·o·log'i·cal·ly
ecol'o·gist
ecol'o·gy
ec·o·nom'ic
ec·o·nom'i·cal
ec·o·nom'i·cal·ly

ec·o·nom'ics
econ'o·mist
econ'o·mize
econ'o·my
eco'sphere
eco·spher'ic
eco·sys'tem
eco'tone
ec'ru
ec'sta·sy
ec·stat'ic
ec·stat'i·cal·ly
Ec'ua·dor
Ec·ua·dor'an
  or Ec·ua·dor'ian
ec·u·men'i·cal
ec·u·men'i·cal·ly
ec·u·me·nic'i·ty
ec·ze'ma
ec·zem'a·tous
Ed'am
ed'dy
e'del·weiss
ede'ma
edem'a·tous
edge
edge'ways
  or edge'wise
edg'i·ness
edg'ing
edg'y
ed·i·bil'i·ty
ed'i·ble
e'dict
ed·i·fi·ca'tion
ed'i·fice

ed'i·fy
ed'it
edi'tion
ed'i·tor
ed·i·to'ri·al
ed·i·to·ri·al·iza'-
  tion
ed·i·to'ri·al·ize
ed·i·to'ri·al·iz·er
ed·i·to'ri·al·ly
ed'i·tor·ship
Ed'mon·ton
ed'u·ca·ble
ed'u·cate
ed·u·ca'tion
ed·u·ca'tion·al·ly
ed'u·ca·tor
educe'
educ'ible
educ'tion
ee'rie
  also ee'ry
ee'ri·ly
ef·face'
ef·face'able
ef·face'ment
ef·fect'
  result (see affect)
ef·fec'tive
ef·fec'tive·ly
ef·fec'tive·ness
ef·fec'tu·al
ef·fec'tu·al·ly
ef·fec'tu·ate
ef·fem'i·na·cy
ef·fem'i·nate

ef'fer·ent
ef·fer·vesce'
ef·fer·ves'cence
ef·fer·ves'cent
ef·fete'
ef·fi·ca'cious
ef'fi·ca·cy
ef·fi'cien·cy
ef·fi'cient
ef·fi'cient·ly
ef'fi·gy
ef·flo·resce'
ef·flo·res'cence
ef'flu·ence
ef'flu·ent
ef·flu'vi·um
  pl ef·flu'vi·a or
  ef·flu'vi·ums
ef'fort
ef'fort·less·ly
ef·fron'tery
ef·ful'gence
ef·ful'gent
ef·fuse'
ef·fu'sion
ef·fu'sive
egal·i·tar'i·an
egal·i·tar'i·an·ism
egg'beat·er
egg'head
egg'nog
egg'plant
egg'shell
e'gis
e'go
ego·cen'tric

ego·cen·tric'i·ty
e'go·ism
e'go·ist
ego·is'tic
  also ego·is'ti·cal
ego·is'ti·cal·ly
e'go·tism
e'go·tist
ego·tis'tic
  or ego·tis'ti·cal
ego·tis'ti·cal·ly
egre'gious
e'gress
e'gret
E'gypt
Egyp'tian
ei'der
eigh·teen'
eigh·teenth'
eighth
eight'i·eth
eight'y
ei'ther
ejac'u·late
ejac·u·la'tion
eject'
ejec'tion
ejec'tor
eke
ekis·ti'cian
ekis'tics
elab'o·rate
elab'o·rate·ly
elab'o·rate·ness
elab·o·ra'tion
élan'

elapse'
elas'tic
elas·tic'i·ty
elate'
ela'tion
el'bow
el'bow·room
el'der·ber·ry
el'der·ly
el'dest
El Do·ra'do
elec'tion
elec·tion·eer'
elec'tive
elec'tor
elec'tor·al
elec'tor·ate
elec'tric
   or elec'tri·cal
elec'tri·cal·ly
elec·tri'cian
elec·tric'i·ty
elec·tri·fi·ca'tion
elec'tri·fy
elec·tro·anal'y·sis
elec·tro·an·a·lyt'ic
elec·tro·car'dio·
   gram
elec·tro·car'dio·
   graph
elec·tro·car·di·og'
   ra·phy
elec'tro·chem'i·
   cal·ly
elec·tro·chem'is·
   try

elec·tro·en·ceph'
   a·lo·gram
elec·tro·en·ceph'
   a·lo·graph
elec'tro·cute
elec·tro·cu'tion
elec'trode
elec·trol'y·sis
elec'tro·lyte
elec·tro·lyt'ic
elec·tro·mag'net
elec·tro·mag·
   net'ic
elec·tro·mag·ne·
   tism
elec·trom'e·ter
elec·tro·mo'tive
elec'tron
elec·tron'ic
elec·tron'i·cal·ly
elec·tron'ics
elec'tro·plate
elec·tro·sen'si·tive
elec'tr·shock
elec·tro·ther'a·py
elec·tro·ther'mal
elec'tro·type
el·ee·mos'y·nary
el'e·gance
el'e·gant
el·e·gi'ac
el'e·gize
el'e·gy
el'e·ment
el·e·men'tal
el·e·men'ta·ry

el'e·phant
el·e·phan·ti'a·sis
el·e·phan'tine
el'e·vate
el·e·va'tion
el'e·va·tor
elev'enth
elf
   pl elves
elf'in
elf'ish
elic'it
   draw out (see illicit)
elide'
el·i·gi·bil'i·ty
el'i·gi·ble
elim'i·nate
elim·i·na'tion
eli'sion
elite'
elix'ir
Eliz·a·be'than
el·lipse'
el·lip'sis
   pl el·lip'ses
el·lip'tic
el·lip'ti·cal
Eliz'a·beth
el·o·cu'tion
el·o·cu'tion·ist
elon'gate
elon·ga'tion
elope'
elope'ment
el'o·quence
el'o·quent

El Pas'o
El Paso'an
El Sal'va·dor
else'where
elu'ci·date
elu·ci·da'tion
elude'
    evade (see allude)

elu'sive
    evasive (see
    allusive)

elu'sive·ly
elu'sive·ness
Ely'sian
Ely'si·um
ema'ci·ate
ema·ci·a'tion
em'a·nate
em·a·na'tion
eman'ci·pate
eman·ci·pa'tion
eman'ci·pa·tor
emas'cu·late
emas·cu·la'tion
em·balm'
em·balm'er
em·bank'
em·bank'ment
em·bar'go
    pl em·bar'goes

em·bark'
em·bar·ka'tion
em·bar'rass
em·bar'rass·ment
em'bas·sy
em·bat'tle

em·bed'
em·bel'lish
em·bel'lish·ment
em'ber
em·bez'zle
em·bez'zle·ment
em·bez'zler
em·bit'ter
em·bla'zon
em'blem
em·blem·at'ic
    also em·blem·at'i·cal

em·bod'i·ment
em·bod'y
em·bold'en
em·bol'ic
em'bo·lism
em·boss'
em·bou·chure'
em·brace'
em·brace'able
em·bra'sure
em'bro·cate
em·bro·ca'tion
em·broi'der
em·broi'dery
em·broil'
em·broil'ment
em'bryo
em·bry·o·log'i·cal
em·bry·ol'o·gist
em·bry·ol'o·gy
em·bry·on'ic
em·cee'
emend'
    correct (see amend)

emen·da'tion
em'er·ald
emerge'
emer'gence
emer'gen·cy
emer'gent
emer'i·tus
    pl emer'i·ti

em'ery
emet'ic
em'i·grant
em'i·grate
em·i·gra'tion
émi·gré'
    or em·i·gré'

em'i·nence
em'i·nent
    high (see imminent)

emir'
em'is·sary
emis'sion
emis·siv'i·ty
emit'
    emit'ted
    emit'ting

emol'lient
emol'u·ment
emote'
emo'tion
emo'tion·al
emo'tion·al·ly
emo'tive
em·path'ic
em'pa·thy
em·pen·nage'
em'per·or

em'pha·sis
 pl em'pha·ses
em'pha·size
em·phat'ic
em·phat'i·cal·ly
em·phy·se'ma
em'pire
em·pir'i·cal
 or em·pir'ic
em·pir'i·cal·ly
em·pir'i·cism
em·pir'i·cist
em·place'ment
em·ploy'
em·ploy·abil'i·ty
em·ploy'able
em·ploy·ee'
em·ploy'er
em·ploy'ment
em·po'ri·um
 pl em·po'ri·ums *also*
  em·po'ria
em·pow'er
em'press
emp'ti·ness
emp'ty
emp·ty-hand'ed
em·py·re'an
e'mu
em'u·late
em·u·la'tion
em'u·lous
emul'si·fi·able
emul'si·fi·ca·tion
emul'si·fi·er

emul'si·fy
emul'sion
en·a'ble
en·a'bling
en·act'
en·act'ment
enam'el
 enam'eled
  or enam'elled
enam'el·ing
 or enam'el·ling
enam'el·ware
en·am'or
en bloc'
en·camp'
en·camp'ment
en·cap'su·late
en·case'
en·ceph·a·lit'ic
en·ceph·a·li'tis
en·ceph·a·lo·my·
 eli'tis
en·chain'
en·chant'
en·chant'er
en·chant'ment
en·chant'ress
en·chi·la'da
en·ci'pher
en·cir'cle
en·cir'cle·ment
en'clave
en·close'
en·clo'sure
en·code'

en·co'mi·um
 pl en·co'mi·ums *or*
  en·co'mia

en·com'pass
en'core
en·coun'ter
en·cour'age
en·cour'age·ment
en·croach'
en·croach'ment
en·crust'
en·cum'ber
en·cum'brance
en·cyc'li·cal
en·cy·clo·pe'dia
en·cy·clo·pe'dic
en·cyst'
en·dan'ger
en·dear'
en·dear'ment
en·deav'or
en·dem'ic
end'ing
en'dive
end'less
end'most
en'do·crine
en·do·cri·nol'o·gy
en·dog'a·mous
en·dog'a·my
en·dorse'
en·dorse'ment
en'do·scope
en·do·scop'ic
en·dos'co·py

en·dow'
en·dow'ment
en·dur'able
en·dur'ance
en·dure'
end'ways
en'e·ma
en'e·my
en·er·get'ic
en·er·get'i·cal·ly
en'er·gize
en'er·giz·er
en'er·gy
en'er·vate
en·er·va'tion
en·fee'ble
en·fee'ble·ment
en'fi·lade
en·fold'
en·force'
en·force'able
en·force'ment
en·fran'chise
en·fran'chise·
  ment
en·gage'
en·gage'ment
en·gag'ing
en·gen'der
en'gine
en·gi·neer'
En'gland
En'glish
en·graft'
en·grave'

en·grav'er
en·grav'ing
en·gross'
en·gulf'
en·hance'
en·hance'ment
enig'ma
en·ig·mat'ic
  also en·ig·mat'i·cal
en·ig·mat'i·cal·ly
en·jamb'ment
  or en·jambe'ment
en·join'
en·joy'
en·joy'able
en·joy'ably
en·joy'ment
en·large'
en·large'ment
en·larg'er
en·light'en
en·light'en·ment
en·list'
en·list'ment
en·liv'en
en masse'
en·mesh'
en'mi·ty
en·no'ble
en·no'ble·ment
en'nui
enor'mi·ty
enor'mous
enough'
en·plane'

en·quire'
en'qui·ry
en·rage'
en·rap'ture
en·rich'
en·rich'ment
en·roll'
  or en·rol'
en·roll'ed
en·roll'ing
en·roll'ment
en route'
en·sconce'
en·sem'ble
en·sheathe'
en·shrine'
en·shroud'
en'sign
en'si·lage
en·slave'
en·slave'ment
en·snare'
en·sue'
en·sure'
en·tail'
en·tan'gle
en·tan'gle·ment
en·tente'
en'ter
en·ter·i'tis
en'ter·prise
en'ter·pris·ing
en·ter·tain'
en·ter·tain'er
en·ter·tain'ment

en·thrall'
  or en·thral'
en·throne'
en·thuse'
en·thu'si·asm
en·thu'si·ast
en·thu·si·as'tic
en·thu·si·as'ti·
  cal·ly
en·tice'
en·tice'ment
en·tire'
en·tire'ly
en·tire'ty
en·ti'tle
en'ti·ty
en·tomb'
en·tomb'ment
en·to·mo·log'i·cal
en·to·mol'o·gist
en·to·mol'o·gy
en·tou·rage'
en'tr'acte'
en'trails
en·train'
en'trance
  noun
en·trance'
  verb
en'trant
en·trap'
en·trap'ment
en·treat'
en·treat'y
en'trée
  or en'tree

en·trench'
en·trench'ment
en·tre·pre·neur'
en'tro·py
en·trust'
en'try
en·twine'
enu'mer·ate
enu·mer·a'tion
enu'mer·a·tive
enu'mer·a·tor
enun'ci·ate
enun·ci·a'tion
enun'ci·a·tor
en·u·re'sis
en·vel'op
en've·lope
en·vel'op·ment
en·ven'om
en'vi·able
en'vi·ably
en'vi·ous
en'vi·ous·ly
en'vi·ous·ness
en·vi'ron·ment
en·vi·ron·men'tal
en·vi'rons
en·vis'age
en'voy
en'vy
en·wreathe'
en·zy·mat'ic
en'zyme
e'on
ep·au·let'
  also ep·au·lette'

epergne'
ephed'rine
ephem'era
ephem'er·al
ep'ic
  poem (see epoch)

epi'cen·ter
ep'i·cure
ep·i·cu·re'an
ep·i·dem'ic
epi·der'mal
epi·der'mis
epi·glot'tis
ep'i·gram
ep·i·gram·
  mat'ic
ep·i·gram·mat'i·
  cal·ly
ep'i·graph
epig'ra·pher
ep·i·graph'ic
epig'ra·phy
ep'i·lep·sy
ep·i·lep'tic
ep'i·logue
Epiph'a·ny
epis'co·pa·cy
epis'co·pal
Epis·co·pa'lian
epis'co·pate
ep'i·sode
ep·i·sod'ic
ep·i·sod'i·cal·ly
epis'tle
epis'to·lary
ep'i·taph

ep·i·tha·la′mi·um
or ep·i·tha·la′mi·on
pl ep·i·tha·la′mi-
   ums *or* ep·i·tha·
   la′mia

ep·i·the′li·al
ep·i·the′li·um
ep′i·thet
epit′o·me
epit′o·mize
ep′och
   era (see epic*)*

ep′och·al
ep·ox′y
eq·ua·bil′i·ty
eq′ua·ble
eq′ua·bly
e′qual
   e′qualed
      or e′qualled

   e′qual·ing
      or e′qual·ling

equal′i·ty
equal·iza′tion
e′qual·ize
e′qual·iz·er
e′qual·ly
equa·nim′i·ty
equate′
equa′tion
equa′tor
equa·to′ri·al
Equa·to′ri·al
   Guin′ea
eq′uer·ry
eques′tri·an

eques·tri·enne′
equi·an′gu·lar
equi·dis′tant
equi·lat′er·al
equil′i·brate
equil·i·bra′tion
equi·lib′ri·um
   pl equi·lib′ri·ums *or*
      equi·lib′ri·a

e′quine
equi·noc′tial
e′qui·nox
equip′
   equipped′
   equip′ping
eq′ui·page
equip′ment
eq′ui·poise
eq′ui·ta·ble
eq′ui·ta·bly
eq·ui·ta′tion
eq′ui·ty
equiv′a·lence
equiv′a·lent
equiv′o·cal
equiv′o·cal·ly
equiv′o·cate
equiv·o·ca′tion
equiv′o·ca·tor
er′a
erad′i·ca·ble
erad′i·cate
erad·i·ca′tion
erad′i·ca·tor
eras′able
erase′

eras′er
era′sure
erect′
erec′tion
erec′tor
ere·long′
E′rie
er′mine
erode′
erog′e·nous
   also er·o·gen′ic

ero′sion
ero′sive
erot′ic
erot′i·ca
erot′i·cal·ly
erot′i·cism
er′ran·cy
er′rand
er′rant
er·ra′ta
er·rat′ic
er·rat′i·cal·ly
er·ra′tum
   pl er·ra′ta

er·ro′ne·ous
er′ror
er′satz
erst′while
er′u·dite
er·u·di′tion
erupt′
erup′tion
erup′tive
er·y·sip′e·las
es′ca·late

es·ca·la'tion
es'ca·la·tor
es·cal'lop
es'ca·pade
es·cape'
es·cap·ee'
es·cap'ism
es·cap'ist
es'ca·role
es·carp'
es·carp'ment
es'char
es·cha·rot'ic
es·cha·to·log'i·
  cal·ly
es·cha·tol'o·gy
es·cheat'
es·chew'
es'cort
es·cri·toire'
es'crow
es·cu'do
es·cutch'eon
Es'ki·mo
eso·pha·geal'
esoph'a·gus
es·o·ter'ic
es·o·ter'i·cal·ly
es'pa·drille
es·pal'ier
es·pe'cial
es·pe'cial·ly
Es·pe·ran'to
es'pi·o·nage
es'pla·nade
es·pous'al

es·pouse'
espres'so
es·prit' de corps
es·py'
es'quire
es·say'
  verb, attempt (see
  assay)

es'say
  noun

es'say·ist
es'sence
es·sen'tial
es·sen'tial·ly
es·tab'lish
es·tab'lish·ment
es·tate'
es·teem'
es'ter
es'thete
es·thet'ic
es'ti·ma·ble
es'ti·mate
es·ti·ma'tion
es'ti·ma·tor
Es·to'nia
Es·to'ni·an
es·trange'
es·trange'ment
es'tro·gen
es'tu·ary
etch
etch'er
etch'ing
eter'nal
eter'nal·ly

eter'ni·ty
eth'ane
e'ther
ethe're·al
ethe're·al·ly
eth'i·cal
eth'i·cal·ly
eth'ics
Ethi·o'pia
Ethi·o'pi·an
eth'nic
eth'ni·cal·ly
eth·no·cen'tric
eth·no·cen'tri·
  cal·ly
eth·no·cen'trism
eth·nog'ra·pher
eth·no·graph'ic
eth·no·graph'i·
  cal·ly
eth·nog'ra·phy
eth·no·log'ic
eth·no·log'i·cal·ly
eth·nol'o·gist
eth·nol'o·gy
e'thos
eth'yl
eti·o·log'ic
eti·ol'o·gy
et'i·quette
é'tude
et·y·mo·log'i·cal
et·y·mol'o·gist
et·y·mol'o·gy
eu·ca·lyp'tus
Eu'cha·rist

eu·cha·ris′tic
eu′chre
eu·gen′ic
eu·gen′i·cal·ly
eu·gen′ics
eu·lo·gis′tic
eu′lo·gize
eu′lo·gy
eu′nuch
eu′phe·mism
eu·phe·mis′tic
eu·phe·mis′ti·
  cal·ly
eu·phon′ic
eu·pho′ni·ous
eu′pho·ny
eu·pho′ria
eu·phor′ic
Eur·a′sian
eu·re′ka
Eu′ro·bond
Eu′ro·dol·lar
Eu′rope
Eu·ro·pe′an
eu·sta′chian
eu·tha·na′sia
eu·then′ic
eu·then′ics
evac′u·ate
evac·u·a′tion
evac·u·ee′
evade′
eval′u·ate
eval·u·a′tion
ev·a·nes′cence
ev·a·nes′cent

evan·gel′i·cal
Evan·gel′i·cal·
  ism
evan·gel′i·cal·ly
evan′ge·lism
evan′ge·list
evan·ge·lis′tic
evan·ge·lis′ti·
  cal·ly
evan′ge·lize
Ev′ans·ville
evap′o·rate
evap·o·ra′tion
evap′o·ra·tor
eva′sion
eva′sive
even·hand′ed
eve′ning
e′ven·ly
e′ven·ness
e′ven·song
event′
event′ful
e′ven·tide
even·tu′al
even·tu·al′i·ty
even′tu·al·ly
even′tu·ate
ev′er
ev·er·bloom′ing
ev′er·glade
ev′er·green
ev·er·last′ing
ev·er·more′
ev′ery
ev′ery·body

ev′ery·day
ev′ery·one
ev′ery·thing
ev′ery·where
evict′
evic′tion
ev′i·dence
ev′i·dent
ev·i·den′tial
ev·i·den′tial·ly
evil·do′er
e′vil·ly
evil-mind′ed
evince′
evis′cer·ate
evis·cer·a′tion
evo·ca′tion
evoke′
ev·o·lu′tion
ev·o·lu′tion·ary
ev·o·lu′tion·ist
evolve′
ewe
  *female sheep (see
  yew)*

ew′er
ex·ac′er·bate
ex·ac·er·ba′tion
ex·act′
ex·act′ing
ex·ac′tion
ex·ac′ti·tude
ex·act′ly
ex·act′ness
ex·ag′ger·ate
ex·ag·ger·a′tion

ex·ag'ger·a·tor
ex·alt'
ex·al·ta'tion
ex·am·i·na'tion
ex·am'ine
ex·am'in·er
ex·am'ple
ex·as'per·ate
ex·as·per·a'tion
ex'ca·vate
ex'ca·va'tion
ex'ca·va·tor
ex·ceed'
    surpass (see accede)
ex·ceed'ing·ly
ex·cel'
    ex·celled'
    ex·cel'ling
ex'cel·lence
ex'cel·len·cy
ex'cel·lent
ex·cel'si·or
ex·cept'
    leave out (see accept)
ex·cep'tion
ex·cep'tion·able
ex·cep'tion·al
ex·cep'tion·al·ly
ex'cerpt
ex·cerp'tion
ex·cess'
    surplus (see access)
ex·ces'sive
ex·ces'sive·ly
ex·change'

ex·change'able
ex'che·quer
ex'cis·able
ex·cise'
ex·ci'sion
ex·cit·abil'i·ty
ex·cit'able
ex·ci'tant
ex·ci·ta'tion
ex·cite'
ex·cit'ed·ly
ex·cite'ment
ex·claim'
ex·cla·ma'tion
ex·clam'a·to·ry
ex·clude'
ex·clu'sion
ex·clu'sive
ex·clu'sive·ness
ex·clu·siv'i·ty
ex·com·mu'ni·cate
ex·com·mu·ni·ca'tion
ex·co'ri·ate
ex·co·ri·a'tion
ex'cre·ment
ex·cres'cence
ex·cres'cent
ex·crete'
ex·cre'tion
ex'cre·to·ry
ex·cru'ci·at·ing
ex'cul·pate
ex·cul·pa'tion
ex·cul'pa·to·ry

ex·cur'sion
ex·cur'sion·ist
ex·cur'sive
ex·cus'able
ex·cus'ably
ex·cuse'
ex'e·cra·ble
ex'e·crate
ex·e·cra'tion
ex'e·cute
ex·e·cu'tion
ex·e·cu'tion·er
ex·ec'u·tive
ex·ec'u·tor
ex·ec'u·trix
ex·e·ge'sis
    pl ex·e·ge'ses
ex'e·gete
ex·em'plar
ex·em'pla·ry
ex·em·pli·fi·ca'tion
ex·em'pli·fy
ex·empt'
ex·emp'tion
ex'er·cis·able
ex'er·cise
    exert (see exorcise)
ex'er·cis·er
ex·ert'
ex·er'tion
ex·ha·la'tion
ex·hale'
ex·haust'
ex·haust·ibil'i·ty
ex·haust'ible

ex·haus′tion
ex·haus′tive
ex·haust′less
ex·hib′it
ex·hi·bi′tion
ex·hi·bi′tion·ism
ex·hib′i·tor
ex·hil′a·rate
ex·hil·a·ra′tion
ex·hort′
ex·hor·ta′tion
ex·hu·ma′tion
ex·hume′
ex′i·gen·cy
ex′i·gent
ex·i·gu′i·ty
ex·ig′u·ous
ex′ile
ex·ist′
ex·is′tence
ex·is′tent
ex·is·ten′tial
ex·is·ten′tial·ism
ex′it
ex′o·dus
ex of·fi′ci·o
ex·og′a·mous
ex·og′a·my
ex·og′e·nous
ex·on′er·ate
ex·on·er·a′tion
ex·o′ra·ble
ex·or′bi·tant
ex′or·cise
   expel (see exercise)
ex′or·cism

ex′or·cist
ex·o·ter′ic
ex·o·ter′i·cal·ly
ex·ot′ic
ex·ot′i·cal·ly
ex·ot′i·cism
ex·pand′
ex·pand′able
ex·pand′er
ex·panse′
ex·pan′sion
ex·pan′sive
ex par′te
ex·pa′ti·ate
ex·pa·ti·a′tion
ex·pa′tri·ate
ex·pa·tri·a′tion
ex·pect′
ex·pect′able
ex·pect′ably
ex·pec′tan·cy
ex·pec′tant
ex·pec·ta′tion
ex·pec′to·rant
ex·pec′to·rate
ex·pec·to·ra′tion
ex·pe′di·en·cy
  or ex·pe′di·ence
ex·pe′di·ent
ex′pe·dite
ex′pe·dit·er
ex·pe·di′tion
ex·pe·di′tion·ary
ex·pe·di′tious
ex·pel′
  ex·pelled′

ex·pel′ling
ex·pel′lant
ex·pend′
ex·pend·abil′i·ty
ex·pend′able
ex·pen′di·ture
ex·pense′
ex·pen′sive
ex·pen′sive·ly
ex·pe′ri·ence
ex·pe′ri·enced
ex·pe·ri·en′tial
ex·pe·ri·en′tial·ly
ex·per′i·ment
ex·per·i·men′tal
ex·per·i·men′tal·ly
ex·per·i·men·ta′
  tion
ex·per′i·ment·er
ex′pert
ex·per·tise′
ex′pert·ly
ex′pert·ness
ex′pi·a·ble
ex′pi·ate
ex·pi·a′tion
ex′pi·a·tor
ex′pi·a·to·ry
ex·pi·ra′tion
ex·pire′
ex·plain′able
ex·plain′
ex·pla·na′tion
ex·plan′a·to·ry
ex′ple·tive
ex·plic′a·ble

ex'pli·cate
ex·pli·ca'tion
ex'pli·ca·tor
ex·pli'ca·to·ry
ex·plic'it
ex·plode'
ex'ploit
ex·ploit'able
ex·ploi·ta'tion
ex·ploit'ative
ex·ploit'er
ex·plo·ra'tion
ex·plor'a·to·ry
ex·plore'
ex·plor'er
ex·plo'sion
ex·plo'sive
ex·po'nent
ex·po·nen'tial
ex·port'
  verb
ex'port
  noun
ex·por·ta'tion
ex'port·er
ex·pose'
ex·po·sé'
ex·po·si'tion
ex·pos'i·tor
ex·pos'i·to·ry
ex post fac'to
ex·pos'tu·late
ex·pos·tu·la'tion
ex·po'sure
ex·pound'
ex·press'

ex·press'ible
ex·pres'sion
ex·pres'sion·ism
ex·pres'sion·ist
ex·pres·sion·is'tic
ex·press'man
ex·press'way
ex·pro'pri·ate
ex·pro·pri·a'tion
ex·pul'sion
ex·punge'
ex'pur·gate
ex·pur·ga'tion
ex·quis'ite
ex'tant
  existent (see extent)
ex·tem·po·ra'ne·
  ous
ex·tem'po·rary
ex·tem'po·re
ex·tem'po·rize
ex·tend'
ex·ten'sion
ex·ten'sive
ex·tent'
  size (see extant)
ex·ten'u·ate
ex·ten·u·a'tion
ex·te'ri·or
ex·ter'mi·nate
ex·ter·mi·na'tion
ex·ter'mi·na·tor
ex'tern
ex·ter'nal
ex·ter'nal·ly

ex·ter·ri·to'ri·al
ex·ter·ri·to·ri·al'
  i·ty
ex·tinct'
ex·tinc'tion
ex·tin'guish
ex·tin'guish·able
ex·tin'guish·er
ex'tir·pate
ex·tir·pa'tion
ex·tol'
  also ex·toll'
  ex·tolled'
  ex·tol'ling
ex·tort'
ex·tor'tion
ex·tor'tion·ate
ex·tor'tion·er
ex·tor'tion·ist
ex'tra
ex·tract'
  verb
ex'tract
  noun
ex·tract'able
ex·trac'tion
ex·trac'tor
ex·tra·cur·ric'u·
  lar
ex'tra·dit·able
ex'tra·dite
ex·tra·di'tion
ex·tra·ga·lac'tic
ex·tra·le'gal
ex·tra·le'gal·ly
ex·tral'i·ty

ex·tra·mar'i·tal
ex·tra·mu'ral
ex·tra'ne·ous
ex·traor·di·nar'i·ly
ex·traor'di·nary
ex·trap'o·late
ex·trap·o·la'tion
ex·tra·sen'so·ry
ex·tra·ter·ri·to'
　ri·al
ex·tra·ter·ri·to·ri·
　al'i·ty
ex·trav'a·gance
ex·trav'a·gant
ex·trav·a·gan'za
ex·tra·ve·hic'u·lar
ex·treme'
ex·treme'ly
ex·trem'ism
ex·trem'ist
ex·trem'i·ty
ex'tri·cate
ex·tri·ca'tion
ex·trin'sic
ex·trin'si·cal·ly
ex·tro·ver'sion
ex'tro·vert
ex'tro·vert·ed
ex·trude'
ex·tru'sion
ex·u'ber·ance
ex·u'ber·ant
ex·u·da'tion
ex·ude'
ex·ult'
ex·ul'tant

ex·ul·ta'tion
ex'urb
ex·ur'ban·ite
ex·ur'bia
eye'ball
eye'brow
eye'ful
eye'glass
eye'ing
　or ey'ing
eye'lash
eye'let
　hole (see islet)
eye'lid
eye'-open·er
eye'piece
eye'sight
eye'sore
eye'spot
eye'strain
eye'tooth
eye'wash
eye·wit'ness
ey'rir
　pl au'rar

F

Fa'bi·an
Fa'bi·an·ism
fa'ble
fa'bled
fab'ric
fab·ri·ca·bil'i·ty
fab'ri·ca·ble
fab'ri·cate

fab·ri·ca'tion
fab'ri·ca·tor
fab'u·lous
fa·cade'
　also fa·çade'
face·down
face'-lift·ing
fac'et
fa·ce'tious
fa·ce'tious·ness
fa'cial
fac'ile
fa·cil'i·tate
fa·cil'i·ty
fac'ing
fac·sim'i·le
fac'tion
fac'tion·al·ism
fac'tion·al·ly
fac'tious
fac·ti'tious
　artificial (see
　fictitious)
fac'tor
fac'tor·able
fac·to'ri·al
fac'to·ry
fac·to'tum
fac'tu·al
fac'tu·al·ly
fac'ul·ty
fad'dish
fad'dist
fade'less
fag
　fagged

fag′ging
fag′ot
  or fag′got
fag′ot·ing
  or fag′got·ing
Fahr′en·heit
fa·ience′
  or fa·ience′
fail′ing
faille
fail-safe
fail′ure
faint
  weak (see feint)
faint′ness
faint·heart′ed
fair′ground
fair′ing
fair′ly
fair′-mind′ed
fair′ness
fair′-spo′ken
fair-trade
fair′way
fair′-weath′er
fair′y
fair′y·land
fait ac·com·pli
  pl faits ac·com·plis
faith′ful
faith′ful·ly
faith′ful·ness
faith′less
faith′less·ness
fak′er
  imposter (see fakir)

fa·kir′
  dervish (see faker)
fal′con
fal′con·er
fal′con·ry
fall
fell
fall′en
fall′ing
fal·la′cious
fal′la·cy
fal·li·bil′i·ty
fal′li·ble
fal′li·bly
fall·ing-out′
  pl fallings-out′
fal·lo′pi·an
fall′out
fal′low
false′hood
false′ly
false′ness
fal·set′to
fal·si·fi·ca′tion
fal′si·fi·er
fal′si·fy
fal′si·ty
fal′ter
fal′ter·ing·ly
fa·mil′ial
fa·mil′iar
fa·mil·iar′i·ty
fa·mil·iar·iza′tion
fa·mil′iar·ize
fam′i·ly
fam′ine

fam′ish
fa′mous
fa′mous·ly
fan
fanned
fan′ning
fa·nat′ic
fa·nat′i·cal
fa·nat′i·cal·ly
fa·nat′i·cism
fan′ci·er
fan′ci·ful
fan′ci·ful·ly
fan′ci·ly
fan′cy
fan′cy-free
fan′cy·work
fan·dan′go
fan′fare
fan′-jet
fan′light
fan′tail
fan·ta′sia
fan·tas′tic
  also fan·tas′ti·cal
fan·tas′ti·cal·ly
fan′ta·sy
far′ad
far′a·day
far′away
far·ceur′
far′ci·cal
far′ci·cal·ly
fare·well′
far·fetched
far-flung′

fa·ri′na
far·i·na′ceous
farm′er
farm′hand
farm′house
farm′ing
farm′land
farm′stead
farm′yard
far-off
far-out
far·ra′go
  pl far·ra′goes
far′-reach′ing
far′row
far′see′ing
far′sight′ed
far′sight′ed·ness
far′ther
far′thest
far′thing
fas′ci·cle
fas′ci·nate
fas·ci·na′tion
fas·ci·na·tor
fas′cism
fas′cist
fas·cis′tic
fash′ion
fash′ion·able
fash′ion·ably
fast′-back
fas′ten
fas′ten·er
fas′ten·ing
fas·tid′i·ous

fas·tid′i·ous·ness
fast′ness
fa′tal
fa′tal·ism
fa′tal·ist
fa·tal·is′tic
fa·tal·is′ti·cal·ly
fa·tal′i·ty
fa′tal·ly
fat′back
fat′ed
fate′ful
fate′ful·ly
fa′ther
fa′ther·hood
fa′ther-in-law
  pl fa′thers-in-law
fa′ther·land
fa′ther·less
fa′ther·li·ness
fa′ther·ly
fath′om
fath′om·able
fa′thom·less
fa·tigue′
fat′ten
fat′ty
fa·tu′i·ty
fat′u·ous
fau′ces
fau′cet
fault′find·er
fault′find·ing
fault′i·ly
fault′less
fault′y

faun
  deity (see fawn)
fau′na
  pl fau′nas *or*
  fau′nae
faux pas′
  pl faux pas′
fa′vor
fa′vor·able
fa′vor·ably
fa′vored
fa′vor·ite
fa′vor·it·ism
fawn
  grovel, deer (see
  faun)
faze
  daunt (see phase)
fe′al·ty
fear′ful
fear′ful·ly
fear′less
fear′less·ness
fear′some
fea·si·bil′i·ty
fea′si·ble
fea′si·bly
feat
  deed (see feet)
feath′er
feath′er·bed
feath′er·bed·ding
feath′ered
feath′er·edge
feath′er·weight
feath′er·y

fea′ture
  fea′tured
  fea′tur·ing
fea′ture·less
feb′ri·fuge
fe′brile
Feb′ru·ary
fe′cal
fe′ces
feck′less
fe′cund
fec′un·date
fec·un·da′tion
fe·cun′di·ty
fed′er·al
fed′er·al·ism
fed′er·al·ist
fed·er·al·iza′tion
fed′er·al·ize
fed′er·ate
fed·er·a′tion
fed′er·a·tive
fe·do′ra
fee′ble
fee′ble·ness
fee′ble·mind·ed
fee′ble·mind·ed·
  ness
fee′bly
feed
  fed
  feed′ing
feed′back
feed′er
feel
  felt
  feel′ing

feel′er
feel′ing
feel′ing·ly
feet
  pl of foot,
  measure (see
  feat)
feign
feint
  feigned (see faint)
fe·lic′i·tate
fe·lic·i·ta′tion
fe·lic′i·tous
fe·lic′i·ty
fe′line
fel′lah
  pl fel′la·hin
fel′low
fel·low·man′
fel′low·ship
fel′on
fe·lo′ni·ous
fel′o·ny
fe′male
fem′i·nine
fem·i·nin′i·ty
fem′i·nism
fem′i·nist
fe′mur
  pl fe′murs *or*
  fem′o·ra
fen
  pl fen
fenc′er
fenc′ing
fend′er
fen·es·tra′tion

fen′nel
fer·ment′
  verb
fer′ment
  noun
fer·men·ta′·
  tion
fe·ro′cious
fe·ro′cious·ness
fe·roc′i·ty
fer′ret
fer′ric
Fer′ris wheel
fer′rous
fer′rule
  metal ring (see
  ferule)
fer′ry
fer′ry·boat
fer′tile
fer·til′i·ty
fer·til·iza′tion
fer′til·ize
fer′til·iz·er
fer′ule
  rod (see ferrule)
fer′ven·cy
fer′vent
fer′vid
fer′vor
fes′tal
fes′ter
fes′ti·val
fes′tive
fes·tiv′i·ty
fes·toon′
fe′tal

fetch
fetch′ing
fete
   or fête
fet′id
fet′ish
   or fet′ich
fe′tish·ism
fe′tish·ist
fet′lock
fet′ter
fet′tle
fe′tus
feu′dal
feu′dal·ism
feu·dal·is′
   tic
feu′da·to·ry
fe′ver
fe′ver·ish·ly
fez
   pl fez′zes
fi·an·cé′
   masc
fi·an·cée′
   fem
fi·as′co
   pl fi·as′coes
fi′at
fib
   fibbed
   fib′bing
fib′ber
fi′ber
   or fi′bre
fi′ber·board
fib′ril·ate

fib′ril·la′
   tion
fi′brin
fi′brin·ous
fi′broid
fi′brous
fib′u·la
   pl fib′u·lae *or*
   fib′u·las

fib′u·lar
fiche
fick′le
fick′le·ness
fic′tion
fic′tion·al
fic·ti′tious
   imaginary (see
   factitious)

fid′dle
fid′dler
fid′dle·stick
fi·del′i·ty
fid′get
fid′gety
fi·du′ci·ary
field′er
field′piece
fiend′ish
fierce′ly
fierce′ness
fi′ery
fi·es′ta
fif·teen′
fif·teenth′
fifth
   pl fifths
fif′ty

fif′ti·eth
fif·ty-fif′ty
fight
   fought
   fight′ing
fight′er
fig′ment
fig·u·ra′tion
fig′u·ra·tive
fig′ure
fig′ure·head
fig·u·rine′
fil′a·ment
fil·a·men′
   tous
fil′bert
filch
fil′er
fi·let mi·gnon′
   pl fi·lets mi·gnons′
fil′i·al
fil′i·bus·ter
fil′i·bus·ter·er
fil′i·gree
fil′ing
Fil·i·pi′no
fill′er
   that which fills
fil′ler
   pl fil′lers *or* fil′ler
   currency unit

fil′let
   also fi′let

fill′ing
fil′lip
fil′ly
film′card

film′dom
film′strip
film′y
fils
   pl fils
fil′ter
   strainer (see philter)
fil′ter·able
   also fil′tra·ble
filth′i·ness
filth′y
fil′trate
fil·tra′tion
fi·na′gle
fi·na′gler
fi′nal
fi·na′le
fi′nal·ist
fi·nal′i·ty
fi′nal·ize
fi′nal·ly
fi·nance′
fi·nan′cial
fi·nan′cial·ly
fin·an·cier′
find
  found
  find′ing
find′er
fin de siè′cle
find′ing
fine′ly
fine′ness
fin′ery
fine·spun
fi·nesse′

fin′ger
fin′ger·board
fin′gered
fin′ger·ing
fin′ger·nail
fin′ger·print
fin′ger·tip
fin′i·al
fin′i·cal
fin′i·cal·ly
fin′ick·i·ness
fin′ick·ing
fin′icky
fin′is
fin′ish
fin′ished
fin′ish·er
fi′nite
Fin′land
Fin′land·er
Finn
fin·nan had′die
Finn′ish
fiord
fir
   tree (see fur)
fire′arm
fire′ball
fire′boat
fire′box
fire′brand
fire′break
fire′brick
fire′bug
fire′clay
fire′crack·er

fire′damp
fire′dog
fire′-eat·er
fire′fly
fire′house
fire′light
fire′man
fire′place
fire′plug
fire′pow·er
fire′proof
fire′side
fire′stone
fire′trap
fire′wa·ter
fire′wood
fire′work
fir′ing
fir′ma·ment
firm′ly
firm′ness
first·born
first·fruits
first·hand
first′ly
first-rate
first-string
firth
fis′cal
fis′cal·ly
fish
   pl fish *or* fish′es
fish-and-chips′
fish′er
fish′er·man
fish′ery

flat

fish′hook
fish′ing
fish′like
fish′mon·ger
fish′tail
fish′wife
fish′y
fis′sion
fis′sion·able
fis′sure
fist′i·cuffs
fis′tu·la
   pl fis′tu·las *or*
   fis′tu·lae

fis′tu·lous
fit
   fit′ted
   fit′ting
fit′ful
fit′ful·ly
fit′ly
fit′ness
fit′ter
fit′ting
fix·a′tion
fix′a·tive
fix′ed·ly
fix′ed·ness
fix′i·ty
fix′ture
fiz′zle
fjord
flab′ber·gast
flab′bi·ly
flab′bi·ness
flab′by

flac′cid
flac′on
flag
   flagged
   flag′ging
fla·gel′lant
flag′el·late
flag·el·la′tion
fla·gel′lum
   pl fla·gel′la *also*
   fla·gel′lums

fla·geo·let′
flag′ging
flag′on
flag′pole
fla′gran·cy
fla′grant
fla·gran·te
   de·lic′to
fla′grant·ly
flag′ship
flag′staff
flag′stone
flag′wav·ing
flair
   aptitude (*see* flare)

flak′i·ness
flak′y
flam′beau
   pl flam′beaux *or*
   flam′beaus

flam·boy′ance
   also flam·boy′an·cy

flam·boy′ant
fla·men′co
flam′er

flam′ing
flame′out
flame′proof
flame′throw·er
fla·min′go
flam·ma·bil′i·ty
flam′ma·ble
flange
flang′er
flank′er
flan′nel
flan·nel·ette′
flap
   flapped
   flap′ping
flap′jack
flap′per
flap′py
flare
   flame (*see* flair)

flare′back
flar′ing
flare′-up
flash′back
flash′bulb
flash′cube
flash′gun
flash′i·ly
flash′i·ness
flash′ing
flash′light
flash′y
flask
flat
   flat′ted
   flat′ting

flat′bed
flat′boat
flat′car
flat′fish
flat′foot′ed
flat′iron
flat′ly
flat′ness
flat′ten
flat′ter
flat′ter·er
flat′tery
flat′top
flat′u·lence
flat′u·lent
fla′tus
flat′ware
flat′work
flat′worm
flaunt
flau′tist
fla′vor
fla′vored
fla′vor·ful
fla′vor·ing
fla′vor·less
fla′vor·
  some
flaw′ed
flaw′less
flax′en
flea′bit·ten
fledg′ling
flee
  fled
  flee′ing

fleec′y
fleet′ing
fleet′ly
fleet′ness
Flem′ing
Flem′ish
flesh′i·ness
flesh′ly
flesh′pot
flesh′y
fleur-de-lis′
  or fleur-de-lys′
  pl fleurs-de-lis′ *or*
    fleurs-de-lis′ *or*
    fleurs-de-lys′ *or*
    fleur-de-lys′
flex·i·bil′i·ty
flex′i·ble
flex′i·bly
flex′or
flex′ure
flick′er
fli′er
flight′i·ness
flight′less
flight′y
flim′flam
flim′si·ly
flim′si·ness
flim′sy
fling
  flung
  fling′ing
flint′i·ly
flint′i·ness
flint′y
flint′lock

flip
  flipped
  flip′ping
flip′-flop
flip′pan·cy
flip′pant
flip′per
flir·ta′tion
flir·ta′tious
flit
  flit′ted
  flit′ting
flit′ter
fliv′ver
float′er
float′ing
flock·ing
floe
  ice (see flow)

flog
  flogged
  flog′ging
flog′ger
flood′gate
flood′light
flood′plain
flood′wat·er
flood′way
floor′board
floor′ing
floor′-length
floor′walk·er
floo′zy
flop
  flopped
  flop′ping

flop'py
flo'ra
  pl flo'ras also flo'rae
flo'ral
flo·res'cence
  flourishing (see fluoresence)
flo·res'cent
flo'ri·cul·ture
flor'id
Flor'i·da
Flo·rid'i·an
flor'in
flo'rist
floss'y
flo·ta'tion
flo·til'la
flot'sam
flounc'ing
flounc'y
floun'der
flour'ish
flout
flow
  stream (see floe)
flow'chart
flow'er
flow'ered
flow'er·i·ness
flow'er·pot
flow'ery
flu
  influenza (see flue)
flub
  flubbed

flub'bing
fluc'tu·ate
fluc·tu·a'tion
flue
  chimney (see flu)
flu'en·cy
flu'ent
fluff'i·ness
fluff'y
flu'id
flu·id'ic
flu·id'i·ty
flu·id·ounce'
flum'mox
flun'ky
  or flun'key
flu·o·resce'
flu·o·res'cence
  light (see florescence)
flu·o·res'cent
flu'o·ri·date
flu·o·ri·da'tion
flu'o·ride
flu·o·rin·ate
flu·o·rin·a'tion
flu'o·rine
flu'o·ro·scope
flu·o·ros'co·py
flur'ry
flus'ter
flut'ed
flut'ing
flut'ist
flut'ter
flut'tery

fly
  flew
  flown
  fly'ing
fly'able
fly'blown
fly'by
fly'-by-night
fly'cast·er
fly'catch·er
fly'ing
fly'leaf
fly'over
fly'pa·per
fly'speck
fly'weight
fly'wheel
foam'i·ly
foam'i·ness
foam'y
fob
  fobbed
  fob'bing
fo'cal
fo'cal·ly
fo·cal·iza'tion
fo'cal·ize
fo'cus
  pl fo'cus·es or fo'ci
fo'cus
  fo'cused
    also fo'cussed
  fo'cus·ing
    also fo'cus·sing
fod'der
foe

foe'tal
foe'tus
fog
  fogged
  fog'ging
fog'bound
fog'gi·ly
fog'gi·ness
fog'gy
fog'horn
fo'gy
  also fo'gey
foi'ble
fold'away
fold'er
fol'de·rol
fo'liage
fo'li·ate
fo'li·at·ed
fo·li·a'tion
fo'lio
folk'lore
folk'lor·ist
folk-rock
folks'y
folk'way
fol'li·cle
fol'low
fol'low·er
fol'low·ing
fol'low-through
fol'low-up
fol'ly
fo·ment'
fo·men·ta'tion

fon'dant
fon'dle
fond'ly
fond'ness
fon·due'
  also fon·du'
food'stuff
fool'har·di·ly
fool'har·di·ness
fool'har·dy
fool'ish
fool'ish·ly
fool'ish·ness
fool·proof
fools'cap
foot
  pl feet
  also foot
foot'age
foot'ball
foot'board
foot'bridge
foot'can·dle
foot'ed
foot'fall
foot'hill
foot'hold
foot'ing
foot'lights
foot'lock·er
foot'loose
foot'man
foot'mark
foot'note
foot'pad

foot'path
foot-pound
foot'print
foot'race
foot'rest
foot'sore
foot'step
foot'stool
foot-ton
foot'wear
foot'work
fop'pery
fop'pish
for'age
for'ag·er
for'ay
for·bear'
  abstain (*see* forebear)

for·bore'
for·borne'
for·bear'ing
for·bear'ance
for·bid'
  for·bade'
  or for·bad'
for·bid'den
for·bid'ding
for·bid'ding
force'ful
force'ful·ly
for'ceps
  pl for'ceps
forc'ible
forc'ibly

fore-and-aft
fore′arm
fore′bear
  or for′bear
  ancestor (*see*
    forbear)

fore·bode′
  also for·bode′

fore·bod′ing
fore′cast
  fore′cast
    or for′cast·ed

  fore′cast·ing
fore′cast·er
fore′cas·tle
fore·close′
fore·clo′sure
fore·doom′
fore·fa·ther
fore′fin·ger
fore′foot
fore′front
fore·go′
fore·go′ing
fore·gone′
fore′ground
fore′hand
fore·hand′ed
fore′head
for′eign
for′eign·er
fore·know′
fore·knowl′edge
fore′la·dy
fore′land

fore′leg
fore′limb
fore′lock
fore′man
fore′mast
fore′most
fore′name
fore′named
fore′noon
fo·ren′sic
fo·ren′si·cal·ly
fore·or·dain′
fore·or·di·na′tion
fore′quar·ter
fore′run·ner
fore′said
fore′sail
fore·see′
  fore·saw′
  fore·seen′
  fore·see′ing
fore·see′able
fore·shad′ow
fore′sheet
fore′shore
fore·short′en
fore′sight
fore·sight′ed·ness
fore′skin
for′est
fore·es·ta′tion
fore·stall′
for′est·ed
for′est·er
for′est·ry

fore′taste
fore·tell′
  fore·told′
  fore·tell′ing
fore′thought
fore·to′ken
fore′top
for·ev′er
for·ev·er·more′
fore·warn′
fore′wom·an
fore′word
  preface (*see*
    forward)

for′feit
for′fei·ture
for·gath′er
  or fore·gath′er

forg′er
forg′ery
for·get′
  for·got′
  for·got′ten
    or for·got′

  for·get′ting
for·get′ful
for·get′ta·ble
forg′ing
for·giv′able
for·give′
  for·gave′
  for·giv′en
  for·giv′ing
for·give′ness
for·giv′ing

for·go'
  or fore·go'

fo'rint

fork'ed

fork'lift

for·lorn'

for'mal

form·al'de·hyde

for'mal·ism

for·mal'i·ty

for·mal·iza'tion

for'mal·ize

for'mal·ly

for'mat

for·ma'tion

for'ma·tive

for'mer

for'mer·ly

form·fit'ting

for'mi·da·ble

for'mi·da·bly

form'less

For·mo'sa

For·mo'san

for'mu·la

for'mu·late

for·mu·la'tion

for'mu·la·tor

for'ni·cate

for·ni·ca'tion

for'ni·ca·tor

for·sake'
  for·sook'
  for·sak'en
  for·sak'ing

for·sak'en

for·sooth'

for·swear'
  or fore·swear'

for·syth'i·a

fort
  fortified place (see forte)

forte
  special skill (see fort)

for'te
  music, loudly

forth·com'ing

forth'right

forth·with'

for'ti·eth

for·ti·fi·ca'tion

for'ti·fi·er

for'ti·fy

for·tis'si·mo

for'ti·tude

for·ti·tu'di·nous

Fort Lau'der·dale

fort'night·ly

for'tress

for·tu'i·tous

for·tu'i·ty

for'tu·nate

for'tune

for'tune-tel·ler

for'tune-tell·ing

Fort Wayne'

Fort Worth'

for'ty

for·ty-nin'er

fo'rum
  pl fo'rums *also* fo'ra

for'ward
  brash (see foreword)

for'ward·er

for'ward·ing

fos'sil

fos'sil·ize

fos'ter

foul
  dirty (see fowl)

fou·lard'

foul'ly

foul·mouthed

foul'ness

foun·da'tion

foun'der
  verb, collapse

found'er
  noun, establisher

found'ling

found'ry

foun'tain

foun'tain·head

four'-flush·er

four'fold

four'-foot'ed

four'-hand'ed

four'-in-hand

four'-post'er

four'score

four'some

four·square

four·teen'

four·teenth'
fourth
four'-wheel'er
fowl
bird (see foul)
fox
pl fox'es *or* fox
fox'glove
fox'hole
fox'hound
fox'i·ly
fox'i·ness
fox'-trot
fox'y
foy'er
fra'cas
frac'tion
frac'tion·al
frac'tion·al·ize
frac'tion·al·ly
frac'tious
frac'ture
frag'ile
fra·gil'i·ty
frag'ment
frag·men'tal·ly
frag'men·tary
frag·men·ta'tion
frag'men·tize
fra'grance
fra'grant
frail'ty
fram'er
frame'-up
frame'work

franc
currency (see frank)
France
fran'chise
fran·chi·see'
fran·gi·bil'i·ty
fran'gi·ble
frank
open (see franc)
Fran'ken·stein
Frank'fort
frank'furt·er
or frank'fort·er *or*
frank'furt *or*
frank'fort
frank'in·cense
fran'tic
fran'ti·cal·ly
frap·pé'
or frappe
fra·ter'nal
fra·ter'nal·ly
fra·ter'ni·ty
frat·er·ni·za'tion
frat'er·nize
frat'ri·cide
fraud'u·lence
fraud'u·lent
fraught
fraz'zle
fray'ing
freak'ish
freck'le
free'boot·er
free·born'

freed'man
free'dom
free'-for-all
free'hand
free'hold
free'ly
free'man
Free'ma·son
Fre'mont
free·stand'ing
free'stone
free·think'er
free'way
free·wheel'
freeze
chill (see frieze)

froze
fro'zen
freez'ing
freeze'-dry
freez'er
freight'age
freight'er
French
French'man
French'wom·an
fre·net'ic
fre·net'i·cal·ly
fren'zied
fren'zy
fre'quen·cy
fre'quent
fres'co

pl fres'coes *or*
fres'cos

fresh'en
fresh'et
fresh'ly
fresh'man
fresh'ness
fresh·wa'ter
Fres'no
fret
  fret'ted
  fret'ting
fret'ful
fret'ful·ly
fret'ful·ness
fret'work
fri'a·ble
fri'ar
fric·as·see'
fric'tion
fric'tion·al·ly
Fri'day
friend'less
friend'li·ness
friend'ly
friend'ship
frieze
  ornamental (see
  freeze)

frig'ate
fright'en
fright'ful
fright'ful·ly
frig'id
fri·gid'i·ty
frill'y
frip'pery
frisk'i·ly

frisk'i·ness
frisk'y
frit'ter
fri·vol'i·ty
friv'o·lous
frizz'i·ly
frizz'i·ness
friz'zle
friz'zly
frog'man
frol'ic
  frol'icked
  frol'ick·ing
frol'ic·some
fron'tal
front'age
fron'tal
fron·tier'
fron·tiers'man
fron'tis·piece
frost'bite
frost'ed
frost'i·ly
frost'i·ness
frost'ing
frost'y
froth'i·ly
froth'i·ness
froth'y
frou'frou
fro'ward
frown
frow'zy
  or frow'sy
fro'zen
fruc·ti·fi·ca'tion

fruc'ti·fy
fruc'tose
fru'gal
fru·gal'i·ty
fru'gal·ly
fruit'cake
fruit'ful·ly
fru·i'tion
fruit'less
fruit'y
frump'ish
frump'y
frus'trate
frus·tra'tion
fry
  fried
  fry'ing
fry'er
fuch'sia
fud'dle
fudge
fu'el
  fu'eled
    or fu'elled
  fu'el·ing
    or fu'el·ling
fu'gi·tive
fugue
füh'rer
  or fueh'rer
ful'crum
  pl ful'crums *or*
  ful'cra

ful·fill'
  or ful·fil'
ful·filled'

ful·fill′ing
ful·fill′ment
full′back
full′blood′ed
full-blown
full′-bod′ied
full′er
full′-fash′ioned
full-fledged
full-length
full′ness
full-scale
ful′ly
ful′mi·nate
ful·mi·na′tion
ful′min·a·tor
ful′some
fu′ma·role
fum′ble
fu′mi·gant
fu′mi·gate
fu·mi·ga′tion
fu′mi·ga·tor
func′tion
func′tion·al
func′tion·al·ism
func′tion·al·ly
func′tion·ary
func′tion·less
fun·da·men′tal
fun·da·men′tal·
  ism
fun·da·men′tal·ist
fun·da·men′tal·ly
fu′ner·al
fu′ner·ary

fu·ne′re·al
fun·gi·cid′al
fun′gi·cide
fun′gus
  pl fun′gi *also*
   fun′gus·es
fu·nic′u·lar
funk′y
fun′nel
fun′neled
  also fun′nelled
fun′nel·ing
  also fun′nel·ling
fun′ni·ly
fun′ni·ness
fun′ny
fur
  coat (see fir*)*
fur′be·low
fur′bish
fu′ri·ous
furl
fur′long
fur′lough
fur′nace
fur′nish
fur′nish·ings
fur′ni·ture
fu′ror
fur′ri·er
fur′row
fur′ry
fur′ther
fur′ther·ance
fur′ther·more
fur′ther·most

fur′thest
fur′tive
fur′tive·ness
fu′ry
fu′se·lage
fus·ibil′i·ty
fus′ible
fu′sil·lade
fu′sion
fuss′bud·get
fuss′i·ly
fuss′i·ness
fuss′y
fus′tian
fus′ti·ly
fus′ti·ness
fus′ty
fu′tile
fu·til′i·ty
fu′ture
fu′tur·ism
fu′tur·ist
fu·tur·is′tic
fu·tu′ri·ty
fuzz′i·ly
fuzz′i·ness
fuzz′y

G

gab
  gabbed
  gab′bing
gab′ar·dine
gab′ble
gab′bling

gab'by
gab'fest
ga'ble
ga'bled
Ga·bon'
Gab·o·nese'
gad
  gad'ded
  gad'ding
gad'about
gad'fly
gad'get
gad'get·ry
Gael'ic
gaff
  spear, hook (see gaffe)

gaffe
  blunder (see gaff)

gaf'fer
gag
  gagged
  gag'ging
gage
  pledge (see gauge)

gag'gle
gag'ster
gai'ety
gai'ly
gain'er
gain'ful
gain'ful·ly
gain·say'
  gain·said'
  gain·say'ing

gain·say'er
gait
  walk (see gate)

gai'ter
ga'la
ga·lac'tic
gal'axy
gal·lant'
gal'lant·ry
gall'blad·der
gal'le·on
gal'ler·ied
gal'lery
gal'ley
Gal'lic
gall'ing
gal'li·vant
gal'lon
gal'lop
gal'lop·er
gal'lows
gall'stone
ga·lore'
ga·losh'
gal·van'ic
gal'va·nism
gal·va·ni·za'tion
gal'va·nize
gal·va·nom'e·ter
Gam'bia
Gam'bi·an
gam'bit
gam'ble
  wager (see gambol)

gam'bler

gam'bol
  frisk (see gamble)

gam'boled
  or gam'bolled

gam'bol·ing
  or gam'bol·ling

gam'brel
game'cock
game'keep·er
game'ly
game'ster
ga·mete'
gam'in
gam'i·ness
gam'ma glob'u·lin
gam'ut
gam'y
gan'der
gang'land
gan'gling
gan'gli·on
  pl gan'glia *also*
  gan'gli·ons

gang'plank
gan'grene
gan'gre·nous
gang'ster
gang'way
gant'let
gan'try
gaol
gap'ing
ga·rage'
ga·rage'man
gar'bage

gar'ble
gar·çon'
gar'den
gar'den·er
Gar·den Grove
gar·de'nia
gar·gan'tu·an
gar'gle
gar'gling
gar'goyle
gar'ish
gar'land
gar'lic
gar'licky
gar'ment
gar'ner
gar'net
gar'nish
gar·nish·ee'
gar·nish·eed'
gar'nish·ment
gar'ni·ture
gar'ret
gar'ri·son
gar·rote'
   or ga·rotte'
gar·ru'li·ty
gar'ru·lous
gar'ru·lous·ness
gar'ter
Gar'y
gas'eous
gas'si·ness
gas'ket
gas'light

gas·o·line'
   or gas·o·lene'
gas'ser
gas'sy
gas'tric
gas·tri'tis
gas·tro·en·ter·ol'
   o·gist
gas·tro·en·ter·ol'
   o·gy
gas·tro·in·tes'ti·
   nal
gas·tro·nom'ic
gas·tron'o·my
gas'works
gate
   door (see gait)
gate'-crash·er
gate'post
gate'way
gath'er
gath'er·er
gauche
   crude (see gouache)
gau·che·rie'
gau'cho
gaud'i·ly
gaud'i·ness
gaud'y
gauge
   measure (see gage)
gaunt
gaunt'let
gauze
gauz'y

gav'el
ga·votte'
gawk'ish
gawk'y
gay'ety
gay'ly
ga·ze'bo
ga·zelle'
gaz'er
ga·zette'
gaz·et·teer'
gear'box
gear'ing
gear'shift
gee'zer
Gei'ger
gei'sha
   pl gei'sha or gei'shas
gel
   gelled
gel'ling
gel'a·tin
   also gel'a·tine
ge·la·ti·ni·za'tion
ge·la'ti·nize
ge·lat'i·nous
geld'ing
gel'id
ge·lid'i·ty
gel·ig'nite
gem'i·nate
gem·i·na'tion
gem'stone
gen'darme
gen·dar'mer·ie

gen′der
gen′der·ing
ge·ne·a·log′i·cal
ge·ne·a·log′i·cal·ly
ge·ne·al′o·gist
ge·ne·al′o·gy
gen′er·al
gen′er·a·ble
gen·er·a·lis′si·mo
gen·er·al′i·ty
gen′er·al·iza′tion
gen′er·al·ize
gen′er·al·ly
gen′er·al·ship
gen′er·ate
gen′er·a′tion
gen′er·a·tive
gen′er·a·tor
ge·ner′ic
ge·ner′i·cal·ly
gen·er·os′i·ty
gen′er·ous
gen′e·sis
   pl gen′e·ses
ge·net′ic
ge·net′i·cal·ly
ge·net′ics
ge′nial
ge·nial′i·ty
ge′nial·ly
gen′ic
ge′nie
   pl ge′nies *also* ge′nii
gen′i·tal
gen·i·ta′lia
gen′i·tive

gen·i·to·ur′i·nary
ge′nius
gen·o·ci′dal
gen′o·cide
genre
gens
   pl gen′tes
gen·teel′
gen′tian
gen′tile
gen·til′i·ty
gen′tle
gen′tle·folk
   also gen′tle·folks
gen′tle·man
gen′tle·man·ly
gen′tle·wom·an
gen′tly
gen′try
gen′u·flect
gen·u·flec′tion
   or gen·u·flex′ion
gen′u·ine
gen′u·ine·ly
gen′u·ine·ness
ge′nus
   pl gen′era
geo·cen′tric
geo·cen′tri·cal·ly
geo·chem′i·cal
geo·chem′i·cal·ly
geo·chem′is·try
geo·chron·o·log′
   i·cal
geo·chro·nol′o·gy
geo·des′ic

ge·od′e·sy
geo·det′ic
geo·det′i·cal·ly
ge·o·graph′ic
ge·o·graph′i·cal
ge·o·graph′i·cal·ly
ge·og′ra·phy
geo·log′ic
geo·log′i·cal
geo·log′i·cal·ly
ge·ol′o·gist
ge·ol′o·gy
geo·mag·net′ic
geo·mag′ne·tism
ge·o·met′ric
ge·o·met′ri·cal
ge·o·met′ri·cal·ly
geo·me·tri′cian
ge·om′e·try
geo·phys′i·cal
geo·phys′i·cist
geo·phys′ics
geo·po·lit′i·cal
geo·po·lit′i·cal·ly
geo·pol·i·ti′cian
geo·pol′i·tics
Geor′gia
geo·ther′mal
ge·ra′ni·um
ger·i·at′ric
ger·i·at′rics
Ger′man
Ger·man′ic
ger·mane′
Ger′ma·ny
ger·mi·cid′al

ger'mi·cide
ger'mi·nal
ger'mi·nate
ger·mi·na'tion
ger·on·tol'o·gist
ger·on·tol'o·gy
ger·ry·man'der
ger'und
ge·sta'po
ges'tate
ges·ta'tion
ges·tic'u·late
ges·tic·u·la'tion
ges'ture
ge·sund'heit
get
  got
  got
    or got'ten
  get'ting
get'away
get'-to·geth·er
get'up
gew'gaw
gey'ser
Gha'na
Gha·na'ian
  or Gha'nian
ghast'li·ness
ghast'ly
gher'kin
ghet'to
  pl ghet'tos *or*
  ghet'toes

ghet·to·iza'tion
ghet'to·ize

ghost'li·ness
ghost'ly
ghost'write
ghost'-writ·er
ghoul'ish
gi'ant
gi'ant·ess
gi'ant·ism
gib
gib'ber
gib'ber·ing
gib'ber·ish
gib'bet
gib'bon
gib·bos'i·ty
gib'bous
gibe
  taunt (*see* jibe)
gib'er
gib'let
Gib'son
gid'di·ly
gid'di·ness
gid'dy
gift'ed
gig
  gigged
  gig'ging
gi·gan'tic
gi·gan'ti·cal·ly
gig'gle
gig'gly
gig'o·lo
gild
  overlay with gold
  (*see* guild)

gilded
  or gilt
gild'ing
gilt
  gold (*see* guilt)
gilt-edged
gim'crack
gim'let
gim'mick
gim'mick·ry
gim'micky
gimp'y
gin
  ginned
  gin'ning
gin'ger
gin'ger·bread
gin'ger·ly
gin'ger·snap
ging'ham
gin·gi·vi'tis
gi·raffe'
gird
  or girt
gird'ed
gird'ing
gird'er
gir'dle
girl'hood
girl'ish
girth
gist
give
  gave
  giv'en
  giv'ing

give-and-take'
give'away
giv'en
giz'mo
  or gis'mo
giz'zard
gla'brous
gla·cé'
gla'cial
gla'ci·ate
gla·ci·a'tion
gla'cier
gla·ci·ol'o·gist
gla·ci·ol'o·gy
glad'den
glad'i·a·tor
glad·i·a·to'ri·al
glad·i·o'lus
  pl glad·i·o'li *or*
  glad·i·o'lus *or*
  glad·i·o'lus·es
glad'ly
glad'ness
glad'some
glad'stone
glam'or·ize
  also glam'our·ize
glam'or·ous
  also glam'our·ous
glam'our
  or glam'or
glanc'ing
glan'du·lar
glar'ing
glass'ful
glass'i·ly
glass·ine'

glass'i·ness
glass'ware
glass'y
glau·co'ma
gla'zier
glaz'ing
glean'able
glean'er
glean'ings
glee'ful
glee'ful·ly
Glen'dale
glib'ly
glib'ness
glid'er
glim'mer
glimpse
glis'ten
glit'ter
glit'tery
gloam'ing
gloat
glob'al
glob'al·ly
globe'-trot·ter
glob'u·lar
glob'ule
glob'u·lin
glock'en·spiel
gloom'i·ly
gloom'i·ness
gloom'y
glo·ri·fi·ca'tion
glo'ri·fy
glo'ri·ous
glor'y
glos'sa·ry

gloss'i·ly
gloss'i·ness
gloss'y
glot'tal
glot'tis
  pl glot'tis·es *or*
  glot'ti·des
glot'tal
glow'er
glow'worm
glu'cose
glue
glue'y
glu'i·ly
glut
  glut'ted
  glut'ting
glu'ta·mate
glu'ten
glu'ten·ous
  having the quality
  of gluten (see
  glutinous)
glu'ti·nous
  sticky (see
  glutenous)
glut'ton
glut'ton·ous
glut'tony
glyc'er·in
  or glyc'er·ine
glyc'er·ol
gly'co·gen
G'-man
gnarled
gnash
gnat

gnaw
gneiss
gnome
gnom′ish
Gnos′tic
gnos′ti·cism
gnu
go
   went
   gone
   go′ing
goad
go′-ahead
goal′ie
goal′keep·er
goal′post
goa·tee′
goat′skin
gob′ble
gob·ble·dy·gook′
  or gob·ble·de·gook′
gob′bler
go′-be·tween
gob′let
gob′lin
god′child
god′daugh·ter
god′dess
god′fa·ther
god′less
god′like
god′li·ness
god′ly
god′moth·er
god′par·ent
god′send
god′son

go′-get·ter
gog′gle
gog′gles
go′-go
go·ings-on′
goi′ter
  also goi′tre
gold′brick
gold′en
gold′en·rod
gold′field
gold-filled
gold′finch
gold′fish
gold′smith
golf′er
go′nad
gon′do·la
gon·do·lier′
gon′er
gon′fa·lon
go′-no-go
gon·or·rhe′a
gon·or·rhe′al
good
   bet′ter
   best
good-bye′
  or good-by′
good′-heart′ed
good′-hu′mored
good′-look′ing
good′ly
good′-na′tured
good′ness
good′-tem′pered
good·will

goody-good′y
goo′ey
goof′i·ness
goof′y
goo′i·er
goo′i·ness
goose
  pl geese
goose′ber·ry
goose′flesh
goose′neck
go′pher
Gor′di·an
gorge
gor′geous
Gor·gon·zo′la
go·ril′la
gor′man·dize
gor′man·diz·er
gor′y
gos′hawk
gos′ling
gos′pel
gos′sa·mer
gos′sip
Goth′ic
got′ten
gouache
  painting (see gauche)
Gou′da
gouge
gou′lash
gourd
  plant (see gourde)
gourde
  currency (see gourd)

gour'mand
gour'met
gout
gov'ern
gov'er·nance
gov'ern·ess
gov'ern·ment
gov·ern·men'tal
gov'er·nor
gov'er·nor-gen'
  er·al
    pl gov'er·nors-
    gen'er·al *or*
    gov'er·nor-
    gen'er·als

grab
  grabbed
  grab'bing
grace'ful
grace'ful·ly
grace'less
gra'cious
grack'le
gra·da'tion
gra'di·ent
grad'u·al
grad'u·al·ism
grad'u·al·ly
grad'u·ate
grad·u·a'tion
graf·fi'to
  pl graf·fi'ti
graft'er
gra'ham
grain'field
grain'y

gram
  or gramme
gram'mar
gram·mar'i·an
gram·mat'i·cal
gram·mat'i·cal·ly
gra'na·ry
gran'dam
grand'child
grand'daugh·ter
gran·dee'
gran'deur
grand'fa·ther
gran·dil'o·quence
gran·dil'o·quent
gran'di·ose
grand'ly
grand'moth·er
grand'par·ent
Grand' Ra'pids
grand'son
grand'stand
grange
gran'ite
gran'ite-ware
gran'ny
gran·tee'
grant-in-aid'
  pl grants-in-aid'
grant'or
gran'u·lar
gran'u·late
gran'u·lat·ed
gran·u·la'tion
gran'ule
grape'fruit

grape'shot
grape'vine
graph'ic
graph'i·cal·ly
graph'ics
graph'ite
grap'nel
grap'ple
grap'pling
grasp'er
grass'hop·per
grass'land
grass'y
grate'ful
grate'ful·ly
grat'er
grat·i·fi·ca'tion
grat'i·fy
grat'ing
gra'tis
grat'i·tude
gra·tu'i·tous
gra·tu'i·ty
gra·va'men
grave
  graved
  grav'en
    or graved
  grav'ing
grave'clothes
grav'el
  grav'eled
    or grav'elled
  grav'el·ing
    or grav'el·ling
grav'el·ly

grave'ly
grave'stone
grave'yard
grav'i·tate
grav·i·ta'tion
grav'i·ty
gra'vy
gray'ish
greas'i·ness
grease'paint
greas'y
Great Brit'ain
great'coat
great'ly
great'ness
Gre'cian
Greece
greed'i·ly
greed'i·ness
greed'y
Greek
green'back
green'belt
green'ery
green'gro·cer
green'horn
green'house
green'ish
green'ness
green'room
Greens'boro
green'sward
greet'er
greet'ing
gre·gar'i·ous
grem'lin

gre·nade'
gren·a·dier'
gren·a·dine'
grey'hound
grid'dle
grid'dle cake
grid'iron
griev'ance
griev'ous
grill
   cooking (see grille)
gril'lage
grille
   or grill
   grating (see grill)
grill'work
grim'ace
grim'i·ness
grim'ly
grim'y
grin
   grinned
   grin'ning
grind
   ground
   grind'ing
grind'er
grind'stone
grip
   hold (see gripe,
   grippe)
   gripped
   grip'ping
gripe
   complain (see grip,
   grippe)

grippe
   influenza (see grip,
   gripe)

gris'-gris
   pl gris'-gris

gris'li·ness
gris'ly
grist
gris'tle
gris'tli·ness
gris'tly
grist'mill
grit
   grit'ted
   grit'ting
grit'ti·ness
grit'ty
griz'zled
griz'zly
gro'cer
gro'cery
grog'gi·ly
grog'gi·ness
grog'gy
gro'gram
groin
grom'met
gro'schen
   pl groschen
gros'grain
gross'ly
gross'ness
grosz
   pl gro'szy
gro·tesque'
gro·tesque'ly

gro·tes'que·rie

grot'to
   pl grot'toes, grot'tos

grouch'i·ly

grouch'i·ness

grouch'y

ground'er

ground'hog

ground'less

ground'wa·ter

ground'work

group'ing

grouse
   pl grouse

grov'el
  grov'eled
   or grov'elled

  grov'el·ing
   or grov'el·ling

grov'el·er
   or grov'el·ler

grow
  grew
  grown
  grow'ing

grow'er

growl'er

growl'ing

grown'-up

growth

grub
  grubbed
  grub'bing

grub'bi·ly

grub'bi·ness

grub'by

grub'stake

grudge

grudg'ing·ly

gru'el

gru'el·ing
   or gru'el·ling

grue'some

gruff'ly

grum'ble

grum'bler

grump'i·ly

grump'i·ness

grump'y

Gru·yère'

G'-string

gua'no

gua·ra·ni'
   pl gua·ra·nis' *or*
   gua·ra·nies'

guar·an·tee'

guar·an·tor'

guar'an·ty

guard'house

guard'ian

guard'room

guards'man

Gua·te·ma'la

Gua·te·ma'lan

gua'va

gu·ber·na·to'ri·al

guern'sey

guer·ril'la
   or gue·ril'la

guess'ti·mate

guess'work

guest

guf·faw'

guid'able

guid'ance

guide'book

guide'line

gui'don

guild
   association (*see* gild)

guild'hall

guil'der

guile

guile'ful

guile'ful·ly

guile'less

guil'lo·tine

guilt
   blame (*see* gilt)

guilt'i·ly

guilt'i·ness

guilt'less

guilt'y

Guin'ea

Guin'ean

guise

gui·tar'

gulch

gul'den
   pl gul'dens *or*
   gul'den

gul'let

gull·ibil'i·ty

gull'ible

gull′i·bly
gul′ly
gum
  gummed
  gum′ming
gum′bo
gum′boil
gum′drop
gum′mi·ness
gum′my
gump′tion
gum′shoe
gun
  gunned
  gun′ning
gun′boat
gun′cot·ton
gun′fight
gun′fire
gun′lock
gun′man
gun′met·al
gun′ner
gun′ner·y
gun′ny
gun′ny·sack
gun′point
gun′pow·der
gun′run·ner
gun′ship
gun′shot
gun′-shy
gun′smith
gun′wale
  or gun′nel

gup′py
gur′gle
gu·ru′
gush′er
gush′y
gus′set
gus′ta·to·ry
gust′i·ly
gust′i·ness
gus′to
gust′y
gut
  gut′ted
  gut′ting
gut′less
gut·ta-per′cha
gut′ter
gu′ter·snipe
gut′tur·al
gut′tur·al·ly
Guy·an′a
Guy·a·nese′
guz′zle
guz′zling
gym·na′si·um
  pl gym·na′si·ums *or*
    gym·na′sia

gym′nast
gym·nas′tic
gym·nas′tics
gym′no·sperm
gyn·e·co·log′i·cal
gyn·e·col′o·gist
gyn·e·col′o·gy
gyp

gypped
gyp′ping
gyp′sum
Gyp′sy
gy′rate
gy·ra′tion
gy′ro·com·pass
gy′ro·scope
gy·ro·sta′bi·liz·er
gy′ro·stat

H

ha·ba·ne′ra
ha·be·as cor′pus
hab′er·dash·er
hab′er·dash·ery
ha·bil′i·ment
hab′it
hab·it·abil′i·ty
hab′it·a·ble
hab′it·ably
hab′i·tant
hab′i·tat
hab·i·ta′tion
hab′it-form·ing
ha·bit′u·al
ha·bit′u·al·ly
ha·bit′u·ate
ha·bit·u·a′tion
ha·bi′tué
ha·ci·en′da
hack′le
hack′man
hack′ney

hack′neyed
hack′saw
hack′work
had′dock
Ha′des
haem′or·rhage
hag′gard
hag′gis
hag′gle
hag′gler
hag·i·og′ra·pher
hag·i·og′ra·phy
hail
  ice, greet (see hale)
hail′stone
hail′storm
hair′breadth
  or hairs′breadth
hair′brush
hair′cloth
hair′cut
hair′do
hair′dress·er
hair′i·ness
hair′less
hair′line
hair′pin
hair′-rais·ing
hair′split·ter
hair′split·ting
hair′spring
hair′trigger
hair′y
Hai′ti
Hai′tian

ha·la′la
  pl ha·la′la
ha·la′tion
hal′berd
  or hal′bert
hal′cy·on
hale
  healthy, haul (see hail)
ha′ler
half
  pl halves
half′back
half-baked
half′-breed
half′-caste
half-cocked
half′-dol′lar
half′heart′ed
half-length
half′-life
half′-light
half′-mast
half′-moon
half′-slip
half-staff
half′tone
half′-track
half′-truth
half·way
half′-wit
half-wit′ted
hal′i·but
hal′ide
Hal′i·fax

hal′ite
hal·i·to′sis
hal·le·lu′jah
hall′mark
hal′low
hal′lowed
Hal·low·een′
hal·lu′ci·nate
hal·lu·ci·na′tion
hal·lu′ci·na·to·ry
hal·lu′ci·no·gen
hal·lu′ci·no·
  gen′ic
hall′way
ha′lo
  pl ha′los *or* ha′loes
hal′o·gen
hal′ter
halt′ing
halve
hal′yard
  or hal′liard
ham
  hammed
  ham′ming
ham′burg·er
Ham′il·ton
ham′let
ham′mer
ham′mer·head
ham′mer·lock
ham′mock
Ham′mond
ham′per
Hamp′ton

ham′ster
ham′string
hand′bag
hand′ball
hand′bar·row
hand′bill
hand′book
hand′car
hand′clasp
hand′cuff
hand′ful
hand′gun
hand′i·cap
  hand′i·capped
  hand′i·cap·ping
hand′i·cap·per
hand′i·craft
hand′i·crafts·man
hand′i·ly
hand′i·ness
hand′i·work
hand′ker·chief
  pl hand′ker·chiefs
  also
    hand′ker·chieves

han′dle
han′dle·bar
hand′made
hand′maid
  or hand′maid·en
hand′-me-down
hand′off
hand′out
hand′pick
hand′rail

hand′saw
hands′-down
hand′set
hand′shake
hand′some
  good looking (see
    hansom)
hand′spike
hand′spring
hand-to-hand′
hand′wo·ven
hand′writ·ing
hand′writ·ten
hand′y
hand′y·man
hang
  hung
    also hanged
hang′ing
hang′ar
  airplanes (see
    hanger)
hang′dog
hang′er
  that which hangs
    (see hangar)
hang·er-on′
  pl hangers-on′
hang′ing
hang′man
hang′nail
hang′out
hang′over
han′ker
han·ky-pan′ky

han′som
  cab (see handsome)
Ha′nuk·kah
hao′le
hap·haz′ard
hap′less
hap′pen
hap′pen·ing
hap′pen·stance
hap′pi·ly
hap′pi·ness
hap′py
hap′py-go-lucky
hara-kir′i
ha·rangue′
ha·rangu′er
ha·rass′
ha·rass′ment
har′bin·ger
har′bor
har′bor·age
hard-and-fast′
hard′back
hard′ball
hard′-bit′ten
hard-boiled
hard′edge
hard′en
hard′ened
hard′head′ed
hard′heart′ed
har′di·hood
har′di·ly
har′di·ness
hard′ly

hard-of-hear'ing
hard'pan
hard'-shell
hard'ship
hard'stand
hard-sur'face
hard'tack
hard'top
hard'ware
hard'wood
hard·work'ing
har'dy
hare·brained
hare·lip
hare·lipped
har'em
har'le·quin
har'lot
harm'ful
harm'ful·ly
harm'less
har·mon'ic
har·mon'i·cal·ly
har·mon'i·ca
har·mon'ics
har·mo'ni·ous
har·mo'ni·um
har·mo·ni·za'tion
har'mo·nize
har'mo·ny
har'ness
harp'er
har·poon'
harp'si·chord
har'py
har'ri·dan

har'ri·er
Har'ris·burg
har'row
har'ry
harsh'ness
Hart'ford
har·um-scar'um
har'vest
har'vest·er
has'-been
hash'ish
has'sle
has'sock
haste
has'ten
hast'i·ly
hast'i·ness
hast'y
hat'box
hatch
hatch'ery
hatch'et
hatch'ing
hatch'way
hate'ful
hate'ful·ly
ha'tred
hat'ter
haugh'ti·ly
haugh'ti·ness
haugh'ty
haul'age
haul'er
haunch
haunt
haunt'ing·ly

haute cou·ture'
hau·teur'
have
    had
    hav'ing
    has
ha'ven
have'-not
hav'er·sack
hav'oc
Ha·waii'
Ha·wai'ian
hawk
hawk'er
hawk'ish
haw'ser
haw'thorn
hay'cock
hay'fork
hay'loft
hay'mow
hay'rack
hay'rick
hay'seed
hay'wire
haz'ard
haz'ard·ous
ha'zel
ha'zel·nut
haz'i·ly
haz'i·ness
haz'y
head'ache
head'band
head'board
head'dress

head'ed
head'er
head·first'
head'gear
head'hunt·er
head'i·ly
head'i·ness
head'ing
head'land
head'less
head'light
head'line
head'lin·er
head'lock
head'long
head·man
head'mas·ter
head'mis·tress
head'most
head'note
head-on
head'phone
head'piece
head'pin
head'quar·ters
head'rest
head'set
head'ship
heads'man
head'stock
head·stall
head'stone
head'strong
head'wait'er
head'wa·ter
head'way

head'word
head'work
head'y
heal
  cure (*see* heel)
heal'er
health'ful
health'ful·ly
health'i·ly
health'i·ness
health'y
heap
hear
  heard
  hear'ing
hear'er
hear'ing
hear'ken
hear'say
hearse
heart'ache
heart'beat
heart'break
heart'bro·ken
heart'burn
heart'en
heart'felt
hearth
hearth'side
hearth'stone
heart'i·ly
heart'i·ness
heart'land
heart'less
heart'rend·ing
heart'sick

heart'sore
heart'strings
heart'throb
heart-to-heart
heart'y
heat'ed·ly
heat'er
heath
hea'then
heath'er
heat'stroke
heave
  heaved
  or hove
  heav'ing
heav'en
heav'en·ward
heav'i·ly
heav'i·ness
heav'y
heav'y-du'ty
heav'y-hand'ed
heav'y·heart'ed
heav'y·set'
heav'y·weight
He·bra'ic
He'brew
heck'le
heck'ler
hect'are
hec'tic
hec'ti·cal·ly
hedge
hedge'hog
hedge'hop
hedge'row

he'do·nism
he'do·nist
he·do·nis'tic
heed'ful
heed'ful·ly
heed'less
heel
   foot (see heal)
heft'y
he·gem'o·ny
he·gi'ra
heif'er
height
height'en
hei'nous
heir
   inheritor (see air)
heir'ess
heir'loom
Hel'e·na
hel'i·cal
hel'i·coid
hel·i·coi'dal
hel'i·cop·ter
he·lio·cen'tric
he'lio·trope
hel'i·port
he'li·um
he'lix
   pl hel'i·ces *also*
   he'lix·es
hell'-bent
hell'cat
Hel·len'ic
Hel'le·nist
Hel·le·nis'tic

hel'lion
hell'ish
hel·lo'
helm
hel'met
helms'man
hel'ot
help'er
help'ful
help'ful·ly
help'less
help'mate
hel·ter-skel'ter
hem
   hemmed
   hem'ming
he'mal
he-man
hem'a·tite
hem·a·tol'o·gist
hem·a·tol'o·gy
hemi·sphere
hemi·spher'i·cal
hemi·line
hem'lock
he'mo·glo·bin
   or hae'mo·glo·bin
he·mol'y·sis
he·mo·lyt'ic
he·mo·phil'ia
he·mo·phil'i·ac
hem'or·rhage
hem·or·rhag'ic
hem'or·rhoid
hem'stitch
hence'forth

hence·for'ward
hench'man
hen'na
hen'peck
he·pat'ic
hep·a·ti'tis
hep'ta·gon
hep·tam'e·ter
her'ald
he·ral'dic
her'ald·ry
her·ba'ceous
her·bar'i·um
her·bi·cid'al
her'bi·cide
her'bi·vore
her·biv'o·rous
her·cu·le'an
herd'er
herds'man
here'about
   or here'abouts
here·af'ter
here·by'
he·red'i·tary
he·red'i·ty
here·in'
here·of'
here·on'
her'e·sy
her'e·tic
he·ret'i·cal
here·to'
here'to·fore
here·un'der
here·un'to

here'up·on
here·with'
her'i·ta·ble
her'i·tage
her·met'ic
her·met'i·cal
her·met'i·cal·ly
her'mit
her'mit·age
her'nia
her'ni·ate
he'ro
he·ro'ic
he·ro'i·cal·ly
he·ro'ics
her'o·in
   narcotic (see
   heroine)
her'o·ine
   female hero (see
   heroin)
her'o·ism
her'on
her'pes
her·pe·tol'o·gist
her·pe·tol'o·gy
her'ring
her'ring·bone
her·self'
hes'i·tance
hes'i·tan·cy
hes'i·tant
hes'i·tate
hes·i·ta'tion
het'er·o·dox
het'er·o·doxy

het·er·o·ge·ne'i·ty
het·er·o·ge'ne·
   ous
het·ero·sex'u·al
het·ero·sex·u·al'
   i·ty
hew
   cut (see hue)
hewed
hewed
   or hewn
hew'ing
hexa·chlo'ro·
   phene
hex'a·gon
hex·ag'o·nal
hex'a·gram
hex·am'e·ter
hey'day
Hi·a·le'ah
hi·a'tus
hi·ba'chi
hi'ber·nate
hi·ber·na'tion
hi'ber·na·tor
hi·bis'cus
hic'cup
   also hic'cough
hic'cuped
   also hic'cupped
hic'cup·ing
   also hic'cup·ping
hick'o·ry
hi·dal'go
hide
hid

hid'den
   or hid
hid'ing
hide-and-seek'
hide'away
hide'bound
hid'eous
hide'out
hie
hied
hy'ing
   or hie'ing
hi·er·ar'chi·cal
hi·er·ar'chi·cal·ly
hi'er·ar·chy
hi·er·o·glyph'ic
hi-fi
hig·gle·dy-pig'
   gle·dy
high'ball
high'born
high'boy
high'bred
high'brow
high·er-up'
high·fa·lu'tin
high-flown
high'-fly'ing
high'-hand'ed
high-hat
high'land
high'land·er
high'-lev'el
high'light
high'-mind'ed
high'ness

high-octane
high-pressure
high·rise
high'road
high'-sound'ing
high'-spir'it·ed
high-strung
high'tail
high-tension
high-test
high-toned
high-water
high'way
high'way·man
hi'jack
  or high'-jack

hi'jack·er
hik'er
hi·lar'i·ous
hi·lar'i·ty
hill'bil·ly
hill'ock
hill'side
hill'top
hill'y
him·self'
hin'der
hind'most
hind'quar·ter
hin'drance
hind'sight
Hin'du·ism
hin'ter·land
hip·bone
hip'pie
  or hip'py

Hip·po·crat'ic
hip'po·drome
hip·po·pot'a·mus
  pl hip·po·pot'a·mus·
  es *or* hip·po·pot'
  a·mi
hip'py
hip'ster
hire'ling
hir'sute
His·pan'ic
his'ta·mine
his'to·gen
his·to·gen'e·sis
his'to·gram
his·tol'o·gist
his·tol'o·gy
his·to'ri·an
his·tor'ic
his·tor'i·cal
his·tor'i·cal·ly
his·to·ric'i·ty
his·to·ri·og'ra·
  pher
his·to·ri·og'ra·
  phy
his'to·ry
his·tri·on'ic
his·tri·on'i·cal·ly
his·tri·on'ics
hit
  hit
  hit'ting
hitch'hike
hitch'hik·er
hith'er·to
hit'ter

hive
  bee house (see
  hives)

hives
  pl hives
  allergic disorder (see
  hive)

hoard
  accumulate (see
  horde)

hoar'frost
hoar'i·ness
hoarse'ly
hoar'y
hoax
hob'ble
hob'by
hob'by·horse
hob'gob·lin
hob'nail
hob'nob
  hob'nobbed
  hob'nob·bing
ho'bo
  pl ho'boes *also*
  ho'bos

hob'by·ist
hock'ey
ho·cus-po'cus
hodge'podge
ho'gan
hog'gish
hogs'head
hog'-tie
hog'wash
hoi pol·loi'

hop

hoist
ho'kum
hold
  held
  hold'ing
hold'ing
hold'out
hold'over
hold'up
hol'i·day
ho'li·ness
Hol'land
Hol'land·er
hol'low
hol'ly
hol'ly·hock
Hol'ly·wood
hol'o·caust
hol'o·gram
hol'o·graph
ho·log'ra·phy
hol'stein
hol'ster
ho'ly
hom'age
hom'bre
hom'burg
home'body
home'bred
home'com·ing
home·grown
home'land
home'less
home'li·ness
home'ly
home·made

home'mak·er
ho·meo·path'ic
ho·me·op'a·thy
hom'er
home'room
home'sick
home'spun
home'stead
home'stead·er
home·stretch
home'ward
home'work
hom'ey
hom·i·cid'al
hom'i·cide
hom·i·let'ic
hom·i·let'ics
hom'i·ly
hom'i·nid
hom'i·noid
hom'i·ny
ho·mo·ge·ne'i·ty
ho·mo·ge'ne·ous
ho·mog·e·ni·za'·
  tion
ho·mog'e·nize
ho·mog'e·nous
hom'o·graph
ho·mol'o·gous
hom'onym
ho'mo·phone
ho·mo sa'pi·ens
ho·mo·sex'u·al
ho·mo·sex·u·al'·
  i·ty
Hon·du'ras

Hon·du'ran
hone
hon'est
hon'esty
hon'ey
hon'ey·bee
hon'ey·comb
hon'ey·dew
hon'ey·moon
hon'ey·suck·le
hon'ky-tonk
Ho·no·lu'lu
hon'or
hon'or·able
hon'or·ably
hon·o·rar'i·um
  pl hon·o·rar'ia *also*
  hon·o·rar'i·ums
hon'or·ary
hon·or·if'ic
hood'ed
hood'lum
hoo'doo
hood'wink
hoo'ey
hoof
  pl hooves *or* hoofs
hook'ah
hook'up
hook'worm
hoo'li·gan
hoop'la
hoo'te·nan·ny
hop
hopped
hop'ping

hope'ful

hope'ful·ly

hope'less

hop'per

hop'scotch

horde
throng (see hoard)

hore'hound

ho·ri'zon

hor·i·zon'tal

hor·i·zon'tal·ly

hor'mon·al

hor'mone

horn'book

hor'net

horn'pipe

horn'swog·gle

horn'y

hor·o·log'i·cal

ho·rol'o·gist

ho·rol'o·gy

hor'o·scope

hor·ren'dous

hor'ri·ble

hor'ri·bly

hor'rid

hor'ri·fy

hor'ror

hors d'oeuvre'

horse'back

horse'flesh

horse'fly

horse'hair

horse'hide

horse'laugh

horse'man

horse'play

horse'pow·er

horse'rad·ish

horse'shoe

horse'whip

horse'wom·an

hors'ey
or hors'y

hor'ta·tive

hor'ta·to·ry

hor·ti·cul'tur·al

hor·ti·cul'ture

hor·ti·cul'tur·ist

ho·san'na

hose
pl hose *or* hos'es

ho'siery

hos'pice

hos·pit'a·ble

hos·pit'a·bly

hos'pi·tal

hos·pi·tal'i·ty

hos·pi·tal·iza'tion

hos'pi·tal·ize

hos'tage

hos'tel

hos'tel·er

hos'tel·ry

host'ess

hos'tile

hos'tile·ly

hos·til'i·ty

hos'tler

hot'bed

hot'-blood'ed

hot'box

ho·tel'

hot'foot
pl hot'foots

hot'head'ed

hot'house

hot'-rod'der

hot'shot

hour'glass

hour'ly

house
pl hous'es

house'boat

house'boy

house'break·ing

house'bro·ken

house'clean

house'coat

house'fly

house'ful

house'hold

house'keep·er

house'lights

house'man

house'maid

house'moth·er

house'top

house'warm·ing

house'wife

house'work

hous'ing

Hous'ton

hov'el

hov'er

hov'er·craft

how·be'it

how'dah

how·ev'er
how'it·zer
howl'er
how·so·ev'er
hoy'den
hua·ra'che
hub'bub
hu'bris
huck'le·ber·ry
huck'ster
hud'dle
hue
   color (see hew)
huff'ish
huff'y
hug
  hugged
  hug'ging
huge'ly
Hu'gue·not
hu'la
hulk'ing
hul'la·ba·loo
hum
  hummed
  hum'ming
hu'man
hu·mane'
hu·mane'ly
hu'man·ism
hu'man·ist
hu·man·is'tic
hu·man·i·tar'i·an
hu·man'i·ty
hu·man·iza'tion
hu'man·ize

hu'man·kind
hu'man·ly
hum'ble
hum'bler
hum'bly
hum'bug
hum'ding'er
hum'drum
hu'mer·al
hu'mer·us
hu'mid
hu·mid·i·fi·ca'tion
hu·mid'i·fi·er
hu·mid'i·fy
hu·mid'i·ty
hu'mi·dor
hu·mil'i·ate
hu·mil·i·a'tion
hu·mil'i·ty
hum'ming·bird
hum'mock
hu'mor
hu'mor·ist
hu'mor·ous
hump'back
hu'mus
hunch'back
hun'dred
hun'dredth
hun'dred·weight
Hun·gar'i·an
Hun'ga·ry
hun'ger
hun'gri·ly
hun'gry
hun·ky-do'ry

hunt'er
Hun'ting·ton
hunt'ress
hunts'man
Hunts'ville
hur'dle
  obstacle (see hurtle)
hur·dy-gur'dy
hurl'er
hur·ly-bur'ly
hur·rah'
hur'ri·cane
hur'ried·ly
hur'ried·ness
hur'ry
hurt
hurt
hurt'ing
hurt'ful
hur'tle
  hurl (see hurdle)
hus'band
hus'band·man
hus'band·ry
hush'-hush
husk'er
husk'i·ly
husk'i·ness
husk'ing
husk'y
hus·sar'
  cavalry (see huzzah)
hus'sy
hus'tings
hus'tle

hus'tler

huz·zah'
   or huz·za'
   exclamation (*see*
    hussar)

hy'a·cinth

hy'brid

hy·brid·iza'tion

hy'brid·ize

hy·dran'gea

hy'drant

hy'drate

hy·drau'lic

hy·drau'lics

hy'dride

hy'dro

hy·dro·car'bon

hy·dro·chlo·ric

hy·dro·elec'tric

hy'dro·foil

hy'dro·gen

hy·drog'e·nate

hy·drog·e·na'tion

hy·drog'e·nous

hy·dro·log'ic

hy·drol'o·gist

hy·drol'o·gy

hy·drol'y·sis

hy·drom'e·ter

hy'dro·naut

hy·dron'ic

hy·dro·pho'bia

hy'dro·plane

hy·dro·pon'ics

hy·dro·stat'ic

hy·dro·ther'a·py

hy'drous

hy·drox'ide

hy·e'na

hy'giene

hy·gien'ic

hy·gien'i·cal·ly

hy·gien'ist

hy·grom'e·ter

hy·gro·scop'ic

hy'men

hy·me·ne'al

hymn

hym'nal

hym'no·dy

hym·nol'o·gy

hy·per·acid'i·ty

hy·per·ac'tive

hy·per·bar'ic

hy·per'bo·la
   curve (*see*
    hyperbole)

hy·per'bo·le
   exaggeration (*see*
    hyperbola)

hy·per·bol'ic

hy·per·crit'i·cal

hy·per·crit'i·cal·ly

hy·per·gly·ce'mia
   excess sugar (*see*
    hypoglycemia)

hy·per·sen'si·tive

hy·per·sen·si·tiv'
  i·ty

hy·per·son'ic

hy·per·ten'sion

hy·per·tro'phic

hy·per'tro·phy

hy'phen

hy'phen·ate

hy·phen·a'tion

hyp·no'sis

hyp·not'ic

hyp·not'i·cal·ly

hyp'no·tism

hyp'no·tist

hyp'no·tize

hy·po·chon'dria

hy·po·chon'dri·ac

hy·poc'ri·sy

hyp'o·crite

hyp·o·crit'i·cal

hyp·o·crit'i·cal·ly

hy·po·der'mic

hy·po·gly·ce'mia
   decrease of sugar
   (*see* hyperglyce-
   mia)

hy·pot'e·nuse

hy·poth'e·cate

hy·poth'e·sis

hy·poth'e·size

hy·po·thet'i·cal

hy·po·thet'i·cal·ly

hys·ter·ec'to·my

hys·te'ria

hys·ter'ic

hys·ter'i·cal

hys·ter'i·cal·ly

hys·ter'ics

I

iam'bic

ib'i·dem
ice'berg
ice'boat
ice'bound
ice'box
ice'break·er
ice-cold
ice'house
Ice'land
Ice'land·er
Ice·lan'dic
ice'man
ice'-skate
ich·thy·ol'o·gist
ich·thy·ol'o·gy
i'ci·cle
i'ci·ly
i'ci·ness
ic'ing
i'con
icon'o·clasm
icon'o·clast
i'cy
I'da·ho
ide'a
ide'al
ide'al·ism
ide'al·ist
ide·al·is'tic
ide·al·is'ti·cal·ly
ide·al·iza'tion
ide'al·ize
ide'al·ly
ide'ate
ide'ation
id'em

iden'ti·cal
iden'ti·cal·ly
iden'ti·fi·able
iden'ti·fi·ably
iden·ti·fi·ca'tion
iden'ti·fi·er
iden'ti·fy
iden'ti·ty
id'eo·gram
id'eo·graph
ideo·log'i·cal
    or ideo·log'ic
ideo·log'i·cal·ly
ide·ol'o·gist
ide·ol'o·gy
id'i·o·cy
id'i·om
id·i·om·at'ic
id·i·om·at'i·cal·ly
id·io·syn'cra·sy
id·io·syn·crat'ic
id·io·syn·crat'i·
    cal·ly
id'i·ot
id·i·ot'ic
id·i·ot'i·cal·ly
id'le
    doing nothing (see
    idol, idyll)
id'le·ness
id'ler
id'ly
id'ol
    object of worship
    (see idle, idyll)
idol'a·ter

id'ol·a·trous
idol'a·try
idol·iza'tion
id'ol·ize
id'yll
    or id'yl
    poem (see idle, idol)
idyl'lic
if'fy
ig'loo
ig'ne·ous
ig·nit'able
    also ig·nit'ible
ig'nite
ig·ni'tion
ig·no'ble
ig·no'bly
ig·no·min'i·ous
ig'no·mi·ny
ig·no·ra'mus
ig'no·rance
ig'no·rant
ig·nore'
igua'na
i'kon
il'e·um
    pl il'ea
    intestine (see ilium)
il·e·it'is
il'i·um
    pl il'ia
    bone (see ileum)
ill
    worse
    worst
ill-ad·vised'
ill'-be'ing
ill'-bod'ing

ill-bred
il·le′gal
il·le·gal′i·ty
il·le′gal·ly
il·leg·i·bil′i·ty
il·leg′i·ble
il·leg′i·bly
il·le·git′i·ma·cy
il·le·git′i·mate
il·le·git′i·mate·ly
ill′-fat′ed
ill′-fa′vored
ill′-got′ten
ill′-hu′mored
il·lib′er·al
il·lic′it
unlawful (see elicit)
il·lim′it·able
il·lim′it·ably
Il·li·nois′
il·lit′er·a·cy
il·lit′er·ate
ill′-man′nered
ill′-na′tured
ill′ness
il·log′i·cal
il·log′i·cal·ly
ill′-sort′ed
ill-starred
ill′-tem′pered
ill-treat
il·lu′mi·nate
il·lu·mi·na′tion
il·lu′mi·na·tor
il·lu′mine
ill′-us′age
ill-use

il·lu′sion
  mistaken idea (see
  allusion)
il·lu′sion·ist
il·lu′sive
  deceptive (see
  allusive)
il·lu′so·ry
il′lus·trate
il·lus·tra′tion
il·lus′tra·tive
il′lus·tra·tor
il·lus′tri·ous
im′age
im′ag·ery
imag′in·able
imag′in·ably
imag′i·nary
imag·i·na′tion
imag′i·na·tive
imag′ine
im′ag·ism
im′ag·ist
im·bal′ance
im′be·cile
im·be·cil′i·ty
im·bed′
im·bibe′
im·bib′er
im′bri·cate
im·bri·ca′tion
im·bro′glio
im·brue′
im·bue′
im′i·ta·ble
im′i·tate
im·i·ta′tion

im′i·ta·tive
im′i·ta·tor
im·mac′u·late
im′ma·nent
  in dwelling (see
  imminent)
im·ma·te′ri·al
im·ma·ture′
im·ma·tu′ri·ty
im·mea′sur·able
im·mea′sur·ably
im·me′di·a·cy
im·me′di·ate
im·me′di·ate·ly
im·me·mo′ri·al
im·mense′
im·mense′ly
im·men′si·ty
im·merse′
im·mer′sion
im′mi·grant
im′mi·grate
im·mi·gra′tion
im′mi·nence
im′mi·nent
  impending (see
  eminence,
  immanent)

im·mis′ci·ble
im·mit′i·ga·ble
im·mo′bile
im·mo·bil′i·ty
im·mo·bi·li′za′
  tion
im·mo′bi·lize
im·mod′er·a·cy
im·mod′er·ate

im·mod'est
im·mod'es·ty
im'mo·late
im·mo·la'tion
im·mor'al
im·mo·ral'i·ty
im·mor'al·ly
im·mor'tal
im·mor·tal'i·ty
im·mor'tal·ize
im·mor'tal·ly
im·mov·abil'i·ty
im·mov'able
im·mov'ably
im·mune'
im·mu'ni·ty
im·mu·ni·za'tion
im'mu·nize
im·mu·nol'o·gist
im·mu·nol'o·gy
im·mure'
im·mu·ta·bil'i·ty
im·mu'ta·ble
im·mu'ta·bly
im·pact'
   verb

im'pact
   noun

im·pact'ed
im·pair'
im·pair'ment
im·pale'
im·pal·pa·bil'i·ty
im·pal'pa·ble
im·pal'pa·bly
im·pan'el
im·part'

im·part'able
   able to
    communicate
   (*see* impartible)

im·part'ably
im·par'tial
im·par·tial'i·ty
im·par'tial·ly
im·par'ti·ble
   not partible

im·pass'able
   not passable (*see*
   impassible)

im·pass'ably
im'passe
im·pas'si·ble
   unfeeling (*see*
   impassable)

im·pas'si·bly
im·pas'sioned
im·pas'sive
im·pas·siv'i·ty
im·pa'tience
im·pa'tient
im·peach'
im·peach'ment
im·pec·ca·bil'i·ty
im·pec'ca·ble
im·pec'ca·bly
im·pe·cu'nious
im·ped'ance
im·pede'
im·ped'i·ment
im·ped·i·men'ta
im·pel'
im·pelled'
im·pel'ling

im·pend'
im·pend'ing
im·pen·e·tra·bil'i·ty
im·pen'e·tra·ble
im·pen'e·tra·bly
im·pen'i·tent
im·per'a·tive
im·per·ceiv'able
im·per·cep·ti·bil'i·ty
im·per·cep'ti·ble
im·per·cep'ti·bly
im·per·cep'tive
im·per'fect
im·per·fec'tion
im·per'fo·rate
im·pe'ri·al
im·pe'ri·al·ism
im·pe'ri·al·ist
im·pe·ri·al·is'tic
im·pe·ri·al·is'ti·cal·ly
im·pe'ri·al·ly
im·per'il
im·per'iled
   or im·per'illed

im·per'il·ing
   or im·per'il·ling

im·pe'ri·ous
im·per·ish·abil'i·ty
im·per'ish·able
im·per'ish·ably
im·per'ma·nence
im·per'ma·nen·cy
im·per'ma·nent

im·per·me·
  abil′i·ty
im·per′me·able
im·per′me·ably
im·per·mis·si·
  bil′i·ty
im·per·mis′si·ble
im·per′son·al
im·per·son·al′i·ty
im·per′son·al·ize
im·per′son·al·ly
im·per′son·ate
im·per·son·a′tion
im·per′son·ator
im·per′ti·nence
im·per′ti·nent
im·per·turb·
  abil′i·ty
im·per·turb′able
im·per·turb′ably
im·per′vi·ous
im·pe·ti′go
im·pet·u·os′i·ty
im·pet′u·ous
im′pe·tus
im·pi′ety
im·pinge′
im·pinge′ment
im′pi·ous
imp′ish
im·plac′a·ble
im·plac′a·bly
im·plant′
im·plan·ta′tion
im·plau·si·bil′i·ty
im·plau′si·ble

im·plau′si·bly
im′ple·ment
im·ple·men·
  ta′tion
im′pli·cate
im·pli·ca′tion
im·plic′it
im·plode′
im·plore′
im·plo′sion
im·plo′sive
im·ply′
im·po·lite′
im·pol′i·tic
im·pon·der·
  a·bil′i·ty
im·pon′der·a·ble
im·pon′der·a·bly
im·port′
  verb
im′port
  noun
im·port′a·ble
im·por′tance
im·por′tant
im·por·ta′tion
im·port′er
im·por′tu·nate
im·por·tune′
im·por·tu′ni·ty
im·pose′
im·pos′ing
im·po·si′tion
im·pos·si·bil′i·ty
im·pos′si·ble
im·pos′si·bly

im′post
im·pos′tor
  or im·pos′ter
im·pos′ture
im′po·tence
im′po·ten·cy
im′po·tent
im·pound′
im·pov′er·ish
im·prac′ti·ca·
  bil′i·ty
im·prac′ti·ca·ble
im·prac′ti·ca·bly
im·prac′ti·cal
im·prac·ti·cal′i·ty
im′pre·cate
im·pre·ca′tion
im·pre·cise′
im·pre·ci′sion
im·preg·na·bil′i·ty
im·preg′na·ble
im·preg′na·bly
im·preg′nate
im·preg·na′tion
im·pre·sa′rio
im·press′
im·press′ible
im·pres′sion
im·pres·sion·
  abil′i·ty
im·pres′sion·able
im·pres′sion·ably
im·pres′sion·ism
im·pres′sion·ist
im·pres′sion·is′tic
im·pres′sive

im·pres'sive·ly
im·press'ment
im·pri·ma'tur
im·print'
verb

im'print
noun

im·pris'on
im·pris'on·ment
im·prob·a·bil'i·ty
im·prob'a·ble
im·prob'a·bly
im·promp'tu
im·prop'er
im·pro·pri'e·ty
im·prov·abil'i·ty
im·prov'able
im·prove'
im·prove'ment
im·prov'i·dence
im·prov'i·dent
im·pro·vi·sa'tion
im·pro·vise'
im·pro·vis'er
or im·pro·vi'sor

im·pru'dence
im·pru'dent
im'pu·dence
im'pu·dent
im·pugn'
im'pulse
im·pul'sion
im·pul'sive
im·pul'sive·ly
im·pu'ni·ty
im·pure'

im·pu'ri·ty
im·put·abil'i·ty
im·put'able
im·pu·ta'tion
im·pute'
in·abil'i·ty
in ab·sen'tia
in·ac·ces·si·
  bil'i·ty
in·ac·ces'si·ble
in·ac'cu·ra·cy
in·ac'cu·rate
in·ac'tion
in·ac'ti·vate
in·ac·ti·va'tion
in·ac'tive
in·ac·tiv'i·ty
in·ad'e·qua·cy
in·ad'e·quate
in·ad·mis·si·
  bil'i·ty
in·ad·mis'si·ble
in·ad·ver'tence
in·ad·ver'ten·cy
in·ad·ver'tent
in·ad·vis·abil'i·ty
in·ad·vis'able
in·alien·abil'i·ty
in·al'ien·able
in·al'ien·ably
in·al·ter·abil'i·ty
in·al'ter·able
in·al'ter·ably
in·amo·ra'ta
inane'
in·an'i·mate

inan'i·ty
in·ap·pli·ca·bil'i·ty
in·ap'pli·ca·ble
in·ap'pli·ca·bly
in·ap·pre'cia·ble
in·ap·pre'cia·bly
in·ap·pro'pri·ate
in·apt'
*not suitable (see
inept)*

in·ap'ti·tude
in·ar·tic'u·late
in·as·much as
in·at·ten'tion
in·at·ten'tive
in·au·di·bil'i·ty
in·au'di·ble
in·au'di·bly
in·au'gu·ral
in·au'gu·rate
in·au·gu·ra'tion
in·aus·pi'cious
in'board
in'born
in'bound
in'bred
in'breed·ing
in·cal·cu·la·
  bil'i·ty
in·cal'cu·la·ble
in·cal'cu·la·bly
in·can·des'cence
in·can·des'cent
in·can·ta'tion
in·ca·pa·bil'i·ty
in·ca'pa·ble

in·ca·pac'i·tant
in·ca·pac'i·tate
in·ca·pac·i·ta'tion
in·ca·pac'i·ty
in·car'cer·ate
in·car·cer·a'tion
in·car'nate
in·car·na'tion
in·cau'tious
in·cen'di·a·rism
in·cen'di·ary
in'cense
  noun

in·cense'
  verb

in·cen'tive
in·cep'tion
in·cep'tive
in·cer'ti·tude
in·ces'sant
in'cest
in·ces'tu·ous
in·cho'ate
in'ci·dence
in'ci·dent
in·ci·den'tal
in·ci·den'tal·ly
in·cin'er·ate
in·cin·er·a'tion
in·cin'er·a·tor
in·cip'i·en·cy
  also in·cip'i·ence

in·cip'i·ent
in·cise'
in·ci'sion
in·ci'sive

in·ci'sive·ly
in·ci'sor
in·ci·ta'tion
in·cite'
in·cite'ment
in·ci·vil'i·ty
in·clem'en·cy
in·clem'ent
in·clin'able
in·cli·na'tion
in·cline'
  verb

in'cline
  noun

in·clin'ing
in·cli·nom'e·ter
in·clud'able
  or in·clud'ible

in·clude'
in·clu'sion
in·clu'sive
in·cog·ni'to
in'cog'ni·zant
in·co·her'ence
in·co·her'ent
in·com·bus'ti·ble
in'come
in'com·ing
in·com·men'su·
  ra·ble
in·com·men'su·
  ra·bly
in·com·men'su·
  rate
in·com·mode'
in·com·mo'di·ous

in·com·mu·ni·ca·
  bil'i·ty
in·com·mu'ni·
  ca·ble
in·com·mu'ni·
  ca·bly
in·com·mu·ni·
  ca'do
in·com·mu'ni·
  ca·tive
in·com·mut'able
in·com·mut'ably
in·com·pa·ra·
  bil'i·ty
in·com'pa·ra·ble
in·com'pa·ra·bly
in·com·pat·i·
  bil'i·ty
in·com·pat'i·ble
in·com'pe·tence
in·com'pe·ten·cy
in·com'pe·tent
in·com·plete'
in·com·pre·
  hen'si·ble
in·com·press'ible
in·con·ceiv·
  abil'i·ty
in·con·ceiv'able
in·con·ceiv'ably
in·con·clu'sive
in·con·gru'ent
in·con·gru'i·ty
in·con'gru·ous
in·con·se·
  quen'tial

in·con·se·
  quen'tial·ly
in·con·sid'er·able
in·con·sid'er·ate
in·con·sid'er·
  ate·ly
in·con·sis'ten·cy
  also in·con·sis'tence
in·con·sis'tent
in·con·sol'able
in·con·sol'ably
in·con·spic'u·ous
in·con'stan·cy
in·con'stant
in·con·test·
  abil'i·ty
in·con·test'able
in·con·test'ably
in·con'ti·nence
in·con'ti·nent
in·con·trol'la·ble
in·con·tro·
  vert'ible
in·con·tro·
  vert'ibly
in·con·ve'nience
in·con·ve'nient
in·con·vert·
  ibil'i·ty
in·con·vert'ible
in·con·vert'ibly
in·cor'po·rate
in·cor'po·rat·ed
in·cor·po·ra'tion
in·cor'po·ra·tor
in·cor·po're·al

in·cor·po're·al·ly
in·cor·rect'
in·cor·ri·gi·bil'i·ty
in·cor'ri·gi·ble
in·cor'ri·gi·bly
in·cor·rupt'
in·cor·rupt·ibil'i·ty
in·cor·rupt'ible
in·cor·rupt'ibly
in·creas'able
in·crease'
  verb
in'crease
  noun
in·creas'ing·ly
in·cred·i·bil'i·ty
in·cred'i·ble
in·cred'i·bly
in·cre·du'li·ty
in·cred'u·lous·ly
in'cre·ment
in·cre·men'tal
in·crim'i·nate
in·crim·i·na'tion
in·crim'i·na·to·ry
in·crust'
in·crus·ta'tion
in'cu·bate
in·cu·ba'tion
in'cu·ba·tor
in'cu·bus
  pl in'cu·bi *also*
  in'cu·bus·es
in·cul'cate
in·cul·ca'tion
in·cul'pa·ble

in·cul'pate
in·cul·pa'tion
in·cul'pa·to·ry
in·cum'ben·cy
in·cum'bent
in·cu·nab'u·lum
  pl in·cu·nab'u·la
in·cur'
  in·curred'
  in·cur'ring
in·cur·abil'i·ty
in·cur'able
in·cur'ably
in·cu'ri·ous
in·cur'sion
in·cur'sive
in·debt'ed
in·de'cen·cy
in·de'cent
in·de·ci'pher·able
in·de·ci'sion
in·de·ci'sive
in·de·clin'able
in·dec'o·rous
in·de·co'rum
in·deed'
in·de·fat·i·ga·
  bil'i·ty
in·de·fat'i·ga·ble
in·de·fat'i·ga·bly
in·de·fea'si·ble
in·de·fea'si·bly
in·de·fen·si·
  bil'i·ty
in·de·fen'si·ble
in·de·fen'si·bly

in·de·fin′able
in·def′i·nite
in·del′i·ble
in·del′i·bly
in·del′i·ca·cy
in·del′i·cate
in·dem·ni·fi·
  ca′tion
in·dem′ni·fy
in·dem′ni·ty
in·dent′
in·den·ta′tion
in·den′tion
in·den′ture
in·de·pen′dence
in·de·pen′den·cy
in·de·pen′dent
in·de·scrib′able
in·de·scrib′ably
in·de·struc′ti·
  bil′i·ty
in·de·struc′ti·ble
in·de·struc′ti·bly
in·de·ter′min·able
in·de·ter′min·ably
in·de·ter′mi·na·cy
in·de·ter′mi·nate
in·de·ter′mi·
  nate·ly
in·de·ter·mi·
  na′tion
in·de·ter′min·ism
in′dex
  pl in′dex·es or
  in′di·ces

in′dex·er

In′dia
In′di·an
In·di·an′a
In·di·a·nap′o·lis
in′di·cate
in·di·ca′tion
in·dic′a·tive
in′di·ca·tor
in·di′cia
in·dict′able
in·dict′
  charge (see indite)

in·dict′ment
in·dif′fer·ence
in·dif′fer·ent
in·dif′fer·ent·ism
in′di·gence
in′di·gene
  also in′di·gen

in·dig′e·nous
in′di·gent
in·di·gest·ibil′i·ty
in·di·gest′ible
in·di·ges′tion
in·dig′nant
in·dig·na′tion
in·dig′ni·ty
in′di·go
  pl in′di·gos or
  in′di·goes

in·di·rect′
in·di·rec′tion
in·dis·cern′ible
in·dis·creet′
  imprudent (see
  indiscrete)

in·dis·crete′
  *not separated (see
  indiscreet)*

in·dis·cre′tion
  imprudence

in·dis·crim′i·nate
in·dis·pens·
  abil′i·ty
in·dis·pens′able
in·dis·pens′ably
in·dis·pos′ed
in·dis·po·si′tion
in·dis·put′able
in·dis·put′ably
in·dis·sol′u·ble
in·dis·sol′u·bly
in·dis·tinct′
in·dis·tin′guish·
  able
in·dis·tin′guish·
  ably
in·dite′
  compose (see indict)

in·di·vid′u·al
in·di·vid′u·al·ism
in·di·vid′u·al·ist
in·di·vid·u·al·is′tic
in·di·vid·u·al·is′ti·
  cal·ly
in·di·vid·u·al′i·ty
in·di·vid′u·al·
  iza′tion
in·di·vid′u·al·ize
in·di·vid′u·al·ly
in·di·vis·i·bil′i·ty
in·di·vis′i·ble

in·di·vis'i·bly
in·doc'tri·nate
in·doc·tri·na'tion
in·doc'tri·na·tor
in'do·lence
in'do·lent
in·dom·i·ta·
  bil'i·ty
in·dom'i·ta·ble
in·dom'i·ta·bly
In·do·ne'sia
In·do·ne'sian
in·door
in·doors'
in·dorse'
in·du·bi·ta·bil'i·ty
in·du'bi·ta·ble
in·du'bi·ta·bly
in·duce'
in·duce'ment
in·duct'
in·duct·ee'
in·duc'tance
in·duc'tion
in·duc'tive
in·duc'tor
in·dulge'
in·dul'gence
in·dul'gent
in'du·rate
in·du·ra'tion
in·dus'tri·al
in·dus'tri·al·ism
in·dus'tri·al·ist
in·dus·tri·al·
  iza'tion

in·dus'tri·al·ize
in·dus'tri·al·ly
in·dus'tri·ous
in'dus·try
ine'bri·ate
ine·bri·a'tion
in·ebri'ety
in·ed'i·ble
in·ed'it·ed
in·ed'u·ca·ble
in·ef·fa·bil'i·ty
in·ef'fa·ble
in·ef'fa·bly
in·ef·fac'a·bly
in·ef·face·abil'i·ty
in·ef·face'able
in·ef·fec'tive
in·ef·fec'tu·al
in·ef·fec'tu·al·ly
in·ef·fi·ca'cious
in·ef'fi·ca·cy
in·ef·fi'cien·cy
in·ef·fi'cient
in·elas'tic
in·elas·tic'i·ty
in·el'e·gance
in·el'e·gant
in·el·i·gi·bil'i·ty
in·el'i·gi·ble
in·el'o·quent
in·eluc·ta·bil'i·ty
in·eluc'ta·ble
in·eluc'ta·bly
in·ept'
  unfit (see inapt)
in·ep'ti·tude

in·equal'i·ty
in·eq'ui·ta·ble
in·eq'ui·ty
  injustice (see
  iniquity)

in·erad'i·ca·ble
in·erad'i·ca·bly
in·er'ran·cy
in·er'rant
in·ert'
in·er'tia
in·er'tial
in·es·cap'able
in·es·cap'ably
in·es·sen'tial
in·es'ti·ma·ble
in·es'ti·ma·bly
in·ev·i·ta·bil'i·ty
in·ev'i·ta·ble
in·ev'i·ta·bly
in·ex·act'
in·ex·cus'able
in·ex·cus'ably
in·ex·haust·ibil'
  i·ty
in·ex·haust'ible
in·ex·haust'ibly
in·ex'o·ra·ble
in·ex'o·ra·bly
in·ex·pe'di·en·cy
in·ex·pe'di·ent
in·ex·pen'sive
in·ex·pe'ri·ence
in·ex'pert
in·ex'pi·a·ble
in·ex·pli·ca·bil'i·ty

in·ex·plic'a·ble
in·ex·plic'a·bly
in·ex·press·ibil'i·ty
in·ex·press'ible
in·ex·press'ibly
in·ex·press'ive
in·ex·pug'na·ble
in·ex·pug'na·bly
in·ex·ten'si·ble
in·ex·ten'so
in·ex·tin'guish·able
in·ex·tin'guish·ably
in ex·tre'mis
in·ex·tri·ca·bil'i·ty
in·ex·tric'a·ble
in·ex·tric'a·bly
in·fal·li·bil'i·ty
in·fal'li·ble
in·fal'li·bly
in'fa·mous
in'fa·my
in'fan·cy
in'fant
in·fan'ti·cide
in'fan·tile
in'fan·til·ism
in·fan·til'i·ty
in'fan·try
in'fan·try·man
in·fat'u·ate
in·fat·u·a'tion
in·fect'
in·fec'tion

in·fec'tious
in·fec'tive
in·fec'tor
in·fe·lic'i·tous
in·fe·lic'i·ty
in·fer'
in·ferred'
in·fer'ring
in·fer'able
  or in·fer'ri·ble
in'fer·ence
in·fer·en'tial
in·fer·en'tial·ly
in·fe'ri·or
in·fe·ri·or'i·ty
in·fer'nal
in·fer'nal·ly
in·fer'no
in·fer'tile
in·fer·til'i·ty
in·fest'
in·fes·ta'tion
in'fi·del
in·fi·del'i·ty
in'field
in'field·er
in'fight·ing
in·fil'trate
in'fil·tra'tion
in'fil·tra·tor
in'fi·nite
in'fi·nite·ly
in·fin·i·tes'i·mal
in·fin·i·tes'i·mal·ly
in·fin'i·tive

in·fin'i·tude
in·fin'i·ty
in·firm'
in·fir'ma·ry
in·fir'mi·ty
in·flame'
in·flam'ma·ble
in·flam·ma'tion
in·flam'ma·to·ry
in·flate'
in·flat'able
in·fla'tion
in·fla'tion·ary
in·flect'
in·flec'tion
in·flex·i·bil'i·ty
in·flex'i·ble
in·flex'i·bly
in·flict'
in·flic'tion
in·flo·res'cence
in'flow
in'flu·ence
in·flu·en'tial
in·flu·en'za
in'flux
in·fold'
in·form'
in·for'mal
in·for·mal'i·ty
in·for'mal·ly
in·for'mant
in·for·ma'tion
in·for'ma·tive
in·formed'
in·form'er

in'fra
in·frac'tion
in·fran·gi·bil'i·ty
in·fran'gi·ble
in·fran'gi·bly
in·fra·red'
in·fra·son'ic
in·fre'quent
in·fringe'
in·fringe'ment
in·fu'ri·ate
in·fu·ri·a'tion
in·fuse'
in·fus'ible
in·fu'sion
in'gath·er·ing
in·ge'nious
  clever (see
   ingenuous)
in'ge·nue
  or in'gé·nue
in·ge·nu'i·ty
in·gen'u·ous
  straightforward (see
   ingenious)
in·gest'
in·gest'ible
in·ges'tion
in·glo'ri·ous
in'got
in'grain'
in'grained
in'grate
in·gra'ti·ate
in·gra'ti·at·ing
in·grat'i·tude

in·gre'di·ent
in'gress
in'group
in'grow·ing
in'grown
in·hab'it
in·hab'it·able
in·hab'i·tan·cy
in·hab'i·tant
in·hal'ant
in·ha·la'tion
in·ha·la'tor
in·hale'
in·hal'er
in·har·mon'ic
in·har·mo'ni·ous
in·har'mo·ny
in·here'
in·her'ence
in·her'ent
in·her'it
in·her'it·able
in·her'i·tance
in·her'i·tor
in·hib'it
in·hi·bi'tion
in·hib'i·tor
  or in·hib'it·er
in·hib'i·to·ry
in·hos·pi'ta·ble
in·hos·pi'ta·bly
in-house
in·hu'man
in·hu·mane'
in·hu·man'i·ty
in·hu·ma'tion

in·im'i·cal
in·im'i·cal·ly
in·im'i·ta·ble
in·im'i·ta·bly
in·iq'ui·tous
in·iq'ui·ty
  wickedness (see
   inequity)
ini'tial
ini'tialed
  or ini'tialled
ini'tial·ing
  or ini'tial·ling
ini'tial·ly
ini'ti·ate
ini·ti·a'tion
ini'tia·tive
ini'ti·a·tor
ini'tia·to·ry
in·ject'
in·jec'tion
in·jec'tor
in·ju·di'cious
in·junc'tion
in'jure
in·ju'ri·ous
in'ju·ry
in·jus'tice
ink'blot
in'kling
ink'stand
ink'well
ink'y
in·laid
in'land
in'-law

in·lay′
verb

in′lay
noun

in′let

in′mate

in me·di·as res′

in me·mo′ri·am

in′most

in′nards

in·nate′

in·nate′ly

in′ner

in′ner-di·rect′ed

in′ner·most

in′ner·sole′

in′ning

inn′keep·er

in′no·cence

in′no·cent

in·noc′u·ous

in′no·vate

in′no·va′tion

in′no·va·tor

in′no·va·tive

in·nu·en′do
pl in·nu·en′dos *or*
in·nu·en′does

in·nu′mer·a·ble

in·nu′mer·a·bly

in·oc′u·late

in·oc·u·la′tion

in·of·fen′sive

in·op′er·a·ble

in·op′er·a·tive

in·op·por·tune′

in·or′di·nate

in·or·gan′ic

in′pa·tient

in′put

in′quest

in·qui′etude

in·quire′

in·quir′er

in·quir′ing·ly

in′qui·ry

in·qui·si′tion

in·quis′i·tive

in·quis′i·tor

in re′

in rem′

in′road

in′rush

in·sa·lu′bri·ous

in·sane′

in·san′i·tary

in·san′i·ty

in·sa·tia·bil′i·ty

in·sa′tia·ble

in·sa′tia·bly

in·sa′tiate

in·scribe′

in·scrip′tion

in·scru·ta·bil′i·ty

in·scru′ta·ble

in·scru′ta·bly

in′seam

in′sect

in·sec′ti·cide

in·se·cure′

in·se·cu′ri·ty

in·sem·i·na′tion

in·sem′i·nate

in·sen′sate

in·sen·si·bil′i·ty

in·sen′si·ble

in·sen′si·bly

in·sen′si·tive

in·sen·si·tiv′i·ty

in·sen′tience

in·sen′tient

in·sep·a·ra·bil′i·ty

in·sep′a·ra·ble

in·sep′a·ra·bly

in·sert′
verb

in′sert
noun

in·ser′tion

in′set

in′set
or in′set·ted

in′set·ting

in·shore

in·side′

in·sid′er

in·sid′i·ous

in′sight

in·sig′nia
or in·sig′ne
pl in·sig′nia *or*
in·sig′nias

in·sig·nif′i·cance

in·sig·nif′i·cant

in·sin·cere′

in·sin·cere′ly

in·sin·cer′i·ty

in·sin′u·ate

in·sin·u·a'tion
in·sin'u·at·ing
in·sip'id
in·si·pid'i·ty
in·sist'
in·sis'tence
in·sis'tent
in si'tu
in·so·far'
in'sole
in'so·lence
in'so·lent
in·sol·u·bil'i·ty
in·sol'u·ble
in·sol'u·bly
in·solv'able
in·solv'ably
in·sol'ven·cy
in·sol'vent
in·som'nia
in·so·much'
in·sou'ci·ance
in·sou'ci·ant
in·spect'
in·spec'tion
in·spec'tor
in·spi·ra'tion
in·spire'
in·spir'er
in·spir'it
in·sta·bil'i·ty
in·stall'
   or in·stal'

   in·stalled'
   in·stall'ing
in·stal·la'tion

in·stall'ment
   or in·stal'ment

in'stance
in'stant
in·stan·ta'ne·ous
in·stan'ter
in'state'
in sta·tu quo'
in·stead'
in'step
in'sti·gate
in·sti·ga'tion
in'sti·ga'tor
in·still'
   also in·stil'

   in·stilled'
   in·still'ing
in'stinct
in·stinc'tive
in'sti·tute
in·sti·tu'tion
in·sti·tu'tion·al·
   ize
in·sti·tu'tion·al·ly
in·struct'
in·struc'tion
in·struc'tive
in·struc'tor
in'stru·ment
in·stru·men'tal
in·stru·men'tal·ist
in·stru·men·tal'
   i·ty
in·stru·men'tal·ly
in·stru·men·ta'
   tion

in·sub·or'di·nate
in·sub·or·di·na'
   tion
in·sub·stan'tial
in·sub·stan·ti·al'
   i·ty
in·suf'fer·able
in·suf'fer·ably
in·suf·fi'cien·cy
in·suf·fi'cient
in'su·lant
in'su·lar
in·su·lar'i·ty
in'su·late
in·su·la'tion
in'su·la·tor
in'su·lin
in·sult'
   verb

in'sult
   noun

in·su'per·a·ble
in·su'per·a·bly
in·sup·port'able
in·sup·port'ably
in·sup·press'ible
in·sup·press'ibly
in·sur·abil'i·ty
in·sur'able
in·sur'ance
in·sure'
in·sured'
in·sur'er
in·sur'gence
in·sur'gen·cy
in·sur'gent

in·sur·mount′able
in·sur·mount′ably
in·sur·rec′tion
in·sur·rec′tion·
  ary
in·sur·rec′tion·ist
in·sus·cep·ti·bil′
  i·ty
in·sus·cep′ti·ble
in·sus·cep′ti·bly
in·tact′
in·ta′glio
in′take
in·tan·gi·bil′i·ty
in·tan′gi·ble
in·tan′gi·bly
in′te·ger
in′te·gral
in′te·grate
in·te·gra′tion
in·teg′ri·ty
in·teg′u·ment
in′tel·lect
in·tel·lec′tu·al
in·tel·lec′tu·al·ize
in·tel·lec′tu·al·ly
in·tel′li·gence
in·tel′li·gent
in·tel·li·gen′tsia
in·tel·li·gi·bil′i·ty
in·tel′li·gi·ble
in·tel′li·gi·bly
in·tem′per·ance
in·tem′per·ate
in·tend′
in·ten′dant
in·tend′ed

in·tense′
in·tense′ly
in·ten·si·fi·ca′tion
in·ten′si·fy
in·ten′si·ty
in·ten′sive
in·tent′
in·ten′tion
in·ten′tion·al
in·ten′tion·al·ly
in·ter′
  in·terred′
  in·ter′ring
in·ter·act′
in·ter·ac′tion
in·ter a′lia
in·ter·breed′
in·ter′ca·late
in·ter·ca·la′tion
in·ter·cede′
in·ter·cept′
in·ter·cep′tion
in·ter·cep′tor
in·ter·ces′sion
in·ter·ces′sor
in·ter·ces′so·ry
in·ter·change′
  verb
in′ter·change
  noun
in·ter·change′able
in·ter·col·le′giate
in′ter·com
in·ter·com·mu·ni·
  ca′tion
in·ter·con·ti·nen′
  tal

in·ter·cos′tal
in′ter·course
in·ter·cul′tur·al
in·ter·de·nom·i·
  na′tion·al
in·ter·de·part·
  men′tal
in·ter·de·pen′
  dence
in·ter·de·pen′
  den·cy
in·ter·de·pen′
  dent
in·ter·dict′
in·ter·dic′tion
in·ter·dis′ci·plin·
  ary
in′ter·est
in′ter·est·ing
in′ter·face
in·ter·faith′
in·ter·fere′
in·ter·fer′ence
in·ter·fer′on
in·ter·fuse′
in′ter·im
in·te′ri·or
in·ter·ject′
in·ter·jec′tion
in·ter·jec′tion·
  al·ly
in·ter·lace′
in·ter·lard′
in′ter·lay·er
in′ter·leaf
in·ter·leave′
in·ter·line′

in·ter·lin′ear
in′ter·lin·ing
in·ter·link′
in·ter·lock′
in·ter·lo·cu′tion
in·ter·loc′u·tor
in·ter·loc′u·
   to·ry
in·ter·lop′er
in′ter·lude
in·ter·lu′nar
in·ter·mar′riage
in·ter·mar′ry
in·ter·me′di·ary
in·ter·me′di·ate
in·ter′ment
in·ter·mez′zo
   pl in·ter·mez′zi or
   in·ter·mez′zos
in·ter′mi·na·ble
in·ter′mi·na·bly
in·ter·min′gle
in·ter·mis′sion
in·ter·mit′tent
in·ter·mix′
in′tern
   confine
in′tern
   or in′terne
   doctor
in·ter′nal
in·ter·nal·iza′
   tion
in·ter·na′tion·al
in·ter·na·tion·al·
   iza′tion

in·ter·na′tion·al·
   ize
in·ter·na′tion·al·ly
in·ter·nec′ine
in·tern·ee′
in·ter′nist
in·tern′ment
in′tern·ship
in·ter·nun′cio
in·ter·of′fice
in·ter·pen′e·trate
in·ter·pen·e·tra′
   tion
in·ter·per′son·al
in·ter·per′son·al·ly
in·ter·plan′e·tary
in′ter·play
in·ter′po·late
in·ter·po·la′tion
in·ter·pose′
in·ter·po·si′tion
in·ter′pret
in·ter·pre·ta′tion
in·ter′pret·er
in·ter′pre·tive
in·ter·ra′cial
in·ter·reg′num
   pl in·ter·reg′nums *or*
   in·ter·reg′na
in·ter·re·late′
in·ter·re·la′tion
in·ter′ro·gate
in·ter·ro·ga′tion
in·ter·rog′a·tive
in·ter·rog′a·tor
in·ter·rog′a·to·ry

in·ter·rupt′
in·ter·rup′tion
in·ter·scho·las′tic
in·ter·school′
in′ter·sect
in·ter·sec′tion
in·ter·sperse′
in·ter·sper′sion
in·ter·state′
in·ter·stel′lar
in·ter·stice
in·ter·sti′tial
in·ter·tid′al
in·ter·twine′
in·ter·twist′
in·ter·ur′ban
in′ter·val
in·ter·vene′
in·ter·ven′tion
in·ter·ven′tion·
   ism
in·ter·ven′tion·ist
in′ter·view
in′ter·view·er
in·ter·weave′
in·ter·wove′
in·ter·wo′ven
in·ter·weav′ing
in·ter·wo′ven
in·tes′tate
in·tes′ti·nal
in·tes′tine
in′ti·ma·cy
in′ti·mate
in·ti·ma′tion
in·tim′i·date

in·tim·i·da′tion
in′to
in·tol′er·a·ble
in·tol′er·a·bly
in·tol′er·ance
in·tol′er·ant
in·to·na′tion
in·tone′
in to′to
in·tox′i·cant
in·tox′i·cate
in·tox·i·ca′tion
in·trac·ta·bil′i·ty
in·trac′ta·ble
in·trac′ta·bly
in·tra·mu′ral
in·tra·mus′cu·lar
in·tran′si·gence
in·tran′si·gent
in·tran′si·tive
in·tra·state′
in·tra·u′ter·ine
in·tra·ve′nous
in·trep′id
in·tre·pid′i·ty
in′tri·ca·cy
in′tri·cate
in·trigue′
in·trin′sic
in·trin′si·cal·ly
in·tro·duce′
in·tro·duc′tion
in·tro·duc′to·ry
in·tro·spec′tion
in·tro·spec′tive
in·tro·ver′sion

in′tro·vert
in·trude′
in·trud′er
in·tru′sion
in·tru′sive
in·tu·i′tion
in·tu′i·tive
in·tu·mes′cence
in·tu·mes′cent
in′un·date
in·un·da′tion
in·ure′
in vac′uo
in·vade′
in·vad′er
in·val′id
   not valid
in′va·lid
   sickly
in·val′i·date
in·val·i·da′tion
in·val′u·able
in·val′u·ably
in·var′i·able
in·var′i·ably
in·va′sion
in·vec′tive
in·veigh′
in·vei′gle
in·vent′
in·ven′tion
in·ven′tive
in·ven′tor
in′ven·to·ry
in·ver′ness′
in·verse′

in·ver′sion
in·vert′
in·ver′te·brate
in·vest′
in·ves′ti·gate
in·ves·ti·ga′tion
in·ves′ti·ga·tor
in·ves′ti·ture
in·vest′ment
in·ves′tor
in·vet′er·ate
in·vid′i·ous
in·vig′o·rate
in·vig·o·ra′tion
in·vin·ci·bil′i·ty
in·vin′ci·ble
in·vin′ci·bly
in·vi·o·la·bil′i·ty
in·vi′o·la·ble
in·vi′o·la·bly
in·vi′o·late
in·vis·i·bil′i·ty
in·vis′i·ble
in·vis′i·bly
in·vi·ta′tion
in·vite′
in·vit′ing
in·vo·ca′tion
in′voice
in·voke′
in·vol·un·tar′·
   i·ly
in·vol′un·tary
in′vo·lute
in·vo·lu′tion
in·volve′

in·vul·ner·a·bil′
  i·ty
in·vul′ner·a·ble
in·vul′ner·a·bly
in′ward
in′ward·ly
in′wards
in·wrought′
i′o·dide
i′o·dine
i′o·dize
i′on
ion′ic
ion·i·za′tion
i′on·ize
ion′o·sphere
io′ta
I′o·wa
ip·so fac′to
Iran′
Ira′ni·an
Iraq′
Iraq′i
iras·ci·bil′i·ty
iras′ci·ble
iras′ci·bly
irate′
ire′ful
I′re·land
ir·i·des′cence
ir·i·des′cent
i′ris
   pl i′ris·es *or* i′ri·des
I′rish
I′rish·man
irk′some

iron·bound′
iron·clad′
iron′ic
iron′i·cal·ly
i′ron·ware
i′ron·work
i′ro·ny
ir·ra′di·ate
ir·ra·di·a′tion
ir·ra′tio·nal
ir·ra·tio·nal′i·ty
ir·ra′tio·nal·ly
ir·re·claim′able
ir·rec·on·cil·abil′
  i·ty
ir·rec·on·cil′able
ir·rec·on·cil′ably
ir·re·cov′er·able
ir·re·cov′er·ably
ir·re·deem′able
ir·re·deem′ably
ir·re·den′tism
ir·re·den′tist
ir·re·duc′ible
ir·re·fut′able
ir·re·fut′ably
ir·reg′u·lar
ir·reg·u·lar′i·ty
ir·rel′e·vance
ir·rel′e·van·cy
ir·rel′e·vant
ir·re·li′gious
ir·re·me′di·a·ble
ir·re·me′di·a·bly
ir·re·mov′able
ir·re·mov′ably

ir·rep′a·ra·ble
ir·rep′a·ra·bly
ir·re·place′able
ir·re·press′ible
ir·re·press′ibly
ir·re·proach′able
ir·re·proach′ably
ir·re·sist′ible
ir·re·sist′ibly
ir·res′o·lute
ir·res·o·lu′tion
ir·re·solv′able
ir·re·spec′tive
ir·re·spon·si·bil′
  i·ty
ir·re·spon′si·ble
ir·re·spon′si·bly
ir·re·triev′able
ir·re·triev′ably
ir·rev′er·ence
ir·rev′er·ent
ir·re·vers′ible
ir·re·vers′ibly
ir·rev′o·ca·ble
ir·rev′o·ca·bly
ir′ri·gate
ir·ri·ga′tion
ir·ri·ta·bil′i·ty
ir′ri·ta·ble
ir′ri·ta·bly
ir′ri·tant
ir′ri·tate
ir·ri·ta′tion
ir·rupt′
ir·rup′tion
i′sin·glass

Is'lam
Is·lam'ic
is'land
isle
  island (*see* aisle)
is'let
  small island (*see* eyelet)
i'so·bar
i'so·late
iso·la'tion
iso·la'tion·ism
iso·la'tion·ist
i'so·mer
iso·met'ric
iso·met'ri·cal·ly
iso·met'rics
isos'ce·les
i'so·therm
iso·ther'mal
i'so·tope
iso·top'ic
Is'ra·el
Is·rae'li
is'su·ance
is'sue
isth'mi·an
isth'mus
It'a·ly
Ital'ian
ital'ic
ital'i·cize
itch
itch'i·ness
itch'y
item·iza'tion

i'tem·ize
it'er·ate
it·er·a'tion
itin'er·ant
itin'er·ary
it·self'
i'vied
i'vo·ry
i'vy

J

jab
  jabbed
  jab'bing
jab'ber
jab'ber·wocky
ja·bot'
ja'cinth
jack'al
jack'a·napes
jack'ass
jack'boot
jack'daw
jack'et
jack'ham·mer
jack'-in-the-box
  pl jack'-in-the-box·es
  or jacks'-in-the-box
jack-in-the-pul'pit
  pl jack-in-the-pul'pits *or* jacks-in-the-pul'pit
jack'knife
jack'-of-all'-trades
  pl jacks-of-all'-trades

jack'-o'-lan·tern
jack'pot
jack'rab·bit
jack'screw
Jack'son
Jack'son·ville
jack'straw
jac'o·net
jac'quard
jac·que·rie'
jad'ed
jad'ite
jag
  jagged
  jag'ging
jag'ged
jag'uar
jai'alai
jail'bird
jail'break
jail'er
  or jail'or
ja·lop'y
jal'ou·sie
  window (*see* jealousy)

jam
  jammed
  jam'ming
Ja·mai'ca
Ja·mai'can
jam·bo·ree'
jan'gle
jan'i·tor
Jan'u·ary
Ja·pan'

Jap·a·nese′
jar
  jarred
  jar′ring
jar·di·niere′
jar′gon
jas′mine
jas′per
ja′to
jaun′dice
jaun′ti·ly
jaun′ti·ness
jaun′ty
jav′e·lin
jaw′bone
jaw′break·er
Jay·cee
jay·vee
jay′walk
jay′walk·er
jazz′i·ly
jazz′i·ness
jazz′y
jeal′ous
jeal′ou·sy
  suspicion (see
   jalousie)

jeans
Jef′fer·son Cit′y
je′hu
je·june′
Jell′-O
jel′ly
jel′ly·fish
jen′ny
jeop′ar·dize

jeop′ar·dy
jer·e·mi′ad
jerk′i·ly
jer′kin
jerk′i·ness
jerk′wa·ter
jerk′y
  in fits and starts
jer′ky
  meat
jer·o·bo′am
jer′ry-built
jer′sey
jes′sa·mine
jest′er
Je′su·it
je·su·it′i·cal
je·su·it′i·cal·ly
jet
  jet′ted
  jet′ting
je·te′
jet-pro·pelled′
jet′sam
jet′ti·son
jet′ty
jeu d'es·prit
  pl jeux d'es·prit
jew′el
jew′el·er
  or jew′el·ler

jew′el·ry
Jew′ish
Jew′ry
jibe
  agree (see gibe)

jif′fy
jig
  jigged
  jig′ging
jig′ger
jig′gle
jig′saw
jim′-dan′dy
jim′my
jim′son·weed
jin′gle
jin′go·ism
jin·go·is′tic
jin·go·is′ti·cal·ly
jin·rik′i·sha
jinx
jit′ney
jit′ter·bug
jit′ters
jit′tery
jiu·jit′su
  or jiu·jut′su
job
  jobbed
  job′bing
job′ber
job′hold·er
job′less·ness
jock′ey
jock′strap
jo·cose′
jo·cos′i·ty
joc′u·lar
joc·u·lar′i·ty
jo′cund
jo·cun′di·ty

jodh′pur
jog
  jogged
  jog′ging
jog′ger
jog′gle
john′ny
joie de vi′vre
join′er
joint′ly
jok′er
jol′li·ty
jol′ly
jon′quil
Jor′dan
Jor·da′ni·an
jos′tle
jot
  jot′ted
  jot′ting
jour′nal
jour·nal·ese′
jour′nal·ism
jour′nal·ist
jour·nal·is′tic
jour′ney
jour′ney·man
jo′vi·al
jo·vi·al′i·ty
jo′vi·al·ly
jowl
joy′ful
joy′ful·ly
joy′ous
joy′ride
joy′rid·er

ju′bi·lant
ju·bi·la′tion
ju·bi·lee′
Ju·da′ic
Ju′da·ism
judg′ment
  or judge′ment

ju′di·ca·ture
ju·di′cial
ju·di′cial·ly
ju·di′ci·ary
ju·di′cious
ju′do
jug′ger·naut
jug′gle
jug′gler
jug′u·lar
juic′er
juic′i·ly
juic′i·ness
juic′y
ju·jit′su
  or ju·jut′su

ju′jube
juke′box
ju′lep
Ju·ly′
jum′ble
jum′bo
jump′er
jump′i·ness
jump·ing-off′
jump′y
jun′co
  pl jun′cos *or*
  jun′coes

junc′tion
junc′ture
June
Ju′neau
jun′gle
ju′nior
ju′ni·per
Jun′ker
jun′ket
jun′ta
Ju′pi·ter
ju·rid′i·cal
ju·rid′i·cal·ly
ju·ris·dic′tion
ju·ris·dic′tion·al
ju·ris·pru′dence
ju·ris·pru·den′
  tial·ly
ju′rist
ju·ris′tic
ju′ror
ju′ry
ju′ry·man
jus′tice
jus·ti′cia·ble
jus′ti·fi·able
jus′ti·fi·ably
jus·ti·fi·ca′tion
jus′ti·fy
just′ly
jut
  jut′ted
  jut′ting
jute
ju′ve·nile
ju·ve·nil′ia

jux'ta·pose
jux·ta·po·si'tion

K

ka'bob
Ka·bu'ki
kaf'fee·klatsch
kai'ser
ka·lei'do·scope
ka·lei·do·scop'ic
ka·ma·ai'na
ka·mi·ka'ze
kan·ga·roo'
Kan'sas
ka'o·lin
ka'pok
ka·put'
kar'a·kul
kar'at
ka·ra'te
kar'ma
ka'ty·did
kat'zen·jam·mer
kay'ak
kay'o
  kay'oed
  kay'o·ing
ka·zoo'
ke·bab'
  or ke·bob'
kedge
keel'boat
keel'haul
keel'son
keen'ly

keep
  kept
  keep'ing
keep'er
keep'sake
keg'ler
Kel'vin
ken'nel
ke'no
Ken·tuck'y
Ken'ya
Ken'yan
ke'pi
ker'a·tin
ker'chief
ker'nel
  seed, core (see
    colonel)
ker'o·sene
  or ker'o·sine
ker'sey
ker'sey·mere
ke'tene
ke'tone
ket'tle
ket'tle·drum
key
  lock (see quay)
key'board
key'hole
key'note
key'not·er
key'stone
key'way
kha'ki
khe·dive'

kib·butz'
  pl kib·but·zim'
kib'itz·er
ki'bosh
kick'back
kick'off
kid
  kid'ded
  kid'ding
kid'nap
  kid'napped
  or kid'naped
  kid'nap·ping
  or kid'nap·ing
kid'nap·per
  or kid'nap·er
kid'ney
kid'skin
kill'er
kill'ing
kill'joy
kiln
ki'lo
kil'o·cy·cle
kil'o·gram
kil'o·li·ter
ki·lo'me·ter
kil'o·volt
kil'o·watt
kil'o·watt-hour
kil'ter
ki·mo'no
kin'der·gar·ten
kind'heart'ed
kin'dle
kind'li·ness

kin′dling
kind′ly
kin′dred
ki·ne·mat′ic
ki·ne·mat′ics
kin′e·scope
ki·ne·si·ol′o·gy
ki·net′ic
ki·net′ics
kin′folk
or kins′folk

king′bolt
king′dom
king′fish
king′fish·er
king′ly
king′mak·er
king′pin
king′-size
or king′-sized

kink′y
kin′ship
kins′man
kins′wom·an
ki′osk
kip
pl kip or kips

kip′per
kir′tle
kis′met
kitch′en
kitch·en·ette′
kitch′en·ware
kitsch
kit′ten
kit′ten·ish

kit′ty
kit·ty-cor′ner
or kit·ty-cor′nered

klep·to·ma′nia
klep·to·ma′ni·ac
knap′sack
knave
rogue (see nave)

knav′ery
knav′ish
knead
massage (see need)

knee′cap
knee-deep
knee-high
knee′hole
kneel
knelt
or kneeled

kneel′ing
knick′ers
knick′knack
knife
pl knives

knife′-edge
knight
rank (see night)

knight′-er′rant
knight′hood
knit
knit
or knit′ted

knit′ting
knit′ter
knit′wear
knob′by

knock′about
knock′down
knock′er
knock′-kneed
knock′out
knoll
knot
knot′ted
knot′ting
knot′hole
knot′ty
know
knew
known
know′ing
know′able
know′-how
know′ing
know′-it-all
knowl′edge
knowl′edge·able
knowl′edge·ably
Knox′ville
knuck′le
knuck′le·bone
knurl
kohl·ra′bi
ko′peck
Ko·ran′
Ko·re′a
Ko·re′an
ko·ru′na
pl ko′ru·ny or
ko′ru·nas

ko′sher
kow·tow′

kro′na
  pl kro′nur
  Icelandic currency

kro′na
  pl kro′nor
  Swedish currency

kro′ne
  pl kro′ner

kryp′ton

ku′dos
  pl ku′dos

ku·lak′

kum′quat

ku·rus′
  pl ku·rus′

Ku·wait′

Ku·wai′ti

kwa′cha
  pl kwa′cha

kwa·shi·or′kor

ky·at′

L

la′bel
  la′beled
    or la′belled
  la′bel·ing
    or la′bel·ling

la′bi·al

la′bile

la′bor

lab′o·ra·to·ry

la′bor·er

la′bored

la·bo′ri·ous

la′bor·sav·ing

la·bur′num

lab′y·rinth

lab·y·rin′thine

lac′er·ate

lac·er·a′tion

la′ches
  pl la′ches

lach′ry·mose

lac′ing

lack·a·dai′si·cal

lack·a·dai′si·cal·ly

lack′ey

lack′lus·ter

la·con′ic

la·con′i·cal·ly

lac′quer

lac′ri·mal
  also lach′ry·mal

la·crosse′

lac′tate

lac·ta′tion

lac′te·al

lac′tic

lac′tose

la·cu′na
  pl la·cu′nae *or*
    la·cu′nas

la·cus′trine

lac′y

lad′der

lad′der-back

lad′en

lad′ing

la′dle

la′dy

la′dy·bug

la′dy·fin·ger

la·dy-in-wait′ing
  pl la·dies-in-wait′
    ·ing

la′dy·like

la′dy·love

la′dy·ship

lag

  lagged

  lag′ging

la′ger

lag′gard

la′gniappe

la·goon′

lair
  den (see layer)

lais·sez-faire′

la′ity

lak′er

la′ma
  monk (see llama)

lam·baste′
  or lam·bast′

lam′bent

lam′bre·quin

lamb′skin

lame
  disabled (see lamé)

la·mé′
  brocade (see lame)

la·ment′

lam′en·ta·ble

lam′en·ta·bly

lam·en·ta′tion

lam'i·na
   pl lam'i·nae
lam'i·nat·ed
lam·i·na'tion
lamp'black
lamp'light·er
lam·poon'
lam'prey
la·nai'
lanc'er
lan'cet
lan'dau
land'ed
land'fall
land'form
land'hold·er
land'ing
land'la·dy
land'locked
land'lord
land'lub·ber
land'mark
land'mass
land'own·er
land'scape
land'slide
lands'man
land'ward
lan'guage
lan'guid
lan'guish
lan'guor
lan'guor·ous
lank'i·ness
lank'y
lan'o·lin

Lan'sing
lan'tern
lan'yard
Laos
Lao'tian
lap
   lapped
   lap'ping
lap'board
lap'dog
la·pel'
lap'i·dary
lap'in
la·pis la'zu·li
lap'pet
lapse
lar'ce·nous
lar'ce·ny
lar'der
large'ly
large-scale
lar·gess'
   or lar·gesse'
lar'go
lar'i·at
lark'spur
lar'va
   pl lar'vae *also*
   lar'vas
lar'val
la·ryn'ge·al
lar·yn·gi'tis
lar'ynx
   pl la·ryn·ges *or*
   lar'ynx·es
las'car

las·civ'i·ous
la'ser
lash'ing
las'si·tude
las'so
   pl lassos *or* lassoes
Las'tex
last'ing
Las Ve'gas
lat·a·ki'a
latch
latch'key
latch'string
la·teen'
late'com·er
late'ly
la'ten·cy
la'tent
lat'er·al
lat'er·al·ly
la'tex
lath
   strip of wood (see
   lathe)
lathe
   machine (see lath)
lath'er
Lat'in
lat'i·tude
lat·i·tu·di·nar'i·an
la·trine'
lat'ter
lat'ter-day
lat'tice
lat'tice·work
Lat'via

Lat'vi·an
laud'able
laud'ably
lau'da·num
lau'da·to·ry
laugh'able
laugh'ing·stock
laugh'ter
launch'er
laun'der
laun'der·er
laun'dress
Laun'dro·mat
laun'dry
laun'dry·man
lau're·ate
lau'rel
la'va
la·va'bo
la·va·liere'
 or la·val·liere'
lav'a·to·ry
lav'en·der
lav'ish
law'-abid·ing
law'break·er
law'ful
law'ful·ly
law'giv·er
law'less
law'mak·er
law'suit
law'yer
lax'a·tive
lax'i·ty
lax'ness

lay
 laid
 lay'ing
lay'er
 level (see lair)
lay'er·ing
lay·ette'
lay'man
lay'off
lay'out
la'zi·ly
la'zi·ness
la'zy
la'zy·bones
leach
 filter (see leech)
lead
 led
 lead'ing
lead'en
lead'er
lead'er·ship
lead'-in
lead'ing
lead'off
lead'-up
leaf
 pl leaves
leaf'age
leaf'let
leaf'y
league
lea'guer
leak
 escape (see leek)
leak'age

leak'y
lean
 incline (see lien)
lean'ness
lean'-to
leap
 leaped
 leapt
 leap'ing
leap'frog
learn'ed
learn'er
learn'ing
lease'hold
leas'ing
least
least'wise
leath'er
leath'er·y
leave
 left
 leav'ing
leav'en
leav'en·ing
leave'-tak·ing
leav'ings
Leb'a·non
Leb'a·nese
lech'er
lech'er·ous
lech'ery
lech·er
lec'tern
lec'tor
lec'ture
lec'tur·er

le′der·ho·sen
ledge
led′ger
leech
  worm (*see* leach)
leek
  plant (*see* leak)
leer′y
lee′ward
lee′way
left′-hand′ed
left′ist
left′over
leg
  legged
  leg′ging
leg′a·cy
le′gal
le′gal·ism
le·gal·is′tic
le·gal′i·ty
le·gal·iza′tion
le′gal·ize
le′gal·ly
leg′ate
leg·a·tee′
le·ga′tion
le·ga′to
le·ga′tor
leg′end
leg′end·ary
leg·er·de·main′
leg′ging
  or leg′gin
leg′gy
leg′horn

leg·i·bil′i·ty
leg′i·ble
leg′i·bly
le′gion
le′gion·ary
le·gion·naire′
leg′is·late
leg·is·la′tion
leg′is·la·tive
leg′is·la·tor
leg′is·la·ture
le′gist
le·git′i·ma·cy
le·git′i·mate
le·git′i·mate·ly
le·git′i·mize
leg′man
leg′ume
le·gu′mi·nous
lei
lei′sure
lei′sure·li·ness
lei′sure·ly
leit′mo·tiv
  or leit′mo·tif
lek
lem′ming
lem′on
lem·on·ade′
lem·pi′ra
le′mur
lend
  lent
  lend′ing
lend′er
lend-lease′

length
length′en
length′wise
length′y
le′ni·en·cy
le′ni·ent
len′i·tive
len′i·ty
lens
Lent′en
len′til
le·one′
le′o·nine
leop′ard
le′o·tard
lep′er
lep′re·chaun
lep′ro·sy
lep′rous
lep·ton′
  pl lep·ta′
les′bi·an
le′sion
Le·so′tho
les·see′
less′en
  make less (*see* lesson)
less′er
  smaller (*see* lessor)
les′son
  instruction (*see* lessen)
les′sor
  one who leases out (*see* lesser)
let

lie

let
let'ting
let'down
le'thal
le'thal·ly
le·thar'gic
leth'ar·gy
let'ter
let'ter·er
let'ter·head
let·ter·per'fect
let'ter·press
let'tuce
let'up
leu
   pl lei

leu·ke'mia
leu'ko·cyte
lev
   pl le'va

lev'ee
   embankment (see levy)

lev'el
  lev'eled
    or lev'elled

  lev'el·ing
    or lev'el·ling

lev'el·er
lev·el·head'ed
lev'el·ly
lev'er
lev'er·age
le·vi'a·than
lev'i·tate
lev·i·ta'tion

lev'i·ty
lev'y
   impose (see levee)

lewd
lewd'ness
lex·i·cog'ra·pher
lex·i·co·graph'ic
lex·i·cog'ra·phy
lex'i·con
Lex'ing·ton
li·a·bil'i·ty
li'a·ble
   responsible (see libel)

li'ai·son
li'ar
   one who lies (see lyre)

li·ba'tion
li'bel
   malign (see liable)

  li'beled
    or li'belled

  li'bel·ing
    or li'bel·ling

  li'bel·er
    or li'bel·ler

  li'bel·ous
    or li'bel·lous

lib'er·al
lib'er·al·ism
lib·er·al'i·ty
lib·er·al·iza'tion
lib'er·al·ize
lib'er·al·ly
lib'er·ate

lib·er·a'tion
lib'er·a·tor
Li·be'ria
Li·be'ri·an
lib·er·tar'i·an
lib'er·tine
lib'er·ty
li·bid'i·nal
li·bid'i·nous
li·bi'do
li·brar'i·an
li'brary
li·bret'tist
li·bret'to
   pl li·bret'tos *or*
   li·bret'ti

Lib'ya
Lib'y·an
li'cense
   or li'cence

li·cens·ee'
li·cen'ti·ate
li·cen'tious
li'chen
lic'it
lick·e·ty-split'
lick'spit·tle
lic'o·rice
li'do
lie
   untruth (see lye)

lie
   position

  lay
  lain
  ly'ing

lie
tell an untruth
  lied
  ly′ing
Liech·ten·stein
Liech·ten·steiner
lied
  pl lie′der
  song
lien
  claim (see lean)
lieu
lieu·ten′an·cy
lieu·ten′ant
life
  pl lives
life·blood
life′boat
life′guard
life′less
life′like
life′line
life′long
life′sav·er
life′sav·ing
life-size
  or life-sized
life′time
life′work
lift′off
lig′a·ment
lig′a·ture
light
  light′ed
  or lit
  light′ing

light′en
ligh′ter
  boat
light′er
  flame
light′face
light′-fin′gered
light′-foot′ed
light′-hand′ed
light′-head′ed
light′heart·ed
light′house
light′ing
light′ly
light′ning
light·proof
light′ship
lights-out
light′weight
light′-year
lig′ne·ous
lig′nite
lik′able
  or like′able
like′li·hood
like′ly
like′-mind′ed
lik′en
like′ness
like′wise
lik′ing
li·ku′ta
  pl ma·ku′ta
li′lac
lil·li·pu′tian
lil′y

lily-white′
limb
  appendage (see limn)
lim′ber
lim′bo
lime·ade′
lime′light
lim′er·ick
lime′stone
lim′it
lim·i·ta′tion
lim′it·ed
limn
  draw (see limb)
lim′ou·sine
lim′pet
lim′pid
limp′ly
lin′age
  lines (see lineage)
linch′pin
Lin′coln
lin′den
lin′eage
  ancestry (see linage)
lin′eal
lin′ea·ment
  outline (see liniment)
lin′ear
line′man
lin′en
lin′er
lines′man

line′up
lin′ger
lin·ger·ie′
lin′go
  pl lin′goes

lin·gua fran′ca
  pl lin·gua fran′cas
  or lin·guae
  fran′cae

lin′gual
lin′guist
lin·guis′tic
lin·guis′tics
lin′i·ment
  balm (see
  lineament)

lin′ing
link′age
link′up
li·no′le·um
Li′no·type
lin′seed
lin·sey-wool′sey
lin′tel
li′on
li′on·ess
li·on·heart′ed
li·on·iza′tion
li′on·ize
lip′ide
  or lip′id
lip′read·ing
lip′stick
liq·ue·fac′tion
liq·ue·fi·a·ble
liq·ue·fi·er

liq′ue·fy
li·ques′cence
li·ques′cent
li·queur′
liq′uid
liq′ui·date
liq·ui·da′tion
liq·ui·da·tor
li·quid′i·ty
li′quor
li′ra
  pl li′re *also* li′ras
lisle
lis′some
  also lis′som
lis′ten
lis′ten·er
list′ing
list′less
lit′a·ny
li′ter
  or li′tre
lit′er·a·cy
lit′er·al
  verbatim (see
  littoral)
lit′er·al·ly
lit′er·ary
lit′er·ate
li·te·ra′ti
lit·ter·a·teur′
lit′er·a·ture
lithe
lithe′some
lith′o·graph
li·thog′ra·pher

li·thog′ra·phy
Lith·u·a′nia
Lith·u·a′ni·an
lit′i·ga·ble
lit′i·gant
lit′i·gate
lit·i·ga′tion
li·ti′gious
lit′mus
lit′ter
lit′ter·bug
lit′tle
Lit′tle Rock
lit′to·ral
  shore (see literal)
li·tur′gi·cal
li·tur′gi·cal·ly
lit′ur·gist
lit′ur·gy
liv′able
  also live′able
live′li·hood
live′li·ness
live′long
live′ly
liv′en
liv′er
liv′er·ied
liv′er·wort
liv′er·wurst
liv′ery
liv′ery·man
live′stock
liv′id
liv′ing
Li·vo′nia

liz'ard

lla'ma
animal (see lama)

lla'no

load
pack (see lode)

load'ed

load'stone

loaf
pl loaves

loaf'er

loam'y

loan
lend (see lone)

loan'word

loath
reluctant (see loathe)

loathe
detest (see loath)

loath'ing

loath'some

lob
  lobbed
  lob'bing

lob'by

lob'by·ist

lo'bar

lob'ster

lo'cal

lo·cale'

lo·cal'i·ty

lo·cal·i·za'tion

lo'cal·ize

lo'cal·ly

lo'cate

lo·ca'tion

lock'er

lock'et

lock'jaw

lock'out

lock'smith

lock'step

lock'up

lo·co·mo'tion

lo·co·mo'tive

lo·co·mo'tor

lo'cus
  pl lo'ci

lo'cust

lo·cu'tion

lode
ore deposit (see load)

lode'star

lode'stone

lodge
contain (see loge)

lodg'er

lodg'ing

lodg'ment
  or lodge'ment

loess

loft'i·ly

loft'i·ness

loft'y

log
  logged
  log'ging

log'a·rithm

loge
theater section (see lodge)

log'ger

log'ger·head

log'gia

log'ic

log'i·cal

log'i·cal·ly

lo·gi'cian

lo·gis'tics

log'jam

log'o·gram

log'o·graph

log'o·type

log'roll·ing

lo'gy

loin'cloth

loi'ter

loi'ter·er

lol'li·pop
  or lol'ly·pop

Lon'don

lone
solitary (see loan)

lone'li·ness

lone'ly

lone'some

Long Beach

long'bow

long'-dis'tance

lon·gev'i·ty

long'hair

long'-haired

long'hand

long'ing

lon'gi·tude

lon·gi·tu'di·nal

lon·gi·tu'di·nal·ly

long-lived
long′-play′ing
long-range
long′shore′man
long′-suf′fer·ing
long-term
long′-wind′ed
look·er-on′
look′out
loo′ny
  or loo′ney
loop′hole
loose′-joint′ed
loose′ly
loos′en
loose′ness
loot′er
lop
  lopped
  lop′ping
lop-eared
lop′sid·ed
lo·qua′cious
lo·quac′i·ty
lord′ly
lor·do′sis
lord′ship
lor·gnette′
lor′ry
Los An′ge·les
lose
  lost
  los′ing
los′er
lo′tion
lot′tery

lo′tus
  or lot′os
loud·mouthed
loud′speak′er
Lou·i·si·an′a
Lou′is·ville
louse
  pl lice
lous′y
lout′ish
lou′ver
  or lou′vre
lov′able
love′li·ness
love′ly
lov·er
love′-sick
lov′ing
low·born
low′boy
low·bred
low′brow
low′down
low′er
low·er·case′
low′er·most
low-key
low′land
low′-lev′el
low′li·ness
low′ly
low′-pres′sure
low′rise
low′-spir′it·ed
low′-ten′sion
lox
  pl lox *or* lox′es

loy′al
loy′al·ist
loy′al·ly
loy′al·ty
loz′enge
lu′au
lub′ber
Lub′bock
lu′bri·cant
lu′bri·cate
lu·bri·ca′tion
lu′bri·ca·tor
lu·bri′cious
lu′cent
lu′cid
lu·cid′i·ty
Lu′cite
luck′i·ly
luck′y
lu′cra·tive
lu′cre
lu·cu·bra′tion
lu′di·crous
lug
  lugged
  lug′ging
lug′gage
lug′ger
lu·gu′bri·ous
lug′worm
luke·warm
lul′la·by
lum·ba′go
lum′ber
lum′ber·jack
lum′ber·yard

lu'men
  pl lu'mi·na *or*
    lu'mens
lu'mi·nary
lu·mi·nos'i·ty
lu'mi·nous
lum'mox
lump'i·ly
lump'i·ness
lump'ish
lump'y
lu'na·cy
lu'nar
lu'na·tic
lun'cheon
lun·cheon·ette'
lunch'room
lung'fish
lung'wort
lunk'head
lu'pine
lu'rid
lus'cious
lush'ness
lus'ter
  or lus'tre
lus'ter·ware
lust'i·ly
lust'i·ness
lus'trous
lust'y
Lu'ther·an
Lu'ther·an·ism
Lux'em·bourg
  or Lux'em·berg
Lux'em·bourg·er
  or Lux'em·berg·er

lux·u'ri·ance
lux·u'ri·ant
lux·u'ri·ate
lux·u'ri·ous
lux'u·ry
ly·ce'um
lye
  corrosive (*see* lie)

ly'ing
ly·ing-in'
  pl ly·ings-in' *or* ly·ing-
    ins'

lymph
lym·phat'ic
lym'pho·cyte
lynch
lynx
  pl lynx *or* lynx'es
lyre
  harp (*see* liar)

lyr'ic
lyr'i·cal
lyr'i·cal·ly
lyr'i·cism
lyr'i·cist

M

ma·ca'bre
mac·ad'am
mac·ad'am·ize
ma·caque'
mac·a·ro'ni
  pl mac·a·ro'nis *or*
    mac·a·ro'nies

mac·a·roon'

ma·caw'
Mc·Coy'
mac'er·ate
mac·er·a'tion
ma·chet'e
mach'i·nate
mach·i·na'tion
ma·chine'
ma·chine'like
ma·chine'ry
ma·chin'ist
mack'er·el
mack'i·naw
mack'in·tosh
Ma'con
mac·ra·me'
mac'ro
mac'ro·cosm
ma'cron
mac·ro·scop'ic
mac'ule
Mad·a·gas'can
Mad·a·gas'car
mad'am
  pl mes·dames'
  form of address (*see*
    madame)

ma·dame'
  pl mes·dames'
  title (*see* madam)

mad'cap
mad'den
mad'der
Ma·dei'ra
ma·de·moi·selle'
  pl ma·de·moi·selles'
  or mes·de·moi·
    selles'

made-up
mad'house
Mad'i·son
mad'ly
mad'man
mad'ness
ma·dras'
mad'ri·gal
mad'wom·an
mael'strom
mae'stro
  pl mae'stros *or*
    mae'stri
Ma'fia
mag'a·zine
ma·gen'ta
mag'got
mag'goty
ma'gi
mag'ic
mag'i·cal
mag'i·cal·ly
ma·gi'cian
mag·is·te'ri·al
mag'is·tra·cy
mag'is·tral
mag'is·trate
mag'ma
mag·na·nim'i·ty
mag·nan'i·mous
mag'nate
  important person
   (*see* magnet)
mag·ne'sia
mag·ne'sium
mag'net
  attracter (*see*
   magnate)

mag·net'ic
mag'ne·tism
mag·ne·ti·za'tion
mag'ne·tize
mag·ne'to
mag·ne·tom'e·ter
mag·net'o·sphere
mag·ni·fi·ca'tion
mag·nif'i·cence
mag·nif'i·cent
mag·ni'fi·er
mag'ni·fy
mag·nil'o·quence
mag·nil'o·quent
mag'ni·tude
mag·no'lia
mag'num
mag'pie
ma·ha·ra'ja
  or ma·ha·ra'jah
ma·ha·ra'ni
  or ma·ha·ra'nee
ma·hat'ma
ma·hog'a·ny
maid'en
maid'en·hair
maid'en·hood
maid'en·ly
maid-in-wait'ing
  pl maids-in-wait'ing
maid'ser·vant
mail'bag
mail'box
mail'er
mail'ing
mail'man

maim
Maine
main'land
main'ly
main'mast
main'sail
main'sheet
main'spring
main'stay
main'stream
main·tain'
main·tain'a·ble
main'te·nance
mai·son·ette'
maî·tre d'hô·tel'
  pl maî·tres d'hô·tel'
maize
  grain (*see* maze)
ma·jes'tic
ma·jes'ti·cal·ly
maj'es·ty
ma·jol'i·ca
ma'jor
ma·jor·do'mo
ma'jor·ing
ma·jor'i·ty
maj'us·cule
mak'able
make
  made
  mak'ing
make'-be·lieve
make'-do
mak'er
make'shift
make'up

mal·ad·ap·ta′tion
mal·adapt′ed
mal·ad·just′ed
mal·ad·min′is·ter
mal·ad·min·is-
    tra′tion
mal·adroit′
mal′a·dy
Mal·a·gas′y
mal·aise′
mal′a·prop·ism
mal·ap·ro·pos′
ma·lar′ia
ma·lar′i·al
Ma·la′wi
Ma·la′wi·an
Ma·lay′sia
Ma·lay′sian
mal·con·tent′
mal de mer′
Mal′dive
Mal·div′i·an
mal·e·dic′tion
mal·e·fac′tion
mal·e·fac′tor
ma·lef′ic
ma·lef′i·cence
ma·lef′i·cent
male′ness
ma·lev′o·lence
ma·lev′o·lent
mal·fea′sance
mal·for·ma′tion
mal·form′ed
mal·func′tion
mal′ice

ma·li′cious
ma·lign′
ma·lig′nan·cy
ma·lig′nant
ma·lig′ni·ty
ma·lin′ger
ma·lin′ger·er
mall
    promenade (see
    maul)
Ma′li
Ma′li·an
mal′lard
mal·le·a·bil′i·ty
mal′le·a·ble
mal′let
mal′low
malm′sey
mal·nour′ished
mal·nu·tri′tion
mal·oc·clu′sion
mal·o′dor·ous
mal·prac′tice
Mal′ta
Mal′tese
malt′ose
mal·treat′
mam′bo
mam′ma
    or ma′ma
mam′mal
mam·ma′li·an
mam′ma·ry
mam′mon
mam′moth
man
    pl men

man
    manned
    man′ning
man-about-town′
    pl men-about-town′
man′a·cle
man′age
man·age·a·bil′i·ty
man′age·able
man′age·ably
man′age·ment
man′ag·er
man·a·ge′ri·al
ma·ña′na
man-at-arms′
    pl men-at-arms′
man·da′mus
man′da·rin
man′date
man′da·to·ry
man′di·ble
man·do·lin′
man′drake
man′drel
    metal bar (see
    mandrill)
man′drill
    baboon (see
    mandrel)
ma·nege′
    horsemanship (see
    ménage)
ma·neu′ver
ma·neu·ver·abil′-
    i·ty
ma·neu′ver·able

man'ful
man'ful·ly
man'ga·nese
mange
man'gel-wur·zel
man'ger
man'gle
man'gler
man'go
 pl man'goes *or*
 man'gos

man'grove
man'gy
man'han·dle
man·hat'tan
man'hole
man'hood
man-hour
man'hunt
ma'nia
ma'ni·ac
ma·ni'a·cal
ma·ni'a·cal·ly
man'ic
man·ic-de·pres'
 sive
man'i·cure
man'i·cur·ist
man'i·fest
man·i·fes·ta'tion
man·i·fes'to
 pl man·i·fes'tos *or*
 man·i·fes'toes

man'i·fold
man'i·kin
 or man'ni·kin

Ma·nil'a
ma·nip'u·late
ma·nip·u·la'tion
ma·nip'u·la·tive
ma·nip'u·la·tor
Man·i·to'ba
man·kind
man'like
man'li·ness
man'ly
man'-made
man'na
manned
man'ne·quin
man'ner
 mode (see manor)

man'nered
man'ner·ism
man'ner·ly
man'nish
ma·noeu'vre
man-of-war'
 pl men-of-war'

man'or
 estate (see manner)

ma·no'ri·al
man'pow·er
man·que'
man'sard
man'ser·vant
 pl men'ser·vants

man'sion
man'-size
 or man'-sized

man'slaugh·ter
man'ta

man·teau'
man'tel
 fireplace shelf (see
 mantle)

man'telet
man'tel·piece
man·til'la
man'tis
 man'tis·es *or*
 man'tes

man'tle
 garment (see
 mantel)

man'u·al
man'u·al·ly
man·u·fac'to·ry
man·u·fac'ture
man·u·fac'tur·er
man·u·mis'sion
man·u·mit'
man·u·mit'ted
man·u·mit'ting
ma·nure'
man'u·script
man'y
 more
 most
many·fold'
many-sid'ed
map
 mapped
 map'ping
ma'ple
mar
 marred
 mar'ring

mar'a·bou
  or mar'a·bout

ma·ra'ca

mar·a·schi'no

ma·ras'mus

mar'a·thon

ma·raud'

ma·raud'er

mar'ble

mar'ble·ize

mar'bling

mar·cel'
  mar·celled'
  mar·cel'ling

March

march'er

mar'chio·ness

march'-past

Mar·di Gras'

mar'ga·rine

mar'gay

mar'gin

mar'gin·al

mar'gin·al·ly

mar·gi·na'lia

mar'grave

ma·ri·a'chi

mar'i·gold

mar·i·jua'na
  or mar·i·hua'na

ma·rim'ba

ma·ri'na

mar'i·nate

ma·rine'

mar'i·ner

mar·i·o·nette'

mar'i·tal

mar'i·time

mar'jo·ram

mark'down

mark'ed

mark'ed·ly

mark'er

mar'ket

mar·ket·abil'i·ty

mar'ket·able

mar'ket·ing

mar'ket·place

mark'ing

mark'ka
  pl mark'kaa *or*
  markkas

marks'man

marks'man·ship

mark'up

marl

mar'lin

mar'line·spike

mar·ma·lade

mar·mo're·al

mar'mo·set

mar'mot

ma·roon'

mar·quee'

mar'quess

mar'que·try

mar·quis

mar·quise'

mar·qui·sette'

mar'riage

mar'riage·able

mar'ried

mar'row

mar'row·bone

mar'ry

Mars

mar'shal
  order (see martial)

mar'shaled
  or mar'shalled

mar'shal·ing
  or mar'shal·ling

marsh'mal·low

marsh'y

mar·su'pi·al

mar'ten
  mammal (see
  martin)

mar'tial
  warlike (see
  marshal)

Mar'tian

mar'tin
  bird (see marten)

mar·ti·net'

mar'tin·gale

mar·ti'ni

mar'tyr

mar'tyr·dom

mar'vel

mar'veled
  or mar'velled

mar'vel·ing
  or mar'vel·ling

mar'vel·ous
  or mar'vel·lous

Marx'ism

Marx'ist

Mar'y·land
mar'zi·pan
mas·car'a
mas'con
mas'cot
mas'cu·line
mas·cu·lin'i·ty
ma'ser
mask
  conceal (see masque)

mas'och·ism
mas'och·ist
mas·och·is'tic
ma'son
Ma·son'ic
ma'son·ry
masque
  play (see mask)
mas·quer·ade'
Mas·sa·chu'setts
mas'sa·cre
mas·sage'
mas·seur'
mas·seuse'
mas·sif'
  mountain (see massive)

mas'sive
  huge (see massif)
mass-pro·duce'
mas'ter
master-at-arms
  pl masters-at-arms
mas'ter·ful
mas'ter·ful·ly

mas'ter·ly
mas'ter·mind
mas'ter·piece
mas'ter·stroke
mas'ter·work
mas'tery
mast'head
mas'ti·cate
mas·ti·ca'tion
mas'tiff
mas'to·don
mas'toid
mas'tur·bate
mas·tur·ba'tion
mat
  mat'ted
  mat'ting
mat'a·dor
match'book
match'less
match'lock
match'mak·er
match'wood
ma·te'ri·al
  of matter (see matériel)

ma·te'ri·al·ism
ma·te'ri·al·ist
ma·te·ri·al·is'tic
ma·te·ri·al·is'ti·cal·ly
ma·te·ri·al·i·za'tion
ma·te'ri·al·ize
ma·te'ri·al·ly
ma·te·ria med'i·ca

ma·té·ri·el'
  or ma·te·ri·el'
  equipment (see material)

ma·ter'nal
ma·ter'nal·ly
ma·ter'ni·ty
math·e·mat'i·cal
math·e·mat'i·cal·ly
math·e·ma·ti'cian
math·e·mat'ics
mat·i·nee'
mat'ins
ma'tri·arch
ma·tri·ar'chal
ma·tri·ar'chy
ma·tri·ci'dal
ma'tri·cide
ma·tric'u·lant
ma·tric'u·late
ma·tric·u·la'tion
mat·ri·lin'eal
mat·ri·lin'eal·ly
mat·ri·mo'ni·al
mat·ri·mo'ni·al·ly
mat'ri·mo·ny
ma'trix
  pl ma'tri·ces or ma'trix·es

ma'tron
ma'tron·ly
mat'ter
mat'ter-of-fact
mat'ting
mat'tins

mat'tock
mat'tress
mat'u·rate
mat·u·ra'tion
ma·ture'
ma·tu'ri·ty
mat'zo
   pl mat'zoth *or*
   mat'zos

maud'lin
maul
   mangle (see mall)
maun'der
Mau·ri·ta'nia
Mau·ri·ta'nian
Mau·ri'tian
Mau·ri'ti·us
mau·so·le'um
mauve
mav'er·ick
ma'vis
mawk'ish
max·il'la
   pl max·il'lae *or*
   maxillas
max'im
max'i·mal
max'i·mal·ly
max'i·mum
   pl max'i·ma *or*
   max'i·mums
May
may'ap·ple
may'be
may'flow·er
may'hem

may'on·naise
may'or
may'or·al·ty
may'pole
maze
   intricate network
   (see maize)

ma·zur'ka
Mc·Coy'
mead'ow
mead'ow·lark
mea'ger
   or mea'gre
mea'ger·ly
meal'time
meal'y
mealy·mouthed'
mean
   intend (see mien)
meant
mean'ing
me·an'der
mean'ing
mean'ing·ful
mean'ing·less
mean'ly
mean'ness
mean'time
mean'while
mea'sles
mea'sly
mea·sur·abil'i·ty
mea'sur·able
mea'sur·ably
mea'sure
mea'sure·less

mea'sure·ment
mea'sur·er
meat
   food (see meet,
   mete)
meat'ball
meat'i·ness
me·a'tus
   pl me·a'tus·es *or*
   me·a'tus
meat'y
mec'ca
me·chan'ic
me·chan'i·cal
me·chan'i·cal·ly
me·chan'ics
mech'a·nism
mech·a·nis'tic
mech·a·nis'ti·
   cal·ly
mech·a·ni·za'tion
mech'a·nize
med'al
   award (see meddle)
med'al·ist
   or med'al·ist
me·dal'lion
med'dle
   interfere (see
   medal)
med'dler
med'dle·some
me'di·a
me'di·al
me'di·an
me'di·ate

me·di·a′tion
me′di·a·tor
med′ic
med′i·ca·ble
med′i·ca·bly
med′ic·aid
med′i·cal
med′i·cal·ly
med′i·care
med′i·cate
med·i·ca′tion
me·dic′i·nal
me·dic′i·nal·ly
med′i·cine
med′i·co
me·di·e′val
　or me·di·ae′val
me·di·e′val·ist
me·di·o′cre
me·di·oc′ri·ty
med′i·tate
med·i·ta′tion
med′i·ta·tive
me′di·um
　pl me′di·ums or
　me′dia
med′ley
me·dul′la
　pl me·dul′las or
　me·dul′lae
me·dul′la
　ob·lon·ga′ta
meek′ly
meek′ness
meer′schaum
meet
　come upon (see
　meat, mete)

met
meet′ing
meet′ing
meet′ing·house
mega′cy·cle
meg′a·death
meg′a·lith
meg·a·lo·ma′nia
meg·a·lo·ma′
　ni·ac
meg·a·lo·ma·ni′a·
　cal
meg·a·lop′o·lis
meg′a·phone
meg′a·ton
mei·o′sis
mel′a·mine
mel·an·cho′lia
mel·an·chol′ic
mel′an·choly
mé·lange′
mel′a·nin
me′lee
me′lio·rate
me·lio·ra′tion
me′lio·ra·tive
mel·lif′lu·ous
mel′low
me·lo′de·on
me·lod′ic
me·lod′i·cal·ly
me·lo′di·ous
mel′o·dra·ma
melo·dra·mat′ic
melo·dra·mat′i·
　cal·ly

mel′o·dy
mel′on
melt
melt′ed
melt′ed
　also mol′ten
melt′ing
mel′ton
melt′wa·ter
mem′ber
mem′ber·ship
mem′brane
mem′bra·nous
me·men′to
　pl me·men′tos or
　me·men′toes
me·men·to mo′ri
mem′o
mem′oir
mem·o·ra·bil′ia
mem′o·ra·ble
mem′o·ra·bly
mem·o·ran′dum
　pl mem·o·ran′dums
　or mem·o·ran′da
me·mo′ri·al
me·mo′ri·al·ize
mem·o·ri·za′tion
mem′o·rize
mem′o·ry
Mem′phis
men′ace
men′ac·ing·ly
mé·nage′
　household (see
　manege)
me·nag′er·ie
men·da′cious

men·dac′i·ty
Men·de′lian
men′di·cant
men′folk
  or men′folks
men·ha′den
me′ni·al
me′ni·al·ly
men·in·gi′tis
me·nis′cus
  pl me·nis′ci *also*
  me·nis′cus·es

meno·paus′al
meno′pause
me·no′rah
men′ses
men′stru·al
men′stru·ate
men·stru·a′tion
men·su·ra·bil′i·ty
men·su·ra·ble
men·su·ra′tion
men′tal
men·tal′i·ty
men′tal·ly
men′thol
men′tho·lat·ed
men′tion
men′tion·able
men′tor
men′u
me·phit′ic
mer′can·tile
mer′can·til·ism
mer′ce·nary
mer′cer·ize

mer′chan·dise
mer′chan·dis·er
mer′chant
mer′ci·ful
mer′ci·ful·ly
mer′ci·less
mer·cu′ri·al
mer·cu′ri·al·ly
mer·cu′ric
mer′cu·ry
mer′cy
mere′ly
mer·e·tri′cious
mer·gan′ser
merg′er
me·rid′i·an
me·ringue′
me·ri′no
mer′it
mer·i·to′ri·ous
mer′maid
mer′ri·ly
mer′ri·ment
mer′ry
mer·ry-an′drew
mer′ry-go-round
mer′ry·mak·er
mer′ry·mak·ing
Mer·thi′o·late
me′sa
més·al·liance′
mes·cal′
mes·ca·line
mes·dames′
mes·de·moi·selles′
mesh′work

mes′mer·ism
mes′mer·ize
me′son
mes·quite′
mes′sage
mes′sen·ger
mes·si′ah
mes·si·an′ic
mes·sieurs′
mess′i·ly
mess′i·ness
mess′mate
mess′y
mes·ti′zo
met·a·bol′ic
me·tab′o·lism
me·tab′o·lize
met′al,
met′al
  chemical element
  (*see* mettle)

met′aled
  or met′alled

met′al·ing
  or met′al·ling
me·tal′lic
met·al·lur′gi·cal
met′al·lur·gist
met′al·lur·gy
met′al·ware
met′al·work
met·a·mor′phic
met·a·mor′phism
met·a·mor′phose
met·a·mor′pho·sis
met′a·phor

met·a·phor′i·cal
met·a·phor′i·cal·ly
meta·phys′ic
meta·phys′i·cal
meta·phys′i·cal·ly
meta·phys′ics
me·tas′ta·sis
   pl me·tas′ta·ses
meta·tar′sal
meta·tar′sus
mete
   allot (*see* meat, meet)
me·tem·psy·cho′sis
me′te·or
me′te·or′ic
me·te·or′i·cal·ly
me′te·or·ite
me′te·or·oid
me·te·o·ro·log′i·cal
me·te·o·ro·log′i·cal·ly
me·te·o·rol′o·gist
me·te·o·rol′o·gy
me′ter
meth′a·done
   or meth′a·don
meth′ane
meth′a·nol
meth′od
me·thod′i·cal
me·thod′i·cal·ly
Meth′od·ist
meth′od·ize

meth·od·olog′i·cal
meth·od·olog′i·cal·ly
meth·od·ol′o·gy
me·tic′u·lous
mé·tier′
me-too
met′ric
met′ri·cal
met′ri·cal·ly
met′ro
met′ro·nome
me·trop′o·lis
met·ro·pol′i·tan
met′tle
   spirit (*see* metal)
met′tle·some
Mex′i·can
Mex′i·co
mez′za·nine
mez·zo-so·pran′o
Mi·am′i
mi·as′ma
   pl mi·as′mas *or* mi·as′ma·ta
mi′ca
Mich′i·gan
mi′crobe
mi′cro·bi·al
mi′cro·cir·cuit
mi′cro·copy
mi′cro·cosm
mi′cro·dot
mi′cro·fiche
mi′cro·film
mi′cro·form

mi′cro·groove
mi·crom′e·ter
mi′cron
mi·cro·or′ga·nism
mi′cro·phone
mi′cro·print
mi′cro·probe
mi′cro·read·er
mi′cro·scope
mi·cro·scop′ic
mi·cro·scop′i·cal·ly
mi·cros′co·py
mi′cro·wave
mid′day
mid′den
mid′dle
mid·dle-aged′
mid′dle·brow
mid′dle·man
mid′dle-of-the-road
mid′dle-of-the-road·er
mid′dle·weight
mid′dling
mid′dy
   midshipman (*see* midi)
midg′et
mid′i
   skirt (*see* middy)
mid′land
mid′most
mid′night
mid′point

mid′riff
mid′sec·tion
mid′ship·man
mid′ships
midst
mid·stream
mid′sum′mer
mid′way
mid′week
mid′wife
mid′wife·ry
mid′win′ter
mid′year
mien
   appearance (see mean)

might
   strength (see mite)

might′i·ly
might′i·ness
might′y
mi·gnon·ette′
mi′graine
mi′grant
mi′grate
mi·gra′tion
mi′gra·to·ry
mi·ka′do
mil′dew
mild′ly
mild′ness
mile′age
mile′post
mil′er
mile′stone
mi·lieu′

mil′i·tan·cy
mil′i·tant
mil·i·tar′i·ly
mil′i·ta·rism
mil·i·ta·ris′tic
mil·i·ta·ri·za′tion
mil′i·ta·rize
mil′i·tary
mil′i·tate
mi·li′tia
mi·li′tia·man
milk′er
milk′i·ness
milk′maid
milk′man
milk′sop
milk′weed
milk′wort
milk′y
mill′dam
mil·len′ni·al
mil·len′ni·um
   pl mil·len′nia *or* mil·len′ni·ums

mill′er
mil′let
mil′li·ard
mil′li·bar
mil·lieme′
mil′li·gram
mil′li·me·ter
mil′li·ner
mil′li·nery
mill′ing
mil′lion
mil·lion·aire′

mil′lionth
mill′pond
mill′race
mill′stone
mill′stream
mill′wright
Mil·wau′kee
mim′e·o·graph
mim′er
mi·me′sis
mi·met′ic
mim′ic
  mim′icked
  mim′ick·ing
mim·ic′ry
mi·mo′sa
min′a·ret
min′a·to·ry
mince′meat
minc′ing
mind′ed
mind′ex·pand·ing
mind′ful
mind′ful·ly
mind′less
mine′lay·er
min′er
   one that mines (see minor)

min′er·al
min·er·al·iza′tion
min′er·al·ize
min·er·al·og′i·cal
min·er·al′o·gist
min·er·al′o·gy
min·e·stro′ne

mine′sweep·er
min′gle
min′ia·ture
min′ia·tur·ist
min·ia·tur·iza′tion
min′ia·tur·ize
min′i·bus
min′i·cab
min′im
min′i·mal
min′i·mal·ly
min·i·mi·za′tion
min′i·mize
min′i·mum
   pl min′i·ma *or*
   min′i·mums

min′ing
min′ion
min′is·cule
min′i·skirt
min′i·state
min′is·ter
min·is·te′ri·al
min′is·trant
min·is·tra′tion
min′is·try
mini′track
min′i·ver
mink
   pl mink *or* minks

Min·ne·ap′o·lis
min′ne·sing·er
Min·ne·so′ta
min′now
mi′nor
   lesser (*see* miner)

mi·nor′i·ty
min′strel
min′strel·sy
mint′age
mint′er
mint′y
min′u·end
min·u·et′
mi′nus
min′us·cule
min′ute
   noun
mi′nute
   adjective
mi·nute′ly
min′ute·man
mi·nu′tia
   pl mi·nu′ti·ae
minx
mir′a·cle
mi·rac′u·lous
mir′a·dor
mi·rage′
mir′ror
mirth′ful
mirth′ful·ly
mir′y
mis·ad·ven′ture
mis·al·li′ance
mis·al·lo·ca′tion
mis′an·thrope
mis·an·throp′ic
mis·an·throp′i·
   cal·ly
mis·an′thro·py
mis·ap·pli·ca′tion

mis·ap·ply′
mis·ap·pre·hend′
mis·ap·pre·hen′
   sion
mis·ap·pro′pri·ate
mis·ap·pro·pri·
   a′tion
mis·be·got′ten
mis·be·have′
mis·be·hav′ior
mis·be·lief′
mis·be·liev′er
mis·brand′
mis·cal′cu·late
mis·cal·cu·la′tion
mis·call′
mis·car′riage
mis·car′ry
mis·cast′
mis·ce·ge·na′tion
mis·cel·la′nea
mis·cel·la′ne·ous
mis′cel·la·ny
mis·chance′
mis′chief
mis′chie·vous
mis·ci·bil′i·ty
mis′ci·ble
mis·con·ceive′
mis·con·cep′tion
mis·con′duct
mis·con·struc′tion
mis·con·strue′
mis·count′
mis′cre·ant
mis·cue′

mis·deal'
mis·deed'
mis·de·mean'ant
mis·de·mean'or
mis·di·rect'
mis·di·rec'tion
mis·do'er
mis·do'ing
mise-en-scène'
mi'ser
mis'er·a·ble
mis'er·a·bly
mi'ser·li·ness
mi'ser·ly
mis'ery
mis·es'ti·mate
mis·es·ti·ma'tion
mis·fea'sance
mis·file'
mis·fire'
mis'fit
mis·for'tune
mis·giv'ing
mis·gov'ern
mis·gov'ern·ment
mis·guid'ance
mis·guide'
mis·han'dle
mis'hap
mish'mash
mis·in·form'
mis·in·for·ma'tion
mis·in·ter'pret
mis·in·ter·pre·ta'
  tion
mis·judge'

mis·judg'ment
mis·lay'
mis·lead'
mis·man'age
mis·man'age·
  ment
mis·match'
mis·mate'
mis·name'
mis·no'mer
mi·sog'a·mist
mi·sog'a·my
mi·sog'y·nist
mi·sog'y·ny
mis·place'
mis·play'
mis·print'
mis·pri'sion
mis·pro·nounce'
mis·pro·nun·ci·a'
  tion
mis·quo·ta'tion
mis·quote'
mis·read'
mis·rep·re·sent'
mis·rep·re·sen·ta'
  tion
mis·rule'
mis'sal
  book (see missile)
mis·send'
  mis·sent'
  mis·sent'
  mis·send'ing
mis·shape'
mis·shap'en

mis'sile
  weapon (see missal)
mis'sile·ry
  also mis'sil·ry
miss'ing
mis'sion
mis'sion·ary
mis'sion·er
Mis·sis·sip'pi
mis'sive
Mis·sou'ri
mis·spell'
mis·spend'
mis·state'
mis·state'ment
mis·step'
mis·tak'able
mis·take'
  mis·took'
  mis·tak'en
  mis·tak'ing
mis·tak'en
mis'ter
mist'i·ly
mis·time'
mist'i·ness
mis'tle·toe
mis'tral
mis·treat'
mis·treat'ment
mis'tress
mis·tri'al
mis·trust'
mist'y
mis·un·der·stand'
mis·us'age

mis·use'

mis·val'ue

mis·ven'ture

mite
   small thing (see might)

mi'ter
   or mi'tre

mi'tered
   or mi'tred

mi'ter·ing
   or mi'tring

mit'i·ga·ble

mit'i·gate

mit·i·ga'tion

mit'i·ga·tive

mit'i·ga·tor

mi·to'sis
   pl mi·to'ses

mitt

mit'ten

mix'able

mix'er

mix'ture

mix'-up

miz'zen
   or miz'en

miz'zen·mast

mne·mon'ic

mne·mon'ics

moat
   trench (see mote)

mob
  mobbed
  mob'bing

Mo·bile'

mo'bile

mo·bil'i·ty

mo·bi·li·za'tion

mo'bi·lize

mo'bi·liz·er

mob·oc'ra·cy

mob'ster

moc'ca·sin

mo'cha

mock'er

mock'ery

mock-he·ro'ic

mock'ing·bird

mock'-up

mod'al

mod'el
  mod'eled
   or mod'elled
  mod'el·ing
   or mod'el·ling

mod'er·ate

mod'er·ate·ly

mod·er·a'tion

mod'er·a'to

mod'er·a·tor

mod'ern

mod'ern·ism

mod·ern·is'tic

mo·der'ni·ty

mod·ern·i·za'tion

mod'ern·ize

mod'ern·iz·er

mod'est

mod'es·ty

mod'i·cum

mod·i·fi·ca'tion

mod'i·fi·er

mod'i·fy

mod'ish

mo·diste'

mod'u·lar

mod'u·late

mod·u·la'tion

mod'u·la·tor

mod'ule

mo·dus ope·ran'di
   pl mo'di ope·ran·di

mo·dus vi·ven'di
   pl mo'di vi·ven·di

mo'gul

mo'hair

moi'e·ty

moi·ré'
   or moire

moist'en

moist'ly

moist'ness

mois'ture

mo'lar

mo·las'ses

mold'board

mold'er

mold'i·ness

mold'ing

mold'y

mo·lec'u·lar

mol'e·cule

mole'hill

mole'skin

mo·lest'

mo·les·ta'tion

mo·lest'er

mol·li·fi·ca′tion
mol′li·fy
mol′lusk
  or mol′lusc
mol′ly·cod·dle
molt
mol′ten
mol′to
mo·lyb′de·num
mo′ment
mo·men·tar′i·ly
mo′men·tary
mo·men′tous
mo·men′tum
  pl mo·men′ta *or*
  mo·men′tums
Mo′na·co
Mo′na·can
mo′nad
mon′arch
mo·nar′chi·cal
  or mo·nar′chic
mon′ar·chism
mon′ar·chist
mon′ar·chy
mon·as·te′ri·al
mon′as·tery
mo·nas′tic
mo·nas′ti·cal·ly
mo·nas′ti·cism
mon·au′ral
Mon′day
Mon·e·gasque′
mon·e·tar′i·ly
mon′e·tary
mon·e·ti·za′tion
mon′e·tize

mon′ey
  pl mon′eys *or*
  mon′ies
mon′ey·bags
mon′eyed
  or mon′ied
mon′ey·lend·er
mon′ey·mak·er
mon′ey·wort
mon′ger
Mon·go′lia
Mon·go′lian
mon′gol·ism
Mon′gol·oid
mon′goose
  pl mon′goos·es
mon′grel
mo′nism
mo′nist
mon′i·tor
mon′i·to·ry
mon′key
mon′key·shine
monk′ish
monks′hood
mono·chro·mat′ic
mono·chro·mat′i·
  cal·ly
mono′chrome
mon′o·cle
mon·oc′u·lar
mon′o·dy
mo·nog′a·mist
mo·nog′a·mous
mo·nog′a·my
mon′o·gram

mon′o·graph
mo·nog′y·ny
mono′lith
mon′o·logue
  also mon′o·log
mon′o·logu·ist
  or mo·nol′o·gist
mono·ma′nia
mono·ma′ni·ac
mo·no·nu·cle·o′sis
mono·phon′ic
mon′o·plane
mo·nop′o·list
mo·nop·o·lis′tic
mo·nop·o·lis′ti·
  cal·ly
mo·nop·o·li·za′·
  tion
mo·nop′o·lize
mo·nop′o·ly
mon′o·rail
mono·syl·lab′ic
mono·syl·lab′i·
  cal·ly
mon′o·syl·la·ble
mon′o·the·ism
mon′o·the·ist
mon′o·tone
mo·not′o·nous
mo·not′o·ny
mon′o·type
mon·ox′ide
mon·sei·gneur′
  pl mes·sei·gneurs′
mon·sieur′
  pl mes·sieurs′

mon·si′gnor
  pl mon·si′gnors *or*
  mon·si·gno′ri

mon·soon′
mon′ster
mon′strance
mon·stros′i·ty
mon′strous
mon·tage′
Mon·tan′a
Mon·tes·so′ri·an
Mont·gom′ery
month′ly
Mont·pe′lier
Mon·tre·al′
mon′u·ment
mon·u·men′tal
mon·u·men′tal·ly
mood′i·ly
mood′i·ness
mood′y
moon′beam
moon-eyed
moon′light
moon′light·er
moon′light·ing
moon′lit
moon′scape
moon′shine
moon′stone
moon′struck
moor′age
moor′ing
moor′land
moose
  pl moose
  animal (*see* mousse)

mop
  mopped
  mop′ping
mop′board
mop′pet
mop′-up
mo·raine′
mor′al
mo·rale′
mor′al·ist
mor·al·is′tic
mor·al·is′ti·cal·ly
mo·ral′i·ty
mor·al·i·za′tion
mor′al·ize
mor′al·iz·er
mor′al·ly
mo·rass′
mor·a·to′ri·um
  pl mor·a·to′ri·ums *or*
  mor·a·to′ria

mor′bid
mor·bid′i·ty
mor′dant
  caustic (*see*
  mordent)

mor′dent
  music (*see* mordant)

more·o′ver
mo′res
mor·ga·nat′ic
mor·ga·nat′i·
  cal·ly
morgue
mor′i·bund
mor·i·bun′di·ty

Mor′mon
Mor′mon·ism
morn′ing
  day (*see* mourning)

Mo·roc′can
Mo·roc′co
mo′ron
mo·ron′ic
mo·ron′i·cal·ly
mo·rose′
mor′pheme
mor·phe′mic
mor′phia
mor′phine
mor·pho·log′i·cal
mor·pho·log′i·
  cal·ly
mor·phol′o·gist
mor·phol′o·gy
mor′ris
mor′row
mor′sel
mor′tal
mor·tal′i·ty
mor′tal·ly
mor′tar
mor′tar·board
mort′gage
mort·gag·ee′
mort·ga·gor′
mor·ti′cian
mor·ti·fi·ca′tion
mor′ti·fy
mor′tise
  also mor′tice

mort′main

mor′tu·ary
mo·sa′ic
mo′sey
mosque
mos·qui′to
  pl mos·qui′toes
moss′back
moss′-grown
moss′y
most′ly
mote
  particle (see moat)
mo·tel′
mo·tet′
moth′ball
moth′-eat·en
moth′er
moth′er·hood
moth′er·house
moth′er-in-law
  pl moth′ers-in-law
moth′er·land
moth′er·less
moth′er·li·ness
moth′er·ly
moth′er-of-pearl′
mo·tif′
mo′tile
mo·til′i·ty
mo′tion
mo′ti·vate
mo′ti·va′tion
mo′tive
mo·tiv′i·ty
mot′ley
mo′tor

mo′tor·boat
mo′tor·cade
mo′tor·car
mo′tor·cy·cle
mo′tor·cy·clist
mo′tor·drome
mo′tor·ist
mo·tor·i·za′tion
mo′tor·ize
mo′tor·man
mo′tor·truck
mot′tle
mot′to
  pl mot′toes *also* mot′tos
mou·lage′
mound
mount′able
moun′tain
moun·tain·eer′
moun·tain·ous
moun′tain·side
moun′tain·top
moun′te·bank
Mount′ie
mount′ing
mourn′er
mourn′ful
mourn′ful·ly
mourn′ing
  grief (see morning)
mouse
  pl mice
  rodent (see mousse)
mous′er
mousse
  dessert (see moose, mouse)

mous·se·line′
mous·se·line′de
  soie
  pl mous·se·lines′ de soie
mous′y
  or mous′ey
mouth′ful
mouth′part
mouth′piece
mouth′wash
mou′ton
  sheepskin (see mutton)
mov·abil′i·ty
  or move·abil′i·ty
mov′able
  or move′able
mov′ably
move′ment
mov′er
mov′ie
mov′ing
mow
  mowed
  mowed
  or mown
  mow′ing
mow′er
much
  more
  most
mu′ci·lage
mu·ci·lag′i·nous
muck′rak·er
mu·cous
  adjective

mu′cus
   noun

mud′di·ly
mud′di·ness
mud′dle
mud·dle·head′ed
mud′dler
mud′dy
mud′guard
mud′sling·er
mu·ez′zin
muf′fin
muf′fle
muf′fler
muf′fling
muf′ti
mug
  mugged
  mug′ging
mug′ger
mug′gi·ness
mug′gy
mug′wump
Mu·ham′mad
muk′luk
mu·lat′to
  pl mu·lat′toes *or*
  mu·lat′tos

mul′ber·ry
mulch
  cover (see mulct)
mulct
  defraud (see mulch)
mul′ish
mul′lah
mul′let

mul′li·gan
mul·li·ga·taw′ny
mul′lion
mul·ti·col′ored
mul·ti·far′i·ous
mul′ti·form
mul·ti·lat′er·al
mul·ti·lat′er·al·ly
mul·ti·me′dia
mul·ti·mil·lion·
  aire′
mul·ti·na′tion
mul·ti·par′tite
mul·ti·par′ty
mul′ti·ple
mul′ti·ple-choice
mul·ti·pli·cand′
mul·ti·pli·ca′tion
mul·ti·plic′i·ty
mul·ti·pli′er
mul′ti·ply
mul′ti·tude
mul·ti·tu′di·nous
mul·ti·ver′si·ty
mul·ti·vi′ta·min
mum′ble
mum′bler
mum′ble·ty-peg
mum·bo jum′bo
mum′mer
mum′mery
mum·mi·fi·ca′tion
mum′mi·fy
mum′my
mun·dane′
mu·nic′i·pal

mu·nic·i·pal′i·ty
mu·nic′i·pal·ly
mu·nif′i·cence
mu·nif′i·cent
mu·ni′tion
mu′ral
mu′ral·ist
mur′der
mur′der·er
mur′der·ess
mur′der·ous
murk′i·ly
murk′i·ness
murk′y
mur′mur
mur′mur·er
mus′ca·dine
mus·ca·tel′
mus′cle
  body tissue (see
  mussel)
mus′cle-bound
mus′cu·lar
mus·cu·lar′i·ty
mus′cu·la·ture
mu·sette′
mu·se′um
mush′i·ly
mush′i·ness
mush′room
mush′y
mu′sic
mu′si·cal
  of music (see
  musicale)
mu·si·cale′
  concert (see
  musical)

mu'si·cal·ly
mu·si'cian
mu·si·col'o·gist
mu·si·col'o·gy
mus'keg
mus'kel·lunge
mus'ket
mus·ke·teer'
mus'ket·ry
musk'i·ness
musk'mel·on
musk'rat
musk'y
Mus'lim
mus'lin
mus'sel
  shell fish (see
  muscle)

muss'i·ly
muss'i·ness
muss'y
mus'tache
mus'tang
mus'tard
mus'ter
must'i·ly
must'i·ness
must'y
mu·ta·bil'i·ty
mu'ta·ble
mu'ta·bly
mu'tant
mu'tate
mu·ta'tion
  mu·tan'dis

mute'ly
mu'ti·late
mu·ti·la'tion
mu'ti·la·tor
mu·ti·neer'
mu'ti·nous
mu'ti·ny
mut'ter
mut'ton
  meat (see mouton)
mut'ton-chops
mu'tu·al
mu·tu·al'i·ty
mu'tu·al·ly
muu'muu
muz'zle
my·col'o·gist
my·col'o·gy
my·co'sis
my'elin
  also my'eline
my·eli'tis
my·i'a·sis
my'na
  or my'nah
myo·gen'ic
my·o'pia
my·o'pic
my·o'pi·cal·ly
myr'i·ad
myr'mi·don
myrrh
myr'tle
my·self'
mys·te'ri·ous
mys·te'ri·um

mys'tery
mys'tic
mys'ti·cal
mys'ti·cal·ly
mys'ti·cism
mys·ti·fi·ca'tion
mys'ti·fy
mys·tique'
myth
myth'i·cal
myth'i·cal·ly
myth·o·log'i·cal
myth·o·log'i·cal·ly
my·thol'o·gist
my·thol'o·gy

N

nab
  nabbed
  nab'bing
na'bob
na·celle'
na'cre
na'dir
nag
  nagged
  nag'ging
na'iad
  pl na'iads *or*
  na'ia·des
nain'sook
na·ive'
  also na·ive'
na·ive'ly

na·ïve·té′
  also na·ive·té′

na·ive·ty
  also na·ïve′ty

na′ked

nam·by-pam′by

name′able
  also nam′able

name′less

name′ly

name′plate

name′sake

nan·keen′
  also nan·kin′

nan′ny goat

nap
  napped
  nap′ping

na′palm

na′pery

naph′tha

naph′tha·lene

nap′kin

na·po′leon

Na·po·le·on′ic

nap′per

nap′py

nar′cis·sism

nar′cis·sist

nar·cis·sis′tic

nar·cis′sus
  pl nar·cis′sus *or*
  nar·cis′sus·es *or*
  nar·cis′si

nar′co·lep·sy

nar·co′sis
  pl nar·co′ses

nar·cot′ic

nar′co·tize

nar′is
  pl nar′es

nar′rate

nar·ra′tion

nar′ra·tive

nar′ra·tor

nar′row

nar·row-mind′ed

nar′whal
  also nar′wal

na′sal

na·sal′i·ty

na·sal·iza′tion

na′sal·ize

na′sal·ly

nas′cence

nas′cent

Nash′ville

na·so·phar′ynx

nas′ti·ly

nas′ti·ness

nas·tur′tium

nas′ty

na′tal

na·tal′i·ty

na′tant

na·ta·to′ri·al
  or na′ta·to·ry

na·ta·to′ri·um

na′tion

na′tion·al

na′tion·al·ism

na′tion·al·ist

na·tion·al·is′tic

na·tion·al·is′ti·
  cal·ly

na·tion·al′i·ty

na·tion·al·iza′tion

na′tion·al·ize

na′tion·al·ly

na′tion·hood

na′tion-state′

na·tion·wide′

na′tive

na′tiv·ism

na′tiv·ist

Na·tiv′i·ty

nat′ti·ly

nat′ti·ness

nat′ty

nat′u·ral

nat′u·ral·ism

nat′u·ral·ist

nat·u·ral·is′tic

nat·u·ral·is′ti·
  cal·ly

nat·u·ral·iza′tion

nat′u·ral·ize

nat′u·ral·ly

na′ture

naught

naught′i·ly

naught′i·ness

naught′y

Na·u′ru

nau′sea

nau′se·ate

nau′se·at·ing

nau′seous

nau′ti·cal

nau'ti·cal·ly

nau'ti·lus
pl nau'ti·lus·es *or*
nau'ti·li

na'val
of a navy (see
navel)

nave
center of a church
(see knave)

na'vel
abdominal
depression (see
naval)

nav·i·ga·bil'i·ty

nav'i·ga·ble

nav'i·gate

nav·i·ga'tion

nav'i·ga·tor

na'vy

nay
no (see née, neigh)

na·ya pai·sa'
pl na·ye pai·se'

Na'zi

Na'zism
or Na'zi·ism

Ne·an'der·thal

near·by'

near'ly

near'ness

near'sight·ed

neat'ly

neat'ness

Ne·bras'ka

neb'u·la
pl neb'u·las *or*
neb'u·lae

neb'u·lar

neb'u·lize

neb·u·los'i·ty

neb'u·lous

nec·es·sar'i·ly

nec'es·sary

ne·ces'si·tate

ne·ces'si·tous

ne·ces'si·ty

neck'band

neck'er·chief
pl neck'er·chiefs
also
neck'er·chieves

neck'lace

neck'line

neck'piece

neck'tie

ne·crol'o·gist

ne·crol'o·gy

nec'ro·man·cer

nec'ro·man·cy

ne·crop'o·lis
pl ne·crop'o·lis·es *or*
ne·crop'o·les

nec'rop·sy

ne·cro'sis
pl ne·cro'ses

nec'tar

nec'tar·ine'

née
or nee
born (see nay,
neigh)

need
require (see knead)

need'ful

need'ful·ly

need'i·ness

nee'dle

nee'dle·like

nee'dle·point

nee'dler

need'less

nee'dle·work

nee'dling

need'y

ne'er'-do-well

ne·far'i·ous

ne·gate'

ne·ga'tion

neg'a·tive

neg'a·tive·ly

neg'a·tiv·ism

neg·a·tiv'i·ty

ne·glect'

ne·glect'ful

neg·li·gee'
also neg·li·gé'

neg'li·gence

neg'li·gent

neg·li·gi·bil'i·ty

neg'li·gi·ble

neg'li·gi·bly

ne·go·tia·bil'i·ty

ne·go'tia·ble

ne·go'tia·bly

ne·go'tiant

ne·go'ti·ate

ne·go·ti·a'tion

ne·go'ti·a·tor

ne'gri·tude

Ne'gro
pl Ne'groes

ne′groid
ne′gus
neigh
  horse cry (see
    nay, née)

neigh′bor
neigh′bor·hood
neigh′bor·ing
neigh′bor·li·ness
neigh′bor·ly
nei′ther
  neither one (see
    nether)

nel′son
nem′a·tode
Nem′bu·tal
nem′e·sis
  pl nem′e·ses

ne·moph′i·la
neo·clas′sic
neo·clas′si·cal
neo·clas′si·cism
neo·co·lo′nial
neo·co·lo′ni·al·
  ism
neo·lith′ic
ne·ol′o·gism
ne·ol′o·gy
neo·my′cin
ne′on
ne′o·phyte
ne′o·plasm
ne′o·prene
Ne·pal′
Nepa·lese′
Ne·pal′i

ne·pen′the
neph′ew
ne·phri′tis
ne plus ul′tra
nep′o·tism
Nep′tune
Ne′re·id
nerve′less
nerve′-rack·ing
  or nerve′-wrack·ing
ner′vous
nerv′y
nes′tle
nest′ling
net
  net′ted
  net′ting
neth′er
  lower (see neither)

Neth′er·land·er
Neth′er·lands
neth′er·most
neth′er·world
net′ting
net′tle
net′tle·some
net′work
neu′ral
neu·ral′gia
neu·ral′gic
neur·as·the′nia
neu·ras·then′ic
neu·rit′ic
neu·ri′tis
neu·ro·log′i·cal
neu·rol′o·gist

neu·rol′o·gy
neu·ro·mus′cu·lar
neu′ron
  also neu′rone
neu·ro′sis
  pl neu·ro′ses
neu·rot′ic
neu·rot′i·cal·ly
neu′ter
neu′tral
neu′tral·ism
neu·tral′i·ty
neu·tral·iza′tion
neu′tral·ize
neu′tral·iz·er
neu·tri′no
neu′tron
Ne·vad′a
nev′er
nev·er·more′
nev·er-nev′er land
nev·er·the·less′
ne′vus
  pl ne′vi

New′ark
New Bed′ford
new·born
New Bruns′wick
new′com·er
new deal′er
new′el
new′fan′gled
new′-fash′ioned
new·found
New′found·land
New Hamp′shire

New Ha'ven
new'ish
New Jer'sey
new'ly
new'ly·wed
New Mex'i·co
new'ness
New Or'leans
New'port News
news'boy
news'break
news'cast
news'cast·er
news'let·ter
news'man
news'mon·ger
news'pa·per
news'pa·per·man
news'print
news'reel
news'stand
news'wor·thy
New York
New Zea'land
New Zea'land·er
nex'us
   pl nex'ux·es *or*
     nex'us

ngwee
   pl ngwee

ni'a·cin
Ni·ag'a·ra
nib'ble
Nic·a·ra'gua
Nic·a·ra'guan
nice'ly

nice'ness
nice'ty
niche
   recess (see nick)

nick
   notch (see niche)

nick'el
nick·el·od'e·on
nick'name
nic'o·tine
nic·o·ti'nic
niece
nif'ty
Ni'ger
Ni·ge'ri·a
Ni·ge'ri·an
Ni·ge·rois'
   pl Ni·ge·rois'

nig'gard·li·ness
nig'gard·ly
nig'gling
night
   dark (see knight)

night'cap
night'clothes
night'club
night'dress
night'fall
night'gown
night'hawk
night'in·gale
night'long
night'ly
night'mare
night'shade
night'shirt

night'stick
night'time
night'walk·er
ni'hil·ism
ni'hil·ist
ni·hil·is'tic
Ni'ke
nim'ble
nim'bly
nim'bus
   pl nim'bi *or*
     nim'bus·es

Nim'rod
nin'com·poop
nine'pins
nine·teen'
nine·teenth'
nine'ti·eth
nine'ty
nin'ny
ni'non
ninth
nip
   nipped
   nip'ping
nip'per
nip'ple
nip'-up
nip'py
nir·va'na
ni'sei
   pl ni'sei *also* ni'seis

nit'-pick·ing
ni'ter
   also ni'tre

ni'trate

ni·tra′tion
ni′tric
ni′tro
ni′tro·gen
ni·trog′e·nous
ni·tro·glyc′er·in
  or ni·tro·glyc′er·ine
nit·ty-grit′ty
nit′wit
no·bil′i·ty
no′ble
no′ble·man
no·blesse oblige′
no′bly
no′body
noc·tur′nal
noc·tur′nal·ly
noc′turne
noc′u·ous
nod
  nod′ded
  nod′ding
nod′al
node
nod′u·lar
nod′ule
nod′u·lose
no·el′
nog′gin
no′-good
noise′less
noise′mak·er
nois′i·ly
nois′i·ness
noi′some
nois′y

no·lo con·ten′
  de·re
no′mad
no·mad′ic
no′-man's-land
nom de guerre′
  pl noms de guerre′
nom de plume′
  pl noms de plume′
no′men·cla·ture
nom′i·nal
nom′i·nal·ly
nom′i·nate
nom′i·na′tion
nom′i·na·tive
nom′i·na·tor
nom·i·nee′
non′age
no·na·ge·nar′i·an
non·aligned′
non·align′ment
non′book
non′can·di·date
nonce
non·cha·lance′
non·cha·lant′
non′com
non·com·bat′ant
non′com·mis′-
  sioned
non·com·mit′tal
non com·pos
  men′tis
non·con·duc′tor
non·con·form′ist
non·con·for′mi·ty

non·con·trib′u-
  to·ry
non·co·op·er·a′-
  tion
non·de·script′
non·en′ti·ty
none′such
none·the·less′
non′fic′tion
non′grad′ed
non·in·ter·ven′-
  tion
non′met′al
non·me·tal′lic
non·pa·reil′
non′par′ti·san
non·plus′
  non·plussed′
  also non·plused′
  non·plus′sing
  also non·plus′ing
non′prof′it
non′res′i·dent
non·re·sis′tance
non·re·stric′tive
non′sched′uled
non′sense
non·sen′si·cal
non·sen′si·cal·ly
non seq′ui·tur
non′sked
non′skid
non′stop
non·sup·port′
non′ trop′po
non·u′nion

non'vi'o·lence
noo'dle
noon'day
noon'time
no-par
Nor'folk
nor'mal
nor'mal·cy
nor·mal'i·ty
nor'mal·iza'tion
nor'mal·ize
nor'mal·ly
nor'ma·tive
Norse
north'bound
North Car·o·li'na
North Da·ko'ta
north·east'
north·east'er·ly
north·east'ern
north'er·ly
north'ern
north'ern·most
north'ward
north'wards
Nor'way
Nor·we'gian
north·west'
north·west'er·ly
north·west'ern
nose'band
nose'bleed
nose'gay
nose'piece
no-show

nos'i·ly
nos'i·ness
nos·tal'gia
nos·tal'gic
nos·tal'gi·cal·ly
nos'tril
nos'trum
nos'y
  or nos'ey
no·ta be'ne
no·ta·bil'i·ty
no'ta·ble
no'ta·bly
no·tar'i·al
no·ta·ri·za'tion
no'ta·rize
no'ta·ry public
  pl no'ta·ries public
  or no'ta·ry publics

no'tate
no·ta'tion
no·ta'tion·al
notch
notch'back
note'book
note'case
not'ed
note'wor·thi·ly
note'wor·thi·ness
note'wor·thy
noth'ing
noth'ing·ness
no'tice
no'tice·able
no'tice·ably

no'ti·fi·ca'tion
no'ti·fi·er
no'ti·fy
no'tion
no'tion·al
no·to·ri'ety
no·to'ri·ous
no-trump
not·with·stand'ing
nou'gat
nought
nour'ish
nour'ish·ing
nour'ish·ment
nou·veau riche'
  pl nou·veaux riches'
no'va
  pl no'vas *or* no'vae
No·va Sco'tia
nov'el
nov·el·ette'
nov'el·ist
nov·el·iza'tion
nov'el·ize
nov'el·ty
no·vel'la
  pl no·vel'las *or*
  no·vel'le
No·vem'ber
no·ve'na
nov'ice
no·vi'tiate
now'a·days
no'way
  or no'ways

no'where
no'wise
nox'ious
noz'zle
nth
nu'ance
nub'ble
nub'bly
nu'bile
nu'cle·ar
nu'cle·ate
nu·cle'ic
nu'cle·on
nu·cle·on'ics
nu'cle·us
  pl nu'clei *also*
    nu'cle·us·es

nu'clide
nude
nudge
nud'ism
nud'ist
nu'di·ty
nu'ga·to·ry
nug'get
nui'sance
nul·li·fi·ca'tion
nul'li·fi·er
nul'li·fy
nul'li·ty
numb
num'ber
numb'ing
numb'ly
numb'ness

num'ber·less
nu'mer·a·ble
nu'mer·al
nu'mer·ate
nu·mer·a'tion
nu'mer·a·tor
nu·mer'i·cal
nu·mer'i·cal·ly
nu·mer·ol'o·gy
nu'mer·ous
nu·mis·mat'ic
nu·mis·mat'ics
nu·mis·ma·tist
num'skull
nun'ci·a·ture
nun'cio
nun'nery
nup'tial
nurse'maid
nur'sery
nur'sery·man
nur'ture
nut'crack·er
nut'meg
nut'pick
nu'tria
nu'tri·ent
nu'tri·ment
nu·tri'tion
nu·tri'tious
nu'tri·tive
nut'shell
nut'ty
nuz'zle
ny'lon

nym·pho·ma'nia
nym·pho·ma'
  ni·ac

O

oaf'ish
oak'en
Oak'land
oa'kum
oar
  propellant (see ore)
oar'lock
oars'man
oa'sis
  pl oa'ses
oat'en
oat'cake
oath
oat'meal
ob·bli·ga'to
ob·du·ra·cy
ob'du·rate
obe'di·ence
obe'di·ent
obei'sance
obei'sant
ob'e·lisk
obese'
obe·si·ty
obey'
ob·fus'cate
ob·fus·ca'tion
ob·fus'ca·to·ry
o'bi

obit′

obi·ter dic′tum
　　pl obi·ter dic′ta

obit′u·ary

ob′ject

ob·jec′ti·fy

ob·jec′tion

ob·jec′tion·able

ob·jec′tion·ably

ob·jec′tive

ob·jec′tive·ly

ob·jec·tiv′i·ty

ob·jec′tor

ob·jet d′art′
　　pl ob·jets d′art′

ob′jur·gate

ob·jur·ga′tion

ob·late′

obla′tion

ob′li·gate

ob′li·ga′tion

oblig′a·to·ry

oblige′

oblig′ing

oblique′

oblique′ly

obliq′ui·ty

oblit′er·ate

oblit·er·a′tion

obliv′i·on

obliv′i·ous

ob′long

ob′lo·quy

ob·nox′ious

o′boe

o′bo·ist

ob·scene′

ob·scene′ly

ob·scen′i·ty

ob·scu′ran·tism

ob·scu′ran·tist

ob·scure′

ob·scure′ly

ob·scu′ri·ty

ob·se′qui·ous

ob′se·quy

ob·serv′able

ob·serv′ably

ob·ser′vance

ob·ser′vant

ob·ser·va′tion

ob·ser′va·to·ry

ob·serve′

ob·serv′er

ob·sess′

ob·ses′sion

ob·ses′sive

ob·sid′i·an

ob·so·lesce′

ob·so·les′cence

ob·so·les′cent

ob·so·lete′

ob′sta·cle

ob·stet′ric

ob·stet′ri·cal

ob·ste·tri′cian

ob·stet′rics

ob′sti·na·cy

ob′sti·nate

ob′sti·nate·ly

ob·strep′er·ous

ob·struct′

ob·struc′tion

ob·struc′tion·ism

ob·struc′tion·ist

ob·struc′tive

ob·struc′tor

ob·tain′

ob·tain′able

ob·trude′

ob·tru′sion

ob·tru′sive

ob·tuse′

ob·verse′
　　adjective

ob′verse
　　noun

ob·vert′

ob′vi·ate

ob·vi·a′tion

ob′vi·ous

oc·a·ri′na

oc·ca′sion

oc·ca′sion·al

oc·ca′sion·al·ly

oc·ci·den′tal

oc·clude′

oc·clu′sion

oc·clu′sive

oc·cult′

oc·cul·ta′tion

oc′cu·pan·cy

oc′cu·pant

oc·cu·pa′tion

oc·cu·pa′tion·al

oc·cu·pa′tion·al·ly

oc′cu·pi·er

oc′cu·py

oc·cur′

oc·cur′rence

o′cean

oleomargarine

o'cean·go·ing
oce·an'ic
ocean·og'ra·pher
ocean·o·graph'ic
ocean·og'ra·phy
ocean·ol'o·gy
oc'e·lot
o'cher
or o'chre
o'clock'
oc'ta·gon
oc·tag'o·nal
oc·tag'o·nal·ly
oc'tane
oc'tave
oc·ta'vo
oc·tet'
Oc·to'ber
oc·to·ge·nar'i·an
oc'to·pod
oc'to·pus
oc·to·roon'
oc'u·lar
oc'u·list
odd'ball
odd'ity
odd'ly
odd'ment
odds-on
od'i·ous
od'i·um
odom'e·ter
od'or
od'or·ant
od'or·ous
od'ys·sey
oed'i·pal

Oed'i·pus
of'fal
off'beat
off'-col'or
or off'-col'ored
of·fend'
of·fend'er
of·fense'
or of·fence'
of·fen'sive
of'fer
of'fer·ing
of'fer·to·ry
off'hand
off'hand'ed
of'fice
of'fice·hold·er
of'fi·cer
of·fi'cial
of·fi'cial·dom
of·fi'cial·ly
of·fi'ci·ant
of·fi'ci·ate
of·fi·ci·a'tion
of·fi'cious
off'ing
off'ish
off'print
off'set
off'shoot
off·shore
off'spring
pl off'spring also
off'springs

off'stage
off-the-rec'ord
off-white

of'ten
of'ten·times
or oft'times
o'gle
o'gre
o'gre·ish
Ohi'o
ohm
ohm'me·ter
oil'cloth
oil'er
oil'i·ly
oil'i·ness
oil'seed
oil'skin
oil'stone
oil'y
oint'ment
OK
or okay'
OK'd
or okay'ed
OK'ing
or okay'ing
Okla·ho'ma
o'kra
old'en
old'-fash'ioned
old'ish
old-line
old'ster
old'-tim'er
old-world
ole·ag'i·nous
o'le·an·der
o'leo
oleo·mar'ga·rine

ol·fac'tion
ol·fac'to·ry
ol'i·garch
ol·i·gar'chic
  or ol·i·gar'chi·cal
ol'i·gar·chy
ol·i·gop'o·ly
ol'ive
Olym'pi·a
olym'pi·ad
Olym'pic
O'ma·ha
om'buds·man
  pl om'buds·men
ome'ga
om'e·let
  also om'e·lette
o'men
om'i·nous
omis'si·ble
omis'sion
omit
  omit'ted
  omit'ting
om'ni·bus
om·ni·di·rec'-
  tion·al
om·ni·fo'cal
om·nip'o·tence
om·nip'o·tent
om·ni·pres'ence
om·ni·pres'ent
om'ni·range
om·ni'science
om·ni'scient
om·niv'o·rous

once'-over
on'com·ing
one'ness
on'er·ous
one·self'
one'-shot
one'-sid'ed
one'time
one-to-one'
one'-track
one-up'man·ship
one-way
on'go·ing
on'ion
on'ion·skin
on-line
on'look·er
on'ly
on·o·mat·o·poe'ia
on·o·mat·o·poe'ic
  or
   on·o·mat·o·po·et'ic
on·o·mat·o·poe'i·
  cal·ly
  or
   on·o·mat·o·po·et'i·
   cal·ly
on'rush
on'set
on·shore
on'slaught
On·tar'io
on'to
o'nus
on'ward
  also on'wards

on'yx
oo'dles
ooz'y
opac'i·ty
o'pal
opal·es'cence
opal·es'cent
opaque'
opaque'ly
open-air'
open-and-shut'
open-end'
op'en·er
open-eyed'
open·hand'ed
open·heart'ed
o'pen-hearth
op'en·ing
open-mind'ed
open-mouthed'
o'pen·ness
o'pen·work
op'era
op'er·a·ble
op'er·a·bly
op'er·ate
op·er·at'ic
op·er·at'i·cal·ly
op·er·a'tion
op·er·a'tion·al
op'er·a·tive
op'er·a·tor
op·er·et'ta
oph·thal'mic
oph·thal·mol'o·
  gist

oph·thal·mol'o·gy
o'pi·ate
opin'ion
opin'ion·at·ed
o'pi·um
opos'sum
  pl opos'sums *also*
  opos'sum
op·po'nent
op·por·tune'
op·por·tune'ly
op·por·tun'ism
op·por·tun'ist
op·por·tu·nis'tic
op·por·tu'ni·ty
op·pose'
op'po·site
op·po·si'tion
op·press'
op·pres'sion
op·pres'sive
op·pres'sive·ly
op·pres'sor
op·pres·sion
op·pro'bri·ous
op·pro'bri·um
op'tic
op'ti·cal
op'ti·cal·ly
op·ti'cian
op'tics
op'ti·mal
op'ti·mal·ly
op'ti·mism
op'ti·mist
op·ti·mis'tic

op·ti·mis'ti·cal·ly
op'ti·mize
op'ti·mum
  pl op'ti·ma *also*
  op'ti·mums
op'tion
op'tion·al
op'tion·al·ly
op·to·met'ric
op·tom'e·trist
op·tom'e·try
op'u·lence
op'u·lent
o'pus
  pl o'pera *also*
  o'pus·es
or'a·cle
orac'u·lar
or'al
  spoken (see aural)
or'al·ly
or'ange
or·ange·ade'
orang'u·tan
  or orang'ou·tan
o'rate
ora'tion
or'a·tor
or·a·tor'i·cal
or·a·tor'i·cal·ly
or·a·to'rio
or'a·to·ry
or·bic'u·lar
or'bit
or'bit·al
or'chard

or'ches·tra
or·ches'tral
or'ches·trate
or·ches·tra'tion
or'chid
or·dain'
or·deal'
or'der
or'dered
or'der·li·ness
or'der·ly
or'di·nal
or'di·nance
  law (see ordnance)
or·di·nar'i·ly
or'di·nary
or'di·nate
or·di·na'tion
ord'nance
  military supplies
  (see ordinance)
or'dure
ore
  mineral (see oar)
öre
  pl öre
oreg'a·no
Or'e·gon
or'gan
or'gan·dy
  also or'gan·die
or·gan'ic
or·gan'i·cal·ly
or'ga·nism
or'gan·ist
or'ga·niz·able

or·ga·ni·za'tion
or·ga·ni·za'tion·al
or'ga·nize
or'ga·niz·er
or·gan'za
or'gasm
or·gi·as'tic
or·gi·as'ti·cal·ly
or'gu·lous
or'gy
or'i·el
or'i·ent
Or'i·en·tal
or'i·en·tate
ori·en·ta'tion
or'i·fice
or'i·flamme
ori·ga'mi
or'i·gin
orig'i·nal
orig·i·nal'i·ty
orig'i·nal·ly
orig'i·nate
orig·i·na'tion
orig'i·na·tor
or'i·ole
or'i·son
Or'lon
or'mo·lu
or'na·ment
or·na·men'tal
or·na·men·ta'tion
or·nate'
or·nate'ly
or'nery
or·ni·thol'o·gist

or·ni·thol'o·gy
orog'e·ny
or'o·tund
or'phan
or'phan·age
or'ris
or·tho·don'tics
or·tho·don'tist
or'tho·dox
or'tho·doxy
or·tho·graph'ic
or·thog'ra·phy
or·tho·pe'dic
or·tho·pe'dics
or·tho·pe'dist
os'cil·late
os·cil·la'tion
os'cil·la·tor
os·cil'la·to·ry
os·cil'lo·scope
os'cu·late
os·cu·la'tion
o'sier
os·mo'sis
os·mot'ic
os'prey
os·si·fi·ca'tion
os'si·fy
os'su·ary
os·ten'si·ble
os·ten'si·bly
os·ten·ta'tion
os·ten·ta'tious
os'te·o·path
os·te·o·path'ic
os·te·op'a·thy

os'tra·cism
os'tra·cize
os'trich
oth'er
oth'er·wise
oth'er·world
o'ti·ose
Ot'ta·wa
ot'ter
ot'to·man
our·selves'
oust'er
out'age
out-and-out'
out·bal'ance
out·bid'
  out·bid'
  out·bid'ding
out'board
out'bound
out'break
out'build·ing
out'burst
out'cast
out·class'
out'come
out'crop
out'cry
out·dat'ed
out·dis'tance
out·do'
out'door
out·doors'
out'draw'
out'er
out·er-di·rect'ed

out'er·most
out·face'
out'field
out'field·er
out·fight'
out'fit
  out·fit'ted
  out·fit'ting
out'fit·ter
out·flank'
out'flow
out·fox'
out·gen'er·al
  out·gen'er·aled
  or out·gen'er·alled
  out·gen'er·al·ing
  or out·gen'er·al·ling
out'go
out'go·ing
out·grow'
out'growth
out·guess'
out'house
out'ing
out·land'ish
out·last'
out'law
out'law·ry
out'lay
out'let
out'li·er
out'line
out·live'
out'look
out'ly·ing
out·ma·neu'ver

out·match'
out·mod'ed
out'most
out·num'ber
out-of-bounds'
out-of-date'
out-of-door'
  or out-of-doors'
out-of-the-way'
out'pa·tient
out'play'
out'point'
out'post
out·pour'
out·put
out·rage
out·ra'geous
out·rank'
ou·tré'
out·reach'
out·ride'
out'rid·er
out'rig·ger
out·right'
out·run'
out·sell'
out'set
out·shine'
out·side'
out·sid'er
out·sit'
out'size
out'skirts
out·smart'
out·spo'ken
out·spread

out·stand'ing
out'sta·tion
out·stay'
out·stretched'
out·strip'
out'ward
out'ward·ly
out·wear'
out·weigh'
out·wit'
  out·wit'ted
  out·wit'ting
out·work'
out·worn'
o'val
o'val·ly
ovar'i·an
ov'a·ry
ova'tion
ov'en
ov'en·bird
over·abun'dance
over·abun'dant
over·act'
over·ac'tive
over·age'
  adjective
ov'er·age
  noun
over·all'
o'ver·alls
o'ver·arm
over·awe'
over·bal'ance
over·bear'ing
over·bid'

over·blown'
o'ver·board
over·build'
over·bur'den
over·call'
over·cap'i·tal·ize
o'ver·cast
over·charge'
over·cloud'
o'ver·coat
over·come'
over·con'fi·dence
over·crowd'
over·do'
o'ver·dose
o'ver·draft
over·draw'
o'ver·dress
o'ver·drive
over·due'
over·em'pha·size
over·es'ti·mate
over·ex·pose'
over·ex·po'sure
over·ex·tend'
o'ver·flight
over·flow'
over·grow'
o'ver·hand
o'ver·hang
over·haul'
over·head'
over·head'
over·hear'
over·heat'
over·in·dulge'

over·in·dul'gence
over·joy'
o'ver·kill
o'ver·land
over·lap'
over·lay'
over·leap'
over·lie'
over·load'
over·long'
over·look'
o'ver·lord
o'ver·ly
over·match'
over·much'
over·night'
o'ver·pass
over·play'
over·pow'er
over·price'
over·print'
over·pro·tect'
over·rate'
over·reach'
over·ride'
over·rode'
over·rid'den
over·rid'ing
over·ripe'
over·rule'
over·run'
over·ran'
over·run'
over·run'ning
over·seas'
over·see'

over·saw'
over·seen'
over·see'ing
o'ver·seer
over·sell'
over·sold'
over·sel'ling
over·sen'si·tive
over·set'
over·sexed'
over·shad'ow
o'ver·shoe
over·shoot'
over·shot'
over·shoot'ing
o'ver·sight
over·sim·pli·fi·ca'-
tion
over·sim'pli·fy
over·size'
or over·sized'
over·sleep'
over·spend'
over·spent'
over·spend'ing
over·spread'
over·state'
over·state'ment
over·stay'
over·step'
over·strung'
over·stuffed'
over·sub·scribe'
over·sup·ply'
overt'
over·take'

over·took'
over·tak'en
over·tak'ing
over·tax'
over-the-count'er
over·throw'
over·threw'
over·thrown'
over·throw'ing
o'ver·time
o'ver·tone
over·train'
o'ver·trick
over·trump'
o'ver·ture
over·turn'
over·use'
over·ween'ing
over·weigh'
o'ver·weight
over·whelm'
over·wind'
over·wound'
also over·wind'ed
over·wind'ing
over·work'
over·write'
over·writ'ten
also over·writ'
over·writ'ing
over·wrought'
ovip'a·rous
o'void
ov'u·late
ov·u·la'tion
o'vule

o'vum
pl o'va
owe
owl'ish
own'er
ox
pl ox'en
ox'blood
ox'bow
ox'cart
ox'ford
ox·i·da'tion
ox'ide
ox·i·dize'
oxy·acet'y·lene
ox'y·gen
ox'y·gen·ate
ox·y·gen·a'tion
oys'ter
o'zone

P

pa·'an'ga
pl pa·'an'ga
pab'u·lum
pace'mak·er
pac'er
pach'y·derm
pach·ys·an'dra
pa·cif'ic
pac·i·fi·ca'tion
pac'i·fi·er
pac'i·fism
pac'i·fist
pac'i·fy

pack'age
pack'ag·er
pack'er
pack'et
pack'ing
pack'ing·house
pack'rat
pack'sack
pack'sad·dle
pack'thread
pact
pad
pad'ded
pad'ding
pad'ding
pad'dle
pad'dle·ball
pad'dock
pad'dy
pad'lock
pa'dre
pae'an
song (see peon)
pa'gan
pag'eant
pag'eant·ry
page'boy
pag'i·nate
pag·i·na'tion
pa·go'da
pail
bucket (see pale)
pail'ful
pain
hurt (see pane)
pain'ful

pain'ful·ly
pain'less
pains'tak·ing
paint'brush
paint'er
paint'ing
pair
  two (see pare, pear)
pai'sa
  pl pai'sa
pais'ley
pa·ja'mas
Pak·i·stan'
Pak·i·stan'i
pal'ace
pal'a·din
pal·an·quin'
pal'at·able
pal'at·ably
pal'a·tal
pal·a·tal·iza'tion
pal'ate
  roof of the mouth
    (see palette, pallet)
pa·la'tial
pal'a·tine
pa·lav'er
pale
  light (see pail)
pale'face
pa·le·og'ra·pher
pa·le·og'ra·phy
pa·leo·lith'ic
pa·le·on·tol'o·gist
pa·le·on·tol'o·gy

pal'ette
  painter's tablet (see
    palate, pallet)

pal'imp·sest
pal'in·drome
pal'ing
pal·i·sade'
pal·la'di·um
pall'bear·er
pal'let
  bed (see palate,
    palette)

pal'li·ate
pal'li·a·tive
pal'lid
pal'lor
pal'mate
pal·met'to
  pl pal·met'tos *or*
    pal·met'toes

palm'ist·ry
pal·o·mi'no
pal'pa·ble
pal'pa·bly
pal'pate
pal'pi·tate
pal·pi·ta'tion
pal'sied
pal'sy
pal'tri·ness
pal'try
pam'pa
  pl pam'pas
pam'per
pam'phlet

pam'phle·teer'
pan
  panned
  pan'ning
pan·a·ce'a
pa·nache'
Pan'a·ma
Pan·a·ma'ni·an
Pan-Amer'i·can
pan·a·tel'a
pan'cake
pan·chro·mat'ic
pan'cre·as
pan·cre·at'ic
pan'da
pan·dem'ic
pan·de·mo'ni·um
pan'der
pan'der·er
pan·dow'dy
pane
  glass (see pain)
pan·e·gyr'ic
pan·e·gyr'ist
pan'el
pan'el·ing
pan'el·ist
pan'fish
pan'han·dle
pan'han·dler
pan'ic
  pan'icked
  pan'ick·ing
  pan'icky
pan'i·cle

pan'ic-strick·en
pan·jan'drum
pan'nier
  or pan'ier
pan'o·plied
pan'o·ply
pan·o·ram'a
pan·o·ram'ic
pan'sy
pan·ta·loons'
pan'the·ism
pan'the·ist
pan·the·is'tic
pan'the·on
pan'ther
pant'ie
  or pant'y
pant'i·hose
  or pant'y·hose
pan·to·mime
pan·to·mim'ic
pan'try
pant'suit
pa'pa·cy
pa'pal
pa·paw'
pa·pa'ya
pa'per
pa'per·back
pa'per·hang·er
pa'per·weight
pa'pery
pa·pier-mâ·ché'
pa·pil'la
pap'il·lary

pap·il·lo'ma
  pl pap·il·lo'mas *or*
  pap·il·lo'ma·ta
pa·pil·lote'
pa·poose'
pa·pri'ka
pap'ule
pa·py'rus
pa'ra
par'a·ble
pa·rab'o·la
par·a·bol'ic
par'a·chute
par·a·chut'ist
pa·rade'
par'a·digm
par'a·dise
par·a·di·si'a·cal
par·a·di·si'a·cal·ly
par'a·dox
par·a·dox'i·cal
par·a·dox'i·cal·ly
par'af·fin
par'a·gon
par'a·graph
Par'a·guay
Par'a·guay·an
par'a·keet
par'al·lax
par'al·lel
par'al·lel·ism
par·al·lel'o·gram
pa·ral'y·sis
  pl pa·ral'y·ses
par·a·lyt'ic

par·a·ly·za'tion
par'a·lyze
par·a·me'cium
  pl par·a·me'cia *also*
  par·a·me'ciums
pa·ram'e·ter
  mathematics (*see*
  perimeter)
par'a·mount
par'a·mount·cy
par'a·mour
par·a·noi'a
par·a·noi'ac
par'a·noid
par'a·pet
par·a·pher·na'lia
par'a·phrase
par·a·ple'gia
par·a·ple'gic
para·psy·chol'o·gy
par'a·site
par·a·sit'ic
par·a·sit'i·cal·ly
par'a·sit·ism
par·a·si·tol'o·gist
par·a·si·tol'o·gy
par'a·sol
para·thy'roid
par'a·troop·er
par'a·troops
para·ty'phoid
par'boil
par'buck·le
par'cel
  par'celed
    or par'celled

par'cel·ing
  or par'cel·ling

parch'ment

par'don

par'don·able

par'don·ably

pare
  trim (see pair, pear)

par·e·gor'ic

par'ent

par'ent·age

pa·ren'tal

pa·ren'the·sis
  pl pa·ren'the·ses

pa·ren'the·size

par·en·thet'ic
  or par·en·thet'i·cal

par·en·thet'i·
  cal·ly

par'ent·hood

pa·re'sis
  pl pa·re'ses

par ex·cel·lence'

par·fait'

pa·ri'ah

pa·ri'e·tal

pari-mu'tu·el

par'ing

pa·ri pas'su

par'ish

pa·rish'io·ner

par'i·ty

par'ka

park'way

par'lance

par'lay
  bets (see parley)

par'ley
  discussion (see
  parlay)

par'lia·ment

par·lia·men·tar'
  i·an

par·lia·men'ta·ry

par'lor

Par'ma

Par'me·san

pa·ro'chi·al

pa·ro'chi·al·ly

par'o·dist

par'o·dy

pa·role'

pa·rol·ee'

par'ox·ysm

par·ox·ys'mal

par·quet'

par'que·try

par'ra·keet

par'ri·cide

par'rot

par'ry

parse

par'sec

par·si·mo'ni·ous

par'si·mo·ny

pars'ley

pars'nip

par'son

par'son·age

par·take'

par·took'

par·tak'en

par·tak'ing

par·tak'er

par·terre'

par·the·no·gen'e·
  sis

par'tial

par·tial'i·ty

par'tial·ly

part'ible

par·tic'i·pant

par·tic'i·pate

par·tic·i·pa'tion

par·tic'i·pa·tor

par·tic'i·pa·to·ry

par·ti·cip'i·al

par·ti·cip'i·al·ly

par'ti·ci·ple

par'ti·cle

par·ti·col'ored

par·tic'u·lar

par·tic·u·lar'i·ty

par·tic·u·lar·iza'
  tion

par·tic'u·lar·ize

par·tic'u·lar·ly

par·tic'u·late

part'ing

par'ti·san
  or par'ti·zan

par'ti·san·ship

par'tite

par·ti'tion

par'ti·tive

part′ly
part′ner
part′ner·ship
par′tridge
part′-song
part-time′
par·tu′ri·ent
par·tu·ri′tion
par′ty
par′ve·nu
par′y·lene
Pas·a·de′na
pa′sha
pass′able
pass′ably
pas′sage
pas′sage·way
pass′book
pas·sé′
passed
   pass (see past)

pas′sel
pas′sen·ger
passe-par·tout′
pass′er
pas·ser·by′
   pl pas·sers·by′

pas′ser·ine
pas′si·ble
pas′sim
pass′ing
pas′sion
pas′sion·ate
pas′sion·ate·ly
pas′sive

pas′sive·ly
pas·siv′i·ty
pass′key
Pass′over
pass′port
pass′word
past
   ago, beyond (see passed)

pas′ta
paste
paste′board
pas·tel′
pas′tern
pas·teur·iza′tion
pas′teur·ize
pas′teur·iz·er
pas·tiche′
pas·tille′
pas′time
past′i·ness
pas′tor
pas′to·ral
pas′tor·ate
pas·tra′mi
past′ry
pas′tur·age
pas′ture
past′y
pat
   pat′ted
   pat′ting
patch
patch′board
patch′work

pa·tel′la
   pl pa·tel′lae *or*
   pa·tel′las

pat′en
pa′tent
pat′ent·able
pat·en·tee′
pa·ter·fa·mil′i·as
pa·ter′nal
pa·ter′nal·ism
pa·ter·nal·is′tic
pa·ter′nal·ly
pa·ter′ni·ty
Pat′er·son
pa·thet′ic
pa·thet′i·cal·ly
path′find·er
path′o·gen
path·o·gen′ic
path·o·ge·nic′i·ty
path·o·log′i·cal
path·o·log′i·cal·ly
pa·thol′o·gist
pa·thol′o·gy
pa′thos
path′way
pa′tience
pa′tient
pat′i·na
pat′io
pa′tois
   pl pa′tois

pa′tri·arch
pa·tri·ar′chal
pa′tri·arch·ate

pa′tri·ar·chy
pa·tri′cian
pat′ri·cide
pat·ri·lin′e·al
pat′ri·mo·ny
pa′tri·ot
pa·tri·ot′ic
pa·tri·ot′i·cal·ly
pa′tri·o·tism
pa·tris′tic
pa·trol′
  pa·trolled′
  pa·trol′ling
pa·trol′man
pa′tron
pat′ron·age
pa′tron·ess
pa′tron·ize
pat·ro·nym′ic
pa·troon′
pat′sy
pat′ten
pat′ter
pat′tern
pat′ty
pau′ci·ty
paunch′i·ness
paunch′y
pau′per
pau′per·ize
pa·vane′
  also pa·van′
pave′ment
pa·vil′ion
pav′ing
pawn′bro·ker

pawn′shop
pay
  paid
    also payed
  pay′ing
pay′able
pay′check
pay·ee′
pay′load
pay′mas·ter
pay′ment
pay′off
pay′roll
pea
  pl peas, *also* pease
peace
  tranquillity (*see*
  piece)
peace′able
peace′ably
peace′ful
peace′ful·ly
peace′mak·er
peace′time
peach
pea′cock
pea′fowl
pea′hen
peak
  mountain (*see* peek,
  pique)
peal
  resound (*see* peel)
pea′nut
pear
  fruit (*see* pair, pare)

pearl
  gem (*see* purl)
pearl′y
pear′-shaped
peas′ant
peas′ant·ry
pea′shoot·er
peb′ble
peb′bly
pe·can′
pec·ca·dil′lo
  pl pec·ca·dil′loes *or*
  pec·ca·dil′los
pec′ca·ry
pec′tate
pec′tin
pec′to·ral
pec′u·late
pec·u·la′tion
pe·cu′liar
pe·cu·liar′i·ty
pe·cu′liar·ly
pe·cu′ni·ary
ped·a·gog′ic
ped·a·gog′i·cal·ly
ped′a·gogue
  also ped′a·gog
ped′a·gogy
ped′al
  ped′aled
    also ped′alled
  ped′al·ing
    also ped′al·ling
ped′ant
pe·dan′tic
pe·dan′ti·cal·ly

penny

ped'ant·ry
ped'dle
ped'dler
  or ped'lar

ped'er·ast
ped'er·as·ty
ped'es·tal
pe·des'tri·an
pe·di·at'ric
pe·di·a·tri'cian
pe·di·at'rics
pedi'cab
ped'i·cure
ped'i·gree
ped'i·greed
ped'i·ment
pe·dol'o·gist
pe·dol'o·gy
pe·dom'e·ter
pe'dun·cle
peek
  look (see peak,
    pique)

peel
  skin (see peal)

peel'ing
peen
  or pein

peep'hole
peer
  equal, look (see pier)

peer'age
peer'less
peeve
pee'vish
pee'wee

peg
  pegged
  peg'ging
pei·gnoir'
pe·jor'a·tive
Pe·king·ese'
pe'koe
pel'age
pe·lag'ic
pel'i·can
pel·lag'ra
pel'let
pell-mell
pel·lu'cid
pel'vic
pel'vis
  pl pel'vis·es *or*
    pel'ves
pem'mi·can
pen
  penned
  pen'ning
pe'nal
pe·nal·iza'tion
pe'nal·ize
pen'al·ty
pen'ance
pen'chant
pen'cil
  pen'ciled
    or pen'cilled
  pen'cil·ing
    or pen'cil·ling
pen'dant
  noun
pen'dent
  or pen'dant
  adjective

pend'ing
pen'du·lous
pen'du·lum
pe'ne·plain
  also pe'ne·plane

pen·e·tra·bil'i·ty
pen'e·tra·ble
pen'e·tra·bly
pen'e·trate
pen'e·trat·ing
pen·e·tra'tion
pen'e·tra·tive
pen'guin
pen'hold·er
pen·i·cil'lin
pen·in'su·la
  noun

pen·in'su·lar
  adjective

pe'nis
  pl pe'nes *or*
    pe'nis·es
pen'i·tence
pen'i·tent
pen·i·ten'tial
pen·i·ten'tial·ly
pen·i·ten'tia·ry
pen'knife
pen'man·ship
pen'nant
pen'ni
  pl pen'nis *or* pen'nia
pen'ni·less
pen'non
Penn·syl·va'nia
pen'ny
  pl pen'nies

pen′ny-pinch
pen′ny·weight
pen′ny·wise
pen′ny·wort
pe·no·log′i·cal
pe·nol′o·gist
pe·nol′o·gy
pen′sion
pen′sion·er
pen′sive
pen′sive·ly
pen′ta·cle
pen′ta·gon
pen·tag′o·nal
pen·tam′e·ter
pen·ta·ton′ic
Pen′te·cost
Pen·te·cos′tal
pent′house
pen·tom′ic
pe·nu′che
pen·ul′ti·mate
pen·um′bra
  pl pen·um′brae *or*
    pen·um′bras

pe·nu′ri·ous
pen′u·ry
pe′on
  laborer (see paean*)*
pe′on·age
pe′o·ny
peo′ple
  pl peo′ple
Pe·o′ria
pep
  pepped

pep′ping
pep′lum
pep′per
pep′per·box
pep′per·corn
pep′per·mint
pep′pery
pep′pi·ness
pep′py
pep′sin
pep′tic
pep′tone
per·am′bu·late
per·am·bu·la′tion
per·am′bu·la·tor
per an′num
per·cale′
per cap′i·ta
per·ceiv′able
per·ceiv′ably
per·ceive′
per·ceiv′able
per·cent′
  pl per·cent′ *or*
    per·cents′
per·cent′age
per·cen′tile
per′cept
per·cep·ti·bil′i·ty
per·cep′ti·ble
per·cep′ti·bly
per·cep′tion
per·cep′tive
per·cep′tu·al
per·cep′tu·al·ly
per·chance′

Per′che·ron
per·cip′i·ence
per·cip′i·ent
per′co·late
per·co·la′tion
per·co·la′tor
per·cus′sion
per·cus′sive
per di′em
per·di′tion
per·du·ra·bil′i·ty
per·du′ra·ble
per·du′ra·bly
per·e·gri·na′tion
pe·remp′to·ri·ly
pe·remp′to·ri·ness
pe·remp′to·ry
pe·ren′ni·al
pe·ren′ni·al·ly
per′fect
  adjective
per·fect′
  verb
per·fect·ibil′i·ty
per·fect′ible
per·fec′tion
per·fec′tion·ist
per·fec′to
per·fid′i·ous
per′fi·dy
per′fo·rate
per·fo·ra′tion
per′fo·ra·tor
per·force′
per·form′
per·form′able

persimmon

per·for'mance
per'fume
   noun
per·fume'
   verb
per·fum'ery
per·func·to'ri·ly
per·func'to·ri·
   ness
per·func'to·ry
per'go·la
per·haps'
peri·cyn'thi·on
per'i·gee
peri·he'lion
per'il
   per'illed
   per'il·ing
     also per'il·ling
per'il·ous
per'i·lune
pe·rim'e·ter
   boundary (see
     parameter)
pe'ri·od
pe·ri·od'ic
pe·ri·od'i·cal
pe·ri·od'i·cal·ly
pe·ri·od·ic'i·ty
peri·odon'tal
per·i·pa·tet'ic
pe·riph'er·al
pe·riph'er·al·ly
pe·riph'ery
pe·riph'ra·sis
   pl pe·riph'ra·ses
peri·phras'tic

pe·rique'
per'i·scope
peri·scop'ic
per'ish
per·ish·abil'i·ty
per'ish·able
per·i·stal'sis
   pl per·i·stal'ses
per·i·stal'tic
per'i·style
per·i·to·ni'tis
per'i·win·kle
per'jure
per'jur·er
per'ju·ry
perk'i·ly
perk'i·ness
perk'y
per'ma·frost
per'ma·nence
per'ma·nen·cy
per'ma·nent
per·man'ga·nate
per·me·a·bil'i·ty
per'me·a·ble
per'me·a·bly
per'me·ance
per'me·ate
per·me·a'tion
per·mis·si·bil'i·ty
per·mis'si·ble
per·mis'si·bly
per·mis'sion
per·mis'sive
per·mit'
   verb

per·mit'ted
per·mit'ting
per'mit
   noun
per·mu·ta'tion
per·mute'
per·ni'cious
per'orate
per·ora'tion
per·ox'ide
per·pen·dic'u·lar
per'pe·trate
per·pe·tra'tion
per'pe·tra·tor
per·pet'u·al
per·pet'u·al·ly
per·pet'u·ate
per·pet·u·a'tion
per·pet'u·a·tor
per·pe·tu'i·ty
per·plex'
per·plexed'
per·plex'ed·ly
per·plex'i·ty
per'quis·ite
   privilege (see
     prerequisite)

per se'
per'se·cute
per·se·cu'tion
per'se·cu·tor
per·se·ver'ance
per·se·vere'
Per'sian
per'si·flage
per·sim'mon

per·sist'
per·sis'tence
per·sis'ten·cy
per·sis'tent
per·snick'e·ty
per'son
per'son·able
per'son·age
per'son·al
   private (see personnel)
per·son·al'i·ty
per'son·al·ize
per'son·al·ly
per'son·al·ty
per·so·na non gra'ta
   pl per·so·nae non gra'tae *or* per·so·na non gra'ta
per'son·ate
per·son·i·fi·ca'tion
per·son'i·fi·er
per·son'i·fy
per·son·nel'
   employees (see personal)
per·spec'tive
per·spi·ca'cious
per·spi·cac'i·ty
per·spi·cu'i·ty
per·spic'u·ous
per·spi·ra'tion
per·spi·ra·to·ry
per·spire'
per·suad'able

per·suade'
per·sua'si·ble
per·sua'sion
per·sua'sive
per·tain'
per·ti·na'cious
per·ti·nac'i·ty
per'ti·nence
per'ti·nen·cy
per'ti·nent
pert'ly
pert'ness
per·turb'
per·tur·ba'tion
Pe·ru'
pe·rus'al
pe·ruse'
Pe·ru'vi·an
per·vade'
per·va'sive
per·verse'
per·verse'ly
per·ver'sion
per·ver'si·ty
per·ver'sive
per·vert'
   verb
per'vert
   noun
per'vi·ous
pe·se'ta
pe·se'wa
pes'ky
pe'so
pes'si·mism
pes'si·mist

pes·si·mis'tic
pes·si·mis'ti·cal·ly
pes'ter
pest'hole
pes'ti·cide
pes·tif'er·ous
pes'ti·lence
pes'ti·lent
pes·ti·len'tial
pes'tle
pet
   pet'ted
   pet'ting
pet'al
pe·tard'
pe'ter
pet'i·ole
pet'it
pe·tite'
pe·tit four'
   pl petits fours' *or* petit fours'
pe·ti'tion
pe·ti'tion·er
pet'rel
pet·ri·fac'tion
pet'ri·fy
pet·ro·chem'i·cal
pe·trog'ra·phy
pet'rol
pet·ro·la'tum
pe·tro'le·um
pet·ro·log'ic
pe·trol'o·gist
pe·trol'o·gy
pet'ti·coat

phonetic

pet'ti·fog
  pet'ti·fogged
  pet'ti·fog·ging
pet'ti·fog·ger
pet'ti·ly
pet'ti·ness
pet'tish
pet'ty
pet'u·lance
pet'u·lant
pe·tu'nia
pew'ter
pey·o'te
  or pey·ot'l

pfen'nig
pha'eton
phag'o·cyte
pha'lanx
  pl pha'lanx·es *or*
  pha·lan'ges

phal'a·rope
phal'lic
phal'lus
  pl phal'li *or*
  phal'lus·es

phan'tasm
phan·tas·ma·go'-
  ria
phan·tas·ma·go'-
  ric
phan'tom
phar'aoh
phar·i·sa'ic
phar·i·sa'ical
phar·i·sa'ical·ly
phar'i·see

phar·ma·ceu'tic
phar·ma·ceu'ti·cal
phar·ma·ceu'tics
phar'ma·cist
phar·ma·cog'no·sy
phar·ma·co·log'i·-
  cal
phar·ma·co·log'i·-
  cal·ly
phar·ma·col'o·gist
phar·ma·col'o·gy
phar·ma·co·poe'ia
phar'ma·cy
phar'os
pha·ryn'ge·al
phar'ynx
  pl pha·ryn'ges *also*
  phar'ynx·es

phase
  aspect (see faze)
phase'out
pheas'ant
phe·no·bar'bi·tal
phe'nol
phe·no'lic
phe·nom'e·nal
phe·nom'e·non
  pl phe·nom'e·na
phi'al
Phil·a·del'phia
phi·lan'der
phi·lan'der·er
phil·an·throp'ic
phil·an'thro·pist
phi·lan'thro·py
phil·a·tel'ic

phi·lat'e·list
phi·lat'e·ly
phil·har·mon'ic
phi·lip'pic
Phil'ip·pine
Phil'ip·pines
phil'is·tine
phil·o·den'dron
  pl phil·o·den'drons
  or phil·o·den'dra

phil·o·log'i·cal
phi·lol'o·gist
phi·lol'o·gy
phi·los'o·pher
phil·o·soph'ic
phil·o·soph'i·-
  cal·ly
phi·los'o·phize
phi·los'o·phy
phil'ter
  or phil'tre
  potion (see filter)

phle·bi'tis
phlegm
phleg·mat'ic
phleg·mat'i·cal·ly
phlox
  pl phlox *or* phlox'es

pho'bia
pho'bic
Phoe'nix
pho'neme
pho·ne'mic
pho·ne'mi·cal·ly
pho·ne'mics
pho·net'ic

pho·net′i·cal·ly
pho·ne·ti′cian
pho·net′ics
phon′ic
phon′i·cal·ly
phon′ics
pho′ni·ly
pho′ni·ness
pho′no·graph
pho·no·graph′ic
pho·no·log′i·cal
pho·no·log′i·cal·ly
pho·nol′o·gist
pho·nol′o·gy
pho′ny
phos′phate
phos·phat′ic
phos·pho·res′cence
phos·pho·res′cent
phos·phor′ic
phos′pho·rus
pho′to
pho′to·cell
pho·to·chro′mic
pho·to·chron′o·graph
pho·to·com·po·si′tion
pho′to·copy
pho·to·elec′tric
pho·to·elec′tron
pho·to·emis′sive
pho·to·en·grave′
pho·to·en·grav′ing
pho′to·flash

pho′to·flood
pho·to·gen′ic
pho′to·graph
pho·tog′ra·pher
pho·to·graph′ic
pho·to·graph′i·cal·ly
pho·tog′ra·phy
pho·to·gra·vure′
pho·to·lith′o·graph
pho·to·li·thog′ra·phy
pho′to·map
pho·tom′e·ter
pho·to·met′ric
pho·tom′e·try
pho·to·mi′cro·graph
pho·to·mu′ral
pho′ton
pho·to·off′set
pho′to·scan·ner
pho·to·sen′si·tive
pho·to·sen·si·ti·za′tion
pho′to·stat
pho·to·syn′the·sis
phra·se·ol′o·gy
phras′ing
phre·net′ic
phre·nol′o·gy
phy·lac′tery
phy·log′e·ny
phy′lum
pl phy′la

phys′ic
phys′i·cal
phys′i·cal·ly
phy·si′cian
phys′i·cist
phys′ics
phys·i·og′no·my
phys·i·o·graph′ic
phys·i·og′ra·phy
phys·i·o·log′i·cal
phys·i·o·log′i·cal·ly
phys·i·ol′o·gist
phys·i·ol′o·gy
phys·io·ther′a·py
phy·sique′
phy·to·gen′ic
pi
 mathematics (see pie)
pi
 jumble type (see pie)
pied
pi′ing
pi·a·nis′si·mo
pi·an′ist
pi·an′o
 also pi·an′o·forte
pi·as′ter
pi·az′za
pi′ca
pic·a·resque′
pic·a·yune′
pic·ca·lil′li
pic′co·lo

pice
pl pice

pick'ax
or pick'axe

pick'er·el

pick'et

pick'ings

pick'le

pick'pock·et

pick'up

pick'y

pic'nic
pic'nicked
pic'nick·ing
pic'nick·er

pi'cot

pic'to·graph

pic·to'ri·al

pic·to'ri·al·ly

pic'ture

pic·tur·esque'

pid'dle

pid'dling

pid'gin

pie
pastry (see pi)

pie'bald

piece
fragment (see
peace)

pièce de ré·sis·
tance'

piece'-dye

piece'meal

piece'work

piece'work·er

pied-à-terre'

pied'mont

pier
landing (see peer)

pierce

Pierre

pi·etism

pi'ety

pi'geon

pi'geon·hole

pi·geon-toed'

pig'gish

pig'gy·back

pig'head'ed

pig'ment

pig·men·ta'tion

pig'pen

pig'skin

pig'sty

pig'tail

pik'er

pi'las·ter

pil'chard

pil'fer

pil'fer·age

pil'fer·er

pil'grim

pil'grim·age

pil'ing

pil'lage

pil'lar

pill'box

pil'lion

pil'lo·ry

pil'low

pil'low·case

pi'lot

pi'lot·age

pi'lot·house

pil'sner
also pil'sen·er

pi'ma

pi·men'to

pim'per·nel

pim'ple

pim'pled

pim'ply

pin
pinned
pin'ning

pin'afore

pi·ña'ta
or pi·na'ta

pin'ball

pince-nez'

pin'cer

pinch'cock

pinch-hit'
pinch-hit'
pinch-hit'ting

pin'cush·ion

pine'ap·ple

pine'wood

pin'feath·er

pin'fish

Ping'-Pong

pin'head

pin'hole

pin'ion

pink'eye

pin'kie
or pin'ky

pin'nace
pin'na·cle
pin'nate
pi'noch·le
pi'ñon
pin'point
pin'prick
pin'set·ter
pin'stripe
pin'-striped
pin'to
  pl pin'tos also
  pin'toes
pint'-size
  or pint'-sized
pin'up
pin'wale
pin'wheel
pin'work
pin'worm
pi·o·neer'
pi'ous
pipe'ful
pipe'line
pip'er
pi·pette'
  also pi·pet'
pip'ing
pip'pin
pip'-squeak
pi'quan·cy
pi'quant
pique
  resentment (see
  peak, peek)
pi·qué'
  or pi'que
  fabric

pi'ra·cy
pi'rate
pi·rat'i·cal
pi·rat'i·cal·ly
pir·ou·ette'
pis·ca·to'ri·al
pis·mire
pis·tach'io
pis'til
  flower part (see
  pistol)
pis'til·late
pis'tol
  handgun (see pistil)
pis'tol-whip
  pis'tol-whipped
  pis'tol-whip·
  ping
pis'ton
pit
  pit'ted
  pit'ting
pit-a-pat'
pitch
pitch-black
pitch'blende
pitch-dark
pitch'er
pitch'fork
pitch'man
pitch'out
pit'e·ous
pit'fall
pit'head
pith·ec·an'thro·
  pus

pith'i·ly
pith'i·ness
pith'y
pit'i·able
pit'i·ably
pit'i·ful
pit'i·ful·ly
pit'i·less
pi'ton
pit'tance
pit'ted
pit'ter-pat·ter
Pitts'burg
  Calif., Kans.
Pitts'burgh
  Penna.
pi·tu'i·tary
pit'y
pit'y·ing
piv'ot
piv'ot·al
pix'ie
  or pix'y
pix'ie·ish
piz'za
piz·ze·ri'a
piz·zi·ca'to
pla·ca·bil'i·ty
plac'a·ble
plac'a·bly
plac'ard
pla'cate
pla·ce'bo
place'ment
pla·cen'ta
pla·cen'tal

pleasurable

plac′er
plac′id
pla·cid′i·ty
plack′et
pla′gia·rism
pla′gia·rist
pla′gia·rize
plague
plain
  clear (see plane)
plain′clothes′man
plain′ly
plain′ness
plain′spo′ken
plaint
plain′tiff
plain′tive
plain′tive·ly
plait
  pleat (see plate)
plan
  planned
  plan′ning
plane
  level (see plain)
plane′side
plan′et
plan·e·tar′i·um *n*
plan·e·tary
plan·e·tes′i·mal
plan·e·toid
plan·e·tol′o·gy
plan′gen·cy
plan′gent
plank′ing
plank′ton

plan′ner
plan′tain
plan·ta′tion
plant′er
plaque
plas′ma
plas′ter
plas′ter·board
plas′ter·er
plas′tic
plas′ti·cal·ly
plas·tic′i·ty
plas′ti·cize
plat
  plat′ted
  plat′ting
plate
  dish (see plait)
pla·teau′
  pl pla·teaus′ *or*
  pla·teaux′
plate′ful
plat′en
plat′form
plat′ing
plat′i·num
plat′i·tude
plat·i·tu′di·nous
pla·ton′ic
pla·ton′i·cal·ly
pla·toon′
plat′ter
plat′y·pus
plau′dit
plau·si·bil′i·ty
plau′si·ble

plau′si·bly
pla′ya
play′able
play′act·ing
play′back
play′bill
play′book
play′boy
play′-by-play′
play′er
play′ful
play′ful·ly
play′ful·ness
play′go·er
play′ground
play′house
play′land
play′mate
play′-off
play′pen
play′room
play′suit
play′thing
play′wright
pla′za
plea
plead
  plead′ed
   or pled
  plead′ing
plead′er
pleas′ant
pleas′ant·ry
please
pleas′ing
plea′sur·able

plea′sur·ably
plea′sure
ple·be′ian
pleb′i·scite
plec′trum
  pl plec′tra
pledge
ple′na·ry
pleni·po·ten′tia·ry
plen′i·tude
  or plent′i·tude
plen′te·ous
plen′ti·ful
plen′ti·ful·ly
plen′ty
ple′num
  pl ple′nums *or*
  ple′na
pleth′o·ra
pleu′ri·sy
plex′us
pli·abil′i·ty
pli′a·ble
pli′ably
pli′an·cy
pli′ant
pli′ers
plight
plis·sé′
  or plis·se′
plod
  plod′ded
  plod′ding
plod′der
plop
  plopped

plop′ping
plot
  plot′ted
  plot′ting
plot′ter
plov′er
  pl plov′er *or* plov′ers
plow
  or plough
plow′boy
plow′share
pluck′i·ly
pluck′i·ness
pluck′y
plug
  plugged
  plug′ging
plum
  fruit (*see* plumb)
plum′age
plumb
  weight (*see* plum)
plumb′er
plumb′ing
plum′met
plump′ish
plump′ness
plun′der
plun′der·er
plunge
plung′er
plu·per′fect
plu′ral
plu′ral·ism
plu·ral·is′tic
plu·ral′i·ty

plu·ral·iza′tion
plu′ral·ize
plush′ly
plush′y
plu·toc′ra·cy
plu′to·crat
plu·to·crat′ic
plu·to·crat′i·cal·ly
plu·to′ni·um
plu′vi·al
ply
plied
ply′ing
ply′wood
pneu·mat′ic
pneu·mo′nia
poach′er
po′chard
pock′et
pock′et·book
pock′et·ful
pock′et·knife
pock′mark
po·co a po′co
po·co′sin
po·di′a·trist
po·di′a·try
po′di·um
  pl po′di·ums *or*
  po′dia
po′em
po′esy
po′et
po′et·ess
po·et′ic
  or po·et′i·cal

po·et'i·cal·ly
po'etry
po·grom'
poi'gnan·cy
poi'gnant
poin·ci·an'a
poin·set'tia
point-blank
point'ed
point'ed·ly
point'er
poin'til·ism
poin'til·ist
point'less
poi'son
poi'son·ous
pok'er
pok'y
  or pok'ey
Po'land
po'lar
Po·lar'is
po·lar'i·ty
po·lar·i·za'tion
po'lar·ize
Po'lar·oid
pol'der
pole
  staff (see poll)
pole'ax
pole'cat
po·lem'ic
po·lem'i·cal
po·lem'i·cal·ly
po·lem'i·cist
pole'star

po·lice'
po·lice'man
poli·clin'ic
  outpatient
  dispensary (see
  polyclinic)

pol'i·cy
pol'i·cy·hold·er
po'lio
po·lio·my·e·li'tis
Pol'ish
pol'ish
po·lite'
po·lite'ly
po·lite'ness
po·li·tesse'
po·lit'ic
po·lit'i·cal
po·lit'i·cal·ly
pol·i·ti'cian
pol'i·tick
po·lit'i·co
  pl po·lit'i·cos *also*
  po·lit'i·coes

pol'i·tics
pol'i·ty
pol'ka
poll
  survey (see pole)

pol'lack
  or pol'lock

pol'len
pol'li·nate
pol·li·na'tion
pol·li·na'tor
pol'li·nize

pol'li·wog
  or pol'ly·wog

poll'ster
pol·lu'tant
pol·lute'
pol·lut'er
pol·lu'tion
po'lo
po·lo·naise'
pol'ter·geist
pol·troon'
poly·an'drous
pol'y·an·dry
poly·clin'ic
  hospital (see
  policlinic)

pol'y·es·ter
poly·eth'yl·ene
po·lyg'a·mous
po·lyg'a·my
pol'y·glot
pol'y·gon
po·lyg'o·nal
pol'y·graph
pol'y·mer
pol·y·mer'ic
po·lym·er·iza'tion
Pol·y·ne'sian
poly·no'mi·al
pol'yp
poly·phon'ic
po·lyph'o·ny
poly·sty'rene
poly·syl·lab'ic
poly·syl·la·ble
poly·tech'nic

pol'y·the·ism
poly·the·is'tic
poly·un·sat'u·rate
poly·un·sat'u·
  rat·ed
po·made'
pome'gran·ate
pom'mel
  pom'meled
    or pom'melled
  pom'mel·ing
    or pom'mel·ling
pom'pa·dour
pom'pa·no
pom'pon
pom·pos'i·ty
pomp'ous
Pon'ce
pon'cho
pon'der
pon'der·a·ble
pon'der·ous
pon·gee'
pon'iard
pon'tiff
pon·tif'i·cal
pon·tif'i·cal·ly
pon·tif'i·cate
pon·toon'
po'ny
po'ny·tail
poo'dle
pooh'-pooh
pool'room
poor'house
poor'ly
pop

popped
  pop'ping
pop'corn
pop'eyed
pop'gun
pop'in·jay
pop'lar
pop'lin
pop'-off
pop'over
pop'py
pop'py·cock
pop'u·lace
  masses (see
    populous)

pop'u·lar
pop·u·lar'i·ty
pop·u·lar·iza'tion
pop·u·lar·ize
pop·u·lar·iz·er
pop'u·lar·ly
pop'u·late
pop·u·la'tion
pop'u·lous
  crowded (see
    populace)

pop'-up
por'ce·lain
por'ce·lain·ize
por'cine
por'cu·pine
pore
  ponder (see pour)
pork'er
por·nog'ra·pher
por·no·graph'ic
por·nog'ra·phy

po·ro·mer'ic
po·ros'i·ty
po'rous
por'phy·ry
por'poise
por'ridge
por'rin·ger
por·ta·bil'i·ty
por'ta·ble
por'ta·bly
por'tage
por'tal
portal-to-portal
port·cul'lis
porte co·chere'
por·tend'
por'tent
por·ten'tous
por'ter
por'ter·house
port·fo'lio
port'hole
por'ti·co
  pl por'ti·coes *or*
    por'ti·cos

por·ti·ere'
por'tion
Port'land
port'li·ness
port'ly
port·man'teau
  pl port·man'teaus *or*
    port·man'teaux

por'trait
por'trait·ist
por'trai·ture
por·tray'

por-tray′al
Ports′mouth
Por′tu-gal
Por-tu-guese′
  pl Por-tu-guese′

pos′er
  one who poses (see
  poseur)

po-seur′
  affected person (see
  poser)

pos′it
po-si′tion
pos′i-tive
pos′i-tive-ly
pos′i-tiv-ism
pos′i-tron
pos′se
pos-sess′
pos-sessed′
pos-ses′sion
pos-ses′sive
pos-ses′sor
pos-si-bil′i-ty
pos′si-ble
pos′si-bly
pos′sum
post′age
post′al
post′box
post′card
post-clas′si-cal
post-con-so-nan′
  tal
post-date′
post-di-lu′vi-an
post-doc′tor-al

post′er
pos-te′ri-or
pos-ter′i-ty
post-grad′u-ate
post-haste
post-hole
post′hu-mous
post-hyp-not′ic
pos-til′ion
  or pos-til′lion

post′lude
post′man
post′mark
post′mas-ter
post me-ri′di-em
post′mis-tress
post-mor′tem
post-na′sal
post-na′tal
post-op′er-a-tive
post-paid
post-par′tum
post-pone′
post-pone′ment
post′script
pos′tu-lant
pos′tu-late
pos-tu-la′tion
pos′tu-la-tor
pos′ture
post-war
po′sy
pot
  pot′ted
  pot′ting
po′ta-ble
pot′ash

po-ta′tion
po-ta′to
  pl po-ta′toes
pot′bel-lied
pot′bel-ly
pot′boil-er
po′ten-cy
po′tent
po′ten-tate
po-ten′tial
po-ten-ti-al′i-ty
po-ten′tial-ly
pot′ful
poth′er
pot′herb
pot′hole
pot′hook
po′tion
pot′latch
pot′luck
pot-pie
pot-pour-ri′
pot′sherd
pot′shot
pot′tage
pot′ter
pot′tery
pou′chy
poul′tice
poul′try
poul′try-man
pounce
pound′-fool′ish
pour
  flow (see pore)
pour-par-ler′
pout

pov′er·ty
pov′er·ty-
  strick·en
pow′der
pow′dery
pow′er
pow′er·ful
pow′er·ful·ly
pow′er·house
pow′er·less
pow′wow
pox
prac·ti·ca·bil′i·ty
prac′ti·ca·ble
prac′ti·ca·bly
prac′ti·cal
prac′ti·cal′i·ty
prac′ti·cal·ly
prac′tice
  or prac′tise
prac′ticed
  or prac′tised
prac′tic·er
prac·ti′tion·er
prae·to′ri·an
prag·mat′ic
prag·mat′i·cal·ly
prag′ma·tism
prag′ma·tist
prai′rie
praise′wor·thy
pra′line
prance
pranc′er
prank′ster
prat′fall

pra·tique′
prat′tle
pray
  entreat (see prey)
prayer′ful
prayer′ful·ly
preach′er
preach′ment
pre·ad·o·les′cence
pre·ad·o·les′cent
pre′am·ble
pre·ar·range′
pre·ar·range′
  ment
pre·as·signed′
pre·can′cel
pre·can·cel·la′tion
pre·car′i·ous
pre·cau′tion
pre·cau′tion·ary
pre·cede′
prec′e·dence
  ranking ahead of
pre·ced′ent
  prior
prec′e·dent
  example
pre·ced′ing
  foregoing
pre′cept
pre·cep′tor
pre′cinct
pre·ci·os′i·ty
pre′cious
prec′i·pice
pre·cip′i·tan·cy

pre·cip′i·tate
pre·cip′i·tate·ly
pre·cip′i·ta′tion
pre·cip′i·tous
pré·cis′
  pl pré·cis′
  summary (see
   precise)

pre·cise′
  definite (see précis)

pre·cise′ly
pre·ci′sion
pre·clude′
pre·clu′sive
pre·co′cious
pre·coc′i·ty
pre·con·ceive′
pre·con·cep′tion
pre·con·cert′ed
pre·con·di′tion
pre·cook
pre·cur′sor
pre·da′cious
  or pre·da′ceous
pre·dac′i·ty
pre·date
pred′a·tor
pred·a·to′ri·ly
pred′a·to·ry
pre·de·cease′
pred′e·ces·sor
pre·des′ig·nate
pre·des·ig·na′tion
pre·des·ti·na′tion
pre·des′tine
pre·de·ter′mine

pred′i·ca·ble
pre·dic′a·ment
pred′i·cate
pred·i·ca′tion
pre·dict′
pre·dict·abil′i·ty
pre·dict′able
pre·dict′ably
pre·dic′tion
pre·di·gest′
pre·di·ges′tion
pred·i·lec′tion
pre·dis·pose′
pre·dis·po·si′tion
pre·dom′i·nance
pre·dom′i·nant
pre·dom′i·nate
pre·em′i·nence
pre·em′i·nent
pre·empt′
pre·emp′tion
pre·emp′tive
pre·emp′tor
pre·ex·ist′
pre·ex·is′tence
pre·ex·is′tent
pre·fab
pre·fab′ri·cate
pre·fab·ri·ca′tion
pref′ace
pref′a·to·ry
pre′fect
pre′fec·ture
pre·fer′
pre·ferred′
pre·fer′ring

pref·er·a·bil′i·ty
pref′er·a·ble
pref′er·a·bly
pref′er·ence
pref·er·en′tial
pre·fer′ment
pre·fig·u·ra′tion
pre·fig′u·ra·tive
pre·fig′ure
pre′fix
pre·flight
pre·form
preg′nan·cy
preg′nant
pre·heat
pre·hen′sile
pre·his·tor′ic
pre·judge
prej′u·dice
prej·u·di′cial
prel′a·cy
prel′ate
pre·lim′i·nary
prel′ude
pre·ma·ture′
pre·ma·ture′ly
pre·med
pre·med′i·cal
pre·med′i·tate
pre·med·i·ta′tion
pre·mier′
    chief (see premiere)
pre·miere′
    first performance
    (see premier)
prem′ise

pre′mi·um
pre·mix
pre·mo·ni′tion
pre·mon′i·to·ry
pre·na′tal
pre·oc′cu·pan·cy
pre·oc·cu·pa′tion
pre·oc′cu·pied
pre·oc′cu·py
pre·op′er·a·tive
pre·or·dain′
prep·a·ra′tion
pre·par′a·to·ry
pre·pare′
pre·par′ed·ness
pre·pay
pre·pon′der·ance
pre·pon′der·ant
pre·pon′der·ate
prep·o·si′tion
prep·o·si′tion·al
pre·pos·sess′
pre·pos·sess′ing
pre·pos·ses′sion
pre·pos′ter·ous
pre′puce
pre·re·cord′
pre·req′ui·site
    required beforehand
    (see perquisite)

pre·rog′a·tive
pres′age
pres′by·ter
Pres·by·te′ri·an
pres′by·tery
pre′school

pre′science
pre′sci·ent
pre·scribe′
    direct (see
        proscribe)

pre·scrip′tion
pre·scrip′tive
pre·sell′
pres′ence
pres′ent
    noun

pre·sent′
    verb
pre·sent·abil′i·ty
pre·sent′able
pre·sent′ably
pre·sen·ta′tion
pres·ent-day′
pre·sen′ti·ment
    premonition (see
        presentment)

pres′ent·ly
pre·sent′ment
    presentation (see
        presentiment)

pre·serv′able
pres·er·va′tion
pre·ser′va·tive
pre·serve′
pre·serv′er
pre·set
pre·shrunk
pre·side′
pres′i·den·cy
pres′i·dent
pres·i·den′tial

pre·si′dio
pre·sid′i·um
    pl pre·sid′ia or
        pre·sid′i·ums

pre·sig′ni·fy
pre·sort
press′er
press′ing
press′man
press′room
press′run
pres′sure
pres·sur·iza′tion
pres′sur·ize
press′work
pres·ti·dig·i·ta′·
    tion
pres·ti·dig′i·ta·tor
pres·tige′
pres·ti′gious
pres·tis′si·mo
pres′to
pre·stress′
pre·sum′able
pre·sum′ably
pre·sume′
pre·sump′tion
pre·sump′tive
pre·sump′tu·ous
pre·sup·pose′
pre·sup·po·si′tion
pre·tend′
pre·tend′er
pre′tense
    or pre′tence
pre·ten′sion

pre·ten′tious
pre·ten′tious·ness
pret′er·it
    or pret′er·ite
pre·ter·nat′u·ral
pre·ter·nat′u·
    ral·ly
pre′test
pre′text
pret′ti·fy
pret′ti·ly
pret′ti·ness
pret′ty
pret′zel
pre·vail′
pre·vail′ing
prev′a·lence
prev′a·lent
prev′a·lence
pre·var′i·cate
pre·var·i·ca′tion
pre·var′i·ca·tor
pre·vent′
pre·vent·abil′i·ty
pre·vent′able
pre·ven′ta·tive
pre·ven′tion
pre·ven′tive
pre′view
pre′vi·ous
pre·vi′sion
pre·war
prey
    victim (see pray)

price′-cut·ting
price′less

proctology

prick'le
prick'li·ness
prick'ly
pride'ful
pride'ful·ly
prie-dieu'
   pl prie-dieux'
priest'ess
priest'hood
priest'ly
prig'gish
pri'ma·cy
prima don'na
pri·ma fa'cie
pri'mal
pri·mar'i·ly
pri'ma·ry
pri'mate
prim'er
pri·me'val
prim'i·tive
pri·mo·gen'i·tor
pri·mo·gen'i·ture
pri·mor'di·al
prim'rose
Prince Ed·ward
  Is·land
prince'ly
prin'cess
prin'ci·pal
  chief (see principle)
prin·ci·pal'i·ty
prin'ci·pal·ly
prin'ci·ple
  fundamental law
  (see principal)

prin'ci·pled
print'able
print'er
print'ing
print'out
pri'or
pri'or·ess
pri·or'i·ty
pri'o·ry
prism
pris·mat'ic
pris'on
pris'on·er
pris'si·ness
pris'sy
pris'tine
pri'va·cy
pri'vate
pri·va·teer'
pri'vate·ly
pri·va'tion
priv'et
priv'i·lege
priv'i·leged
priv'y
prize'fight
prize'win·ner
prob·a·bil'i·ty
prob'a·ble
prob'a·bly
pro'bate
pro·ba'tion
pro·ba'tion·ary
pro·ba'tion·er
pro'ba·tive
pro'ba·to·ry

pro'bi·ty
prob'lem
prob·lem·at'ic
prob·lem·at'i·cal
prob·lem·at'i·
  cal·ly
pro·bos'cis
  pl pro·bos'cises *also*
  pro·bos'ci·des
pro·ca·the'dral
pro·ce'dur·al
pro·ce'dur·al·ly
pro·ce'dure
pro·ceed'
pro·ceed'ing
pro'ceeds
pro'cess
pro·ces'sion
pro·ces'sion·al
pro·cès-ver·bal'
  pl pro·cès-ver·baux'
pro·claim'
proc·la·ma'tion
pro·cliv'i·ty
pro·con'sul
pro·cras'ti·nate
pro·cras·ti·na'tion
pro·cras'ti·na·tor
pro'cre·ant
pro'cre·ate
pro·cre·a'tion
pro'cre·ative
pro'cre·ator
pro·crus'te·an
proc·tol'o·gist
proc·tol'o·gy

proc'tor
proc·to'ri·al
pro·cur'able
proc'u·ra·tor
pro·cure'
pro·cure'ment
pro·cur'er
prod
  prod'ded
  prod'ding
prod'i·gal
prod·i·gal'i·ty
prod'i·gal·ly
pro·di'gious
prod'i·gy
pro·duce'
  verb
prod'uce
  noun
pro·duc'er
prod'uct
pro·duc'tion
pro·duc'tive
pro·duc·tiv'i·ty
prof·a·na'tion
pro·fan'a·to·ry
pro·fane'
pro·fane'ly
pro·fan'i·ty
pro·fess'
pro·fessed'
pro·fess'ed·ly
pro·fes'sion
pro·fes'sion·al
pro·fes'sion·al·
  ism

pro·fes'sion·al·ize
pro·fes'sion·al·ly
pro·fes'sor
pro·fes·so'ri·al
pro·fes'sor·ship
prof'fer
pro·fi'cien·cy
pro·fi'cient
pro'file
prof'it
  gain (see prophet)
prof·it·abil'i·ty
prof'it·able
prof'it·ably
prof·i·teer'
prof'li·ga·cy
prof'li·gate
pro for'ma
pro·found'
pro·fun'di·ty
pro·fuse'
pro·fuse'ly
pro·fu'sion
pro·gen'i·tor
prog'e·ny
prog'na·thous
prog·no'sis
  pl prog·no'ses
prog·nos'tic
prog·nos'ti·cate
prog·nos·ti·ca'tion
prog·nos'ti·ca·tor
pro'gram
  or pro'gramme

pro'grammed
  or pro'gramed

pro'gram·ming
  or pro'gram·ing

pro'gram·ma·ble
  or pro'gram·able

pro·gram·mat'ic
pro'grammed
  or pro'gramed

pro'gram·mer
  or pro'gram·er

pro'gram·ming
  or pro'gram·ing

prog'ress
  noun

pro·gress'
  verb

pro·gres'sion
pro·gres'sive
pro·gres'sive·ly
pro·hib'it
pro·hi·bi'tion
pro·hi·bi'tion·ist
pro·hib'i·tive
pro·hib'i·to·ry
proj'ect
  noun

pro·ject'
  verb

pro·ject'able
pro·jec'tile
pro·jec'tion
pro·jec'tion·ist
pro·jec'tive
pro·jec'tor
pro·le·gom'e·non
  pl pro·le·gom'e·na
pro·le·tar'i·an

pro·le·tar·i·an·iza'·
  tion
pro·le·tar'i·an·ize
pro·le·tar'i·at
pro·lif'er·ate
pro·lif·er·a'tion
pro·lif'ic
pro·lif'i·cal·ly
pro·lix'
pro·lix'i·ty
pro·loc'u·tor
pro'logue
pro·long'
pro·lon'gate
pro·lon·ga'tion
prom·e·nade'
prom'i·nence
prom'i·nent
prom·is·cu'i·ty
pro·mis'cu·ous
prom'ise
prom'is·ing
prom'is·so·ry
prom'on·to·ry
pro·mote'
pro·mot'er
pro·mo'tion
pro·mo'tion·al
prompt'er
promp'ti·tude
prompt'book
prompt'ly
prom'ul·gate
prom·ul·ga'tion
prone'ness
pro'noun

pro·nounce'
pro·nounce'able
pro·nounced'
pro·nounce'ment
pron'to
pro·nun·ci·a·
  men'to
  pl pro·nun·ci·a·men'
  tos *or* pro·nun·ci·
  a·men'toes

pro·nun·ci·a'tion
proof'read
proof'read·er
prop
  propped
  prop'ping
prop·a·gan'da
prop·a·gan'dist
prop·a·gan'dize
prop'a·gate
prop·a·ga'tion
pro'pane
pro·pel'
  pro·pelled'
  pro·pel'ling
pro·pel'lant
  also pro·pel'lent
pro·pel'ler
pro·pen'si·ty
prop'er
prop'er·tied
prop'er·ty
proph'e·cy
  noun, prediction
  (*see* prophesy)
proph'e·si·er

proph'e·sy
  verb, to predict
proph'et
  predictor (*see* profit)
proph'et·ess
proph·et'ic
pro·phet'i·cal·ly
pro·phy·lac'tic
pro·phy·lax'is
  pl pro·phy·lax'es
pro·pin'qui·ty
pro·pi'tia·ble
pro·pi'ti·ate
pro·pi·ti·a'tion
pro·pi'tia·to·ry
pro·pi'tious
prop·jet
prop'man
pro·po'nent
pro·por'tion
pro·por'tion·able
pro·por'tion·ably
pro·por'tion·al
pro·por'tion·al·ly
pro·por'tion·ate
pro·por'tion·ate·ly
pro·pos'al
pro·pose'
pro·pos'er
prop·o·si'tion
pro·pound'
pro·pri'e·tary
pro·pri'e·tor
pro·pri'e·tress
pro·pri'e·ty
pro·pul'sion

pro·pul'sive
pro ra'ta
pro·rate'
pro·ro·ga'tion
pro·rogue'
pro·sa'ic
pro·sa'i·cal·ly
pro·sce'ni·um
pro·scribe'
  prohibit (see
  prescribe)

pro·scrib'er
pro·scrip'tion
pro·scrip'tive
pros'e·cut·able
pros·e·cute
pros·e·cu'tion
pros'e·cu·tor
pros'e·lyte
pros'e·lyt·ism
pros'e·ly·tize
pro·sem'i·nar
pros'o·dy
pros'pect
pro·spec'tive
pro·spec'tive·ly
pros'pec·tor
pro·spec'tus
pros'per
pros·per'i·ty
pros'per·ous
pros'tate
  gland (see prostrate)
pros·the'sis
  pl pros·the'ses
pros·thet'ic

pros'ti·tute
pros·ti·tu'tion
pros'trate
  helpless (see
  prostate)
pros·tra'tion
pros'y
pro·tag'o·nist
pro'te·an
pro·tect'
pro·tec'tion
pro·tec'tion·ism
pro·tec'tion·ist
pro·tec'tive
pro·tec'tor
pro·tec'tor·ate
pro·tec'tress
pro'té·gé
  masc.
pro'té·gée
  fem.
pro'tein
pro tem'
pro tem'po·re
pro'test
  noun
pro·test'
  verb
Prot'es·tant
prot·es·ta'tion
pro·tho·no·tar'i·al
pro·tho'no·ta·ry
pro'to·col
pro·to·his'to·ry
pro'ton
pro'to·plasm
pro'to·type

pro·to·zo'an
pro·tract'
pro·trac'tion
pro·trac'tor
pro·trude'
pro·tru'sion
pro·tu'ber·ance
pro·tu'ber·ant
proud'ly
prov'able
prov'ably
prove
  proved
  proved
    or prov'en
  prov'ing
prov'e·nance
prov'en·der
pro·ve'nience
prov'erb
pro·ver'bi·al
pro·ver'bi·al·ly
pro·vide'
pro·vid'ed
Prov'i·dence
prov'i·dence
prov'i·dent
prov·i·den'tial
prov·i·den'tial·ly
pro·vid'er
pro·vid'ing
prov'ince
pro·vin'cial
pro·vin'cial·ism
pro·vin'cial·ly
pro·vi'sion

puberty

pro·vi′sion·al
pro·vi′sion·al·ly
pro·vi′so
  pl pro·vi′sos *or*
    pro·vi′soes

pro·vi′so·ry
prov·o·ca′tion
pro·voc′a·tive
pro·voke′
pro·vok′ing
pro′vost
pro·vost mar′shal
prow′ess
prowl
prowl′er
prox′i·mal
prox′i·mal·ly
prox′i·mate
prox·im′i·ty
prox′i·mo
prox′y
pru′dence
pru′dent
pru·den′tial
pru′dent·ly
prud′ery
prud′ish
pru·nel′la
  also pru·nelle′
pru′ri·ence
pru′ri·ent
pry
  pried
  pry′ing
psalm
psalm′book

psalm′ist
psalm′o·dy
Psal′ter
psal′tery
  also psal′try
pseu′do
pseud′onym
pseud·on′y·mous
pseu·do·sci·en·
  tif′ic
psit·ta·co′sis
pso·ri′a·sis
psy′che
psy·che·del′ic
psy·che·del′i·cal·ly
psy·chi·at′ric
psy·chi·at′ri·cal·ly
psy·chi′a·trist
psy·chi′a·try
psy′chic
psy′chi·cal
psy′chi·cal·ly
psy′cho
psy·cho·anal′y·sis
psy·cho·an′a·lyst
psy·cho·an·al·yt′ic
psy·cho·an·a·lyt′i·
  cal·ly
psy·cho·an′a·lyze
psy·cho·bio·log′i·
  cal
psy·cho·bi·ol′o·gy
psy·cho·chem′i·
  cal
psy·cho·dra′ma
psy·cho·dy·nam′ic

psy·cho·dy·nam′i·
  cal·ly
psy·cho·dy·nam′·
  ics
psy·cho·gen′e·sis
psy·cho·ge·net′ic
psy·cho·log′i·cal
psy·cho·log′i·cal·ly
psy·chol′o·gist
psy·chol′o·gist
psy·chol′o·gize
psy·chol′o·gy
psy·cho·met′ric
psy·cho·met′ri·
  cal·ly
psy·cho·met′rics
psy·cho·mo′tor
psy·cho·neu·ro′sis
psy·cho·neu·rot′ic
psy′cho·path
psy·cho·path′ic
psy·cho·path′i·
  cal·ly
psy·cho·patho·log′·
  i·cal
psy·cho·phar·ma·
  ceu′ti·cal
psy·cho′sis
psy·cho·so·mat′ic
psy·cho·so·mat′i·
  cal·ly
psy·cho·ther′a·pist
psy·chot′ic
psy·chot′i·cal·ly
pto′maine
pu′ber·ty

pu'bes
pu'bic
pub'lic
pub·li·ca'tion
pub'li·cist
pub·lic'i·ty
pub'li·cize
pub'lic·ly
pub·lic-spir'it·ed
pub'lish
pub'lish·er
puck'er
puck'ish
pud'ding
pud'dle
pud'dling
pudg'i·ness
pudg'y
pueb'lo
pu'er·ile
pu·er·il'i·ty
pu·er'per·al
Puer·to Ri'can
Puer·to Ri'co
puff'ball
puff'ery
puff'y
pu'gi·lism
pu'gi·list
pu·gi·lis'tic
pug·na'cious
pug·nac'i·ty
puk'ka
pul
   pl puls *or* pu'li
pul'chri·tude

pul·chri·tu'di·
   nous
pull'back
pul'let
pul'ley
Pull'man
pull'out
pull'o'ver
pul'mo·nary
pul'mo·tor
pulp'i·ness
pul'pit
pulp'wood
pulp'y
pul'sar
pul'sate
pul·sa'tion
pul'sa·tor
pulse
pul·ver·i·za'tion
pul'ver·ize
pu'ma
pum'ice
pum'mel
  pum'meled
  or pum'melled
  pum'mel·ing
  or pum'mel·ling
pum'per·nick·el
pump'kin
pun
  punned
  pun'ning
punch'board
punch'-drunk
pun'cheon

punch'er
punc·til'io
punc·til'i·ous
punc'tu·al
punc·tu·al'i·ty
punc'tu·al·ly
punc'tu·ate
punc·tu·a'tion
punc'tu·a·tor
punc'ture
pun'dit
pun'gen·cy
pun'gent
pu'ni·ly
pu'ni·ness
pun'ish
pun'ish·able
pun'ish·ment
pu'ni·tive
pun'ster
punt'er
pu'ny
pu'pa
  pl pu'pae *or* pu'pas
pu'pil
pup'pet
pup·pe·teer'
pup'pet·ry
pup'py
pur'blind
pur'chas·able
pur'chase
pur'chas·er
pur'dah
pure'bred
pu·ree'

pure′ly
pur·ga′tion
pur′ga·tive
pur′ga·to·ry
purge
pu·ri·fi·ca′tion
pu·rif′i·ca·to·ry
pu′ri·fi·er
pu′ri·fy
pur′ism
pur′ist
pu′ri·tan
pu·ri·tan′i·cal
pu·ri·tan′i·cal·ly
pu′ri·ty
purl
   knit (see pearl)
pur′lieu
pur·loin′
pur′ple
pur′plish
pur′port
   noun
pur·port′
   verb
pur′pose
pur′pose·ful
pur′pose·ful·ly
pur′pose·less
pur′pose·ly
purs′er
purs′lane
pur·su′ance
pur·su′ant
pur·sue′
pur·su′er

pur·suit′
pu′ru·lence
pu′ru·lent
pur·vey′
pur·vey′ance
pur·vey′or
pur′view
push′-but′ton
push′cart
push′er
push′over
push′pin
push′y
pu·sil·la·nim′i·ty
pu·sil·lan′i·mous
puss′y·foot
pus′tu·lant
pus′tule
put
   place (see putt)
  put
  put′ting
pu′ta·tive
put′-on
put′out
pu·tre·fac′tion
pu′tre·fy
pu·tres′cence
pu·tres′cent
pu′trid
putsch
putt
   golf stroke (see put)
putt′ee
put′ter
   one that puts

putt′er
   golf club
put′ty
puz′zle
puz′zle·ment
puz′zler
pya
pyg′my
py′lon
py·or·rhe′a
pyr′a·mid
py·ram′i·dal
pyre
py·re′thrum
Py′rex
py·rol′y·sis
py·ro·ma′nia
py·ro·ma′ni·ac
pyr′rhic
py·rom′e·ter
py·ro·tech′nics
py·rox′y·lin
py′thon

Q

qin′tar
quack′ery
quack′ish
quad′ran·gle
qua·dran′gu·lar
quad′rant
qua·drat′ic
qua·drat′ics
qua·dren′ni·al
qua·dren′ni·al·ly

qua·dren'ni·um
  pl qua·dren'ni·ums
  or qua·dren'nia

quad·ri·lat'er·al
qua·drille'
qua·dril'lion
quad·ri·par'tite
qua·droon'
quad'ru·ped
qua·dru'ple
qua·dru'plet
qua·dru'pli·cate
quaff
quag'mire
qua'hog
quail
quaint'ly
Quak'er
qual·i·fi·ca'tion
qual'i·fied
qual'i·fi·er
qual'i·fy
qual'i·ta·tive
qual'i·ty
qualm
quan'da·ry
quan'ti·fi·able
quan·ti·fi·ca'tion
quan'ti·fi·er
quan'ti·fy
quan'ti·ta·tive
quan'ti·ty
quan'tum
  pl quan'ta

quar'an·tin·able
quar'an·tine

quark
quar'rel
  quar'reled
    or quar'relled

  quar'rel·ing
    or quar'rel·ling

quar'rel·some
quar'ry
quart
quar'ter
quar'ter·back
quar'ter·deck
quar'ter·fi'nal
quar'ter·ly
quar'ter·mas·ter
quar'ter·saw
quar·tet'
  also quar·tette'

quar'to
quartz
qua'sar
quash
qua'si
qua'si-ju·di'cial
qua'si-pub'lic
qua'ter·na·ry
qua'train
qua'ver
quay
  wharf (see quay)

queas'i·ly
queas'i·ness
quea'sy
Que·bec'
que·bra'cho
queen'ly

queer'ly
quell
quench'able
quer'u·lous
que'ry
quest
ques'tion
ques'tion·able
ques'tion·ably
ques·tion·naire'
quet·zal'
  pl quet·zals' *or*
  quet·za'les

queue
  line (see cue)

quib'ble
quick'en
quick-freeze
quick'ie
quick'ly
quick'sand
quick'silver
quick'step
quick-tem'pered
quick'-wit'ted
quid pro quo'
qui·es'cence
qui·es'cent
qui'et·ly
qui'etude
qui·et'us
quince
qui'nine
quin·quen'ni·al
quin·quen'ni·al·ly
quin'sy

quin'tal
quin·tes'sence
quint·es·sen'tial
quin·tet'
  also quin·tette'
quin·til'lion
quin·tu'ple
quin·tup'let
quin·tu'pli·cate
quip
  quipped
  quip'ping
quire
  paper (see choir)
quirk
quis'ling
quit
  quit
    also quit'ted
  quit'ting
quit'claim
quit'tance
quit'ter
quiv'er
quix·ot'ic
quix·ot'i·cal·ly
quiz
  pl quiz'zes
quiz
  quizzed
  quiz'zing
quiz'zi·cal
quoit
quon'dam
Quon'set
quo'rum

quo'ta
quot'able
quo·ta'tion
quote
quo·tid'i·an
quo'tient
qursh
  or qu'rush

R

rab'bet
  groove (see rabbit)
rab'bi
rab·bin·ate
rab·bin'i·cal
rab'bit
  animal (see rabbet)
rab'ble
rab'ble-rous·er
rab'id
ra'bies
rac·coon'
race'course
race'horse
ra·ceme'
rac'er
race'track
race'way
ra'cial
ra'cial·ism
ra'cial·ly
rac'i·ly
rac'i·ness
rac'ing
rac'ism

rac'ist
rack'et
rack·e·teer'
ra·con·teur'
rac'y
ra'dar
ra'dar·scope
ra'di·al
ra'di·al·ly
ra'di·ance
ra'di·an·cy
ra'di·ant
ra'di·ate
ra·di·a'tion
ra'di·a·tor
rad'i·cal
rad'i·cal·ism
rad'i·cal·ly
ra'dio
ra·dio·ac'tive
ra·dio·ac·tiv'i·ty
ra·dio·car'bon
ra·dio·gen'ic
ra'dio·gram
ra'dio·graph
ra·di·og'ra·phy
ra·dio·i'so·tope
ra·di·ol'o·gist
ra·di·ol'o·gy
ra·di·om'e·ter
ra'dio·pho'to
ra·di·os'co·py
ra'dio·sonde
ra·dio·tel'e·graph
ra·dio·te·leg'ra·
  phy

ra·dio·tel'e·phone
ra·dio·ther'a·pist
ra·dio·ther'a·py
rad'ish
ra'di·um
ra'di·us
   pl ra'dii *also*
   ra'di·us·es

ra'dix
   pl ra'di·ces *or*
   ra'dix·es

ra'don
raf'fia
raff'ish
raf'fle
raf'ter
rag'a·muf·fin
rag'ged
rag'ing
rag'lan
ra·gout'
rag'pick·er
rag'time
rag'weed
rail'ing
rail'lery
rail'road
rail'way
rai'ment
rain
   shower (*see* reign,
   rein)

rain'bow
rain'coat
rain'drop
rain'fall

rain'mak·ing
rain'proof
rain'storm
rain'wear
rain'y
raise
   lift (*see* raze)

rai'sin
rai·son d'être'
ra'ja
   or ra'jah

rake'-off
rak'ish
Ra'leigh
ral'ly
ram
   rammed
   ram'ming
ram'ble
ram'bler
ram'bling
ram·bunc'tious
ram'ie
ram·i·fi·ca'tion
ram'i·fy
ram'jet
ram'page
ram·pa'geous
ram'pant
ram'part
ram'rod
ram'shack·le
ranch'er
ran'cid
ran·cid'i·ty
ran'cor

ran'cor·ous
rand
ran'dom
ran·dom·iza'tion
ran'dom·ize
rang'er
rang'i·ness
rang'y
ra·ni'
   or ra·nee'

rank'ing
ran'kle
ran'sack
ran'som
rant'er
rap
   knock (*see* wrap)

   rapped
   rap'ping
ra·pa'cious
ra·pac'i·ty
rape
rape'seed
rap'id
rap·id-fire'
ra·pid'i·ty
rap'id·ly
ra'pi·er
rap'ine
rap'pen
   pl rap'pen
rap'ist
rap·port'
rap·proche·ment'
rap·scal'lion
rapt

rapt'ly
rap'ture
rap'tur·ous
ra·ra a'vis
rare'bit
rar·efac'tion
rar'efy
rare'ly
rar'i·ty
ras'cal
ras·cal'i·ty
ras'cal·ly
rash'er
rash'ly
rash'ness
rasp'ber·ry
rat
  rat'ted
  rat'ting
ratch'et
rath'er
rat·i·fi·ca'tion
rat'i·fy
ra·ti·né'
  or ra·tine'
rat'ing
ra'tio
rat·i·o'ci·nate
rat·i·o·ci·na'tion
ra'tion
ra'tio·nal
ra·tio·nale'
ra'tio·nal·ism
ra'tio·nal·ist
ra·tio·nal·is'tic
ra·tio·nal'i·ty

ra·tio·nal·iza'tion
ra'tio·nal·ize
ra'tio·nal·ly
rat'line
rat·tan'
rat·teen'
rat'tle
rat'tle·brain
rat'tler
rat'tle·snake
rat'tle·trap
rat'tling
rat'trap
rat'ty
rau'cous
rav'age
rav'ag·er
rav'el
  rav'eled
    or rav'elled
  ra'vel·ing
    or rav'el·ling
ra'ven
rav'en·ing
rav'en·ous
ra·vine'
rav·i·o'li
rav'ish
raw·boned
raw'hide
ray'on
raze
  demolish (see raise)
ra'zor
ra·zor-backed'
  or ra·zor·back'

ra'zor·bill
raz·zle-daz'zle
razz·ma·tazz'
reach'able
re·act'
  respond (see re-act)
re-act
  do again (see react)
re·ac'tion
re·ac'tion·ary
re·ac'ti·vate
re·ac·ti·va'tion
re·ac'tive
re·ac·tiv'i·ty
re·ac'tor
read·a·bil'i·ty
read'able
read'ably
read'er
read'i·ly
read'i·ness
read'ing
read'out
read'y
ready-made'
ready-to-wear'
re·a'gent
re'al
  actual (see reel)
re'al·ism
re'al·ist
re·al·is'tic
re·al·is'ti·cal·ly
re·al'i·ty
  real (see realty)
re'al·iz·able

re·al·i·za'tion
re'al·ize
re'al·ly
realm
Re'al·tor
re'al·ty
   real estate (see reality)

ream'er
reap'er
re·ap·prais'al
re·arm'
re·ar'ma·ment
rear'most
rear'ward
rea'son
rea·son·abil'i·ty
rea'son·a·ble
rea'son·a·bly
rea'son·ing
re·as·sur'ance
re·as·sure'
re'bate
reb'el
   noun
re·bel'
   verb

re·belled'
re·bel'ling
re·bel'lion
re·bel'lious
re·bind'
re·birth'
re·born'
re·bound
re·broad'cast

re·buff'
re·build'
re·buke'
re'bus
re·but'
   re·but'ted
   re·but'ting
re·but'tal
re·cal'ci·trance
re·cal'ci·trant
re·cal'cu·late
re·cal·cu·la'tion
re·call'
re·call'able
re·cant'
re·can·ta'tion
re·cap'
   re·capped'
   re·cap'ping
re·ca·pit'u·late
re·ca·pit·u·la'tion
re·cap'pa·ble
re·cap'ture
re·cast'
re·cede'
re·ceipt'
re·ceiv'able
re·ceive'
re·ceiv'er
re·ceiv'er·ship
re'cen·cy
re·cen'sion
re'cent
re·cep'ta·cle
re·cep'tion
re·cep'tion·ist

re·cep'tive
re·cep·tiv'i·ty
re·cep'tor
re'cess
re·ces'sion
re·ces'sion·al
re·ces'sive
re·cher·ché'
re·cid'i·vism
re·cid'i·vist
rec'i·pe
re·cip'i·ent
re·cip'ro·cal
re·cip'ro·cal·ly
re·cip'ro·cate
re·cip·ro·ca'tion
rec·i·proc'i·ty
re·ci'sion
re·cit'al
rec·i·ta'tion
rec·i·ta·tive'
re·cite'
reck'less
reck'on
reck'on·ing
re·claim'
re·claim'able
rec·la·ma'tion
re·cline'
rec'luse
rec·og·ni'tion
rec·og·niz·abil'i·ty
rec·og·niz'able
rec·og·niz'ably
re·cog'ni·zance
rec'og·nize

re·coil'
re·coil'less
rec·ol·lect'
rec·ol·lec'tion
re·com·bi·na'tion
rec·om·mend'
rec·om·men'd·
  able
rec·om·men·da'
  tion
re·com·mit'
re·com·mit'tal
rec'om·pense
rec·on·cil·abil'i·ty
rec·on·cil'able
rec'on·cile
rec'on·cil·er
rec·on·cil·i·a'tion
rec'on·dite
re·con·di'tion
re·con·firm'
re·con·fir·ma'tion
re·con'nais·sance
rec·on·noi'ter
re·con·sid'er
re·con·sid·er·a'
  tion
re·con'sti·tute
re·con·struct'
re·con·struc'tion
re·con·ver'sion
re·con·vert'
re·cord'
  verb

rec'ord
  noun

re·cord'er
re·cord'ist
re·count'
  tell

re'count
  count again

re·coup'
re'course
re·cov'er
  regain (see re-cover)

re'·cov'er
  cover again (see
   recover)*

re·cov'er·able
re·cov'ery
rec're·ant
rec're·ate
  renew (see re-
   create)*

re-cre·ate'
  create again (see
   recreate)*

re-cre·a'tion
rec're·ation
re-cre·a'tion
rec're·ation·al
rec're·ative
re·crim'i·nate
re·crim·i·na'tion
re·crim'i·na·to·ry
re·cruit'
rec'tal
rect'an·gle
rect·an'gu·lar
rec·ti·fi'able
rec·ti·fi·ca'tion

rec'ti·fi·er
rec'ti·fy
rec·ti·lin'ear
rec'ti·tude
rec'to
rec'tor
rec'to·ry
rec'tum
  pl rec'tums *or* rec'ta

re·cum'ben·cy
re·cum'bent
re·cu'per·ate
re·cu·per·a'tion
re·cu'per·a·tive
re·cur'
  re·curred'
  re·cur'ring
re·cur'rence
re·cur'rent
re·cy'cle
re·dact'
re·dac'tion
re·dac'tor
red'-blood'ed
red'cap
red'-car'pet
red'coat
red'den
red'dish
re·dec'o·rate
re·dec·o·ra'tion
re·ded·i·ca'tion
re·deem'
re·deem'able
re·deem'er
re·demp'tion

re·demp'tive
re·demp'to·ry
re·de·sign'
re·de·vel'op·ment
red'-hand'ed
red'head
red-hot
re·di·rect'
re·di·rec'tion
re·dis·trib'ute
re·dis·tri·bu'tion
re·dis'trict
red'-let'ter
red'o·lence
red'o·lent
re·dou'ble
re·doubt'
re·doubt'able
re·doubt'ably
re·dound'
red'-pen·cil
re·dress'
red'skin
red'top
re·duce'
re·duc'ible
re·duc'tion
re·dun'dan·cy
re·dun'dant
re·du'pli·cate
re·du·pli·ca'tion
red'wood
re·ech'o
reed'i·ness
re·ed'u·cate
re·ed·u·ca'tion

reed'y
reek
  smell (see wreak)
reel
  spool (see real)
re·elect'
re·em·ploy'
re·en·act'
re·en'try
re·ex·am·i·na'tion
re·ex·am'ine
re·fash'ion
re·fec'tion
re·fec'to·ry
re·fer
  re·ferred'
  re·fer'ring
ref'er·able
ref·er·ee'
ref'er·ence
ref·er·en'dum
  pl ref·er·en'da *or*
  ref·er·en'dums
re·fer'ent
re·fer'ral
re·fill'
  verb
re'fill
  noun
re·fill'able
re·fi'nance'
re·fine'
re·fined'
re·fine'ment
re·fin'er
re·fin'ery

re·fin'ish
re·fit'
re·flect'
re·flec'tion
re·flec'tive
re·flec'tor
re'flex
re·flex'ive
re·for'est
re·for·es·ta'tion
re·form'
  improve (see re-
  form)

re-form
  form again (see
  reform)

ref·or·ma'tion
re·for'ma·to·ry
re·form'er
re·fract'
re·frac'tion
re·frac'tive
re·frac'tor
re·frac'to·ry
re·frain'
re·fran'gi·ble
re·fresh'
re·fresh'ment
re·frig'er·ant
re·frig'er·ate
re·frig·er·a'tion
re·frig'er·a·tor
ref'uge
ref·u·gee'
re·ful'gence
re·ful'gent

re·fund′
verb

re′fund
noun

re·fund′able

re·fur′bish

re·fus′al

re·fuse′
verb

ref′use
noun

re·fut′able

re·fut′ably

ref·u·ta′tion

re·fute′

re·gain′

re′gal
adjective

re·gale′
verb

re·ga′lia

re′gal·ly

re·gard′

re·gard′ing

re·gard′less

re·gat′ta

re′gen·cy

re·gen′er·a·cy

re·gen′er·ate

re·gen·er·a′tion

re·gen′er·a·tive

re·gen′er·a·tor

re′gent

reg′i·cide

re·gime′

reg′i·men

reg′i·ment

reg·i·men′tal

reg·i·men·ta′tion

Re·gi′na

re′gion

re′gion·al

re′gion·al·ly

reg′is·ter

reg′is·trant

reg′is·trar

reg·is·tra′tion

reg′is·try

re′gress
noun

re·gress′
verb

re·gres′sion

re·gres′sive

re·gret′

re·gret′ted

re·gret′ting

re·gret′ful

re·gret′ful·ly

re·gret′ta·ble

re·gret′ta·bly

re·group′

reg′u·lar

reg·u·lar′i·ty

reg′u·lar·ize

reg′u·lar·ly

reg′u·late

reg·u·la′tion

reg′u·la·tive

reg′u·la·tor

reg′u·la·to·ry

re·gur′gi·tate

re·gur·gi·ta′tion

re·ha·bil′i·tate

re·ha·bil·i·ta′tion

re·ha·bil′i·ta·tive

re·hash′

re·hear′ing

re·hears′al

re·hearse′

reign
rule (see rain, rein*)*

re·im·burs′able

re·im·burse′

re·im·burse′ment

rein
check (see rain, reign*)*

re·in·car′nate

re·in·car·na′tion

rein′deer

re·in·fec′tion

re·in·force′

re·in·force′ment

re·in·state′

re·in·state′ment

re·in·sur′ance

re·in·sure′

re·in·ter′pret

re·in·ter·pre·ta′tion

re·is′sue

re·it′er·ate

re·it·er·a′tion

re·ject′

re·jec′tion

re·joice′

re·join′

re·join'der
re·ju've·nate
re·ju·ve·na'tion
re·lapse'
re·lat'able
re·late'
re·lat'ed
re·la'tion
re·la'tion·ship
rel'a·tive
rel'a·tive·ly
rel·a·tiv·is'tic
rel·a·tiv'i·ty
re·la'tor
re·lax'
re·lax'ant
re·lax·a'tion
re'lay
re·lease'
rel'e·gate
rel·e·ga'tion
re·lent'
re·lent'less
rel'e·vance
   also rel'e·van·cy
rel'e·vant
re·li·a·bil'i·ty
re·li'able
re·li'ably
re·li'ance
re·li'ant
rel'ic
re·lief'
re·liev'able
re·lieve'
re·liev'er

re·li'gion
re·li·gi·os'i·ty
re·li'gious
re·line'
re·lin'quish
rel'i·quary
rel'ish
re·luc'tance
re·luc'tant
re·ly'
re·main'
re·main'der
re·mains'
re·make'
re·mand'
re·mark'
re·mark'able
re·mark'ably
re·me'di·a·ble
re·me'di·al
re·me'di·al·ly
rem'e·dy
re·mem'ber
re·mem'brance
re·mind'
rem·i·nisce'
rem·i·nis'cence
rem·i·nis'cent
re·miss'
re·mis'si·ble
re·mis'sion
re·mit'
  re·mit'ted
  re·mit'ting
re·mit'tal
re·mit'tance

rem'nant
re·mod'el
re·mon'strance
re·mon'strant
re·mon'strate
re·mon·stra'tion
re·mon'stra·tive
re·mon'stra·tor
re·morse'
re·morse'ful
re·mote'
re·mote'ly
re·mote'ness
re·mount
re·mov'able
re·mov'al
re·move'
re·mu'ner·ate
re·mu·ner·a'tion
re·mu'ner·a·tive
re·mu'ner·a·tor
re·nais·sance'
re'nal
re·nas'cence
rend
  rent
  rend'ing
ren'der
ren'dez·vous
  ren'dez·voused
  ren'dez·vous·
    ing
ren·di'tion
ren'e·gade
re·nege'
re·new'

re·new'able
re·new'al
ren'net
ren'nin
re·nom'i·nate
re·nounce'
ren'o·vate
ren·o·va'tion
ren'o·va·tor
re·nown'
re·nowned'
rent'al
re·num'ber
re·nun·ci·a'tion
re·o'pen
re·or'der
re·or·ga·ni·za'tion
re·or'ga·nize
re·pack'age
re·pair'
re·pair'able
re·pair'man
rep'a·ra·ble
rep·a·ra'tion
re·par'a·tive
rep·ar·tee'
re·past'
re·pa'tri·ate
re·pa·tri·a'tion
re·pay'
re·pay'able
re·pay'ment
re·peal'
re·peat'
re·peat'ed
re·pel'

re·pelled'
re·pel'ling
re·pel'lent
re·pent'
re·pen'tance
re·pen'tant
re·per·cus'sion
rep'er·toire
rep'er·tory
rep·e·ti'tion
rep·e·ti'tious
re·pet'i·tive
re·pet·i·tive'ly
re·place'
re·place'able
re·place'ment
re·plen'ish
re·plete'
re·plete'ness
re·ple'tion
rep'li·ca
rep'li·cate
rep·li·ca'tion
re·ply'
    re·plied'
    re·ply'ing
re·port'
re·port'able
re·port'age
re·port'ed·ly
re·port'er
rep·or·to'ri·al
re·pose'
re·pos'i·to·ry
re·pos·sess'
re·pos·ses'sion

rep·re·hend'
rep·re·hen'si·ble
rep·re·hen'si·bly
rep·re·hen'sion
rep·re·sent'
rep·re·sen·ta'tion
rep·re·sen'ta·tive
re·press'
re·pres'sion
re·pres'sive
re·prieve'
rep'ri·mand
re·print'
    verb
re'print
    noun
re·pri'sal
re·prise'
re'pro
re·proach'
re·proach'able
re·proach'ful
re·proach'ful·ly
rep'ro·bate
rep·ro·ba'tion
re·pro·duce'
re·pro·duc'ible
re·pro·duc'tion
re·pro·duc'tive
re·proof'
re·prove'
re·prov'ing·ly
rep'tile
rep·til'i·an
re·pub'lic
re·pub'li·can

re·pub·li·ca′tion
re·pub′lish
re·pu′di·ate
re·pu·di·a′tion
re·pug′nance
re·pug′nant
re·pulse′
re·pul′sion
re·pul′sive
re·pul′sive·ly
rep·u·ta·bil′i·ty
rep′u·ta·ble
rep′u·ta·bly
rep·u·ta′tion
re·pute′
re·put′ed
re·quest′
req′ui·em
re·quire′
re·quire′ment
req′ui·site
req·ui·si′tion
re·quit′al
re·quite′
rer′e·dos
re′run
   noun

re·run′
   verb

  re·ran′
  re·run′
  re·run′ning
re·sal′able
re′sale
re·scale′
re·scind′

re·scis′sion
re′script
res′cue
res′cu·er
re·search′
re·sec′tion
re·seg·re·ga′tion
re·sem′blance
re·sem′ble
re·sent′
re·sent′ful
re·sent′ful·ly
re·sent′ment
re·ser′pine
res·er·va′tion
re·serve′
re·served′
re·serv′ist
res′er·voir
res ges′tae
re·shape′
re·ship′
re·shuf′fle
re·side′
res′i·dence
res′i·den·cy
res′i·dent
res·i·den′tial
res·i·den′tial·ly
re·sid′u·al
re·sid′u·al·ly
re·sid′u·ary
res′i·due
re·sid′u·um
   pl re·sid′ua

re·sign′

res·ig·na′tion
re·signed′
re·sign′ed·ly
re·sil′ience
re·sil′ien·cy
re·sil′ient
res′in
res′in·ate
res′in·ous
re·sist′
re·sis′tance
re·sis′tant
re·sist′er
   one who resists (see
     resistor)

re·sist′ible
re·sis′tor
   electrical device
     (see resister)

res′o·lute
res′o·lute·ly
res·o·lu′tion
re·solv′able
re·solve′
re·solved′
res′o·nance
res′o·nant
res′o·nate
res′o·na·tor
re·sorb′
re·sorp′tion
re·sort′
re·sound′
re·sound′ing
re′source
re·source′ful

re·spect'
re·spect·a·bil'i·ty
re·spect'able
re·spect'ably
re·spect'ful
re·spect'ful·ly
re·spect'ing
re·spec'tive
re·spec'tive·ly
res·pi·ra'tion
res'pi·ra·tor
res'pi·ra·to·ry
re·spire'
res'pite
re·splen'dence
re·splen'dent
re·spond'
re·spon'dent
re·sponse'
re·spon·si·bil'i·ty
re·spon'si·ble
re·spon'si·bly
re·spon'sive
re·start'
re·state'
res'tau·rant
res'tau·ra·teur'
rest'ful
rest'ful·ly
res·ti·tu'tion
res'tive
res'tive·ly
rest'less
re·stor'able
res·to·ra'tion
re·stor'a·tive

re·store'
re·strain'
re·strain'able
re·strained'
re·straint'
re·strict'
re·stric'tion
re·stric'tive
re·sult'
re·sul'tant
re·sume'
ré'su·mé
   or re'su·me
re·sump'tion
re·su'pi·nate
re·sur'gence
re·sur'gent
res·ur·rect'
res·ur·rec'tion
re·sus'ci·tate
re·sus·ci·ta'tion
re·sus'ci·ta·tor
ret
   ret'ted
   ret'ting
re'tail
re'tail·er
re·tain'
re·tain'er
re·take'
   verb
   re·took'
   re·tak'en
   re·tak'ing
re'take
   noun

re·tal'i·ate
re·tal·i·a'tion
re·tal'ia·to·ry
re·tard'
re·tar·da'tion
re·tard'ed
retch
   vomit (see wretch)
re·tell'
   re·told'
   re·tell'ing
re·ten'tion
re·ten'tive
re·ten·tiv'i·ty
re'test
ret'i·cence
ret'i·cent
ret'i·cle
re·tic'u·lar
re·tic'u·late
ret'i·na
   pl ret'i·nas *or*
   ret'i·nae
ret'i·nue
re·tire'
re·tire'ment
re·tir'ing
re·tool'
re·tort'
re·touch'
re·trace'
re·tract'
re·tract'able
re·trac'tile
re·trac'tion
re·trac'tor

re·tread′
verb

re′tread
noun

re·treat′

re·trench′

re·trench′ment

re·tri′al

ret·ri·bu′tion

re·trib′u·tive

re·trib′u·to·ry

re·triev′able

re·triev′al

re·trieve′

re·triev′er

ret·ro·ac′tive

re·tro·cede′

re·tro·ces′sion

ret′ro·fire

ret′ro·grade

ret·ro·gress′

ret·ro·gres′sion

ret′ro·rock·et

ret′ro·spect

ret·ro·spec′tion

ret·ro·spec′tive

re·turn′

re·turn′able

re·turn·ee′

re·u·ni·fi·ca′tion

re·u′ni·fy

re·u′nion

re·unite′

re·us′able

re·use′

rev

revved

rev′ving

re·val′u·ate

re·val·u·a′tion

re·val′ue

re·vamp′

re·vanche′

re·vanch′ism

re·vanch′ist

re·veal′

rev·eil·le

rev′el

rev′eled
or rev′elled

rev′el·ing
or rev′el·ling

rev·e·la′tion

rev′el·ler

rev′el·ry

re·venge′

re·venge′ful

re·veng′er

rev′e·nue

rev′e·nu·er

re·ver′ber·ate

re·ver·ber·a′tion

re·vere′

rev′er·ence

rev′er·end

rev′er·ent

rev·er·en′tial

rev′er·ie
or rev′ery

re·vers′

re·ver′sal

re·verse′

re·vers·ibil′i·ty

re·vers′ible

re·vers′ibly

re·ver′sion

re·ver′sion·ary

re·vert′

re·vert′ible

re·view′

re·view′er

re·vile′

re·vil′er

re·vis′able

re·vise′

re·vis′er
or re·vi′sor

re·vi′sion

re·vi′sion·ism

re·vi′so·ry

re·vi·tal·i·za′tion

re·vi′tal·ize

re·viv′al

re·viv′al·ist

re·vive′

re·viv′i·fy

rev′o·ca·ble

rev·o·ca′tion

re·voke′

re·vok′er

re·volt′

re·volt′ing

rev·o·lu′tion

rev·o·lu′tion·ary

rev·o·lu′tion·ist

rev·o·lu′tion·ize

re·volv′able

re·volve′

re·volv′er
re·volv′ing
re·vue′
re·vul′sion
re·wake′
re·wak′en
re·ward′
re·wind′
   verb

re·wound′
   also re·wind′ed

re·wind′ing
re′wind
   noun

re·work′
re·write′
   verb

re·wrote′
re·writ′ten
   also re·writ′

re·writ′ing
re′write
   noun

re·zone′
rhap·sod′ic
rhap·sod′i·cal·ly
rhap′so·dize
rhap′so·dy
rhe′o·stat
rhe′sus
rhet′o·ric
rhe·tor′i·cal
rhe·tor′i·cal·ly
rhe·to·ri′cian
rheu·mat′ic
rheu·mat′i·cal·ly

rheu′ma·tism
rheu′ma·toid
rheum′y
Rh factor
rhine′stone
rhi·noc′er·os
rhi′zome
Rhode Is·land
Rho·de′sia
Rho·de′sian
rho·do·den′dron
rhom′boid
rhom′bus
rhu′barb
rhyme
rhythm
rhyth′mic
rhyth′mi·cal·ly
ri·al′
rib
   ribbed
   rib′bing
rib′ald
rib′ald·ry
rib′bon
ri·bo·fla′vin
rich′es
rich′ly
rich′ness
Rich′mond
rick′ets
ric·ket′tsia
   pl ric·ket′tsi·as *or*
     ric·ket′tsi·ae
rick′ety
rick′sha
   or rick′shaw

ric′o·chet
   ric′o·cheted
   or ric′o·chet·ted
   ric′o·chet·ing
   or ric′o·chet·ting
ric′tus
rid
rid
   also rid′ded
rid′ding
rid′able
   or ride′able
rid′dance
rid′dle
ride
rode
rid′den
rid′ing
rid′er
ridge
ridge′pole
rid′i·cule
ri·dic′u·lous
ri′ding
ri·el′
rif′fle
riff′raff
ri′fle
ri′fling
rig
   rigged
   rig′ging
rig′ger
   one that rigs (see
     rigor)
rig′ging

right
  correct (see rite)
right'-an'gled
righ'teous
right'ful
right'ful·ly
right'-hand
right-hand'ed
right'ist
right'ly
right-of-way'
right-wing'er
rig'id
ri·gid'i·ty
rig'ma·role
rig'or
  severity (see rigger)
rig'or·ous
rim
  rimmed
  rim'ming
rin'der·pest
ring
  encircle
  ringed
  ring'ing
ring
  sound
  rang
  rung
  ring'ing
ring'er
ring'lead·er
ring'let
ring'mas·ter
ring'side

ring'worm
rink
rins'ing
ri'ot
ri'ot·er
ri'ot·ous
rip
  ripped
  rip'ping
ri·par'i·an
ripe'ly
rip'en
ripe'ness
ri·poste'
rip'per
rip'ple
rip'saw
rip'tide
rise
  rose
  ris'en
  ris'ing
ris'er
ris·i·bil'i·ty
ris'i·ble
ris'ing
risk'i·ness
risk'y
ris·qué'
rite
  ceremony (see right)
rit'u·al
rit'u·al·ism
rit·u·al·is'tic
rit·u·al·is'ti·cal·ly
rit'u·al·ly

ri'val
ri'valed
  or ri'valled
ri'val·ing
  or ri'val·ling
ri'val·ry
rive
  rived
  riv'en
    also rived
  riv'ing
riv'er
riv'er·bed
riv'er·boat
riv'er·side
riv'et
riv'et·er
riv'u·let
ri·yal'
roach
road·a·bil'i·ty
road'bed
road'block
road'house
road'run·ner
road'side
road'ster
road'way
road'work
roam'er
roan
roar'ing
roast'er
rob
  robbed
  rob'bing

rob'ber
rob'bery
rob'in
ro'bot
ro·bust'
Roch'es·ter
rock'bound
rock'er
rock'et
rock'et·ry
rock'fish
Rock'ford
rock-ribbed
rock'y
ro·co'co
ro'dent
ro'deo
roe
   deer, fish eggs (see
   row)

roe'buck
roent'gen
ro·ga'tion
rog'er
rogue
rogu'ery
rogu'ish
roil
   rile (see royal)

rois'ter
rois'ter·er
role
   also rôle
   part (see roll)

roll
   list, bread, move
   (*see* role)

roll'back
roll'er
roll'er-skate
   verb
rol'lick
rol'lick·ing
ro·man à clef'
   pl ro·mans à clef'
ro·mance'
Ro·ma'nia
Ro·ma'ni·an
ro·man'tic
ro·man'ti·cal·ly
ro·man'ti·cism
ro·man'ti·cist
ro·man·ti·ci·za'-
   tion
ro·man'ti·cize
romp'er
ron'do
roof'ing
roof'top
rook'ery
rook'ie
room'er
   lodger (see rumor)
room·ette'
room'ful
room'i·ness
room'mate
room'y
roost'er
root'er
root'less
root'let
root·stock

rop'er
rope'way
ro'sa·ry
ro·sé'
ro'se·ate
rose'-col·ored
rose'mary
ro·se'o·la
ro·sette'
rose'wood
Rosh Ha·sha'nah
ros'i·ly
ros'in
ros'i·ness
ros'in·ous
ros'ter
ros'trum
   pl ros'trums *or*
   ros'tra

ros'y
rot
   rot'ted
   rot'ting
Ro·tar'i·an
ro'ta·ry
ro'tat·able
ro'tate
ro·ta'tion
ro'ta·tor
ro'ti·fer
ro·tis'ser·ie
ro·to·gra·vure'
ro'tor
rot'ten
rot'ten·ness
ro·tund'

ro·tun'da
ro·tun'di·ty
roué'
rouge
rough
  uneven (see ruff)
rough'age
rough-and-read'y
rough-and-tum'ble
rough'cast
rough·dry
rough'en
rough·hew
rough'house
rough'ish
rough'neck
rough'shod
rou·lade'
rou·lette'
round'about
round'ed
roun'de·lay
round'er
round'house
round'ish
round'ly
round'-shoul'dered
round'up
round'worm
rous'ing
roust'about
rout
  mob, rummage, defeat (see route)

route
  way (see rout)
route'man
rou·tine'
row
  propel, quarrel, line (see roe)
row'boat
row'di·ly
row'di·ness
row'dy
row'dy·ish
row'dy·ism
row'el
roy'al
  kingly (see roil)
roy'al·ist
roy'al·ly
roy'al·ty
rub
  rubbed
  rub'bing
rub'ber
rub'ber·ize
rub'bery
rub·ber-stamp'
  verb
rub'bing
rub'bish
rub'ble
  waste (see ruble)
rub'down
ru·bel'la
ru·be'o·la
ru'ble
  currency (see rubble)
ru'bric

ru'by
ruck'sack
ruck'us
rud'der
rud'di·ness
rud'dy
rude'ly
rude'ness
ru'di·ment
ru·di·men'ta·ry
rue
rue'ful
rue'ful·ly
ruff
  collar (see rough)
ruf'fi·an
ruf'fle
rug'ged
ru'in
ru·i·na'tion
ru'in·ous
rul'er
rul'ing
rum'ba
rum'ble
ru'mi·nant
ru'mi·nate
ru·mi·na'tion
rum'mage
rum'my
ru'mor
  hearsay (see roomer)
ru'mor·mon·ger
rum'ple
rum'pus
run

ran
run
run'ning
run'about
run'around
run'away
run-down
   dilapidated (see rundown)
run'down
   summary (see run-down)
rung
   ladder, ring (see wrung)

run'-in
run'ner
run'ner-up
run'ning
run'ny
run'off
run'way
ru·pee'
ru·pi'ah
   pl ru·pi'ah *or* ru·pi'ahs

rup'ture
ru'ral
rush'er
rus'set
Rus'sia
Rus'sian
rus'tic
rus'ti·cal·ly
rus'ti·cate
rus·ti·ca'tion
rust'i·ly

rust'i·ness
rus'tle
rus'tler
rust·proof
rust'y
rut
   rut'ted
   rut'ting
ru·ta·ba'ga
ruth'less
rut'ted
Rwan'da
Rwan'dan
rye
   grain (see wry)

S

Sab'bath
sab·bat'i·cal
sa'ber
   or sa'bre
sa'ble
sa'ble·fish
sa·bot'
sab'o·tage
sab·o·teur'
sac
   pouch (see sack)
sac'cha·rin
   noun
sac'cha·rine
   adjective
sac·er·do'tal
sac·er·do'tal·ly
sa'chem

sa·chet'
sack
   bag, fire (see sac)
sack'cloth
sack'ful
   pl sack'fuls *or* sacks'ful

sack'ing
sac'ra·ment
sac·ra·men'tal
sac·ra·men'tal·ly
Sac·ra·men'to
sa'cred
sac'ri·fice
sac·ri·fi'cial
sac·ri·fi'cial·ly
sac'ri·lege
sac·ri·le'gious
sac'ris·tan
sac'ris·ty
sac·ro·il'i·ac
sac'ro·sanct
sa'crum
   pl sa'cra
sad'den
sad'dle
sad'dle·bag
sad'dle·bow
sad'dle·cloth
sad'iron
sa'dism
sa'dist
sa·dis'tic
sa·dis'ti·cal·ly
sa·fa'ri
safe'-con'duct

safe-de·pos′it
safe′guard
safe′keep′ing
safe′light
safe′ty
saf′flow·er
saf′fron
sag
  sagged
  sag′ging
sa′ga
sa·ga′cious
sa·gac′i·ty
sage′brush
sage′ly
sa′go
sail′boat
sail′cloth
sail′er
  ship (see sailor)
sail′fish
sail′ing
sail′or
  one that sails (see
  sailer)
saint′hood
saint′li·ness
Saint Lou′is
saint′ly
Saint Paul′
Saint Pe′ters·
  burg
sake
  purpose
sa′ke
  or sa′ki
  rice wine

sa·laam′
sal·abil′i·ty
sal′able
  or sale′able
sa·la′cious
sal′ad
sal′a·man·der
sa·la′mi
sal′a·ried
sal′a·ry
Sa′lem
sal·era′tus
sales′clerk
sales′girl
sales′man
sales′man·ship
sales′room
sales′wom·an
sa′lience
sa′lient
sa′line
sa·lin′i·ty
sa·li′va
sal′i·vary
sal′i·vate
sal·i·va′tion
sal′low
sal′ly
salm′on
  pl salm′on *also*
  salm′ons
sal·mo·nel′la
  pl sal·mo·nel′las *or*
  sal·mo·nel′la *also*
  sal·mo·nel′lae
sa·lon′

sa·loon′
salt′box
salt′cel·lar
salt′er
sal·tine′
salt′i·ness
Salt Lake City
salt′pe′ter
  also salt′pe′tre
salt′shak·er
salt·wa·ter
salt′wort
salt′y
sa·lu′bri·ous
sal′u·tary
sal·u·ta′tion
sa·lu·ta·to′ri·an
sa·lu′ta·to·ry
sa·lute′
salv′able
Sal′va·dor
Sal·va·do′ran
sal′vage
sal′vage·able
sal·va′tion
sal′ver
sal′vo
  pl sal′vos *or* sal′voes
sa′ma·ra
Sa·mar′i·tan
sam′ba
same′ness
sam′o·var
sam′pan
sam′ple
sam′pler

sam'pling
San An·to'nio
san·a·to'ri·um
   pl san·a·tor'i·ums *or*
   san·a·tor'ia

San Ber·nar·di'no
sanc·ti·fi·ca'tion
sanc'ti·fy
sanc·ti·mo'ni·ous
sanc'ti·mo·ny
sanc'tion
sanc'ti·ty
sanc'tu·ary
sanc'tum
   pl sanc'tums *also*
   sanc'ta

san'dal
san'dal·wood
sand'bag
sand'bank
sand'bar
sand'blast
sand'er
San Di·e'go
sand'hog
sand'i·ness
sand'lot
sand'man
sand'pa·per
sand'pip·er
sand'soap
sand'stone
sand'storm
sand'wich
sand'y
sane'ly

San Fran·cis'co
sang'froid
san'gui·nary
san'guine
san·i·tar'i·ly
san·i·tar'i·um
san'i·tary
san·i·ta'tion
san'i·tize
san'i·ty
San Jo·se'
San Juan'
San Ma·ri'no
San·ta An'a
San·ta Fe'
sap
   sapped
   sap'ping
sa'pi·ence
sa'pi·ent
sap'ling
sap'phire
sap'py
sap'suck·er
sap'wood
sa·ran'
sa·ra'pe
sar'casm
sar·cas'tic
sar·cas'ti·cal·ly
sar·co'ma
sar·coph'a·gus
   pl sar·coph'a·gi *or*
   sar·coph'a·gus·es

sar·dine'
sar·don'ic

sar·don'i·cal·ly
sa'ri
sa·rong'
sar·sa·pa·ril'la
sar·to'ri·al
Sas·katch'e·wan
sa·shay'
Sas·ka·toon'
sas'sa·fras
sass'y
sa·tang'
sa·tan'ic
sa·tan'i·cal·ly
satch'el
sa·teen'
sat'el·lite
sa'tia·ble
sa'ti·ate
sa·ti'e·ty
sat'in
sat'in·wood
sat'iny
sat'ire
sa·tir'i·cal
sa·tir'i·cal·ly
sat'i·rist
sat'i·rize
sat·is·fac'tion
sat·is·fac'to·ri·ly
sat·is·fac'to·ry
sat·is·fi'able
sat'is·fy
sa'trap
sat'u·rant
sat'u·rate
sat·u·ra'tion

Sat'ur·day
sat'ur·nine
sa'tyr
sa·ty·ri'a·sis
sauce'pan
sau'cer
sauc'i·ly
sauc'i·ness
sauc'y
Sau'di
Sau·di Ara'bia
Sau·di Ara'bi·an
sau'er·kraut
sau'na
saun'ter
sau'sage
sau·té'
  sau·téed'
  sau·té'ing
sau·terne'
sav'age
sav'age·ly
sav'age·ry
Sa·van'nah
sa·vant'
sav'able
  or save'able
sav'er
sav'ing
sav'ior
  or sav'iour
sa·voir-faire'
sa'vor
sa'vor·i·ly
sa'vor·i·ness

sa'vory
  appetizing
sa'vo·ry
  herb
saw
  sawed
  sawed
    or sawn
  saw'ing
saw'dust
sawed-off
saw'horse
saw'mill
saw-toothed
sax'o·phone
sax'o·phon·ist
say
  said
  say'ing
say'able
say'ing
say'-so
scab
  scabbed
  scab'bing
scab'bard
scab'by
sca'bies
scab'rous
scaf'fold
scaf'fold·ing
scal'able
scal'age
scal'a·wag
scald'ing

scaled
scale'-down
scale'less
scale'-up
scal'i·ness
scal'lion
scal'lop
scal'pel
scalp'er
scal'y
scam'per
scam'pi
scan
  scanned
  scan'ning
scan'dal
scan'dal·ize
scan'dal·mon·ger
scan'dal·ous
scan'ner
scant'i·ly
scant'i·ness
scant'ling
scant'y
scape'goat
scape'grace
scap'u·la
  pl scap'u·lae *or*
  scap'u·las
scap'u·lar
scar
  scarred
  scar'ring
scar'ab
scarce'ly

scar'ci·ty
scare'crow
scarf
   pl scarves *or* scarfs
scar·i·fi·ca'tion
scar'i·fy
scar'let
scar'y
   also scar'ey
scat
   scatted
   scat'ting
scath'ing
scat·o·log'i·cal
scat'ter
scat'ter·brained
scat'ter·ing
scav'enge
scav'en·ger
sce·nar'io
sce·nar'ist
scene
sce'nery
sce'nic
sce'ni·cal·ly
scent
   smell (*see* sent)
scep'ter
sched'ule
sche'ma
   pl sche'ma·ta
sche·mat'ic
sche·mat'i·cal·ly
scheme
schem'er

schem'ing
scher'zo
   pl scher'zos *or*
     scher'zi
schil'ling
schism
schis·mat'ic
schis·to·so·mi'a·
   sis
schiz'oid
schizo·phre'nia
schizo·phren'ic
schol'ar
schol'ar·ly
schol'ar·ship
scho·las'tic
scho·las'ti·cal·ly
scho·las'ti·cism
school'bag
school'boy
school'child
   pl school'chil·dren
school'girl
school'house
school'ing
school'marm
school'mate
school'room
school'teach·er
school'work
schoo'ner
sci·at'i·ca
sci'ence
sci·en·tif'ic
sci·en·tif'i·cal·ly

sci'en·tist
scim'i·tar
scin·til'la
scin'til·late
scin·til·la'tion
sci'on
scis'sors
scle·ro'sis
scoff'er
scoff'law
scold'ing
scone
scoop'ful
scoot'er
scorch'er
scorch'ing
score
   pl scores *or* score
scor'er
score'board
score'card
score'keep·er
score'less
scorn'er
scorn'ful
scorn'ful·ly
scor'pi·on
scot-free
scoun'drel
scour
scourge
scout'ing
scout'mas·ter
scowl
scrab'ble

scrag'gly
scrag'gy
scram'ble
Scran'ton
scrap
  scrapped
  scrap'ping
scrap'book
scrap'er
scap'per
scrap'ple
scrap'py
scratch
scratch'i·ness
scratch'y
scrawl
scraw'ni·ness
scraw'ny
scream'er
scream'ing
screech
screen'able
screen'ing
screen'play
screen'writer
screw'ball
screw'driv·er
screw'worm
scrib'ble
scrib'bler
scrim'mage
scrim'mag·er
scrimp'y
scrim'shaw
scrip
  certificate (see script)

script
  writing (see scrip)
scrip'tur·al
scrip'tur·al·ly
scrip'ture
script'writ·er
scriv'en·er
scroll'work
scro'tum
  pl scro'ta *or* scro'tums

scroung'er
scroung'ing
scrub
  scrubbed
  scrub'bing
scrub'by
scruff'y
scrump'tious
scru'ple
scru'pu·lous
scru'ta·ble
scru'ti·nize
scru'ti·ny
scu'ba
scuf'fle
scull
  boat (see skull)
scul'lery
scul'lion
scul'pin
  pl scul'pins *also* scul'pin

sculp'tor
sculp'tur·al
sculp'tur·al·ly
sculp'ture

scum'my
scup'per
scup'per·nong
scur·ril'i·ty
scur'ri·lous
scur'ry
scur'vy
scutch'eon
scut'tle
scut'tle·butt
sea'bag
sea'bed
sea'bird
sea'board
sea'borne
sea'coast
sea'far·er
sea'far·ing
sea'food
sea'go·ing
sea'-lane
seal'ant
seal'skin
sea'man
sea'man·ship
seam'i·ness
seam'less
sea'mount
seam'stress
seam'y
sé'ance
sea'plane
sea'port
sear
  burn (see seer)
search'er
search'light

sea′scape
sea′shell
sea′shore
sea′sick
sea′side
sea′son
sea′son·able
sea′son·ably
sea′son·al
sea′son·ing
seat′ing
Se·at′tle
sea′wall
sea′ward
   also sea′wards
sea′wa·ter
sea′way
sea′weed
sea′wor·thy
se·ba′ceous
se′cant
se·cede′
se·ces′sion
se·ces′sion·ist
se·clude′
se·clu′sion
sec′ond
sec·ond·ar′i·ly
sec′ond·ary
sec·ond-best′
sec·ond-class′
sec·ond-guess′
sec·ond-hand′
sec′ond·ly
sec·ond-rate′
se′cre·cy
se′cret

sec·re·tar′i·al
sec·re·tar′i·at
sec′re·tary
se·crete′
se·cre′tion
se·cre′tive
se·cre′to·ry
sect
sec·tar′i·an
sec′tion
sec′tion·al
sec′tion·al·ly
sec′tion·al·ism
sec′tor
sec′u·lar
sec′u·lar·ism
sec·u·lar·iza′tion
sec′u·lar·ize
se·cure′
se·cure′ly
se·cu′ri·ty
se·dan′
se·date′
se·date′ly
se·da′tion
sed′a·tive
sed′en·tary
sed′i·ment
sed·i·men′ta·ry
sed·i·men·ta′tion
se·di′tion
se·di′tious
se·duce′
se·duc′er
se·duc′tion
se·duc′tive
se·du′li·ty

sed′u·lous
see
  saw
  seen
  see′ing
see′able
seed
  pl seed *or* seeds
seed′er
seed′i·ly
seed′i·ness
seed′ling
seed′time
seek
  sought
  seek′ing
seek′er
seem′ing
seem′li·ness
seem′ly
seep′age
seer
  prophet (*see* sear)
seer′suck·er
sed′u·lous
see′saw
seethe
seeth′ing
seg′ment
seg·men′tal
seg·men′tal·ly
seg′men·tary
seg·men·ta′tion
seg′re·gate
seg′re·gat·ed
seg·re·ga′tion
seg·re·ga′tion·ist

seis'mic
seis'mi·cal·ly
seis'mo·graph
seis·mog'ra·pher
seis·mo·graph'ic
seis·mog'ra·phy
seis·mol'o·gist
seis·mol'o·gy
seize
sei'zure
sel'dom
se·lect'
se·lect·ee'
se·lec'tion
se·lec'tive
se·lec·tiv'i·ty
se·lect'man
se·lec'tor
self
   pl selves

self'-ab'ne·ga·
   tion
self-ac·cu·sa'tion
self'-act'ing
self-ad·dressed'
self-ad·just'ing
self-anal'y·sis
self-ap·point'ed
self-as·sert'ing
self-as·ser'tion
self-as·sur'ance
self-as·sured'
self'-cen'tered
self-com·mand'
self'-con'fi·dence
self'-con'scious

self-con·tained'
self-con·trol'
self-con·trolled'
self-crit'i·cism
self-de·feat'ing
self-de·fense'
self-de·ter·mi·na'
   tion
self'-dis'ci·pline
self'-ed'u·cat·ed
self-ef·fac'ing
self-em·ployed'
self'-ev'i·dent
self-ex·plan'a·
   to·ry
self-ex·pres'sion
self'-gov'erned
self'-gov'ern·ing
self'-im'age
self-im·por'tance
self-im·posed'
self-im·prove'
   ment
self-in·crim'i·na·
   tion
self-in·dul'gence
self-in·flict'ed
self'-in'ter·est
self'ish
self'less
self'-liq'ui·dat·ing
self-load'ing
self-lock'ing
self-made
self'-mail'ing
self'-op'er·at·ing

self-per·pet'u·at·
   ing
self-per·pet·u·a'
   tion
self'-pit'y
self'-pit'y·ing
self'-por'trait
self-pos·sessed'
self-pres·er·va'
   tion
self-pro·claimed'
self-pro·pelled'
self-pro·tec'tion
self'-reg'u·lat·ing
self-re·li'ance
self-re·spect'
self'-righ'teous
self'-ris'ing
self-rule
self'-sac'ri·fice
self'-same
self-sat·is·fac'
   tion
self'sat'is·fied
self'-seal'ing
self-seek'ing
self-ser'vice
self-start'ing
self-styled
self-suf·fi'cien·cy
self-sus·tain'ing
self-taught
self'-wind'ing
sell
   sold
   sell'ing

sell'er
sel'vage
or sel'vedge
selves
se·man'tic
se·man'tics
sem'a·phore
sem'blance
se'men
se·mes'ter
semi·an'nu·al
semi·an'nu·al·ly
semi·ar'id
semi·au·to·mat'ic
semi'cir·cle
semi·cir'cu·lar
semi'co·lon
semi·con·duc'tor
semi·con'scious
semi·fi'nal
adjective
semi'fi·nal
noun
semi·flu'id
semi·for'mal
semi·lu'nar
semi·month'ly
sem'i·nal
sem'i·nar
sem·i·nar'i·an
sem'i·nary
semi·of·fi'cial
semi·o'tic
semi·per'me·able
semi·pre'cious
semi·pri'vate

semi·pro·fes'
  sion·al
semi·pub'lic
semi·rig'id
semi·skilled'
semi·soft'
semi·sol'id
semi·sweet'
Sem'ite
Se·mit'ic
semi·trail·er
semi·trop'i·cal
semi·week'ly
semi·works
semi·year'ly
sen
  pl sen
sen'ate
sen'a·tor
sen·a·to'ri·al
send
  sent
  send'ing
Sen·e·gal'
Sen·e·ga·lese'
  pl Sen·e·ga·lese'
se·nes'cence
sen'gi
  pl sen'gi
se'nile
se·nil'i·ty
se'nior
se·nior'i·ty
sen'na
sen·sa'tion
sen·sa'tion·al

sen·sa'tion·al·ly
sense'less
sen·si·bil'i·ty
sen'si·ble
sen'si·bly
sen'si·tive
sen·si·tiv'i·ty
sen·si·ti·za'tion
sen'si·tize
sen'so·ry
sen'su·al
sen·su·al'i·ty
sen'su·al·ly
sen'su·ous
sen'tence
sen·ten'tious
sen'tient
sen'ti·ment
sen·ti·men'tal
sen·ti·men·tal'i·ty
sen·ti·men'tal·ize
sen·ti·men'tal·ly
sen'ti·nel
sen'try
se'pal
sep'a·ra·ble
sep'a·rate
sep'a·rate·ly
sep·a·ra'tion
sep'a·rat·ist
sep'a·ra·tive
sep'a·ra·tor
se'pia
sep'sis
Sep·tem'ber
sep'tic

sep·ti·ce'mia

sep·tu·a·ge·nar'
i·an

sep'ul·cher
or sep'ul·chre

se·pul'chral

se'quel

se'quence

se·quen'tial

se·ques'ter

se·ques'trate

se·que·stra'tion

se'quin

se·quoi'a

se·ra'glio

ser'aph
pl ser'a·phim or
ser'aphs

se·raph'ic

ser·e·nade'

ser·en·dip'i·ty

se·rene'

se·rene'ly

se·ren'i·ty

serf
peasant (see surf)

serf'dom

serge
cloth (see surge)

ser'geant

se'ri·al
in parts (see cereal)

se·ri·al·iza'tion

se'ri·al·ize

se'ri·al·ly

se'ries
pl se'ries

ser'i·graph

se'ri·ous

ser'mon

se'rous

ser'pent

ser'pen·tine

ser'rate
or ser'rat·ed

se'rum
pl se'rums or se'ra

ser'vant

ser'vice

ser'vice·abil'i·ty

ser'vice·able

ser'vice·man

ser'vile

ser·vil'i·ty

serv'ing

ser'vi·tor

ser'vi·tude

ser·vo·mech'a·
nism

ses'a·me

ses·qui·cen·ten'
ni·al

ses'sion
meeting (see
cession)

set

set

set'ting

set'back

set'screw

set·tee'

set'ter

set'ting

set'tle

set'tle·ment

set'tler

set'-to

set'-up

sev'en

sev·en·teen'

sev'en·ti·eth

sev'en·ty

sev'er

sev'er·al

sev'er·al·ly

sev'er·ance

se·vere'

se·vere'ly

se·ver'i·ty

sew
stitch (see sow)

sewed

sewed
or sewn

sew'ing

sew'age

sew'er

sew'er·age

sew'ing

sex·a·ge·nar'i·an

sex'i·ness

sex'less

sex'linked

sex'tant

sex·tet'
or sex·tette'

sex'ton

sex'u·al

sex·u·al'i·ty

sex'u·al·ly
shab'bi·ly
shab'bi·ness
shab'by
shack'le
shad'i·ly
shad'i·ness
shad'ing
shad'ow
shad'ow·box
shad'owy
shad'y
shaft'ing
shag
  shagged
  shag'ging
shag'gi·ly
shag'gi·ness
shag'gy
shak'able
  or shake'able
shake
  shook
  shak'en
  shak'ing
shake'down
shak'er
shake'-up
shak'i·ly
shak'i·ness
sha'ko
  pl sha'kos *or*
  sha'koes

shak'y
shal'lop
shal'low

sham
  shammed
  sham'ming
sha'man
sham'ble
sham'bles
shame·faced
shame'fac'ed·ly
shame'ful
shame'ful·ly
shame'less
sham'mer
sham·poo'
sham'rock
shang'hai
shan·tung
shan'ty
shan'ty·town
shap'able
  or shape'able
shape'less
shape'li·ness
shape'ly
share'crop·per
shar'er
share'hold·er
shark'skin
sharp'en
sharp-eyed
sharp'shoot·er
sharp'tongued
shat'ter
shave
  shaved
  shaved
  or shav'en

shav'ing
shav'ing
shawl
sheaf
  pl sheaves
shear
  clip (see sheer)
sheared
sheared
  or shorn
shear'ing
shears
sheath
  noun
sheathe
  verb
sheath'ing
she·bang'
shed
shed
shed'ding
sheen
sheep'fold
sheep'ish
sheep'skin
sheer
  thin, swerve (see
  shear)
sheet'ing
Sheet'rock
sheik
  or sheikh
shelf
  pl shelves
shel·lac'
  shel·lacked'

shel·lack′ing
shell′fish
shell·proof
shell′work
shel′ter
shel′ter·belt
shelv·ing
she·nan′i·gan
shep′herd
shep′herd·ess
sher′bet
   also sher′bert

sher′iff
sher′ry
shib′bo·leth
shield
shift′i·ly
shift′i·ness
shift′less
shift′y
shil·le′lagh
   also shil·la′lah

shil′ling
shil′ly-shal·ly
shim′mer
shim′mery
shim′my
shin
  shinned
  shin′ning
shin·bone
shine
  shone
   or shined
  shin′ing
shin′er

shin′gle
shin′gles
shin′i·ness
shin′ing
shin′y
ship
  shipped
  ship′ping
ship′board
ship′build·ing
ship′mate
ship′ment
ship′per
ship′ping
ship·shape
ship′worm
ship′wreck
ship′wright
ship′yard
shirk′er
shirr
  shirr′ing
shirt′ing
shirt′tail
shirt′waist
shiv′er
shoal
shock′er
shock′ing
shod′di·ly
shod′di·ness
shod′dy
shoe
  shod
   also shoed
  shoe′ing

shoe′horn
shoe′lace
shoe′mak·er
sho′er
shoe′string
shoo′fly
shoo′-in
shoot
  let fly (*see* chute)

  shot
  shoot′ing
shoot′er
shop
  shopped
  shop′ping
shop′keep·er
shop′lift·er
shop′per
shop′talk
shop′worn
sho′ran
shore′bird
shor′ing
short′age
short′bread
short′cake
short·change
short′-cir′cuit
short′com′ing
short′cut
short′en
short′en·ing
short′hand
short′hand′ed
short′horn
short-lived

short'ly
short'sight'ed
short'stop
short'-tem'pered
short-term
short·wave
short'-wind'ed
shot'gun
should
shoul'der
shov'el
  shov'eled
    or shov'elled
  shov'el·ing
    or shov'el·ling
shov'el·ful
  pl shov'el·fuls
show
  showed
  shown
    or showed
  show'ing
show'boat
show'case
show'down
show'er
show'ery
show'i·ly
show'i·ness
show'man
show'piece
show'place
show'room
show'y
shrap'nel
shred

shred'ded
shred'ding
Shreve'port
shrew
shrewd
shrew'ish
shriek
shrift
shrike
shrill'ness
shril'ly
shrine
shrink
  shrank
    or shrunk
  shrink'ing
shrink'able
shrink'age
shrive
  shrived
    or shrove
  shriv'en
    or shrived
  shriv'ing
shriv'el
  shriv'eled
    or shriv'elled
  shriv'el·ing
    or shriv'el·ling
shrub'bery
shrug
shrugged
shrug'ging
shuck
shud'der
shuf'fle

shuf'fle·board
shun
  shunned
  shun'ning
shunt
shut
  shut
  shut'ting
shut'down
shut-in
shut'off
shut'out
shut'ter
shut'tle
shut'tle·cock
shy
  shied
  shy'ing
shy
  shi'er
    or shy'er
  shi'est
    or shy'est
shy'ly
shy'ness
shy'ster
Si·a·mese'
  pl Si·a·mese'
sib'i·lant
sib'ling
sib'yl
sib'yl·line
sick'bed
sick'en
sick'le
sick'li·ness

sick'ly
sick'ness
sick'room
side'arm
side'board
side'burns
side'car
side'-glance
side'kick
side'light
side'line
side'long
side'man
side'piece
si·de're·al
side'sad·dle
side'show
side'slip
side'spin
side'split·ting
side'step
side'stroke
side'swipe
side'track
side'walk
side'ways
  or side'wise

sid'ing
si'dle
siege
si·er'ra
si·es'ta
sieve
sift'er
sigh
sight
  view (see cite, site)

sight'ed
sight'less
sight'ly
sight'-read
sight'-see·ing
sight'seer
sign
  mark (see sine)

sig'nal
  sig'naled
    or sig'nalled

  sig'nal·ing
    or sig'nal·ling

sig'nal·ize
sig'nal·ly
sig'na·to·ry
sig'na·ture
sign'board
sign'er
sig'net
sig·nif'i·cance
sig·nif'i·cant
sig·ni·fi·ca'tion
sig'ni·fy
sign'post
si'lage
si'lence
si'lenc·er
si'lent
sil·hou·ette'
sil'i·ca
sil'i·cate
si·li'ceous
  or si·li'cious

sil'i·cone
sil·i·co'sis
silk'en

silk'i·ly
silk'i·ness
silk·screen
silk'weed
silk'worm
silk'y
sil'li·ness
sil'ly
si'lo
sil'ver
sil'ver·fish
sil'ver·smith
sil·ver-tongued'
sil'ver·ware
sil'very
sil'vi·cul·ture
sim'i·an
sim'i·lar
sim·i·lar'i·ty
sim'i·lar·ly
sim'i·le
si·mil'i·tude
sim'mer
si'mo·nize
si'mo·ny
sim'per
sim'ple
sim'ple·mind·ed
sim'ple·ton
sim·plic'i·ty
sim·pli·fi·ca'tion
sim'pli·fi·er
sim'pli·fy
sim'ply
sim'u·late
sim·u·la'tion
sim'u·la·tor

si·mul·ta'ne·ous
sin
  sinned
  sin'ning
sin·cere'
sin·cere'ly
sin·cer'i·ty
sine
  math (*see* sign)
si'ne·cure
si·ne di'e
si·ne qua non'
sin'ew
sin'ewy
sin'ful
sin'ful·ly
sing
  sang
    or sung
  sung
  sing'ing
Sin'ga·pore
singe
  singed
  singe'ing
sing'er
sin'gle
sin·gle-breast'ed
sin·gle-hand'ed
sin·gle-mind'ed
sin·gle-space'
sin'gle·ton
sin'gle-track'
sin'gly
sing'song
sin'gu·lar
sin·gu·lar'i·ty

sin'is·ter
sink
  sank
    or sunk
  sunk
  sink'ing
sink'able
sink'age
sink'er
sink'hole
sin'ner
sin·u·os'i·ty
sin'u·ous
si'nus
si·nus·it'is
sip
  sipped
  sip'ping
si'phon
si'ren
sir'loin
si·roc'co
si'sal
sis'ter
sis'ter·hood
sis'ter-in-law
  pl sis'ters-in-law
sis'ter·ly
sit
  sat
  sit'ting
si·tar'
sit'-down
site
  location (*see* cite, sight)
sit'-in

sit'ter
sit'ting
sit'u·ate
sit·u·at·ed
sit·u·a'tion
six'pack
six'pence
six'pen·ny
six·teen
six'ti·eth
six'ty
siz'able
  or size'able
siz'ably
siz'ing
siz'zle
skate'board
skat'er
skein
skel'e·tal
skel'e·ton
skep'tic
skep'ti·cal
skep'ti·cal·ly
skep'ti·cism
sketch'book
sketch'i·ly
sketch'i·ness
sketch'y
skew'er
ski
  pl skis *or* ski *also* skiis
skid
  skid'ded
  skid'ding
ski'er

ski′ing
skiff
skil′let
skill′ful
   or skil′ful
skill′ful·ly
skim
  skimmed
  skim′ming
skim′mer
skimp′i·ly
skimp′i·ness
skimp′y
skin
  skinned
  skin′ning
skin-deep
skin′flint
skin′ful
skin′ni·ness
skin′ny
skin·tight
skip
  skipped
  skip′ping
skip′jack
skip′per
skir′mish
skit′ter
skit′tish
ski′wear
skul·dug′gery
  or skull·dug′gery
skulk′er
skull
  head skeleton (see
  scull)

skull′cap
sky′borne
sky′diving
sky-high
sky′jack
sky′lark
sky′light
sky′line
sky′lounge
sky′rock·et
sky′scrap·er
sky′ward
sky′way
sky′writ·ing
slack′en
slack′er
slack′ly
sla′lom
slam
  slammed
  slam′ming
slam-bang
slan′der
slan′der·ous
slang′i·ness
slang′y
slant′ways
slant′wise
slap
  slapped
  slap′ping
slap·dash
slap′hap·py
slap′stick
slash′ing
slat

slat′ted
slat′ting
slat′tern
slat′tern·li·ness
slaugh′ter
slaugh′ter·house
slav′er
slav′ery
slav′ish
slay
  kill (see sleigh)

slew
slain
slay·ing
slay′er
slea′zi·ly
slea′zi·ness
slea′zy
sled
  sled′ded
  sled′ding
sledge′ham·mer
sleek′ly
sleep
  slept
  sleep′ing
sleep′er
sleep′i·ly
sleep′i·ness
sleep′less
sleep′walk
sleep′y
sleeve′less
sleigh
  snow vehicle (see
  slay)

sleight
dexterity (see slight)

slen'der

slen'der·ize

sleuth

slic'er

slick'er

slick'ly

slide

  slid

  slid'ing

slid'er

slight
frail (see sleight)

slim

  slimmed

  slim'ming

slim'i·ly

slim'i·ness

slim'ness

slim'y

sling

  slung

  sling'ing

sling'shot

slink

  slunk

  slink'ing

slink'y

slip

  slipped

  slip'ping

slip'case

slip'cov·er

slip'knot

slip'-on

slip'over

slip'page

slip'per

slip'peri·ness

slip'pery

slip·shod

slip'stick

slip'stream

slip'up

slit

  slit

  slit'ting

slith'er

slith'ery

sliv'er

slob'ber

sloe
fruit (see slow)

sloe-eyed

slog

  slogged

  slog'ging

slo'gan

sloop

slop

  slopped

  slop'ping

slop'pi·ly

slop'pi·ness

slop'py

slop'work

slosh

slot

  slot'ted

  slot'ting

sloth'ful

sloth'ful·ly

slouch'er

slouch'y

slough
or sluff

slov'en·li·ness

slov'en·ly

slow
sluggish (see sloe)

slow'down

slow'poke

slow'-wit'ted

sludge

sludg'y

slug

  slugged

  slug'ging

slug'gard

slug'gish

sluice

sluice'way

slum

  slummed

  slum'ming

slum'ber

slum'ber·ous
or slum'brous

slum'lord

slump

slur

  slurred

  slur'ring

slush'i·ness

slush'y

slut'tish

sly
  sli′er
    also sly′er
  sli′est
    also sly′est
sly′ly
small′ish
small′pox
small-scale
small-time
smart′ly
smash′ing
smash′up
smat′ter
smat′ter·ing
smear′y
smell
  smelled
    or smelt
  smell′ing
smell′y
smelt
  pl smelts *or* smelt
smelt′er
smid′gen
  or smid′geon *or*
    smid′gin
smi′lax
smil′ing·ly
smirch
smirk
smite
  smote
  smit′ten
    or smote
  smit′ing

smith·er·eens′
smith′y
smock′ing
smog′gy
smok′able
  or smoke′able
smoke-filled
smoke′less
smok′i·ly
smok′i·ness
smoke′stack
smok′y
smol′der
  or smoul′der
smooth·bore
smooth′en
smooth′ly
smooth-tongued
smor′gas·bord
smoth′er
smudge
smudg·i·ly
smudg·i·ness
smudg′y
smug′gle
smug′gler
smug′ly
smut′ti·ly
smut′ti·ness
smut′ty
snaf′fle
sna·fu′
snag
  snagged
  snag′ging
snail-paced

snake′bite
snake′like
snake′skin
snak′i·ly
snak′y
snap
  snapped
  snap′ping
snap′back
snap′-brim
snap′drag·on
snap′per
snap′pish
snap′py
snap′shot
snar′er
snarl′y
snatch
snaz′zy
sneak′er
sneak′i·ly
sneak′i·ness
sneak′ing
sneak′y
sneer′er
snick′er
  or snig′ger
snif′fle
snif′ter
snip
  snipped
  snip′ping
snip′er·scope
snip′pet
snip′py
sniv′el

sniv′eled
  or sniv′elled

sniv′el·ing
  or sniv′el·ling

snob′bery
snob′bish
snoop′er
snoop′er·scope
snoop′y
snor′kel
snout
snow′ball
snow′blind
snow·bound
snow′cap
snow′drop
snow′drift
snow′fall
snow′flake
snow′man
snow′mo·bile
snow′mo·bil·ing
snow′plow
snow′shoe
snow′storm
snow′suit
snow′y
snub
  snubbed
  snub′bing
snub-nosed
snuff′er
snuf′fle
snug′gle
snug′ly
soak′age

so′-and-so
soap′box
soap′stone
soap′suds
soap′y
soar
  fly (see sore)
sob
  sobbed
  sob′bing
so′ber
so·bri′ety
so′bri·quet
so-called
soc′cer
so·cia·bil′i·ty
so′cia·ble
so′cia·bly
so′cial
so′cial·ism
so′cial·is′tic
so′cial·ite
so·cial·iza′tion
so′cial·ize
so′cial·ly
so·ci′etal
so·ci′etal·ly
so·ci′ety
so·cio·eco·nom′ic
so·ci·o·log′i·cal
so·ci·o·log′i·cal·ly
so·ci·ol′o·gist
so·ci·ol′o·gy
so·ci·om′e·try
so·cio·po·lit′i·cal
so·cio·re·li′gious

sock′et
sock′eye
sod
  sod′ded
  sod′ding
so′da
so·dal′i·ty
sod′den
so′di·um
sod′omy
so·ev′er
so′fa
soft′ball
soft-boiled
soft′bound
soft′en
soft′heart′ed
soft′-ped′al
soft′-shell
  or soft-shelled
soft-soap
soft′-spo′ken
soft′ware
soft′wood
sog′gi·ly
sog′gi·ness
sog′gy
soi′gné′
  or soi·gnée′
soil′borne
soi·ree′
  or soi·rée′
so′journ
sol
  pl so′les
sol′ace

so'lar
so·lar'i·um
  pl so·lar'ia *also*
   so·lar'i·ums

so·lar plex'us
sol'der
sol'dier
sole
  undersurface, fish,
   only (*see* soul)

sol'e·cism
sole'ly
sol'emn
so·lem'ni·fy
so·lem'ni·ty
sol·em·ni·za'tion
sol'em·nize
so'le·noid
so·le·noi'dal
sole'print
sol-fa'
sol·fége'
so·lic'it
so·lic·i·ta'tion
so·lic'i·tor
so·lic'i·tous
so·lic'i·tude
sol'id
sol·i·dar'i·ty
so·lid·i·fi·ca'tion
so·lid'i·fy
so·lid'i·ty
sol'id-state'
so·lil'o·quize
so·lil'o·quy

sol'ip·sism
sol'i·taire
sol'i·tary
sol'i·tude
so'lo
so'lo·ist
so'lon
sol'stice
sol·u·bil'i·ty
sol'u·ble
sol'u·bly
so·lu'tion
solv·abil'i·ty
solv'able
solve
sol'ven·cy
sol'vent
so'ma
So·ma'li
  pl So·ma'li *or*
   So·ma'lis

So·ma'lia
So·ma'lian
so·mat'ic
so·ma·tol'o·gy
som'ber
som·bre'ro
some'body
some'day
some'how
some'one
some'place
som'er·sault
some'thing
some'time

some'times
some'what
some'where
som·me·lier'
som·nam'bu·late
som·nam'bu·lism
som·nam'bu·list
som'no·lence
som'no·lent
so'nar
so·na'ta
son·a·ti'na
sonde
song'bird
song'book
song'ster
song'stress
song'writ·er
son'ic
son'-in-law
  pl sons'-in-law

son'net
so·nor'i·ty
so·no'rous
soon'er
soothe
sooth'er
sooth'ing·ly
sooth'say·er
soot'i·ly
soot'i·ness
soot'y
sop
  sopped
  sop'ping

soph′ism
soph′ist
so·phis′tic
  or so·phis′ti·cal
so·phis′ti·cat·ed
so·phis′ti·ca′tion
soph′ist·ry
soph′o·more
soph·o·mor′ic
so·po·rif′er·ous
sop·o·rif′ic
so·pran′o
sor′bic
sor′cer·er
sor′cer·ess
sor′cery
sor′did
sore
  painful (see soar)
sore′ly
sor′ghum
so·rop′ti·mist
so·ror′i·ty
sor′rel
sor′ri·ly
sor′ri·ness
sor′row
sor′row·ful
sor′row·ful·ly
sor′ry
sor′tie
so-so
sot·to vo′ce
sou·brette′
souf·flé′

soul
  spirit (see sole)
soul′ful
soul′ful·ly
soul′-search·ing
sound′board
sound′ing
sound′ly
sound′proof
soup·çon′
souped′-up
soup′y
sour′dough
sour′ish
sou′sa·phone
sou·tane′
South Af′ri·ca
South Af′ri·can
South Bend′
south′bound
South Car·o·li′na
South Da·ko′ta
south·east′
south·east′er·ly
south·east′ern
south·east′ward
south′er·ly
south′ern
south′ern·most
south′ward
south·west′
south·west′er·ly
south·west′ern
south·west′ward
sou′ve·nir

sov′er·eign
sov′er·eign·ty
so′vi·et
sow
  plant, scatter (see sew)
sowed
sown
  or sowed
sow′ing
sow′er
soy·bean
space′borne
space′craft
space′flight
space′man
space′port
space′ship
space-time
spac′ing
spa′cious
spack′le
spade′ful
spade′work
spa·ghet′ti
Spain
span
spanned
span′ning
span′drel
  or span′dril
span′gle
Span′glish
Span′iard
span′iel

Span'ish
spank'ing
span'ner
spar
  sparred
  spar'ring
spar'ing·ly
spare'ribs
spar'kle
spark'ler
spar'row
sparse'ly
Spar'tan
spasm
spas·mod'ic
spas·mod'i·cal·ly
spas'tic
spat
  spat'ted
  spat'ting
spa'tial
spa'tial·ly
spat'ter
spat'u·la
spav'in
spav'ined
speak
  spoke
  spo'ken
  speak'ing
speak'easy
speak'er
spear'fish
spear'head
spear'mint
spear'wort

spe'cial
spe'cial·ist
spe·cial·iza'tion
spe'cial·ize
spe'cial·ly
spe'cial·ty
spe'cie
  money (see species)
spe'cies
  pl spe'cies
  kind (see specie)
spec·i·fi'able
spe·cif'ic
spe·cif'i·cal·ly
spec·i·fi·ca'tion
spec'i·fi·er
spec'i·fy
spec'i·men
spe'cious
speck'le
spec'ta·cle
spec'ta·cled
spec·tac'u·lar
spec'ta·tor
spec'ter
  or spec'tre
spec'tral
spec·trom'e·ter
spec'tro·scope
spec·tro·scop'ic
spec·tro·scop'i·cal·ly
spec·tros'co·pist
spec·tros'co·py
spec'trum
  pl spec'tra *or*
  spec'trums

spec'u·late
spec·u·la'tion
spec'u·la·tive
spec'u·la·tive·ly
spec'u·la·tor
speech'less
speed
  sped
    or speed'ed
  speed'ing
speed'boat
speed'i·ly
speed'i·ness
speed·om'e·ter
speed'up
speed'way
speed'well
speed'y
spe·le·ol'o·gist
spe·le·ol'o·gy
spell'bind·er
spell'bound
spell'er
spe·lunk'er
spend
  spent
  spend'ing
spend'able
spend'thrift
sperm
  pl sperm *or* sperms
sper·ma·ce'ti
sper·ma·to·zo'on
  pl sper·ma·to·zo'a
spew
sphere

spher'i·cal
spher'i·cal·ly
spher'oid
sphinc'ter
sphinx
   pl sphinx'es *or*
     sphin'ges

spic'i·ly
spic'i·ness
spick'-and-span'
spic'y
spi'der
spi'dery
spig'ot
spill
   spilled
   also spilt
   spill'ing
spill'age
spill'way
spin
   spun
   spin'ning
spin'ach
spi'nal
spi'nal·ly
spin'dle
spin'dling
spin'dly
spin'drift
spine'less
spin'et
spin'ner
spin'-off
spin'ster
spin'y

spi'ral
spi'raled
   or spi'ralled
spi'ral·ing
   or spi'ral·ling
spi'ral·ly
spir'it
spir'it·ed
spir'it·less
spir'i·tu·al
spir'i·tu·al·ism
spir'i·tu·al'i·ty
spir'i·tu·al·ly
spir'i·tu·ous
spi'ro·chete
spit
   impale
   spit'ted
   spit'ting
spit
   eject saliva
   spit
   or spat
   spit'ting
spite'ful
spite'ful·ly
spit'fire
spit'tle
spit·toon'
splash'board
splash'down
splat'ter
splay'foot
spleen'ful
splen'did
splen'dor

sple·net'ic
sple'nic
splic'er
splin'ter
split
   split'ting
split'-lev·el
split'ting
splotch
splurge
splut'ter
spoil
   spoiled
   or spoilt
   spoil'ing
spoil'able
spoil'age
spoil'er
spoil'sport
Spo·kane'
spo'ken
spoke'shave
spokes'man
spo·li·a'tion
sponge
spong'er
spong'i·ness
spong'y
spon'sor
spon·ta·ne'i·ty
spon·ta'ne·ous
spoo'ner·ism
spoon'-feed
   spoon'fed
   spoon'feed·ing

spoon'ful
  pl spoon'fuls *or*
    spoons'ful
spo·rad'ic
spo·rad'i·cal·ly
sport'i·ly
sport'i·ness
sport'ing
sport'ive
sports'cast
sports'man
sports'wear
sports'writ·er
spot
  spot'ted
  spot'ting
spot'-check
spot'less
spot'light
spot'ter
spot'ti·ly
spot'ti·ness
spot'ty
sprawl
spray'er
spread
  spread
  spread'ing
spread'-ea·gle
spread'er
spright'li·ness
spright'ly
spring
  sprang
   or sprung
  sprung
  spring'ing

spring'board
spring'-clean'ing
Spring'field
spring'house
spring'i·ly
spring'i·ness
spring'time
spring'y
sprin'kle
sprin'kler
sprin'kling
sprint'er
sprock'et
spruce'ly
spry
spri'er
  or spry'er
spri'est
  or spry'est
spunk'i·ly
spunk'i·ness
spunk'y
spur
  spurred
  spur'ring
spu'ri·ous
sput'nik
sput'ter
spu'tum
  pl spu'ta
spy
  spied
  spy'ing
spy'glass
squab'ble
squad'ron
squal'id

squall
squal'or
squan'der
square'ly
square-rigged
square'-shoul'-
  dered
squash'i·ly
squash'i·ness
squash'y
squat
  squat'ted
   or squat
  squat'ting
squat'ter
squawk
squeak'er
squeak'y
squeal'er
squea'mish
squee·gee
squeez'er
squelch
squig'gle
squint'y
squirm'y
squir'rel
squish'y
stab
  stabbed
  stab'bing
sta'bile
sta·bil'i·ty
sta·bi·li·za'tion
sta'bi·lize
sta'bi·liz·er
sta'ble

stac·ca′to

sta′di·um
　pl sta′dia *or*
　　sta′diums

staff
　pl staves
　pole, sustenance,
　　music
　pl staffs
　assistants

stage′coach
stage′craft
stage′hand
stage′-man·age
stage′struck
stag′ger
stag′i·ly
stag′i·ness
stag′ing
stag′nan·cy
stag′nant
stag′nate
stag·na′tion
stag′y
staid
stain′able
stain′less
stair′case
stair′way
stair′well
stake
　post, bet (see steak*)*
stake′hold·er
sta·lac′tite
sta·lag′mite
stale′ly
stale′mate
stale′ness

stalk′ing-horse
stal′lion
stal′wart
sta′men
Stam′ford
stam′i·na
stam′mer
stam·pede′
stamp′er
stance
stanch
stan′chion
stand
　stood
　stand′ing
stan′dard
stan′dard-bear·er
stan·dard·iza′tion
stan′dard·ize
stand′by
stand·ee′
stand′-in
stand′ing
stand′off
stand′out
stand′pat
stand′pipe
stand′point
stand′still
stand-up
stan′za
staph·y·lo·coc′cus
　pl staph·y·lo·coc′ci
sta′ple
sta′pler
star
　starred

star′ring
star′board
star′-cham′ber
starch′i·ness
starch′y
star′-crossed
star′dom
star′dust
sta·re·de·ci′sis
star′fish
star′gaze
stark′ly
star′less
star′light
star′like
star′ling
star′lit
star′ry
star·ry-eyed′
star′-span·gled
start′er
star′tle
star′tling
star·va′tion
starve′ling
stat′able
　or state′able
state′craft
state′hood
state′house
state′less
state′li·ness
state′ly
state′ment
state′room
state′side
states′man

stat′ic
stat′i·cal·ly
sta′tion
sta′tion·ary
   fixed (see stationery)
sta′tio·ner
sta′tio·nery
   writing materials
   (see stationary)
sta′tion·mas·ter
stat′ism
sta·tis′tic
sta·tis′ti·cal
sta·tis′ti·cal·ly
stat·is·ti′cian
sta·tis′tics
stat′u·ary
stat′ue
stat·u·esque′
stat·u·ette′
stat′ure
sta′tus
sta·tus quo′
stat′ute
stat′u·to·ry
staunch
stave
  staved
  or stove
  stav′ing
stay
  stayed
  or staid
  stay′ing
stay′-at-home′
stead′fast

stead′i·ly
stead′i·ness
stead′y
steak
  meat (see stake)
steal
  take (see steel)
  stole
  sto′len
  steal′ing
stealth′i·ly
stealth′i·ness
stealth′y
steam′boat
steam′er
steam′i·ly
steam′i·ness
steam′roll′er
steam′ship
steam′y
steel
  metal (see steal)
steel′i·ness
steel′work
steel′y
steel′yard
stee′ple
stee′ple·chase
stee′ple·jack
steep′ly
steer′able
steer′age
steer′er
steers′man
stein
stel′lar

stem
  stemmed
  stem′ming
stem′less
stem′ware
sten′cil
  sten′ciled
  or sten′cilled
  sten′cil·ing
  or sten′cil·ling
ste·nog′ra·pher
sten·o·graph′ic
sten·o·graph′i·
  cal·ly
ste·nog′ra·phy
steno′type
steno′typ·ist
sten·to′ri·an
step
  walk (see steppe)
  stepped
  step′ping
step′broth·er
step-by-step′
step′child
step′daugh·ter
step′-down
step′fa·ther
step′-in
step′lad·der
step′moth·er
step′par·ent
steppe
  plain (see step)
step′ping-stone
step′sis·ter

step′son
step′-up
ster′eo
ster·e·o·phon′ic
ster′e·o·scope
ster·e·o·scop′ic
ster·e·os′co·py
ster′e·o·type
ster′e·o·typed
ster′ile
ste·ril′i·ty
ster·il·iza′tion
ster′il·ize
ster′il·iz·er
ster′ling
stern′ly
ster′num
  pl ster′nums *or*
  ster′na
stet
  stet′ted
  stet′ting
steth′o·scope
ste′ve·dore
stew′ard
stew′ard·ess
stick
  stuck
  stick′ing
stick′er
stick′i·ly
stick′i·ness
stick′-in-the-mud
stick′ler
stick-to′-it·ive·
  ness

stick′y
stiff′en
stiff-necked
sti′fle
sti′fling
stig′ma
  pl stig·ma′ta *or*
  stig′mas
stig·mat′ic
stig′ma·tism
stig′ma·tize
stile
  steps (*see* style)
sti·let′to
  pl sti·let′tos *or*
  sti·let′toes
still′birth
still·born
stilt′ed
Stil′ton
stim′u·lant
stim′u·late
stim·u·la′tion
stim′u·la·tive
stim′u·la·tor
stim′u·lus
  pl stim′u·li
sting
  stung
  sting′ing
sting′er
stin′gi·ly
stin′gi·ness
sting′ray
stin′gy
stink

stank
  or stunk
stunk
stink′ing
sti′pend
stip′ple
stip′u·late
stip·u·la′tion
stip′u·la·tor
stir
  stirred
  stir′ring
stir′ring
stir′rup
stitch
sto·chas′tic
stock·ade′
stock′bro·ker
stock′hold·er
stock·i·net′
stock′ing
stock-in-trade′
stock′man
stock′pile
stock′room
Stock′ton
stock′y
stock′yard
stodg′i·ly
stodg′i·ness
stodg′y
sto′gie
  or sto′gy
sto′ic
sto′ical
sto′ical·ly

sto'icism
stok'er
stoke'hole
stol'id
sto·lid'i·ty
stom'ach
stom'ach·ache
stone-blind
stone-broke
stone'cut·ter
stone-deaf
stone'ma·son
stone'ware
stone'work
ston'i·ly
ston'i·ness
ston'y
stop
  stopped
  stop'ping
stop'cock
stop'gap
stop'light
stop'over
stop'page
stop'per
stop'watch
stor'able
stor'age
store'house
store'keep·er
store'room
store·wide
sto'ried
storm'bound
storm'i·ly

storm'i·ness
storm'y
sto'ry
sto'ry·book
sto'ry·tell·er
sto·tin'ka
  pl sto·tin'ki

stout'heart·ed
stout'ly
stove'pipe
stow'age
stow'away
stra·bis'mus
strad'dle
strafe
strag'gle
strag'gler
strag'gly
straight
  not crooked (see
  strait)

straight'-arm
straight'away
straight'edge
straight'en
  make straight (see
  straiten)

straight-faced
straight·for'ward
strain'er
strait
  channel (see
  straight)

strait'en
  confine (see
  straighten)

strait'jack·et
  or straight'jack·et
strait·laced
strange'ly
strang'er
stran'gle
stran'gle·hold
stran'gler
stran'gu·late
stran·gu·la'tion
strap
  strapped
  strap'ping
strap'hang·er
strap'less
strap'ping
strat'a·gem
stra·te'gic
stra·te'gi·cal·ly
strat'e·gist
strat'e·gy
strat·i·fi·ca'tion
strat'i·fy
stra·tig'ra·phy
stra·to·cu'mu·lus
strat'o·sphere
stra'tum
  pl stra'ta
stra'tus
  pl stra'ti
straw'ber·ry
straw'flow·er
straw'worm
streak'i·ness
streak'y
stream'er

stream'line
stream·lined'
street'car
strength'en
stren'u·ous
strep·to·coc'cus
   pl strep·to·coc'ci
strep·to·my'cin
stretch·abil'i·ty
stretch'able
stretch'er
stretch'er-bear·er
strew
  strewed
  strewed
    or strewn
  strew'ing
stri'at·ed
stri·a'tion
strick'en
strict'ly
stric'ture
stride
  strode
  strid'den
  strid'ing
stri'den·cy
stri'dent
strife
strike
  struck
  struck
    or strick'en
  strik'ing
strike'bound
strike'break·er

strike'out
strike'over
strik'er
strik'ing
string
  strung
  string'ing
strin'gen·cy
strin'gent
string'er
string'i·ness
string'ing
string'y
strip
  stripped
  strip'ping
strip'-crop·ping
strip'ling
strip'per
strip'tease
strive
  strove
  striv'en
    or strived
  striv'ing
stro'bo·scope
stro·bo·scop'ic
stroll'er
strong-arm
strong'box
strong'hold
strong'-mind·ed
stron'tium
strop
  stropped
  strop'ping

stro'phe
stroph'ic
struc'tur·al
struc'tur·al·ly
struc'ture
strug'gle
strum
  strummed
  strum'ming
strum'pet
strut
  strut'ted
  strut'ting
strych'nine
stub
  stubbed
  stub'bing
stub'ble
stub'bly
stub'born
stub'born·ness
stub'by
stuc'co
  stuc'coed
  stuc'co·ing
stud
  stud'ded
  stud'ding
stud'book
stud'ding
stu'dent
stud'horse
stud'ied
stu'dio
stu'di·ous
stuff'i·ly

stuff'i·ness
stuff'ing
stuff'y
stul·ti·fi·ca'tion
stul'ti·fy
stum'ble
stun
  stunned
  stun'ning
stun'ning
stu·pe·fac'tion
stu'pe·fy
stu·pen'dous
stu'pid
stu·pid'i·ty
stu'por
stur'di·ly
stur'dy
stur'geon
stut'ter
sty
  pl sties *also* styes
  pig pen

sty
  or stye
  pl sties *or* styes
  eyelid swelling

style
  fashion (see stile)
style'book
styl'ish
styl'ist
sty·lis'ti·cal·ly
sty·lis'tics
styl·iza'tion
styl'ize

sty'lus
  pl sty'li *also*
   sty'lus·es
sty'mie
  sty'mied
  sty'mie·ing
styp'tic
sty'rene
su'able
sua'sion
sua'sive
suave'ly
sua'vi·ty
sub
  subbed
  sub'bing
sub·a'gen·cy
sub'ar·ea
sub·as·sem'bly
sub·atom'ic
sub·av'er·age
sub'base·ment
sub'bing
sub'class
sub'com·mit·tee
sub'con'scious
sub'con'ti·nent
sub·con'tract
sub·con'trac·tor
sub'cul·ture
sub·cu·ta'ne·ous
sub·dis'ci·pline
sub·di·vide'
sub·di·vi'sion
sub·due'
sub'en·try

sub'fam·i·ly
sub'freez'ing
sub'group
sub·hu'man
sub'ject
  noun
sub·ject'
  verb
sub·jec'tion
sub·jec'tive
sub·jec·tiv'i·ty
sub·join'
sub ju'di·ce
sub'ju·gate
sub·ju·ga'tion
sub·junc'tive
sub·lease
sub·les·see'
sub·les·sor'
sub·let'
sub'li·mate
sub·li·ma'tion
sub·lime'
sub·lim'i·nal
sub·lim'i·nal·ly
sub·lim'i·ty
sub·lu'nar
sub·mar'gin·al
sub·mar'gin·al·ly
sub'ma·rine
sub·merge'
sub·mer'gence
sub·mers'ible
sub·mer'sion
sub·mis'sion
sub·mis'sive

sub·mit'
  sub·mit'ted
  sub·mit'ting
sub'nor'mal
sub·nor·mal'i·ty
sub·or'bit·al
sub·or'der
sub·or'di·nate
sub·or·di·na'tion
sub·orn'
sub·or·na'tion
sub'plot
sub·poe'na
sub're·gion
sub ro'sa
sub·scribe'
sub·scrib'er
sub·scrip'tion
sub'se·quent
sub·ser'vi·ence
sub·ser'vi·ent
sub·side'
sub·sid'ence
sub·sid'i·ary
sub·si·di·za'tion
sub'si·dize
sub'si·dy
sub·sist'
sub·sis'tence
sub'soil
sub·son'ic
sub'spe·cies
sub'stance
sub·stan'dard
sub·stan'tial
sub·stan'tial·ly

sub·stan'ti·ate
sub·stan·ti·a'tion
sub'stan·tive
sub·sta'tion
sub'sti·tut·able
sub'sti·tute
sub·sti·tu'tion
sub'stra·tum
  pl sub'stra·ta
sub'struc·ture
sub·sume'
sub'sur·face
sub'ter·fuge
sub·ter·ra'ne·an
sub'ti·tle
sub'tle
sub'tle·ty
sub'tly
sub·tract'
sub·trac'tion
sub'tra·hend
sub·trop'i·cal
sub'urb
sub·ur'ban
sub·ur'ban·ite
sub·ur'bia
sub·ven'tion
sub·ver'sion
sub·ver'sive
sub·vert'
sub'way
suc·ceed'
suc·cess'
suc·cess'ful
suc·cess'ful·ly
suc·ces'sion

suc·ces'sive
suc·ces'sive·ly
suc·ces'sor
suc·cinct'
suc'cor
  help (see sucker)
suc'co·tash
suc'cu·lence
suc'cu·lent
suc·cumb'
such'like
suck'er
  one that sucks (see succor)
suck'le
suck'ling
su'cre
su'crose
suc'tion
Su·dan'
Su·da·nese'
sud'den
sud'den·ness
su·do·rif'ic
suds'y
suede
  or suède
su'et
suf'fer
suf'fer·able
suf'fer·ably
suf'fer·ance
suf'fer·ing
suf·fice'
suf·fi'cien·cy
suf·fi'cient

suf'fix
suf'fo·cate
suf·fo·ca'tion
suf'fra·gan
suf'frage
suf'frag·ette'
suf'frag·ist
suf·fuse'
suf·fu'sion
sug'ar
sug'ar·cane
sug·ar·coat'
sug'ar·plum
sug'ary
sug·gest'
sug·gest·ibil'i·ty
sug·gest'ible
sug·ges'tion
sug·ges'tive
su·i·cid'al
su'i·cide
sui·ge'ner·is
sui·ju'ris
suit
  legal action, set,
   fitting (see suite,
   sweet)

suit·abil'i·ty
suit'able
suit'ably
suit'case
suite
  retinue, apartment
  (see suit, sweet)

suit'ing
suit'or
sul'fa

sul·fa·nil'a·mide
sul'fate
  or sul'phate
sul'fide
  or sul'phide
sul'fur
  or sul'phur
sul·fu'ric
  or sul·phu'ric
sul'fu·rous
  or sul'phu·rous
sulk'i·ly
sulk'i·ness
sulk'y
sul'len
sul'len·ness
sul'ly
sul'tan
sul·tan'a
sul'tan·ate
sul'tri·ness
sul'try
sum
  summed
  sum'ming
su'mac
  or su'mach
sum·mar'i·ly
sum·ma·ri·za'tion
sum'ma·rize
sum'ma·ry
  concise (see
  summery)

sum·ma'tion
sum'mer
sum'mer·house
sum'mer·time

sum'mery
  like summer (see
  summary)

sum'mit
sum'mon
sum'mons
  pl sum'mon·ses
sump'tu·ous
sun
  sunned
  sun'ning
sun'baked
sun'bathe
sun'beam
sun'bon·net
sun'burn
sun'burst
sun'dae
Sun'day
sun'der
sun'di·al
sun'down
sun'dries
sun'dry
sun'fish
sun'flow·er
sun'glass·es
sunk'en
sun'lamp
sun'light
sun'lit
sun'ny
sun'rise
sun'set
sun'shade
sun'shine
sun'spot

sun'stroke
sun'suit
sun'tan
sun'up
sup
  supped
  sup'ping
su'per
su·per·a·bun'dance
su·per·a·bun'dant
su·per·an·nu·ate
su·per·an·nu·at·ed
su·perb'
su·per·car'go
su·per·cil'i·ous
su·per·con·duc·
  tiv'i·ty
su·per·con·duc'tor
su·per·e'go
su·per·fi'cial
su·per·fi'ci·al·i·ty
su·per·fi'cial·ly
su·per·flu'i·ty
su·per'flu·ous
su·per·high'way
su·per·hu'man
su·per·im·pose'
su·per·in·duce'
su·per·in·duc'tion
su·per·in·tend'
su·per·in·ten'
  dence
su·per·in·ten'
  den·cy
su·per·in·ten'dent
su·pe'ri·or
su·pe·ri·or'i·ty

su·per'la·tive
su'per·lin·er
su'per·man
su'per·mar·ket
su·per'nal
su·per·nat'u·ral
su·per·nat'u·ral·ly
su·per·nu'mer·ary
su'per·pow·er
su'per·scribe
su'per·script
su·per·scrip'tion
su·per·sede'
su·per·se'dure
su·per·sen'si·tive
su·per·son'ic
su·per·son'i·cal·ly
su·per·sti'tion
su·per·sti'tious
su'per·struc·ture
su'per·tank·er
su·per·vene'
su·per·ven'tion
su'per·vise
su·per·vi'sion
su'per·vi·sor
su·per·vi'so·ry
su·pine'
sup'per
sup'per·time
sup·plant'
sup'ple
sup'ple·ment
sup·ple·men'tal
sup·ple·men'ta·ry
sup'pli·ant
sup'pli·cant

sup'pli·cate
sup·pli·ca'tion
sup·pli'er
sup·ply'
sup·port'
sup·port'able
sup·port'ive
sup·pose'
sup·posed'
sup·pos'ed·ly
sup·pos'ing
sup·po·si'tion
sup·pos'i·to·ry
sup·press'
sup·pres'sant
sup·press'ible
sup·pres'sion
sup·pres'sor
sup'pu·rate
sup·pu·ra'tion
su'pra
su·prem'a·cist
su·prem'a·cy
su·preme'
sur'cease
sur'charge
sur'cin·gle
sure·fire
sure'foot·ed
sure'ly
sure'ty
surf
  sea swell (*see* serf)
sur'face
surf'board
surf'boat
sur'feit

surf′er
surf′ing
surge
  sweep (see serge)
sur′geon
sur′gery
sur′gi·cal
sur′gi·cal·ly
sur′li·ness
sur′ly
sur·mise′
sur·mount′
sur·name
sur·pass′
sur′plice
  vestment (see
  surplus)
sur′plus
  excess (see surplice)
sur·prise′
sur·pris′ing
sur·re′al·ism
sur·re′al·ist
sur·re·al·is′ti·
  cal·ly
sur·ren′der
sur·rep·ti′tious
sur′rey
sur′ro·gate
sur·round′
sur·round′ings
sur′tax
sur·veil′lance
sur·vey′
  verb

sur′vey
  noun
sur·vey′ing
sur·vey′or
sur·viv′al
sur·vive′
sur·vi′vor
sus·cep·ti·bil′i·ty
sus·cep′ti·ble
sus·cep′ti·bly
sus·pect′
  verb
sus′pect
  adjective, noun
sus·pend′
sus·pend′er
sus·pense′
sus·pen′sion
sus·pen′so·ry
sus·pi′cion
sus·pi′cious
sus·tain′
sus·tain′able
sus′te·nance
su′ture
su′zer·ain
su′zer·ain·ty
svelte
swab
  swabbed
  swab′bing
swad′dle
swad′dling
swag′ger
swal′low

swal′low·tail
swal′low-tailed
swamp′y
swank′y
swans′down
swap
  swapped
  swap′ping
swarth′i·ness
swarth′y
swash′buck·ler
swas′ti·ka
swat
  swat′ted
  swat′ting
swatch
swath
  noun, cut row (see
  swathe)
swathe
  noun, verb, bandage
  (see swath)
sway·back
Swa′zi
  pl Swa′zi *or* Swa′zis
Swa′zi·land
swear
  swore
  sworn
  swear′ing
sweat
  sweat
  or sweat′ed
  sweat′ing
sweat′band

sweat′box
sweat′er
sweat′i·ly
sweat′i·ness
sweat′shop
sweat′y
Swe′den
Swed′ish
sweep
  swept
  sweep′ing
sweep′back
sweep′er
sweep′ing
sweep′-sec·ond
sweep′stakes
  also sweep′stake
  pl sweep′stakes

sweet
  pleasing, candy (see
    suit, suite)

sweet′bread
sweet′bri·er
sweet′en
sweet′heart
sweet′meat
sweet′-talk
swell
  swelled
  swelled
  or swol′len

  swell′ing
swel′ter
swept-back
swept·wing

swerve
swift′ly
swig
  swigged
  swig′ging
swill
swim
  swam
  swum
  swim′ming
swim′mer
swim′suit
swin′dle
swin′dler
swine
  pl swine
swing
  swung
  swing′ing
swing′-by
swing-wing
swin′ish
Swiss
  pl Swiss
switch
switch′back
switch′board
switch′-hit′ter
switch′man
switch′yard
Swit′zer·land
swiv′el
  swiv′eled
  or swiv′elled
  swiv′el·ing
  or swiv′el·ling

swollen
sword′fish
sword′play
swords′man
sword′tail
syb′a·rite
syb·a·rit′ic
syc′a·more
syc′o·phant
syc·o·phan′tic
syl·lab′ic
syl·lab·i·ca′tion
syl·lab·i·fi·ca′tion
syl·lab′i·fy
syl′la·ble
syl′la·bus
  pl syl′la·bi *or*
    syl′la·bus·es

syl′lo·gism
syl·lo·gis′tic
sylph
syl′van
sym·bi·o′sis
sym·bi·ot′ic
sym′bol
  representation (see
    cymbal)

sym·bol′ic
sym·bol′i·cal·ly
sym′bol·ism
sym·bol·iza′tion
sym′bol·ize
sym·met′ri·cal
sym·met′ri·cal·ly
sym′me·try

sym·pa·thet′ic
sym·pa·thet′i·cal·ly
sym′pa·thize
sym′pa·thiz·er
sym′pa·thy
sym·phon′ic
sym′pho·ny
sym·po′si·um
  pl sym·po′sia *or*
  sym·po′si·ums

symp′tom
symp·tom·at′ic
syn′a·gogue
syn′apse
syn′chro·mesh
syn′chro·nism
syn·chro·ni·za′tion
syn′chro·nize
syn′chro·nous
syn′chro·tron
syn′co·pate
syn′co·pa′tion
syn′co·pe
syn·cret′ic
syn′cre·tism
syn′di·cal·ism
syn′di·cate
syn·di·ca′tion
syn′drome
syn·ec′do·che
syn·ecol′o·gy
syn′er·gism
syn′er·gist
syn·er·gis′ti·cal·ly

syn′od
syn·od′i·cal
syn′onym
syn·on′y·mous
syn·on′y·my
syn·op′sis
  pl syn·op′ses
syn·op′size
syn·op′tic
syn·tac′tic
syn·tac′ti·cal
syn·tac′ti·cal·ly
syn′tax
syn′the·sis
  pl syn′the·ses
syn′the·size
syn·thet′ic
syn·thet′i·cal·ly
syph′i·lis
syph·i·lit′ic
Syr′a·cuse
Syr′ia
Syr′i·an
sy·ringe′
syr′up
syr′upy
sys′tem
sys·tem·at′ic
sys·tem·at′i·cal·ly
sys·tem·ati·za′tion
sys′tem·a·tize
sys·tem′ic
sys′tem·iza′tion
sys′tem·ize

T

tab
tabbed
tab′bing
Ta·bas′co
tab′by
tab′er·na·cle
ta′ble
tab′leau
  pl tab′leaux *also*
  tab′leaus
ta′ble·cloth
ta·ble d'hôte′
ta′ble-hop
ta′ble·land
ta′ble·spoon
ta·ble·spoon′ful
  pl ta·ble·spoon′fuls
  or
  ta·ble·spoons′ful

tab′let
ta′ble·top
ta′ble·ware
tab′loid
ta·boo′
  or ta·bu′
ta′bor
  also ta′bour
tab·o·ret′
  or tab·ou·ret′
tab′u·lar
tab′u·late
tab·u·la′tion
tab′u·la·tor
tac′an

ta·chom'e·ter
tac'it
tac'i·turn
tac·i·tur'ni·ty
tack'i·ness
tack'le
tack'y
ta'co
   pl ta'cos
Ta·co'ma
tact'ful
tact'ful·ly
tac'tic
tac'ti·cal
tac·ti'cian
tac'tics
tac'tile
tact'less
tad'pole
taf'fe·ta
taff'rail
taf'fy
tag
  tagged
  tag'ging
tai·ga'
tail'board
tail'coat
tail'gate
tail'less
tail'light
tai'lor
tai·lor-made'
tail'piece
tail'spin
Tai·wan

take
  took
  tak'en
  tak'ing
take'off
take'out
take'-over
tak'er
tak'ing
talc
tal'cum
tal'ent
tales'man
  juror (see talisman)
tal'is·man
  charm (see
  talesman)
talk'ative
talk'er
talk'ing-to
talk'y
Tal·la·has'see
tal'low
tal'ly
tal·ly·ho'
Tal'mud
tal·mu'dic
tal'on
tam'able
  or tame'able
ta·ma'le
tam'a·rack
tam'a·rind
tam'bour
tam·bou·rine'
tame'ly

tam'er
tam'-o'-shan·ter
Tam'pa
tam'per
tam'pon
tan
  tanned
  tan'ning
tan'a·ger
tan'bark
tan'dem
tan'ge·lo
tan'gent
tan·gen'tial
tan'ger·ine
tan·gi·bil'i·ty
tan'gi·ble
tan'gi·bly
tan'gle
tan'go
tang'y
tank'age
tan'kard
tank'er
tan'ner
tan'nery
tan'nic
tan'nin
tan'ta·lize
tan'ta·mount
tan'trum
Tan·za·ni'a
Tan·za·ni'an
tap
  tapped
  tap'ping

ta'per
  candle, diminish
    (*see* tapir)

tape-re·cord'
tap'es·tried
tap'es·try
tape'worm
tap'hole
tap·i·o'ca
ta'pir
  animal (*see* taper)

tap'pet
tap'room
tap'root
tar
  tarred
  tar'ring
tar·an·tel'la
ta·ran'tu·la
tar'brush
tar'di·ly
tar'di·ness
tar'dy
tare
  weed, weight
    allowance (*see*
    tear)

tar'get
tar'iff
tar'mar
tar'nish
ta'ro
tar·pau'lin
tar'pon
tar'ra·gon
tar'ry

tar'tan
tar'tar
tar·tar'ic
tart'ly
task'mas·ter
tas'sel
  tas'seled
  or tas'selled
  tas'sel·ing
  or tas'sel·ling
taste'ful
taste'ful·ly
taste'less
tast'er
tast'i·ly
tast'i·ness
tast'y
tat
  tat'ted
  tat'ting
tat'ter
tat·ter·de·ma'lion
tat'tered
tat'ter·sall
tat'ting
tat'tle
tat'tle·tale
tat·too'
taught
  past of teach (*see*
    taut)

taunt'er
taupe
taut
  tense (*see* taught)
tau·to·log'i·cal

tau·to·log'i·cal·ly
tau·tol'o·gy
tav'ern
taw'dri·ly
taw'dri·ness
taw'dry
taw'ny
tax·abil'i·ty
tax'able
tax·a'tion
tax-ex·empt'
tax'i
  pl tax'is *also* tax'ies
tax'i
  tax'ied
  taxi'ing
  or taxy'ing
tax'i·cab
tax'i·der·mist
tax'i·der·my
tax'i·me·ter
tax'ing
tax·o·nom'ic
tax·on'o·my
tax'pay·er
T-bar
T'-bone
tea
  beverage (*see* tee)

teach
  taught
  teach'ing
teach·abil'i·ty
teach'able
teach'er
teach'-in

tea′cup
tea′cup·ful
   pl tea′cup·fuls *or*
   tea′cups·ful
tea′house
tea′ket·tle
teak′wood
team
   group (*see* teem)
team′mate
team′ster
team′work
tea′pot
tear
   rip (*see* tare)
   tore
   torn
   tear′ing
tear
   cry (*see* tare, tier)
tear′drop
tear′ful
tear′ful·ly
tea′room
tear′stained
tea′sel
teas′er
tea′spoon
tea′spoon·ful
   pl tea′spoon·fuls *or*
   tea′spoons·ful
teat
tea′time
tech′nic
tech′ni·cal
tech·ni·cal′i·ty

tech′ni·cal·ly
tech·ni′cian
tech·nique′
tech′no·crat
tech·noc′ra·cy
tech·no·log′i·cal
tech·no·log′i·
   cal·ly
tech·nol′o·gist
tech·nol′o·gy
tec·ton′ic
tec·ton′ics
te′dious
te′di·um
tee
   golf (*see* tea)
   teed
   tee′ing
teem
   abound (*see* team)
teen′-age
   or teen′-aged
teen′-ag·er
tee′ter
tee′to·tal·er
   or tee′to·tal·ler
tee′to·tal·ism
Tel·Au′to·graph
tel′e·cast
tel′e·cast
   also tel′e·cast·ed
   tel′e·cast·ing
tele′cast·er
tele·com·mu·ni·
   ca′tion
tel′e·course

tel′e·film
tel·e·gen′ic
tel′e·gram
tel′e·graph
te·leg′ra·pher
tel·e·graph′ic
tel·e·graph′i·cal·ly
te·leg′ra·phy
tele·ki·ne′sis
tel′e·lec·ture
tel′e·me·ter
te·lem′e·try
te·le·o·log′i·cal
te·le·ol′o·gy
tel·e·path′ic
tel·e·path′i·cal·ly
te·lep′a·thy
tel′e·phone
tel·e·phon′ic
tel·e·phon′i·cal·ly
te·leph′o·ny
tele·pho′to
tele·pho′to·graph
tele·pho·tog′ra·phy
tel′e·play
tel′e·print·er
Tel′e·Promp·Ter
tel′er·an
tel′e·scope
tel·e·scop′ic
tel′e·thon
Tel′e·type
tele·type′writ·er
tel′e·view·er
tel′e·vise
tel′e·vi·sion

tel'ex
tell
  told
  tell'ing
tell'er
tel'pher
tell'tale
tem'blor
te·mer'i·ty
tem'per
tem'pera
  also tem'po·ra
tem'per·a·ment
tem·per·a·men'tal
tem·per·a·men'
  tal·ly
tem'per·ance
tem'per·ate
tem'per·a·ture
tem'pest
tem·pes'tu·ous
tem'plate
  or tem'plet
tem'ple
tem'po
  pl tem'pi *or* tem'pos
tem'po·ral
tem·po·rar'i·ly
tem'po·rary
tem·po·ri·za'tion
tem'po·rize
temp·ta'tion
tempt'er
tempt'ress
ten·a·bil'i·ty
ten'a·ble

te·na'cious
te·nac'i·ty
ten'an·cy
ten'ant
ten'ant·ry
ten·den·cy
ten·den'tious
  also ten·den'cious
ten'der
  soft, offer
tend'er
  one that tends
ten'der·foot
  pl ten'der·feet *also*
  ten'der·foots

ten·der·heart'ed
ten'der·ize
ten'der·loin
ten'der·ly
ten'der·ness
ten'don
ten'dril
te·neb'ri·ous
ten'e·brous
ten'e·ment
ten'et
ten'fold
Ten·nes·see'
ten'nis
ten'on
ten'or
ten'pin
tense'ly
tense'ness
ten'sile
ten·sil'i·ty

ten'sion
ten'si·ty
ten'sor
ten'ta·cle
ten'ta·tive
ten'ta·tive·ly
ten'ter
ten'ter·hook
tenth
tenth-rate
te·nu'i·ty
ten'u·ous
ten'ure
ten'ured
te'pee
tep'id
te·qui'la
ter·cen·ten'a·ry
ter'gi·ver·sate
ter'ma·gant
ter'mi·na·ble
ter'mi·na·bly
ter'mi·nal
ter'mi·nal·ly
ter'mi·nate
ter·mi·na'tion
ter'mi·na·tor
ter·mi·nol'o·gy
ter'mi·nus
  pl ter'mi·ni *or*
  ter'mi·nus·es

ter'mite
ter'na·ry
terp·sich·o·re'an
ter'race
ter·ra-cot'ta

ter·ra fir′ma
ter·rain′
Ter·ra·my′cin
ter′ra·pin
ter·rar′i·um
   pl ter·rar′ia *or*
     ter·rar′i·ums

ter·raz′zo
ter·res′tri·al
ter′ri·ble
ter′ri·bly
ter′ri·er
ter·rif′ic
ter·rif′i·cal·ly
ter′ri·fy
ter′ri·fy·ing
ter·ri·to′ri·al
ter·ri·to·ri·al′i·ty
ter′ri·to·ry
ter′ror
ter′ror·ism
ter′ror·ist
ter·ror·iza′tion
ter′ror·ize
ter′ry
terse′ly
ter′ti·ary
tes′sel·late
tes′sel·lat·ed
tes·sel·la′tion
tes′ta·ment
tes·ta·men′ta·ry
tes′tate
tes′ta·tor
tes·ta′trix
tes′ti·cle

tes′ti·fi·er
tes′ti·fy
tes′ti·ly
tes·ti·mo′ni·al
tes′ti·mo·ny
tes′ti·ness
tes·tos′ter·one
tes′ty
tet′a·nus
tête-à-tête′
teth′er
tet·ra·cy′cline
tet·ra·eth′yl
te·tral′o·gy
te·tram′e·ter
Tex′as
text′book
tex′tile
tex′tu·al
tex′tu·al·ly
tex′tur·al
tex′ture
Thai
Thai′land
tha·lid′o·mide
thank′ful
thank′ful·ly
thank′less
thanks·giv′ing
that
   pl those
thatch
thaw
the′ater
  or the′atre
the′ater·go·er

the·at′ri·cal
the·at′rics
theft
the′ism
the′ist
the·is′tic
the·mat′ic
the·mat′i·cal·ly
theme
them·selves′
thence′forth
thence·for′ward
  also
   thence·for′wards

the·oc′ra·cy
the·o·crat′ic
the·od′o·lite
the·o·lo′gian
the·o·log′i·cal
the·ol′o·gy
the′o·rem
the·o·ret′i·cal
the·o·ret′i·cal·ly
the·o·re·ti′cian
the′o·rize
the′o·ry
the·os′o·phist
the·os′o·phy
ther·a·peu′tic
ther·a·peu′ti·
  cal·ly
ther·a·peu′tics
ther′a·pist
ther′a·py
there·abouts′
  or there·about′

there·af'ter
there·at'
there·by'
there·for'
 in return for (see therefore)
there·fore'
 for that reason (see therefor)
there·from'
there·in'
there·of'
there·on'
there·to'
there·upon'
there·with'
ther'mal
therm'ion
ther·mo·dy·nam'i·cal·ly
ther·mo·dy·nam'ics
ther'mo·form
ther·mom'e·ter
ther·mo·nu'cle·ar
ther·mo·phys'i·cal
ther·mo·plas'tic
ther'mos
ther'mo·set·ting
ther'mo·sphere
ther'mo·stat
ther·mo·stat'i·cal·ly
the·sau'rus
 pl the·sau'ri *or* the·sau'rus·es

the'sis
 pl the'ses
thes'pi·an
thi'a·mine
thick'en
thick'et
thick'head'ed
thick'ly
thick'ness
thick·set
thick-skinned
thief
 pl thieves
thieve
thiev'er·y
thigh·bone
thim'ble
thim'ble·ful
thin
thinned
thin'ning
think
 thought
 think'ing
think'able
think'er
thin'ly
thin'ner
thin'ness
thin-skinned
third-class
third-degree
third-rate
thirst'i·ly
thirst'i·ness
thirst'y

thir·teen'
thir·teenth'
thir'ti·eth
thir'ty
this
 pl these
this'tle
this'tle·down
thith'er
thith'er·ward
thole
thong
tho·rac'ic
tho'rax
 pl tho'rax·es *or* tho'ra·ces
thorn'y
thor'ough
thor'ough·bred
thor'ough·fare
thor·ough·go'ing
thor'ough·ness
though
thought
thought'ful
thought'ful·ly
thought'less
thou'sand
 pl thou'sands *or* thou'sand
thou'sandth
thrall'dom
 or thral'dom
thrash'er
thread'bare
thread'i·ness

thread'y
threat'en
3-D
three'-deck'er
three-di·men'-
  sion·al
three'fold
three'-hand'ed
three-legged
three-piece
three-ply
three'-quar'ter
three·score
three'some
thren'o·dy
thresh'er
thresh'old
threw
  past of throw (see
   through)

thrice
thrift'i·ly
thrift'less
thrift'y
thrill'er
thrive
  throve
  or thrived

  thriv'en
  also thrived

  thriv'ing
throat'i·ly
throat'i·ness
throat'y
throb
  throbbed

throb'bing
throe
  pang (see throw)

throm·bo'sis
throne
throng
throt'tle
through
  by way of, finished
  (see threw)

through·out'
throw
  hurl (see throe)

  threw
  thrown
  throw'ing
throw'away
throw'back
thrum
  thrummed
  thrum'ming
thrust
  thrust
  thrust'ing
thrust'or
  or thrust'er

thru'way
  or through'way

thud
  thud'ded
  thud'ding
thumb'hole
thumb'nail
thumb'print
thumb'screw
thumb'tack

thump
thun'der
thun'der·bird
thun'der·bolt
thun'der·clap
thun'der·cloud
thun'der·head
thun'der·ous
thun'der·show·er
thun'der·storm
thun'der·struck
Thurs'day
thwack
thwart
thyme
  herb (see time)

thy'mus
thy'roid
ti·ar'a
tib'ia
  pl tib'i·ae *also*
   tib'i·as

tic
  twitch (see tick)

tick
  beat, insect (see tic)

tick'er
tick'et
tick'ing
tick'le
tick'ler
tick'lish
tick·tack·toe'
  also tic·tac·toe'

tid'al
tid'bit

tid'dle·dy·winks
  or tid'dly·winks
tide'land
tide'mark
tide'wa·ter
tide'way
tid'i·ly
ti'di·ness
tid'ings
ti'dy
tie
  tied
  ty'ing
    or tie'ing
tie'back
tie'-in
tie'pin
tier
  row (see tear)
tie'-up
tif'fa·ny
ti'ger
ti'ger·eye
  also ti'ger's-eye
ti'ger·ish
tight'en
tight'fist'ed
tight-lipped
tight-mouthed
tight'ness
tight'rope
tights
tight'wad
ti'gon
ti'gress
til'ing
till'able

till'age
till'er
  one that tills
til'ler
  steering lever
tim'bal
  drum (see timbale)
tim'bale
  food (see timbal)
tim'ber
  wood (see timbre)
tim'ber·land
tim'ber·line
tim'bre
  sound (see timber)
tim'brel
time
  period (see thyme)
time'-con·sum'
  ing
time'-hon·ored
time'keep·er
time'-lapse
time'less
time'li·ness
time'ly
time-out
time'piece
tim'er
time-release
time'-sav·er
time'sav·ing
time'serv·er
time'-shar·ing
time'ta·ble
time'worn
tim'id

ti·mid'i·ty
tim'id·ly
tim'ing
tim'o·rous
tim'o·thy
tim'pa·ni
tim'pa·nist
tin
  tinned
  tin'ning
tinc'ture
tin'der
tin'der·box
tin'foil
tinge
  tinged
  tinge'ing
    or ting'ing
tin'gle
tin'horn
ti'ni·ly
ti'ni·ness
tin'ker
tin'ker·er
tin'kle
tin'kly
tin'ni·ly
tin'ni·ness
tin'ny
tin·plate
tin'sel
  tin'seled
  or tin'selled
  tin'sel·ing
  or tin'sel·ling
tin'smith
tint'ing

tin·tin·nab·u·la′
  tion
tin′type
tin′ware
tin′work
ti′ny
tip
  tipped
  tip′ping
tip′-off
tip′pet
tip′ple
tip′pler
tip′si·ly
tip′si·ness
tip′ster
tip′sy
tip′toe
tip-top
ti·rade′
tired
tire′less
tire′some
tis′sue
ti′tan
ti·tan′ic
tithe
tith′ing
ti′tian
tit′il·late
tit·il·la′tion
ti′tle
ti′tled
ti′tle·hold·er
tit′mouse
  pl tit′mice
ti·tra′tion

tit′ter
tit′tle-tat·tle
tit′u·lar
tiz′zy
toad′stool
toad′y
to-and-fro′
toast′er
toast′mas·ter
to·bac′co
to·bac′co·nist
to·bog′gan
toc·ca′ta
toc′sin
  alarm (see toxin)
to′day
tod′dle
tod′dler
tod′dy
to-do′
toe
  toed
  toe′ing
toe′-dance
toe′hold
toe′-in
toe′less
toe′nail
toe′piece
tof′fee
  or tof′fy
tog
  togged
  tog′ging
to′ga
to·geth′er
tog′gle

To′go
To·go·lese′
toi′let
toi′let·ry
toil′some
toil′worn
to′ken
to′ken·ism
tole
  metal (see toll)
To·le′do
tol′er·a·ble
tol′er·a·bly
tol′er·ance
tol′er·ant
tol′er·ate
tol·er·a′tion
toll
  tax, sound (see tole)
toll′booth
toll′gate
toll′house
toll′man
tom′a·hawk
to·ma′to
  pl to·ma′toes
tom′boy
tomb′stone
tom′cat
tom·fool′ery
to·mor′row
tom′-tom
ton
  pl tons *also* ton
  weight (see tun)
ton′al
to·nal′i·ty

tone′-deaf
tone′less
tongs
tongue
  tongued
  tongu′ing
tongue′-lash·ing
tongue′-tied
ton′ic
to·night′
ton′nage
ton·neau′
ton′sil
ton·sil·lec′to·my
ton·sil·li′tis
ton·so′ri·al
ton′sure
ton′tine
tool′box
tool′head
tool′hold·er
tool′mak·er
tool′room
tooth
  pl teeth
tooth′ache
tooth′brush
tooth′less
tooth′paste
tooth′pick
tooth′some
tooth′wort
tooth′y
top
  topped
  top′ping

to′paz
top′coat
to·pee′
  or to′pi
To·pe′ka
top′er
top·flight
top′-heavy
top′ic
top′i·cal
top·i·cal′i·ty
top′i·cal·ly
top′knot
top′less
top′mast
top′most
top-notch
to·pog′ra·pher
top·o·graph′ic
top·o·graph′i·cal
top·o·graph′i·
  cal·ly
to·pog′ra·phy
to·po·log′i·cal
to·po·log′i·cal·ly
to·pol′o·gist
to·pol′o·gy
top′ping
top′ple
top′sail
top·side
top′soil
top′stitch
top·sy-tur′vy
toque
To′rah

torch′bear·er
torch′light
tor′e·ador
tor′ment
tor·men′tor
tor·na′do
  pl tor·na′does *or*
  tor·na′dos
To·ron′to
tor·pe′do
  pl tor·pe′does
tor′pid
tor·pid′i·ty
tor′por
torque
Tor′rance
tor′rent
tor·ren′tial
tor·ren′tial·ly
tor′rid
tor′sion
tor′so
  pl tor′sos *or* tor′si
tort
  wrongful act (see
  torte)
torte
  pl tor·ten *or* tortes
  cake (see tort)
tor·til′la
tor′toise
tor′toise·shell
tor′tu·ous
  winding (see
  torturous)
tor′ture

tor'tur·er

tor'tur·ous
painful (see
tortuous)

toss'-up

tot
tot'ted
tot'ting

to'tal
to'taled
or to'talled

to'tal·ing
or to'tal·ling

to·tal·i·tar'i·an

to·tal'i·ty

to'tal·iza·tor
or to'tal·isa·tor

to'tal·ly

to'tem

tot'ter

tou'can

touch'able

touch'back

touch'down

tou·ché'

touch'i·ly

touch'i·ness

touch'ing

touch'-mark

touch'stone

touch'-type

touch'y

tough'en

tough'-mind·ed

tough'ness

tou·pee'

tour de force'
pl tours de force'

tour'ism

tour'ist

tour'ma·line

tour'na·ment

tour'ney

tour'ni·quet

tou'sle

tow'age

to'ward
or to'wards

tow'boat

tow'el
tow'eled
or tow'elled

tow'el·ing
or tow'el·ling

tow'el·ing
or tow'el·ling

tow'er

tow'er·ing

tow'head

tow'head·ed

tow'line

towns'folk

town'ship

towns'man

towns'peo·ple

tow'path

tow'rope

tox·e'mia

tox'ic

tox·ic'i·ty

tox'i·cant

tox·i·co·log'ic

tox·i·co·log'i·
cal·ly

tox·i·col'o·gist

tox·i·col'o·gy

tox'in
poison (see tocsin)

tox'in-an'ti·tox·in

trace'able

trac'er

trac'ery

tra'chea
pl tra'che·ae

tra·cho'ma

trac'ing

track
route, follow (see
tract)

track'age

track-and-field'

track'less

track'walk·er

tract
pamphlet, land (see
track)

trac·ta·bil'i·ty

trac'ta·ble

trac'ta·bly

trac'tile

trac'tion

trac'tor

trade'-in

trade'-last

trade'mark

trad'er

trades'man

trades'peo·ple

tra·di′tion
tra·di′tion·al
tra·di′tion·al·ly
tra·duce′
tra·duc′er
traf′fic
  traf′ficked
  traf′fick·ing
traf·fick′er
tra·ge′di·an
tra·ge·di·enne′
trag′e·dy
trag′ic
trag′i·cal·ly
tragi·com′e·dy
tragi·com′ic
trail′blaz·er
trail′er
train′able
train·ee′
train′er
train′ing
train·load
train′man
trait
trai′tor
trai′tor·ous
trai′tress
tra·jec′to·ry
tram′mel
  tram′meled
  or tram′melled
  tram′mel·ing
  or tram′mel·ling
tram′ple
tram·po·line′
tran′quil

tran′quil·ize
  or tran′quil·lize
tran′quil·iz·er
tran·quil′li·ty
  or tran·quil′i·ty
tran′quil·ly
trans·act′
trans·ac′tion
trans·ac′tion·al
trans·ac′tor
trans·at·lan′tic
trans·ceiv′er
tran·scend′
tran·scen′dence
tran·scen′dent
tran·scen·den′tal
tran·scen·den′-
  tal·ism
trans·con·ti·nen′-
  tal
tran·scribe′
tran′script
tran·scrip′tion
trans·duce′
trans·duc′er
tran·sect′
tran·sec′tion
tran′sept
trans·fer′
  trans·ferred′
  trans·fer′ring
trans·fer′able
trans·fer′al
trans·fer′ence
trans·fig·u·ra′tion
trans·fig′ure
trans·fix′

trans·form′
trans·form′able
trans·for·ma′tion
trans·form′er
trans·fuse′
trans·fus′ible
  or trans·fus′able
trans·fu′sion
trans·gress′
trans·gres′sion
trans·gres′sor
tran′sience
tran′sient
tran·sis′tor
tran·sis′tor·ize
tran′sit
tran·si′tion
tran·si′tion·al
tran·si′tion·al·ly
tran′si·tive
tran′si·tive·ly
tran′si·to·ry
trans·lat′able
trans′late
trans·la′tion
trans′la·tor
trans·lit′er·ate
trans·lit·er·a′tion
trans·lu′cence
trans·lu′cent
trans·mi′grate
trans·mi·gra′tion
trans·mi′gra·to·ry
trans·mis′si·ble
trans·mis′sion
trans·mit′
  trans·mit′ted

trans·mit′ting
trans·mit′ta·ble
trans·mit′tal
trans·mit′tance
trans·mit′ter
trans·mog·ri·fi·
  ca′tion
trans·mog′ri·fy
trans·mut′able
trans·mu·ta′tion
trans·mute′
trans·oce·an′ic
tran′som
tran·son′ic
  also trans·son′ic
trans·pa·cif′ic
trans·par′en·cy
trans·par′ent
tran·spi·ra′tion
tran·spire′
trans·plant′able
trans·plant′
  verb
trans·plant
  noun
trans·po′lar
tran·spon′der
trans·port′
  verb
trans′port
  noun
trans·por·ta′tion
trans·port′er
trans·pos′able
trans·pose′
trans·po·si′tion
trans·ship′

trans·shipped′
trans·ship′ping
trans·ship′ment
tran·sub·stan·ti·
  a′tion
trans·val·u·a′tion
trans·val′ue
trans·ver′sal
trans·verse′
trans·verse′ly
trap
  trapped
  trap′ping
trap·door
tra·peze′
tra·pe′zi·um
trap′e·zoid
trap′per
trap′pings
trap′shoot·ing
tra·pun′to
trash′i·ness
trash′y
trau′ma
  pl trau′ma·ta *or*
  trau′mas
trau·mat′ic
trau·mat′i·cal·ly
trau·ma·tize
tra·vail′
trav′el
trav′eled
  or trav′elled
trav′el·ing
  or trav′el·ling
trav′el·er
  or trav′el·ler

trav′el·ogue
  also trav′el·og
tra·vers′able
tra·verse′
  verb
trav′erse
  adjective, noun
trav′er·tine
  also trav′er·tin
trav′es·ty
trawl′er
treach′er·ous
treach′ery
trea′cle
tread
  trod
  trod′den
  or trod
  tread′ing
trea′dle
tread′mill
trea′son
trea′son·able
trea′son·ous
trea′sur·able
trea′sure
trea′sur·er
trea′sury
treat′able
trea′tise
treat′ment
trea′ty
tre′ble
tre′bly
tree
  treed
  tree′ing

tree′less
tree′nail
   also tre′nail
tree′top
tre′foil
treil′lage
trek
   trekked
   trek′king
trel′lis
trel′lis·work
trem′ble
trem′bly
tre·men′dous
trem′o·lo
trem′or
trem′u·lous
tren′chant
tren′cher
Tren′ton
tre·pan′
   tre·panned′
   tre·pan′ning
trep·i·da′tion
tres′pass
tres′pass·er
tres′tle
   or tres′sel
tres′tle·work
tri′able
tri′ad
tri′al
tri·an′gle
tri·an′gu·lar
tri·an′gu·late
tri·an′gu·la′tion

trib′al
trib′al·ism
trib′al·ly
tribes′man
trib·u·la′tion
tri·bu′nal
trib′une
trib′u·tary
trib′ute
trice
tri′ceps
   pl tri′ceps·es *also*
   tri′ceps
tri·chi′na
   pl tri·chi′nae *also*
   tri·chi′nas
trich·i·no′sis
tri·chot′o·mous
tri·chot′o·my
tri·chro·mat′ic
trick′ery
trick′i·ly
trick′i·ness
trick′le
trick′ster
trick′y
tri′col·or
tri′cor·nered
tri′cot
tri·cus′pid
tri′cy·cle
tri′dent
tri·di·men′sion·al
tri·en′ni·al
tri′er
tri′fle

tri′fler
tri′fling
tri·fo′cals
tri·fur′cate
trig′ger
trig·o·no·met′ric
   or
   trig·o·no·met′ri·cal
trig·o·nom′e·try
tri·lat′er·al
tri·lin′gual
tril′lion
   pl tril′lions *or*
   tril′lion
tril′lionth
tril′o·gy
trim
   trimmed
   trim′ming
tri·ma·ran′
tri·mes′ter
trim′e·ter
trim′mer
tri·month′ly
Trin′i·dad
Trin·i·da′dian
trin′i·ty
trin′ket
tri·no′mi·al
tri′o
tri′ode
trip
   tripped
   trip′ping
tri·par′tite
trip′-ham·mer

triph'thong

tri'ple

tri·ple-space'

trip'let

trip'lex

trip'li·cate

tri'ply

tri'pod

trip'tych

tri'sect

trite

trit'u·rate

tri'umph

tri·um'phal

tri·um'phant

tri·um'vir

tri·um'vi·rate

triv'et

triv'ia

triv'i·al

triv·i·al'i·ty

triv'i·al·ly

tri·week'ly

tro·cha'ic

tro'che
   lozenge (see
   trochee)

tro'chee
   poetic meter (see
   troche)

trod'den

trof'fer

trog'lo·dyte

troi'ka

troll

trol'ley
   or trol'ly

trol'lop

trom·bone'

trom·bon'ist

troop
   soldiers (see troupe)

troop'er

troop'ship

tro'phy

trop'ic

trop'i·cal

tro'pism

tro'po·sphere

trot

trot'ted

trot'ting

trot'line

trot'ter

trou'ba·dour

trou'ble

trou'ble·mak·er

trou'ble·shoot·er

trou'ble·some

trough

trounce

troupe
   stage company (see
   troop)

troup'er

trou'sers

trous'seau

trout
   pl trout also trouts

tro'ver

trow'el

trow'eled
   or trow'elled

trow'el·ing
   or trow'el·ling

tru'an·cy

tru'ant

truck'age

truck'er

truck'ing

truck'le

truck'line

truck·load

truck'-trail·er

truc'u·lence

truc'u·lent

trudge

true

trued

true'ing
   also tru'ing

true-blue

true'heart'ed

true-life

true'love

true'ness

truf'fle

tru'ism

tru'ly

trumped-up

trum'pery

trum'pet

trum'pet·er

trun'cate

trun·ca'tion

trun'cheon

trun'dle

truss

truss'ing

trust·ee′
  guardian (see trusty)

trust·ee′ship
trust′ful
trust′ful·ly
trust′ful·ness
trust′i·ness
trust′wor·thi·ly
trust′wor·thi·ness
trust′wor·thy
trust′y
  dependable (see trustee)

truth′ful
truth′ful·ly
truth′ful·ness
try
  tried
  try′ing
try′out
tryst
T′-shirt
tsu·na′mi
tub
  tubbed
  tub′bing
tu′ba
tub′by
tube′less
tu′ber
tu′ber·cle
tu·ber′cu·lar
tu·ber′cu·late
tu·ber′cu·lin

tu·ber·cu·lo′sis
tu·ber′cu·lous
tube′rose
tu′ber·ous
tub′ing
tu′bu·lar
tu′bule
tuck′er
Tuc′son
Tues′day
tu′fa
tug
  tugged
  tug′ging
tug′boat
tug-of-war′
  pl tugs-of-war′
tu·i′tion
tu·la·re′mia
tu′lip
tulle
Tul′sa
tum′ble
tum′ble·down
tum′bler
tum′ble·weed
tum′bling
tum′brel
  or tum′bril
tu·mes′cence
tu·mes′cent
tu′mid
tu·mid′i·ty
tu′mor
tu·mor·i·gen′ic

tu′mor·ous
tu′mult
tu·mul′tu·ous
tun
  cask, measure (see ton)

tu′na
  pl tu′na *or* tu′nas
tun′able
  also tune′able
tun′dra
tune′ful
tune′ful·ly
tune′less
tun′er
tune′-up
tung′sten
tu′nic
Tu·ni′sia
Tu·ni′sian
tun′nel
  tun′neled
  or tun′nelled
  tun′nel·ing
  or tun′nel·ling
tun′ny
  pl tun′nies *also* tun′ny

tu′pe·lo
tuque
tur′ban
tur′bid
tur′bine
tur′bo
tur′bo·fan

tur′bo·jet
tur′bo·prop
tur′bot
  pl tur′bot *also*
    tur′bots
tur′bu·lence
tur′bu·lent
tu·reen′
turf
  pl turfs *or* turves
tur′gid
tur·gid′i·ty
Tur′key
  country
tur′key
  bird
Turk′ish
tur′mer·ic
tur′moil
turn′about
turn′around
turn′buck·le
turn′coat
turn′down
turn′er
turn′-in
turn′ing
tur′nip
turn′key
turn′off
turn′out
turn′over
turn′pike
turn′spit
turn′stile

turn′ta·ble
tur′pen·tine
tur′pi·tude
tur′quoise
  also tur′quois
tur′ret
tur′tle
tur′tle·back
tur′tle·dove
tur′tle·neck
tusk′er
tus′sle
tus′sock
tu′te·lage
tu′te·lary
tu′tor
tu·to′ri·al
tu′tu
tux·e′do
TV
twad′dle
twain
twang
tweak
tweed′i·ness
tweed′y
tweet′er
tweez′ers
twelfth
twelve
twelve′month
twen′ti·eth
twen′ty
twice-told
twid′dle

twig′gy
twi′light
twi′lit
twill
twin
  twinned
  twin′ning
twinge
twi′night
twin′kle
twin′kler
twin′kling
twin-screw
twirl′er
twist′er
twit
  twit′ted
  twit′ting
twitch
twit′ter
two-bit
two-by-four′
two′-di·men′-
  sion·al
two-faced
two-fac′ed·ly
two′-fist′ed
two′fold
two′-hand′ed
two-ply
two′-sid′ed
two′some
two′-step
two′-time
two′-way

ty·coon'
tyke
tym·pan'ic
tym'pa·num
  pl tym'pa·nums *or*
  tym'pa·na

typ'able
  or type'able
type'cast
type'face
type'found·ry
type'script
type'set
type'set·ter
type'set·ting
type'write
  type'wrote
  type'writ·ten
  also type'writ
  type'writ·ing
type'writ·er
type'writ·ing
ty'phoid
ty·phoon'
ty'phus
typ'i·cal
typ'i·cal·ly
typ'i·fy
typ'ist
ty'po
ty·pog'ra·pher
ty·po·graph'ic
  or ty·po·graph'i·cal
ty·po·graph'i·
  cal·ly
ty·pog'ra·phy

ty·po·log'i·cal
  also ty·po·log'ic
ty·po·log'i·cal·ly
ty·pol'o·gy
ty·ran'ni·cal
  also ty·ran'nic
ty·ran'ni·cal·ly
tyr'an·nize
tyr'an·niz·er
tyr'an·nous
tyr'an·ny
ty'rant
ty'ro
tzar

U

ubiq'ui·tous
ubiq'ui·ty
U-boat
ud'der
ufol'o·gist
Ugan'da
Ugan'dan
ug'li·ness
ug'ly
u'kase
Ukraine
Ukrai'ni·an
uku·le'le
ul'cer
ul'cer·ate
ul·cer·a'tion
ul'cer·ous
ul'lage
ul'ster

ul·te'ri·or
ul'ti·mate
ul'ti·mate·ly
ul·ti·ma'tum
  pl ul·ti·ma'tums *or*
  ul·ti·ma'ta
ul'ti·mo
ul'tra
ul·tra·cen'tri·fuge
ul'tra·cold
ul·tra·con·ser'va·
  tive
ul·tra·fash'ion·
  able
ul·tra·high'
ul'tra·ism
ul·tra·ma·rine'
ul·tra·mi'cro
ul·tra·mi'cro·
  scope
ul·tra·min'ia·ture
ul·tra·mod'ern
ul·tra·mon'tane
ul·tra·na'tion·al·
  ism
ul·tra·pure'
ul'tra·red'
ul·tra·short'
ul·tra·son'ic
ul'tra·sound
ul·tra·vi'o·let
ul·tra vi'res
ul'u·late
ul·u·la'tion
um'bel
um'bel·late

um'ber
um·bil'i·cal
um·bil'i·cus
  pl um·bil'i·ci *or*
    um·bil'i·cus·es

um'bra
  pl um'bras *or*
    um'brae

um'brage
um·bra'geous
um·brel'la
u'mi·ak
um'laut
um'pire
ump'teen
un·abashed'
un·abat'ed
un·a'ble
un·abridged'
un·ac·com'pa·
  nied
un·ac·count'able
un·ac·count'ably
un·ac·count'ed
un·ac·cus'tomed
un·adorned'
un·adul'ter·at·ed
un·ad·vised'
un·af·fect'ed
un·aligned'
un·al·loyed'
un·al'ter·able
un·al'ter·ably
un-Amer'i·can
una·nim'i·ty
unan'i·mous

un·an'swer·able
un·ap·peal'ing
un·armed'
un·asked'
un·as·sail'able
un·as·sail'ably
un·as·sum'ing
un·at·tached'
un·avail'ing
un·avoid'able
un·avoid'ably
un·aware'
un·awares'
un·bal'anced
un·bar'
  un·barred'
  un·bar'ring
un·bear'able
un·bear'ably
un·beat'able
un·beat'en
un·be·com'ing
un·be·known'
  or un·be·knownst'
un·be·lief'
un·be·liev'able
un·be·liev'ably
un·be·liev'er
un·be·liev'ing
un·bend'
  un·bent'
  un·bend'ing
un·bi'ased
un·bid'den
  also un·bid'
un·bind'

un·blush'ing
un·bod'ied
un·bolt'
un·born'
un·bo'som
un·bound'ed
un·bowed'
un·braid'
un·bri'dled
un·bro'ken
un·buck'le
un·bur'den
un·but'ton
un·cage'
un·called'-for
un·can'ni·ly
un·can'ny
un·cap'
un·ceas'ing
un·cer·e·mo'ni·
  ous
un·cer'tain
un·cer'tain·ty
un·chain'
un·change'able
un·change'ably
un·char'i·ta·ble
un·char'i·ta·bly
un·chart'ed
un·chris'tian
un·churched'
un'cial
un·civ'il
un·civ'i·lized
un·clad'
un·clasp'

un·clas'si·fied
un'cle
un·clean'
un·clean'li·ness
un·clench'
Un·cle Sam'
un·cloak'
un·clothe'
  un·clothed'
   or un·clad'
  un·cloth'ing
un·coil'
un·com'fort·able
un·com'fort·ably
un·com·mit'ted
un·com'mon
un·com·mu'ni·
  cat·ive
un·com'pro·mis·
  ing
un·con·cern'
un·con·cerned'
un·con·di'tion·al
un·con·di'tion·
  al·ly
un·con·for'mi·ty
un·con'quer·able
un·con'scio·na·
  ble
un·con'scio·na·
  bly
un·con'scious
un·con·sti·tu'·
  tion·al
un·con·sti·tu·tion·
  al'i·ty

un·con·sti·tu'tion·
  al·ly
un·con·trol'la·ble
un·con·trol'la·bly
un·con·ven'
  tion·al
un·con·ven·tion·
  al'i·ty
un·con·ven'tion·
  al·ly
un·cork'
un·count'ed
un·cou'ple
un·couth'
un·cov'er
un·crit'i·cal
un·crit'i·cal·ly
un·cross'
unc'tion
unc'tu·ous
un·curl'
un·cut'
un·daunt'ed
un·de·cid'ed
un·de·mon'stra·
  tive
un·de·ni'able
un·de·ni'ably
un'der
un·der·a·chiev'er
un·der·act'
un·der·age'
un·der·arm'
un'der·bel·ly
un·der·bid'
un'der·brush

un'der·car·riage
un·der·charge'
  verb
un'der·charge
  noun
un·der·class'man
un'der·clothes
un'der·cloth·ing
un'der·coat
un'der·coat·ing
un·der·cov'er
un'der·cur·rent
un·der·cut'
  verb
un'der·cut
  noun
un·der·de·vel'·
  oped
un'der·dog
un·der·done'
un·der·es'ti·mate
un·der·es·ti·ma'·
  tion
un·der·ex·pose'
un·der·ex·po'sure
un'der·foot'
un'der·gar·ment
un·der·gird'
un·der·glaze'
un·der·go'
  un·der·went'
  un·der·gone'
  un·der·go'ing
un·der·grad'u·ate
un'der·ground
un'der·growth

un′der·hand
un·der·hand′ed
un·der·hung′
un·der·lay′
  un·der·laid′
  un·der·lay′ing
un·der·lie′
  un·der·lay′
  un·der·lain′
  un·der·ly′ing
un′der·line
un′der·ling
un·der·lip′
un·der·ly′ing
un·der·mine′
un′der·most
un·der·neath′
un·der·nour′ished
un′der·pants
un′der·part
un′der·pass
un·der·pay′
  un·der·paid′
  un·der·pay′ing
un′der·pin·ning
un·der·play′
un·der·priv′i·leged
un·der·pro·duc′
  tion
un·der·rate′
un′der·score
un·der·sea′
un·der·sec′re·tary
un·der·sell′
  un·der·sold′
  un·der·sell′ing

un·der·sexed′
un′der·shirt
un·der·shoot′
  un·der·shot′
  un·der·shoot′ing
un·der·shot′
un′der·side
un′der·signed
  pl un′der·signed
un·der·sized′
un′der·skirt
un·der·slung′
un·der·stand′
  un·der·stood′
  un·der·stand′ing
un·der·stand′able
un·der·stand′ably
un·der·stand′ing
un·der·state′
un·der·state′ment
un·der·stood′
un′der·study
un′der·sur·face
un·der·take′
  un·der·took′
  un·der·tak′en
  un·der·tak′ing
un′der·tak·er
un′der·tak·ing
un·der-the-
  count′er
un′der·tone
un′der·tow
un′der·trick
un·der·val·u·a′tion
un·der·val′ue

un′der·wa′ter
un′der·way′
un′der·wear
un′der·weight′
un′der·world
un′der·write
  un′der·wrote
  un′der·writ·ten
  also un·der·writ′
un′der·writ·ing
un′der·writ·er
un·de·sir′able
un·de·sir′ably
un·de′vi·at·ing
un′dies
un·do′
  un·did′
  un·done′
  un·do′ing
un·doubt′ed
un·drape′
un·dress′
un·due′
un′du·lant
un′du·late
un·du·la′tion
un·du′ly
un·dy′ing
un·earned′
un·earth′
un·eas′i·ly
un·eas′i·ness
un·ea′sy
un·em·ploy′able
un·em·ployed′
un·em·ploy′ment

un·end'ing
un·e'qual
un·equaled'
un·equal'ly
un·equiv'o·cal
un·e·quiv'o·cal·ly
un·err'ing
un·es·sen'tial
un·even'
un·event'ful
un·ex·am'pled
un·ex·cep'tion·
   able
un·ex·pect'ed
un·fail'ing
un·fair'
un·faith'ful
un·faith'ful·ly
un·fa·mil'iar
un·fa·mil·iar'i·ty
un·fas'ten
un·fa'vor·able
un·fa'vor·ably
un·feel'ing
un·feigned'
un·fet'ter
un·fit'
un·flap'pa·ble
un·flinch'ing
un·fold'
un·fold'ed
un·for·get'ta·ble
un·for·get'ta·bly
un·formed'
un·for'tu·nate
un·found'ed

un·fre·quent'ed
un·friend'li·ness
un·friend'ly
un·frock'
un·fruit'ful
un·furl'
un·gain'li·ness
un·gain'ly
un·gen'er·ous
un·gird'
un·god'li·ness
un·god'ly
un·gov'ern·able
un·grace'ful
un·grace'ful·ly
un·gra'cious
un·grate'ful
un·grate'ful·ly
un·ground'ed
un·guard'ed
un'guent
un'gu·late
un·hand'
un·hap'pi·ly
un·hap'pi·ness
un·hap'py
un·healthy'
un·heard'
un·heard'-of
un·hinge'
un·hitch'
un·hook'
un·horse'
un·hur'ried
uni·cam'er·al
uni·cel'lu·lar

u'ni·corn
u'ni·cy·cle
uni·di·rec'tion·al
u'ni·fi·able
uni·fi·ca'tion
u'ni·fi·er
u'ni·form
uni·for'mi·ty
u'ni·fy
uni·lat'er·al
uni·lat'er·al·ly
un·im·peach'able
un·im·peach'ably
un·in·hib'it·ed
un·in·tel'li·gent
un·in·tel'li·gi·ble
un·in·tel'li·gi·bly
un·in·ten'tion·al
un·in·ten'tion·
   al·ly
un·in'ter·est·ed
un·in·ter·rupt'ed
u'nion
u'nion·ism
union·iza'tion
u'nion·ize
U'nion of So'vi·et
  So'cial·ist Re·
  pub'lics
unique'
u'ni·son
u'nit
Uni·tar'i·an
u'ni·tary
unite'
unit'ed

Unit'ed States of
   Amer'i·ca
Unit'ed King'dom
Unit'ed Ar'ab Re·
   pub'lic
Unit'ed Na'tions
u'ni·ty
uni·ver'sal
uni·ver·sal'i·ty
uni·ver'sal·ize
u'ni·ver·sal·ly
u'ni·verse
uni·ver'si·ty
un·just'
un·kempt'
un·kind'
un·know'ing
un·known'
un·lace'
un·lade'
un·latch'
un·law'ful
un·law'ful·ly
un·learn'
un·learned'
un·leash'
un·less'
un·let'tered
un·like'
un·like'li·hood
un·like'li·ness
un·like'ly
un·lim'ber
un·lim'it·ed
un·list'ed
un·load'

un·lock'
un·looked'-for
un·loose'
un·loos'en
un·love'ly
un·luck'i·ly
un·luck'i·ness
un·luck'y
un·make'
  un·made'
  un·mak'ing
un·man'
  un·manned'
  un·man'ning
un·man'ly
un·man'ner·ly
un·mask'
un·men'tion·able
un·mer'ci·ful
un·mer'ci·ful·ly
un·mind'ful
un·mis·tak'able
un·mis·tak'ably
un·mit'i·gat·ed
un·moor'
un·moved'
un·muf'fle
un·muz'zle
un·nail'
un·nat'u·ral
un·nat'u·ral·ly
un·nec·es·sar'i·ly
un·nec'es·sary
un·nerve'
un·num'bered
un·ob·tru'sive

un·oc'cu·pied
un·or'ga·nized
un·or'tho·dox
un·pack'
un·par'al·leled
un·peg'
  un·pegged'
  un·peg'ging
un'per·son
un·pile'
un·pin'
  un·pinned'
  un·pin'ning
un·pleas'ant
un·plumbed'
un·pop'u·lar
un·pop·u·lar'i·ty
un·prec'e·dent·ed
un·pre·dict·abil'·
  i·ty
un·pre·dict'able
un·pre·dict'ably
un·prej'u·diced
un·pre·ten'tious
un·prin'ci·pled
un·print'able
un·pro·fes'sion·al
un·pro·fes'sion·
  al·ly
un·prof'it·able
un·prof'it·ably
un·prom'is·ing
un·qual'i·fied
un·ques'tion·able
un·ques'tion·a·bly
un·ques'tion·ing

un'quote
un·rav'el
  un·rav'eled
  or un·rav'elled
  un·rav'el·ing
  or un·rav'el·ling
un·read'
un·read'i·ness
un·read'y
un·re'al
un·re·al·is'tic
un·re·al·is'ti·cal·ly
un·re·al'i·ty
un·rea'son·able
un·rea'son·ably
un·rea'son·ing
un·re·con·
  struct'ed
un·reel'
un·re·gen'er·ate
un·re·lent'ing
un·re·mit'ting
un·re·served'
un·rest'
un·re·strained'
un·rid'dle
un·right'eous
un·ripe'
un·ri'valed
  or un·ri'valled
un·robe'
un·roll'
un·ruf'fled
un·rul'i·ness
un·rul'y
un·sad'dle
un·sat'u·rat·ed

un·sa'vory
un·scathed'
un·schooled'
un·sci·en·tif'ic
un·sci·en·tif'i·
  cal·ly
un·scram'ble
un·screw'
un·scru'pu·lous
un·seal'
un·search'able
un·sea'son·able
un·sea'son·ably
un·seat'
un·seem'ly
un·seen'
un·seg're·gat·ed
un·self'ish
un·set'tle
un·set'tled
un·shack'le
un·shaped'
un·sheathe'
un·shod'
un·sight'ly
un·skilled'
un·skill'ful
un·sling'
  un·slung'
  un·sling'ing
un·snap'
  un·snapped'
  un·snap'ping
un·snarl'
un·so·phis'ti·
  cat·ed
un·sought'

un·sound'
un·spar'ing
un·speak'able
un·speak'ably
un·spot'ted
un·sta'ble
un·stead'i·ly
un·stead'i·ness
un·steady'
un·stop'
  un·stopped'
  un·stop'ping
un·strap'
  un·strapped'
  un·strap'ping
un·stressed'
un·strung'
un·stud'ied
un·sub·stan'tial
un·suc·cess'ful
un·suc·cess'ful·ly
un·suit'able
un·suit'ably
un·sung'
un·tangle'
un·taught'
un·think'able
un·think'ing
un·thought'-of
un·ti'dy
un·tie'
  un·tied'
  un·ty'ing
  or un·tie'ing
un·til'
un·time'li·ness
un·time'ly

un·ti′tled
un′to
un·told′
un·touch·abil′i·ty
un·touch′able
un·tow′ard
un·tried′
un·true′
un·truth′
un·truth′ful
un·truth′ful·ly
un·tu′tored
un·twist′
un·used′
un·u′su·al
un·u′su·al·ly
un·ut′ter·able
un·ut′ter·ably
un·var′nished
un·veil′
un·voiced′
un·war′rant·able
un·wa′ry
un·washed′
un·weave′
  un·wove′
  un·wo′ven
  un·weav′ing
un·well′
un·whole′some
un·wield′i·ness
un·wield′y
un·will′ing
un·wind′,
  un·wound′
  also un·wind′ed
  un·wind′ing

un·wise′
un·wit′ting
un·world′li·ness
un·world′ly
un·wor′thi·ly
un·wor′thi·ness
un·wor′thy
un·wrap′
  un·wrapped′
  un·wrap′ping
un·writ′ten
un·yield′ing
un·yoke′
un·zip′
  un·zipped′
  un·zip′ping
up-and-down′
up′beat
up·braid′
up′bring·ing
up′com′ing
up′-coun′try
up·date′
up′draft
up·end′
up′grade
up′growth
up·heav′al
up′hill′
up·hold′
  up·held′
  up·hold′ing
up·hol′ster
up·hol′ster·er
up·hol′stery
up′keep
up′land

up·lift′
  verb
up′lift
  noun
up′most
up·on′
up′per
up·per·case′
up·per-class′
up·per-class′man
up′per-cut
up′per·most
Up·per Vol′ta
Up·per Vol′tan
up′pish
up′pi·ty
up′right
up′ris·ing
up′roar
up·roar′i·ous
up·root′
up·set′
  verb
  up·set′
  up·set′ting
up′set
  noun
up′shot
up′side
up·stage
up·stairs
up·stand′ing
up′start
up′state
up·stream
up′stroke
up′surge

up'swept
up'swing
up'take
up'thrust
up·tight
up-to-date'
up·town
up'trend
up'turn
up'ward
  or up'wards
up·wind
ura'ni·um
ur'ban
  of the city (see
  urbane)

ur·bane'
  polished (see urban)
ur'ban·ism
ur'ban·ite
ur·ban'i·ty
ur'ban·iza'tion
ur'ban·ize
ur'chin
ure'a
ure'mia
u're·ter
ure'thra
  pl ure'thras *or*
  ure'thrae
urge
ur'gen·cy
ur'gent
u'ric
u'ri·nal

uri·nal'y·sis
u'ri·nary
u'ri·nate
uri·na'tion
urine
urn
uro·log'ic
  or uro·log'i·cal
urol'o·gist
urol'o·gy
ur'sine
Ur'u·guay
Uru·guay'an
us·abil'i·ty
us'able
us'age
use
  used
  us'ing
use'ful
use'ful·ly
use'less
us'er
ush'er
u'su·al
u'su·al·ly
u'su·fruct
u'su·rer
usu'ri·ous
usurp'
usur·pa'tion
usurp'er
u'su·ry
U'tah
uten'sil

u'ter·ine
u'ter·us
  pl u'teri
utile
util·i·tar'i·an
util·i·tar'i·an·ism
util'i·ty
u'ti·liz·able
uti·li·za'tion
u'ti·lize
ut'most
uto'pia
uto'pi·an
ut'ter
ut'ter·ance
ut'ter·most
u'vu·la
  pl u'vu·las *or*
  u'vu·lae

uxo'ri·ous

V

va'can·cy
va'cant
va'cate
va·ca'tion
va·ca'tion·er
vac'ci·nate
vac·ci·na'tion
vac·cine'
vac'il·late
vac'il·la·tor
vac·il·la'tion
va·cu'i·ty

vary

vac'u·ole
vac'u·ous
vac'u·um
   pl vac'u·ums *or*
    vac'ua
vac·u·um-packed'
va·de me'cum
   pl va·de me'cums
vag'a·bond
vag'a·bond·age
va'ga·ry
va·gi'na
   pl va·gi'nae *or*
    va·gi'nas

va'gran·cy
va'grant
vague
vague'ly
vail
vain
   futile, conceited
   (*see* vane, vein)

vain·glo'ri·ous
vain'glo·ry
val'ance
   drapery (*see*
   valence)

vale
   valley (*see* veil)

val·e·dic'tion
val·e·dic'to·ri·an
val·e·dic'to·ry
va'lence
   chemical term (*see*
   valance)

Va·len·ci·ennes'
val'en·tine
val'et
val·e·tu·di·nar'
   i·an
val'iant
val'id
val'i·date
val·i·da'tion
va·lid'i·ty
va·lise'
val'ley
val'or
val·o·ri·za'tion
val'o·rize
val'or·ous
val'u·able
val'u·ably
val·u·a'tion
val'ue
val'ued
val'ue·less
va·lu'ta
valve
val'vu·lar
vam'pire
Van·cou'ver
van'dal
van'dal·ism
van'dal·ize
Van·dyke'
vane
   wind indicator (*see*
   vain, vein)

van'guard

va·nil'la
van'ish
van'i·ty
van'quish
van'quish·able
van'tage
vap'id
va·pid'i·ty
va'por
va·por·iza'tion
va'por·ize
va'por·iz·er
va'por·ous
va·que'ro
vari·abil'i·ty
var'i·able
var'i·ably
var'i·ance
var'i·ant
vari·a'tion
var'i·col·ored
var'i·cose
var·i·cos'i·ty
var'ied
var'ie·gate
var·ie·ga'tion
va·ri'etal
va·ri'etal·ly
va·ri'ety
var·i·o'rum
var'i·ous
var'mint
var'nish
var'si·ty
var'y

vas'cu·lar
vas' de'fer·ens
   pl va·sa de·fer·en'tia
va·sec'to·my
Vas'e·line
vaso·mo'tor
vas'sal
vas'sal·age
vast'ness
vat-dyed
Vat'i·can
vaude'ville
vaude·vil'lian
vault'ed
vault'ing
vaunt
V'-day
vec'tor
veer
veg'e·ta·ble
veg'e·tal
veg·e·tar'i·an
veg'e·tate
veg·e·ta'tion
veg'e·ta·tive
ve'he·mence
ve'he·ment
ve'hi·cle
ve·hic'u·lar
V-eight
veil
   screen (see vail)

veil'ing
vein

   blood vessel, mood
   (*see* vain, vane)

vel'lum
ve·loc'i·pede
ve·loc'i·ty
ve·lour'
   or ve·lours'
   pl ve·lours'
vel'vet
vel·ve·teen'
vel'vety
ve'nal
   mercenary (see
   venial)
ve·nal'i·ty
ve'nal·ly
vend·ee'
ven·det'ta
vend'ible
   or vend'able
ven'dor
ve·neer'
ven'er·a·ble
ven'er·ate
ven·er·a'tion
ve·ne're·al
Ven·e·zu·e'la
Ven·e·zu·e'lan
ven'geance
venge'ful
venge'ful·ly
ve'ni·al
   excusable (see
   venal)
ve·ni're·man
ven'i·son
ven'om
ven'om·ous

ve'nous
ven'ti·late
ven·ti·la'tion
ven'ti·la·tor
ven'tral
ven'tral·ly
ven'tri·cle
ven·tril'o·quism
ven·tril'o·quist
ven'ture
ven'ture·some
ven'tur·ous
ven'ue
ve·ra'cious
   truthful (see
   voracious)

ve·rac'i·ty
ve·ran'da
   or ve·ran'dah

ver'bal
ver·bal·iza'tion
ver'bal·ize
ver'bal·ly
ver·ba'tim
ver·be'na
ver'bi·age
ver·bose'
ver·bos'i·ty
ver·bo'ten
ver'dant
ver'dict
ver'di·gris
ver'dure
verge
ver·i·fi'able
ver·i·fi·ca'tion

vicinity

ver'i·fi·er
ver'i·fy
ver'i·ly
veri·si·mil'i·tude
ver'i·ta·ble
ver'i·ta·bly
ver'i·ty
ver'meil
ver·mi·cel'li
ver'mi·form
ver'mi·fuge
ver·mil'ion
ver'min
   pl ver'min
Ver·mont'
ver·mouth'
ver·nac'u·lar
ver'nal
ver'ni·er
ver'sa·tile
ver·sa·til'i·ty
versed
ver'si·cle
ver·si·fi·ca'tion
ver'si·fy
ver'sion
ver'so
ver'sus
ver'te·bra
   pl ver'te·brae *or*
   ver'te·bras
ver'te·bral
ver'te·brate
ver'tex
   pl ver'tex·es *or*
   ver'ti·ces

ver'ti·cal
ver'ti·cal·ly
ver·ti·cil'late
ver·tig'i·nous
ver'ti·go
   pl ver'ti·goes *or*
   ver·tig'i·nes
ver'vain
verve
ver'y
ves'i·cant
ves'i·cle
ve·sic'u·lar
ves'per
ves'pers
ves'sel
ves'tal
ves'ti·bule
ves'tige
ves·ti'gial
ves·ti'gial·ly
vest'ment
vest'-pock'et
ves'try
ves'try·man
ves'ture
vetch
vet'er·an
vet·er·i·nar'i·an
vet'er·i·nary
ve'to
   pl ve'toes
ve'to·er
vex
  vexed
   also vext

vex'ing
vex·a'tion
vex·a'tious
vi·a·bil'i·ty
vi'a·ble
vi'a·bly
vi'a·duct
vi'al
   small bottle (*see*
   vile, viol)
vi'and
vi'bran·cy
vi'brant
vi'bra·phone
vi'brate
vi·bra'tion
vi·bra'to
vi'bra·tor
vi'bra·to·ry
vi·bur'num
vic'ar
vic'ar·age
vi·car'i·al
vi·car'i·ate
vi·car'i·ous
vice
   depravity (*see* vise)
vice-chan'cel·lor
vice-con'sul
vice-pres'i·den·cy
vice-pres'i·dent
vice'roy
vice ver'sa
vi·chys·soise'
vi'chy
vi·cin'i·ty

vi′cious
vi·cis′si·tude
vic′tim
vic·tim·iza′tion
vic′tim·ize
vic′tim·iz·er
vic′tor
Vic·to′ria
Vic·to′ri·an
vic·to′ri·ous
vic′to·ry
vict′ual
vi·cu′ña
vi′de
vid′eo
vid′eo·tape
vie
 vied
 vy′ing
vi′er
Viet·nam
Viet·nam·ese′
 pl Viet·nam·ese′
view′er
view′point
vig′il
vig′i·lance
vig′i·lant
vig·i·lan′te
vig·i·lan′tism
vi·gnette′
vig′or
vig′or·ous
vile

 repulsive (*see* vial, viol)

vile′ly
vil·i·fi·ca′tion
vil′i·fi·er
vil′i·fy
vil′la
vil′lage
vil′lag·er
vil′lain
vil′lain·ous
vil′lainy
vil′lous
vil′lus
 pl vil′li
vin·ai·grette′
vin′ci·ble
vin′di·ca·ble
vin′di·cate
vin′di·ca·tion
vin′di·ca·tor
vin′di·ca·to·ry
vin·dic′tive
vin·dic′tive·ly
vin′e·gar
vin′e·gary
vine′yard
vin′i·cul·ture
vi′nous
vin′tage
vint′ner
vi′nyl
vi′ol
 musical instrument
 (*see* vial, vile)

vi·o′la
vi′o·la·ble
vi′o·late

vi·o·la′tion
vi′o·la·tor
vi′o·lence
vi′o·lent
vi′o·let
vi·o·lin′
vi·o·lin′ist
vi·o′list
vi·o·lon·cel′list
vi·o·lon·cel′lo
vi·os′ter·ol
VIP
vi′per
vi′per·ous
vi·ra′go
 pl vi·ra′goes *or*
 vi·ra′gos
vi′ral
vir′eo
vir′gin
vir′gin·al
vir′gin·al·ly
Vir·gin′ia
Vir·gin′ia Beach
vir·gin′i·ty
vir′gule
vir′ile
vi·ril′i·ty
vi·rol′o·gist
vi·rol′o·gy
vir·tu′
 objets d'art (*see*
 virtue)

vir′tu·al
vir′tu·al·ly
vir′tue
 goodness (*see* virtu)

voile

vir·tu·os′i·ty
vir·tu·o′so
  pl vir·tu·o′sos or
    vir·tu·o′si

vir′tu·ous
vir′u·lence
  or vir′u·len·cy

vir′u·lent
vi′rus
vi′sa
  vi′saed
  vi′sa·ing
vis′age
vis-à-vis′
  pl vis-à-vis′

vis′cer·al
vis′cer·al·ly
vis′cid
vis·cid′i·ty
vis·co·elas′tic
vis′cose
  noun

vis·cos′i·ty
vis′cous
  adjective
  thick (see viscus)

vis′cus
  pl vis′cera
  body organ (see
    viscous)

vise
  clamp (see vice)

vis·i·bil′i·ty
vis′i·ble
vis′i·bly
vi′sion

vi′sion·ary
vis′it
vis′i·tant
vis·i·ta′tion
vis′i·tor
vi′sor
vis′ta
vi′su·al
vi·su·al·iza′tion
vi′su·al·ize
vi′su·al·iz·er
vi′su·al·ly
vi′ta
  pl vi′tae
vi′tal
vi·tal′i·ty
vi′tal·iza′tion
vi′tal·ize
vi′tal·iz·er
vi′tal·ly
vi′tals
vi′ta·min
vi′ti·ate
vi·ti·a′tion
vi′ti·a·tor
vi′ti·cul·ture
vit′re·ous
vit·ri·fi·ca′tion
vit′ri·fy
vit′ri·ol
vit·ri·ol′ic
vit′tle
vi·tu′per·ate
vi·tu·per·a′tion
vi·tu′per·a·tive
vi′va

vi·va′ce
vi·va′cious
vi·vac′i·ty
vi·va vo′ce
vi·var′i·um
  pl vi·var′ia or
    vi·var′i·ums

viv′id
viv·i·fi·ca′tion
viv′i·fi·er
viv′i·fy
vi·vip′a·rous
viv′i·sect
vivi·sec′tion
vix′en
viz′ard
vi·zier′
vo′ca·ble
vo·cab′u·lary
vo′cal
vo·cal′ic
vo′cal·ist
vo′cal·ize
vo′cal·ly
vo·ca′tion
voc′a·tive
vo·cif′er·ate
vo·cif′er·ous
vod′ka
vogue
vogu′ish
voiced
voice′less
void′able
void′er
voile

vol′a·tile
vol·a·til′i·ty
vol·can′ic
vol·ca′nism
vol·ca′no
  pl vol·ca′noes *or*
  vol·ca′nos

vo·li′tion
vol′ley
vol′ley·ball
volt′age
vol·ta′ic
vol·ta′me·ter
volt′-am·pere
volte-face′
volt′me·ter
vol·u·bil′i·ty
vol′u·ble
vol′u·bly
vol′ume
vol·u·met′ric
vo·lu′mi·nous
vol·un·tar′i·ly
vol′un·tary
vol·un·teer′
vo·lup′tu·ary
vo·lup′tu·ous
vo·lute′
vom′it
voo′doo
vo·ra′cious
  insatiable (see
  veracious)

vo·rac′i·ty
vor′tex
  pl vor′ti·ces *also*
  vor′tex·es

vor′ti·cal
vo′ta·ry
vot′er
vo′tive
vouch′er
vouch·safe′
vow′el
vox po′pu·li
voy′age
voy′ag·er
voy·eur′
vul′can·ite
vul·can·iza′tion
vul′can·ize
vul′can·iz·er
vul′gar
vul·gar′i·an
vul′gar·ism
vul·gar′i·ty
vul·gar·iza′tion
vul′gar·ize
vul′gar·iz·er
vul·ner·a·bil′i·ty
vul′ner·a·ble
vul′ner·a·bly
vul′ture
vul′tur·ous
vul′va
vy′ing

W

wad
wad′ded
wad′ding
wad′able
  or wade′able

wad′ding
wad′dle
wad′er
wa′di
wa′fer
waf′fle
waft
wag
  wagged
  wag′ging
wa′ger
wa′ger·er
wag′gery
wag′gish
wag′gle
wag′gly
wag′on
wag′on·ette
wa·gon-lit
  pl wa·gons-lits *or*
  wa·gon-lits

wa·hi′ne
wa′hoo
waif
wail
  cry (see wale, whale)

wain′scot
  wain′scot·ed
  or wain′scot·ted
  wain′scot·ing
  or wain′scot·ting

wain′wright
waist
  narrow center (see
  waste)

waist′band
waist′coat

waist'line
wait'er
wait'ress
waive
 give up (see wave)

waiv'er
wake
 waked
 or woke

 waked
 or wo'ken

 wak'ing
wake'ful
wak'en
wale
 ridge, texture (see wail, whale)

walk'away
walk'er
walk'ie-talk'ie
walk'-in
walk-on
walk'out
walk'over
walk'-up
walk'way
wal'la·by
wall'board
walled
wal'let
wall'eye
wall'flow·er
wal'lop
wal'lop·ing
wal'low
wall'pa·per
wall'plug

wal'nut
wal'rus
 pl wal'rus *or*
 wal'rus·es

waltz
wam'pum
wan
 wanned
 wan'ning

wan'der
wan'der·lust
wan'gle
wan'i·gan
 or wan'ni·gan

want'ing
wan'ton
wan'ton·ness
wap'i·ti
 pl wap'i·ti *or*
 wap'i·tis

wap·per-jawed'
war
 warred
 war'ring

war'ble
war'bler
war'bon·net
war'den
ward'er
ward'robe
ward'room
ware'house
war'fare
war'head
war'-horse
war'i·ly
war'i·ness

war'like
war'lock
war'lord
warm'-blood'ed
warmed'-o'ver
warm'heart'ed
war'mon·ger
warmth
warm'-up
warn'ing
warp
war'path
war'plane
war'rant
war'rant·able
war·ran·tor'
war'ran·ty
war'ren
war'rior
war'ship
wart
war'time
war'y
wash'able
wash'ba·sin
wash'board
wash'bowl
wash'cloth
washed-out
washed-up
wash'er
wash'er·wom·an
wash'house
wash'ing
Wash'ing·ton
wash'out
wash'room

wash'stand
wash'tub
wash'y
wasp'ish
was'sail
wast'age
waste
    refuse (see waist)
waste'bas·ket
wast'ed
waste'ful
waste'ful·ly
waste'land
waste'pa'per
wast'rel
watch'band
watch'case
watch'dog
watch'ful
watch'ful·ly
watch'mak·er
watch'mak·ing
watch'man
watch'tow·er
watch'word
wa'ter
wa'ter·borne
Wa'ter·bury
wa'ter·col·or
wa'ter-cooled
wa'ter·course
wa'ter·craft
wa'ter·cress
wa'ter·fall
wa'ter·fast
wa'ter·fowl

wa'ter·front
wa'ter·i·ness
wa'ter·leaf
    pl wa'ter·leafs
wa'ter·less
wa'ter·line
wa'ter·logged
wa·ter·loo'
wa'ter·mark
wa'ter·mel·on
wa'ter·pow·er
wa'ter·proof
wa·ter·re·pel'lent
wa·ter·re·sis'tant
wa'ter·scape
wa'ter·shed
wa'ter·side
wa'ter·ski
wa'ter·ski·er
wa'ter·soak
wa'ter·spout
wa·ter·tight'
wa'ter·way
wa'ter·wheel
wa'ter·works
wa'ter·worn
wa'tery
watt'age
watt-hour
wat'tle
watt'me·ter
wave
    flutter, sea swell
    (see waive)

wave'length
wave'let

wa'ver
wav'i·ly
wav'i·ness
wav'y
wax'en
wax'i·ness
wax'ing
wax'wing
wax'work
wax'y
way
    route, method (see
    weigh, whey)

way'bill
way'far·er
way'far·ing
way'lay
    way'laid
    way·lay'ing
way-out
way'side
way'ward
weak'en
weak'fish
weak'heart'ed
weak-kneed
weak'ling
weak'ly
weak'mind'ed
weak'ness
weal
    well-being, welt (see
    wheal, wheel)

wealth'i·ly
wealth'i·ness
wealth'y

wean
weap'on
weap'on·ry
wear
  wore
  worn
  wear'ing
wear'able
wear'er
wea'ri·ly
wea'ri·ness
wea'ri·some
wea'ry
wea'sel
weath'er
  atmospheric
  conditions (see
  whether)
weath·er·abil'i·ty
weath'er-beat·en
weath'er·board
weath'er-bound
weath'er·cock
weath'er·glass
weath'er·ing
weath'er·man
weath'er·proof
weath'er-strip
  weath'er-
  stripped
  also weath'er-stript
  weath'er-strip·
  ping
weath·er·tight'
weath'er-wise
weath'er-worn

weave
  wove
  wo'ven
  weav'ing
weav'er
web
  webbed
  web'bing
web'-foot·ed
wed
  wed'ded
  also wed
  wed'ding
wedge
Wedg'ies
wed'lock
Wednes'day
weed'er
weed'y
week'day
week'end
week'ly
wee'ny
weep
  wept
  weep'ing
weep'er
weep'y
wee'vil
weigh
  measure weight
  (see way, whey)
weight'i·ly
weight'i·ness
weight'less
weight'y

weird
wel'come
weld'er
weld'ment
wel'fare
wel'far·ism
well
  bet'ter
  best
well-ad·vised'
well-ap·point'ed
well'-be·ing'
well-be·loved'
well·born
well-bred
well-con·di'tioned
well-de·fined'
well-dis·posed'
well-done
well'-fa'vored
well-fixed
well'-found'ed
well-groomed
well'-ground'ed
well'-han'dled
well'head
well-heeled
well-knit
well-known
well'-mean'ing
well-nigh
well-off
well'-or'dered
well-read
well-set
well'-spo'ken

well'spring
well-thought'-of
well-timed
well-to-do'
well-turned
well'-wish·er
well-worn
wel'ter
wel'ter·weight
wench'er
were'wolf
　pl were'wolves
wes'kit
west'bound
west'er·ly
west'ern
West'ern Sa·mo'a
West'ern·er
west·ern·iza'tion
west'ern·ize
West Vir·gin'ia
wet
　not dry (see whet)
wet
　or wet'ted
wet'ting
wet
　wet'ter
　wet'test
wet'back
wet'land
wet'ness
wet'tish
whale
　sea animal (see
　wail, wale)

whale'back
whale'boat
whale'bone
whal'er
wharf
　pl wharves *also*
　wharfs
wharf'age
wharf'in·ger
what·ev'er
what'not
what·so·ev'er
wheal
　skin welt (see weal,
　wheel)
wheat
whee'dle
wheel
　turnable disk (see
　weal, wheal)
wheel'bar·row
wheel'base
wheel'chair
wheel'er
wheel·er-deal'er
wheel'horse
wheel'house
wheel'wright
wheeze
wheez'i·ly
wheez'i·ness
wheez'y
whelp
whence
when·ev'er
when'so·ev'er

where'abouts
　also where'about
where·as'
where·at'
where·by'
where'fore
where'from
where·in'
where·of'
where·on'
where'so·ev·er
where'to
where'up·on
wher·ev'er
where'with
where'with·al
wher'ry
whet
　sharpen (see wet)
whet'ted
whet'ting
wheth'er
　if (see weather)
whet'stone
whey
　watery part of milk
　(see way, weigh)
which·ev'er
which·so·ev'er
whiff
while
　time (see wile)
whim
whim'per
whim'si·cal
whim·si·cal'i·ty

whim'si·cal·ly

whim'sy
  or whim'sey

whine
  cry (see wine)

whin'er

whin'ing

whin'ny

whip
  whipped
  whip'ping

whip'cord

whip'lash

whip'per·snap·per

whip'pet

whip'poor·will

whip'saw

whip'stitch

whip'stock

whip'worm

whir
  also whirr
  whirred
  whir'ring

whirl

whirl'i·gig

whirl'pool

whirl'wind

whirl'y·bird

whisk

whisk'er

whis'key
  or whis'ky

whis'per

whis'tle

whis'tler

whis'tle-stop

whis'tling

whit
  bit (see wit)

white'bait

white'cap

white'-col'lar

white'face

white-faced

white'fish

White'horse

white-hot

white'-liv'ered

whit'en·er

white'ness

whit'en·ing

white'wall

white'wash

whith'er
  where (see wither)

whith·er·so·ev'er

whit'ing

whit'ish

whit'tle

whiz
  or whizz
  whizzed
  whiz'zing

whiz
  or whizz
  pl whiz'zes

whiz'er

who·dun'it

who·ev'er

whole'heart'ed

whole·ness

whole'sale

whole'sal·er

whole'some

whol'ly

whom·ev'er

whom·so·ev'er

whoop-de-do'
  or whoop-de-doo'

whoop'ee

whoop'la

whop'per

whop'ping

whore

whorl

who·so·ev'er

Wich'i·ta

Wich'i·ta Falls

wick'ed

wick'er

wick'er·work

wick'et

wick'i·up

wide'-an'gle

wide-awake'

wide-eyed

wid'en

wide-mouthed

wide·spread

wid'geon
  also wi'geon

wid'get

wid'ish

wid'ow

wid'ow·er

width

wield

wield'y
wie'ner
wife
   pl wives
wife'less
wife'li·ness
wife'ly
wig'an
wig'gle
wig'gly
wig'let
wig'mak·er
wig'wag
wig'wam
wil'co
wild'cat
  wild'cat·ted
  wild'cat·ting
wild'cat·ter
wil'de·beest
wil'der·ness
wild-eyed
wild'fire
wild'fowl
wild'life
wild'wood
wile
  trick (see while)
wil'i·ly
wil'i·ness
will'ful
  or wil'ful
will'ful·ly
wil'lies
will'ing
wil'li·waw

will-o'-the-wisp'
wil'low
wil'low·ware
wil'lowy
will'pow·er
wil·ly-nil'ly
wi'ly
wim'ple
win
  won
  win'ning
wince
wind
  wound
  also wind'ed
  wind'ing
wind'age
wind'bag
wind'blown
wind'break
wind'burn
wind'er
wind'fall
wind'i·ly
wind'i·ness
wind'ing-sheet
wind'jam·mer
wind'lass
  machine (see wind-less)
wind·less
  without wind (see windlass)
wind'mill
win'dow
win'dow-dress

win'dow·pane
win'dow-shop
  win'dow-shopped
  win'dow-shop·ping
win'dow-shop·per
win'dow·sill
wind'pipe
wind·proof
wind'row
wind'shield
Wind'sor
wind'storm
wind'swept
wind'up
wind'ward
wind'-wing
wind'y
wine
  beverage (see whine)
wine'glass
wine'grow·er
wine'press
win'ery
wine'shop
wine'skin
wing'back
wing'ding
wing'-foot'ed
wing'span
wing'spread
win'kle
win'na·ble
win'ner

win'ning
Win'ni·peg
win'now
win'some
Win·ston-Sa'lem
win'ter
win'ter·green
win·ter·iza'tion
win'ter·ize
win'ter·tide
win'ter·time
win'try
wip'er
wir'able
wire'draw
wire'hair
wire·haired
wire'less
Wire'pho'to
wire'-pull·er
wir'er
wire'tap
wire'work
wire'worm
wir'i·ness
wir'ing
wir'y
Wis·con'sin
wis'dom
wise'acre
wise'crack
wise'ly
wish'bone
wish'ful
wish'ful·ly
wish'y-washy

wis'py
wis·te'ri·a
  or wis·tar'ia
wist'ful
wist'ful·ly
wit
  sense (see whit)
witch'craft
witch'ery
witch'-hunt
witch'ing
with·al'
with·draw'
  with·drew'
  with·drawn'
  with·draw'ing
with·draw'al
with·drawn'
with·er
  dry up (see whither)
with'ers
with·hold'
  with·held'
  with·hold'ing
with·in'
with·out'
with·stand'
wit'less
wit'ness
wit'ti·cism
wit'ti·ly
wit'ti·ness
wit'ty
wiz'ard
wiz'ard·ry
wiz'ened

wob'ble
wob'bly
woe'be·gone
woe'ful
  also wo'ful
woe'ful·ly
wolf
  pl wolves
wolf'hound
wol'ver·ine
wom'an
  pl wom'en
wom'an·hood
wom'an·ish
wom'an·kind
wom'an·li·ness
wom'an·ly
womb
wom'en·folk
  or wom'en·folks
won
  pl won
  currency
won'der
won'der·ful
won'der·ful·ly
won'der·land
won'der·ment
won'der-work·er
won'drous
wood'bin
wood'bine
wood'-carv·er
wood'chuck
wood'cock
wood'craft

wood'cut
wood'cut·ter
wood'ed
wood'en
wood'en·head
wood'en·ware
wood'land
wood'peck·er
wood'pile
wood'shed
woods'man
wood'sy
wood'wind
wood'work
wood'y
woo'er
woof'er
wool'en
 or wool'len
wool'gath·er·ing
wool'li·ness
wool'ly
 also wool'y
wool·ly-head'ed
wool'pack
woo'zi·ly
woo'zi·ness
woo'zy
Worces'ter
word'age
word'book
word'i·ly
word'i·ness
word'ing
word'less
word-of-mouth'

word'play
word'y
work
 worked
 or wrought
 work'ing
work·abil'i·ty
work'able
work'a·day
work'bas·ket
work'bench
work'book
work'day
work'er
work'horse
work'house
work'ing·man
work'load
work'man
work'man·like
work'man·ship
work'out
work'room
work'shop
work'ta·ble
work'week
world'-beat·er
world'li·ness
world'ly
world'ly-wise
world'-shak·ing
world'-wea·ri·
 ness
world·wide
worm'-eat·en
worm'hole

worm'wood
worn-out
wor'ri·er
wor'ri·ment
wor'ri·some
wor'ry
wor'ry·wart
worse
wors'en
wor'ship
 wor'shiped
 or wor'shipped
 wor'ship·ing
 or wor'ship·ping
wor'ship·er
 or wor'ship·per
wor'ship·ful
wor'ship·ful·ly
worst
wor'sted
wor'thi·ly
wor'thi·ness
worth'less
worth·while
wor'thy
would'-be
wound
wound'wart
wrack
wraith
wran'gle
wran'gler
wrap
 cover (see rap)
 wrapped
 wrap'ping

wrap′around
wrap′per
wrap′ping
wrap′-up
wrath′ful
wrath′ful·ly
wreak
  inflict (see reak)
wreath
  noun
wreathe
  verb
wreck′age
wreck′er
wren
wrench
wrest
wres′tle
wres′tler
wres′tling
wretch
  miserable one (see retch)
wretch′ed
wrig′gle
wrig′gler
wring
  squeeze (see ring)

wrung
wring′ing
wring′er
wrin′kle
wrin′kly
wrist′band
wrist′let
wrist′lock

wrist′watch
writ
write
  wrote
  writ′ten
    also writ
  writ′ing
write′-down
write′-in
write′-off
writ′er
write′-up
writhe
wrong′do′er
wrong′do′ing
wrong′ful
wrong′ful·ly
wrong′head′ed
wrong′ly
wrought
wrung
  past of wring (see rung)
wry
  contorted (see rye)
wry′ly
Wy·o′ming

X

x
x-ed
  also x'd *or* xed
x′ing
x′-ax·is
X′-dis·ease

xe′bec
xen′o·phobe
xeno·pho′bia
xe′ric
xe·ro·graph′ic
xe·rog′ra·phy
xe·roph′i·lous
xe·roph·thal′mia
xe′ro·phyte
Xmas
X′-ray
xy′lo·phone
xy′lo·phon·ist

Y

yacht
yacht′ing
yachts′man
ya′hoo
yam′mer
Yan′kee
yap
  yapped
  yap′ping
yard′age
yard′arm
yard′bird
yard′man
yard′mas·ter
yard′stick
yarn′-dye
yar′row
yawl
yawn
yaws

y′-ax·is
yea
year′book
year′ling
year′long
year′ly
yearn
year-round
yeast′y
yel′low
yel·low-dog′
yel′low·ish
yelp
Ye′men
Ye′me·ni
Ye′men·ite
yen
  pl yen
  currency

yeo′man
ye·shi′va
  or ye·shi′vah
  pl ye·shi′vas *or*
  ye·shi′vahs *or*
  ye·shi′voth

yes′-man
yes′ter·day
yes′ter·year
yew
  tree (see ewe)
yield
yield′ing
yo′del
  yo′deled
  or yo′delled

yo′del·ing
  or yo′del·ling

yo′del·er
yo′ga
yo′gi
  or yo′gin

yo′gurt
  or yo′ghurt

yoke
  couple (see yolk)

yo′kel
yolk
  yellow of eggs (see
  yoke)

Yom Kip′pur
yon′der
Yon′kers
youn′ger
young′ish
young′ster
Youngs′town
your·self′
  pl your·selves′

youth′ful
youth′ful·ly
yowl
yo′-yo
yu′an
  pl yu′an

yuc′ca
Yu·go·slav′
Yu·go·sla′vi·a
Yu·go·sla′vi·an
Yu′kon
yule′tide

Z

zaire
Zam′bia
Zam′bi·an
za′ni·ly
za′ni·ness
zan′y
zar·zue′la
z′-ax·is
zeal
zeal′ot
zeal′ous
ze′bra
zeit′geist
Zen
ze′nith
ze′o·lite
zeph′yr
zep′pe·lin
ze′ro
  pl ze′ros *also* ze′roes

zest′ful
zest′ful·ly
zig′zag
  zig′zagged
  zig′zag·ging
zil′lion
zinc
  zinced
  or zincked
zinc′ing
  or zinck′ing
zin′nia
Zi′on·ism

zymurgy

zip
  zipped
  zip'ping
zip'per
zip'py
zirc'aloy
zir'con
zith'er
zlo'ty
  pl zlo'tys *also* zlo'ty
zo'di·ac
zo·di'a·cal
zom'bi
  or zom'bie

zon'al
zon'al·ly
zoo
zoo-ecol'o·gy
zoo·ge·og'ra·pher
zoo·ge·o·graph'ic
  or zoo·ge·o·graph'i·
  cal
zoo·ge·o·graph'i·
  cal·ly
zoo·ge·og'ra·phy
zoo·graph'ic
zo·og'ra·phy
zo·o·log'i·cal

zo·o·log'i·cal·ly
zo·ol'o·gist
zo·ol'o·gy
zoy'sia
zuc·chet'to
zuc·chi'ni
  pl zuc·chi'ni *or*
  zuc·chi'nis
zwie'back
zy'gote
zy'mase
zy·mol'o·gy
zy·mot'ic
zy'mur·gy

ABBREVIATIONS

Most of the abbreviations included in this list have been normalized to one form. Variation in the use of periods, in typeface, and in capitalization is frequent and widespread (as *mph*, mph, MPH, m.p.h., Mph).

a acre, alto, answer
A ace, argon, assists
AA Alcoholics Anonymous, associate in arts
AAA American Automobile Association
A and M agricultural and mechanical
ab about
AB able-bodied seaman, at bats, bachelor of arts
ABA American Bar Association
abbr abbreviation
ABC American Broadcasting Company
abl ablative
abp archbishop
abr abridged, abridgment
abs absolute
abstr abstract
ac account
Ac actinium
AC alternating current, ante Christum (*Latin*, before Christ), ante

cibum (*Latin*, before meals)
acad academic, academy
accel accelerando
acct account
ack acknowledge, acknowledgment
act active, actual
A.C.T. Australian Capital Territory
actg acting
A.D. after date, anno Domini (*Latin*, in the year of our Lord)
addn addition
addnl additional
ad int ad interim
adj adjective, adjutant
ad loc ad locum (*Latin*, to [at] the place)
adm admiral
admin administration
adv adverb, advertisement
ad val ad valorem (*Latin*, according to value)
advg advertising

advt advertisement
AEF American Expeditionary Force
aeq aequales (*Latin*, equal)
aet, aetat aetatis (*Latin*, of age)
AF air force, audio frequency
AFB air force base
afft affidavit
AFL-CIO American Federation of Labor and Congress of Industrial Organizations
Afr Africa, African
Ag argentum (*Latin*, silver)
AG adjutant general, attorney general
agcy agency
agric, agr agricultural, agriculture
agt agent
AID Agency for International Development
AK Alaska
Al aluminum
AL Alabama
Ala Alabama
ALA American Library Association, Automobile Legal Association
alc alcohol
ald alderman

alg algebra
alk alkaline
alt alternate, altitude
Alta Alberta
alter alteration
a.m. ante meridiem (*Latin*, before noon)
Am America, American, americium
AM amplitude modulation, master of arts
AMA American Medical Association
amb ambassador
amdt amendment
AME African Methodist Episcopal
Amer America, American
amp ampere
amt amount
anal analogy, analysis, analytic
anat anatomy
anc ancient
and andante
ann annals, annual
anon anonymous
ans answer
ant antonym
anthrop anthropology
a/o account of
ap apothecaries'
AP additional premium. Associated Press
APO army post office

app apparatus, appendix
appl applied
appnt appointment
approx approximate,
  approximately
appt appoint,
  appointment
Apr April
apt apartment
aq aqueous
ar arrival, arrive
Ar Arabic, argon
AR Arkansas
ARC American Red
  Cross
arch architecture
archeol archeology
archit architecture
arith arithmetic
Ariz Arizona
Ark Arkansas
arr arranged, arrival,
  arrive
art article, artificial,
  artillery
ARV American Revised
  Version
As arsenic
AS Anglo-Saxon,
  antisubmarine
assn association
assoc associate,
  association
ASSR Autonomous
  Soviet Socialist Republic
asst assistant

astrol astrology
astron astronomer,
  astronomy
ASV American Standard
  Version
At astatine
Atl Atlantic
atm atmosphere,
  atmospheric
att attached, attention,
  attorney
attn attention
attrib attributive
atty attorney
Au aurum (*Latin*, gold)
aud audit, auditor
Aug August
AUS Army of the United
  States
Austral Australian
auth authentic, author,
  authorized
aux auxiliary
av avenue, average,
  avoirdupois
AV ad valorem (*Latin*,
  according to value);
  audiovisual, Authorized
  Version
avdp avoirdupois
ave avenue
avg average
AZ Arizona

b bass, book, born
B bachelor, bishop, boron

Ba barium
BA bachelor of arts
bal balance
bar barometer
Bart baronet
BB bases on balls, best of breed
BBA bachelor of business administration
BBB Better Business Bureau
BBC British Broadcasting Corporation
bbl barrel
B.C. before Christ, British Columbia
BCS bachelor of commercial science
bd board, bound
BD bachelor of divinity, bank draft, bills discounted, brought down
bdl bundle
Be beryllium
BE bill of exchange
BEF British Expeditionary Force
Belg Belgian, Belgium
bet between
bf boldface
BF brought forward
bg bag
bhd bulkhead
Bi bismuth

bib Bible, biblical
bibliog bibliographer, bibliography
BID bis in die (*Latin*, twice a day)
biochem biochemistry
biog biographical, biography
biol biologic, biological, biology
bk bank, book
Bk berkelium
bkg banking
bkgd background
bkt basket, bracket
bl bale, blue
B/L bill of lading
bldg building
bldr builder
blk black, block
blvd boulevard
BM basal metabolism, bowel movement
B/M bill of material
BMR basal metabolic rate
BO body odor, branch office, buyer's option
BOD biochemical oxygen demand
BOQ bachelor officers' quarters
bor borough
bot botanical, botany
bp bishop, boiling point
BP bills payable, blood

pressure, British
Pharmacopoeia
bpl birthplace
BPOE Benevolent and
Protective Order of Elks
br branch, brass, brown
Br British, bromine
BR bills receivable
brig brigade, brigadier
Brit Britain, British
bro brother
bros brothers
BS bachelor of science,
balance sheet, bill of sale
BSA Boy Scouts of
America
BSc bachelor of science
bskt basket
Bt baronet
Btu British thermal unit
bu bushel
bull bulletin
bur bureau
bus business
BV Blessed Virgin
BWI British West Indies
bx box
BX base exchange

c cape, carat, cent,
centimeter, century,
chapter, circa, copyright,
cup
C carbon, centigrade
ca circa
Ca calcium

CA California, chartered
accountant, chief
accountant,
chronological age
CAF cost and freight
cal calendar, caliber,
calorie
calc calculating
Calif, Cal California
Can Canada, Canadian
Canad Canada, Canadian
canc canceled
C and F cost and freight
cap capacity, capital,
capitalize, capitalized
caps capitals, capsule
capt captain
card cardinal
CARE Co-operative for
American Remittances
to Everywhere
cat catalog
CATV community
antenna television
CBC Canadian
Broadcasting
Corporation
CBD cash before delivery
CBS Columbia
Broadcasting System
CBW chemical and
biological warfare
cc cubic centimeter
CC carbon copy
CCC Civilian
Conservation Corps

CCTV closed-circuit television

ccw counterclockwise

cd cord

Cd cadmium

cdr commander

Ce cerium

CE chemical engineer, civil engineer

cen central

cent centigrade, central, century

cert certificate, certification, certified, certify

cf confer (*Latin*, compare)

Cf californium

CF carried forward, cost and freight

CFI cost, freight, and insurance

cg, cgm centigram

CG coast guard, commanding general

ch chain, champion, chapter, church

CH clearinghouse, courthouse, customhouse

chap chapter

chem chemical, chemist, chemistry

chg change, charge

Chin Chinese

hm, chmn chairman

chron chronicle, chronological, chronology

Chron Chronicles

CI cost and insurance

cía compañía (*Spanish*, company)

cie compagnie (*French*, company)

CIF cost, insurance, and freight

C in C commander in chief

cir circle, circular

circ circular

cit citation, cited, citizen

civ civil, civilian

ck cask, check

cl class

Cl chlorine

CL carload

cld called, cleared

clk clerk

clo clothing

clr clear

cm centimeter

CM Congregation of the Mission

cml commerical

CN credit note

CNO chief of naval operations

CNS central nervous system

co company, county

c/o care of

Co cobalt
CO cash order, Colorado, commanding officer, conscientious objector
COD cash on delivery, collect on delivery
C of C Chamber of Commerce
C of S chief of staff
cog cognate
col colonel, colony, column
Col Colossians
coll college
collat collateral
colloq colloquial
Colo Colorado
com commander, commerce, commissioner, committee, common
comb combination, combining
comdg commanding
comdr commander
comdt commandant
coml commercial
comm commission, commonwealth
commo commodore
comp comparative, compiled, compiler, composition, compound
compar comparative
comr commissioner

con consul, contra (*Latin*, against)
conc concentrated
conf conference
Confed Confederate
cong congress
conj conjunction
Conn Connecticut
cons consonant
consol consolidated
const constant, constitution, constitutional
constr construction
cont containing, contents, continent, continental, continued, control
contd continued
contg containing
contr contract, contraction
contrib contribution, contributor
cor corner
Cor Corinthians
CORE Congress of Racial Equality
corp corporal, corporation
corr corrected, correction, correspondence, corresponding, corrugated
cos companies, counties
COS cash on shipment, chief of staff

cp   compare, coupon

CP   chemically pure, Communist party

CPA   certified public accountant

cpd   compound

CPFF   cost plus fixed fee

cpl   corporal

CPO   chief petty officer

CPS   cycles per second

CQ   charge of quarters

cr   credit, creditor, crown

Cr   chromium

cresc   crescendo

crit   critical, criticism

cryst   crystalline

cs   case, cases

c/s   cycles per second

Cs   cesium

CS   chief of staff, civil service

CSA   Confederate States of America

C S S R   Congregatio Sanctissimi Redemptoris (*Latin*, Congregation of the Most Holy Redeemer)

CST   Central standard time

ct   carat, cent, count, court

CT   Central time, Connecticut

ctge   cartage

ctn   carton

ctr   center

cu   cubic

Cu   cuprum (*Latin*, copper)

cum   cumulative

cur   currency, current

cw   clockwise

CWO   cash with order, chief warrant officer

cwt   hundredweight

cyc   cyclopedia

cycl   cyclopedia

cyl   cylinder

CYO   Catholic Youth Organization

CZ   Canal Zone

d   date, daughter, day, degree, died, penny

D   Democrat, Democratic, diameter, doctor, dollar, Dutch

DA   days after acceptance, deposit account, district attorney, don't answer

Dan   Daniel, Danish

DAR   Daughters of the American Revolution

dat   dative

dau   daughter

db   decibel

dbl   double

DC   da capo (*Italian*, from the beginning), decimal classification, direct current, District of

Columbia, doctor of chiropractic, double crochet

DD days after date, demand draft, dishonorable discharge, doctor of divinity

DDD direct distance dialing

DDS doctor of dental science, doctor of dental surgery

DE Delaware

dec deceased, decrease

Dec December

def definite, definition

deg degree

del delegate, delegation

Del Delaware

dely delivery

Dem Democrat, Democratic

Den Denmark

dep depart, departure, deposit, deputy

depr depreciation

dept department

deriv derivation, derivative

det detached, detachment, detail

Deut Deuteronomy

dev deviation

DEW distant early warning

DF damage free

DFC distinguished flying cross

DFM distinguished flying medal

DG Dei gratia (*Late Latin*, by the grace of God), director general

dia diameter

diag diagonal, diagram

dial dialect

diam diameter

dict dictionary

diff difference

dig digest

dil dilute

dim dimension, diminished, diminutive

dir director

disc discount

dist distance, district

distn distillation

distr distribute, distribution, distributor

div divided, dividend, division

dk dark, deck, dock

DLit doctor of letters, doctor of literature

DLitt doctor of letters, doctor of literature

DLO dead letter office

DMD doctor of dental medicine

dn down

do ditto

DOA dead on arrival

doc document
dol dollar
dom domestic, dominant, dominion
doz dozen
DP domestic prelate, double play
dpt department
dr debit, debtor, dram, drive, drum
Dr doctor
DR dead reckoning, dining room
DS dal segno (*Italian*, from the sign), days after sight
DSC distinguished service cross, doctor of surgical chiropody
DSM distinguished service medal
DSO distinguished service order
dsp decessit sine prole (*Latin*, died without issue)
DST daylight saving time
Du Dutch
dup, dupl duplicate
DV Deo volente (*Latin*, God willing), Douay Version
DVM doctor of veterinary medicine
dwt pennyweight
DX distance

dz dozen

E east, eastern, einsteinium, English, errors, excellent
ea each
E and OE errors and omissions excepted
EC east central
eccl ecclesiastic, ecclesiastical
Eccles Ecclesiastes
Ecclus Ecclesiasticus
ecol ecological, ecology
econ economics, economist, economy
Ecua Ecuador
ed edited, edition, editor, education
EDT Eastern daylight time
educ education, educational
EE electrical engineer
eff efficiency
e.g. exempli gratia (*Latin*, for example)
Eg Egypt, Egyptian
ehf extremely high frequency
el elevation
elec electric, electrical, electricity
elect electric, electrical, electricity
elem elementary

elev elevation
embryol embryology
emer emeritus
EMF electromotive force
emp emperor, empress
emu electromagnetic
  unit
enc enclosure
encl enclosure
ency encyclopedia
encyc encyclopedia
ENE east-northeast
eng engine, engineer,
  engineering
Eng England, English
engr engineer, engraved,
  engraving
enl enlarged, enlisted
ens ensign
entom entomology
entomol entomology
env envelope
EOM end of month
Eph Ephesians
eq equal, equation
equip equipment
equiv equivalent
ER earned runs
ERA earned run average
erron erroneous
Es einsteinium
ESE east-southeast
esp especially
ESP extrasensory
  perception
esq esquire

est established, estimate,
  estimated
EST Eastern standard
  time
Esth Esther
ET Eastern time
ETA estimated time of
  arrival
et al et alii (*Latin*, and
  others)
etc et cetera (*Latin*, and
  so forth)
ETD estimated time of
  departure
ethnol ethnology
et seq et sequens (*Latin*,
  and the following one), et
  sequentes *or* et
  sequentia (*Latin*, and
  those that follow)
ety etymology
Eu europium
Eur Europe, European
EV electron volt
EVA extravehicular
  activity
evap evaporate
ex example, express,
  extra
exc excellent, except
exch exchange,
  exchanged
ex div without dividend
exec executive, executor
Exod Exodus
exor executor

exp expense, export, exported, express

expt experiment

exptl experimental

ext extension, exterior, external, extra, extract

Ezek Ezekiel

f female, feminine, filly, focal length, folio, following, forte, frequency

F Fahrenheit, fair, false, fellow, fluorine, French, Friday, furlong

fac facsimile, faculty

FAdm fleet admiral

Fahr Fahrenheit

FAO Food and Agricultural Organization of the United Nations

FAS free alongside

fath fathom

FB freight bill

FBI Federal Bureau of Investigation

fcp foolscap

fcy fancy

FDIC Federal Deposit Insurance Corporation

Fe ferrum (*Latin*, iron)

Feb February

fec fecit (*Latin*, he [she] made it)

fed federal, federation

fedl federal

fedn federation

fem feminine

FEPC Fair Employment Practices Commission

ff folios, following

FICA Federal Insurance Contributions Act

FIFO first in, first out

fig figurative, figuratively, figure

fin finance, financial, finish

Finn Finnish

FIO free in and out

fisc fiscal

fl flourished, fluid

FL Florida

Fla Florida

Flem Flemish

fm fathom

Fm fermium

FM frequency modulation

fn footnote

fo folio

FOB free on board

FOC free of charge

fol folio

for foreign, forestry

FOR free on rail

FOS free on steamer

FOT free on truck

fp freezing point

FPC fish protein concentrate

fpm feet per minute
FPO fleet post office
fr father, friar, from
Fr francium, French,
    Friday
freq frequent, frequently
Fri Friday
front frontispiece
FRS Federal Reserve
    System
frt freight
frwy freeway
FSLIC Federal Savings
    and Loan Insurance
    Corporation
ft feet, foot, fort
fur furlong
furn furnished, furniture
fut future
fwd forward
FYI for your information

g acceleration of gravity,
    gauge, gram, gravity
G German, good
ga gauge
Ga gallium, Georgia
GA general agent,
    general assembly,
    general average,
    Georgia
Gael Gaelic
gal gallon
Gal Galatians
galv galvanized
gar garage

GAR Grand Army of the
    Republic
GAW guaranteed annual
    wage
gaz gazette, gazetteer
GB games behind, Great
    Britain
GCA ground-controlled
    approach
GCT Greenwich civil
    time
Gd gadolinium
gds goods
Ge germanium
gen general, genitive
Gen Genesis
genl general
geog geographic,
    geographical,
    geography
geol geologic, geological,
    geology
geom geometrical,
    geometry
ger gerund
Ger German, Germany
GHQ general
    headquarters
gi gill
GI general issue,
    government issue
Gk Greek
gloss glossary
gm gram
GM general manager
Gmc Germanic

Abbreviations 334

GNP gross national product
GOP Grand Old Party (Republican)
Goth Gothic
gov governor
govt government
gox gaseous oxygen
gp group
GP general practitioner
GPO general post office, Government Printing Office
GQ general quarters
gr grade, grain, gram, gravity, gross
grad graduate
gram grammar
gro gross
GSA Girl Scouts of America
gt great, gutta (*Latin*, drop)
GT gross ton
Gt Brit Great Britain
gtd guaranteed
GU Guam

h hard, hardness, hour, husband
H hits, hydrogen
ha hectare
Hab Habakkuk
Hag Haggai
handbk handbook
Hb hemoglobin

HBM Her Britannic Majesty, His Britannic Majesty
HC Holy Communion, House of Commons
HCL high cost of living
hd head
HD heavy-duty
hdbk handbook
hdkf handkerchief
hdqrs headquarters
hdwe, hdwre hardware
He helium
HE high explosive, His Eminence, His Excellency
Heb Hebrew, Hebrews
hf half, high frequency
Hf hafnium
Hg hydrargyrum (*Latin*, mercury)
HG High German
hgt height
HH Her Highness, His Highness, His Holiness
hhd hogshead
HI Hawaii
hist historian, historical, history
HJ hic jacet (*Latin*, here lies) — used in epitaphs
HL House of Lords
HM Her Majesty, His Majesty
HMS Her Majesty's Ship, His Majesty's Ship

Ho holmium
hon honor, honorable, honorary
hor horizontal
hort horticultural, horticulture
Hos Hosea
hosp hospital
hp horsepower
HP high pressure
HQ headquarters
hr hour
HR home run, House of Representatives
HRH Her Royal Highness, His Royal Highness
HS high school, house surgeon
hse house
ht height
HT high-tension
Hung Hungarian, Hungary
HV high voltage
hvy heavy
hwy highway
hyp, hypoth hypothesis, hypothetical

I iodine, island, isle
Ia Iowa
IA Iowa
ib, ibid ibidem (*Latin*, in the same place)
IBM intercontinental ballistic missile
ICBM intercontinental ballistic missile
ICJ International Court of Justice
id idem (*Latin*, the same)
ID Idaho, identification
i.e. id est (*Latin*, that is)
IE Indo-European
IF intermediate frequency
IGY International Geophysical Year
IHP indicated horsepower
IHS Iesus Hominum Salvator (*Latin*, Jesus, Savior of Men)
IL Illinois
ill illustrated, illustration
Ill Illinois
illus, illust illustrated, illustration
ILS instrument landing system
imit imitative
imp imperative, imperfect, imperial, import, imported
imperf imperfect
in inch
In indium
IN Indiana
inc incorporated, increase
incl including, inclusive

incog   incognito

incr   increase

ind   independent, index, industrial, industry

Ind   Indiana

indef   indefinite

indic   indicative

inf   infantry, infinitive, information

infl   influenced

INP   International News Photo

INRI   Iesus Nazarenus Rex Iudaeorum (*Latin*, Jesus of Nazareth, King of the Jews)

ins   inches, insurance

insol   insoluble

insp   inspector

inst   instant, institute, institution

instr   instructor, instrument

int   interest, interior, internal, international

interj   interjection

interrog   interrogative

intl   international

intrans   intransitive

introd   introduction

inv   invoice

IOOF   Independent Order of Odd Fellows

IP   innings pitched

IPA   International Phonetic Alphabet

i.q.   idem quod (*Latin*, the same as)

IQ   intelligence quotient

Ir   iridium, Irish

IRBM   intermediate range ballistic missile

Ire   Ireland

irreg   irregular

IRS   Internal Revenue Service

Isa   Isaiah

isl   island

Isr   Israel, Israeli

It   Italian

ital   italic, italicized

Ital   Italian

IUCD   intrauterine contraceptive device

IUD   intrauterine device

IV   intravenous

IWW   Industrial Workers of the World

J   jack, journal

Jam   Jamaica

Jan   January

Jap   Japan, Japanese

Jas   James

JCC   Junior Chamber of Commerce

JCS   joint chiefs of staff

jct   junction

Je   June

Jer   Jeremiah

jg   junior grade

Jn   John

jnt, jt joint
Josh Joshua
jour journal
JP jet propulsion, justice of the peace
jr junior
JRC Junior Red Cross
Judg Judges
Jul July
jun junior
Jun June
junc junction
juv juvenile
JV junior varsity

k karat, knit
K kalium (*Latin*, potassium), king
Kans Kansas
kc kilocycle
KC king's counsel, Knights of Columbus
kc/s kilocycles per second
KD kiln-dried, knocked down
kg kilogram
kgm kilogram
KKK Ku Klux Klan
km kilometer
kn knot
K of C Knights of Columbus
KS Kansas
kt karat, knight
kw kilowatt
Ky Kentucky

KY Kentucky

l left, length, line, liter
L lake, large, Latin, libra (*Latin*, pound)
La Louisiana
LA law agent, Los Angeles, Louisiana
Lab Labrador
lam laminated
Lam Lamentations
lang language
lat latitude
Lat Latin
lb pound
LC letter of credit, Library of Congress
LCD lowest common denominator
lcdr lieutenant commander
LCL less than carload
LCM least common multiple
ld load, lord
LD lethal dose
ldg landing, loading
lect lecture
leg legal, legislative, legislature
legis legislative, legislature
LEM lunar excursion model
Lev Leviticus
lf low frequency

lg   large
LG   Low German
lge   large
LGk   Late Greek
LH   left hand, lower half
li   link
Li   lithium
LI   Long Island
lib   liberal, librarian, library
lieut   lieutenant
LIFO   last in, first out
lin   lineal, linear
liq   liquid, liquor
lit   liter, literal, literally, literary, literature
LitD   doctor of letters, doctor of literature
lith, litho   lithography
LittD   doctor of letters, doctor of literature
Lk   Luke
ll   lines
LL   Late Latin
LLD   doctor of laws
LOB   left on bases
loc cit   loco citato (*Latin*, in the place cited)
log   logarithm
Lond   London
long   longitude
loq   loquitur (*Latin*, he [she] speaks)
LP   low pressure
LS   left side, letter signed, locus sigilli (*Latin*,

place of the seal)
lt   lieutenant, light
LT   long ton, low-tension
ltd   limited
LTL   less than truckload
ltr   letter
lub   lubricant, lubricating
lv   leave

m   male, mare, married, masculine, meridian, meridies (*Latin*, noon), meter, mile, mill, minute, month, moon
M   master, medium, mille (*Latin*, thousand), Monday, monsieur
MA   Massachusetts, master of arts, mental age
mach   machine, machinery, machinist
mag   magazine, magnetism, magneto, magnitude
maj   major
Mal   Malachi
man   manual
Man   Manitoba
manuf   manufacture, manufacturing
mar   maritime
Mar   March
masc   masculine
Mass   Massachusetts
math   mathematical,

mathematician, mathematics
MATS Military Air Transport Service
max maximum
mc megacycle
MC master of ceremonies, member of congress
Md Maryland
MD doctor of medicine, Maryland, months after date
mdnt midnight
mdse merchandise
Me Maine
ME Maine, mechanical engineer, Middle English, mining engineer
meas measure
mech mechanical, mechanics
med medical, medicine, medieval, medium
mem member, memoir, memorial
mer meridian
Messrs messieurs
met metropolitan
meteorol meteorology
MEV million electron volts
Mex Mexican, Mexico
mf medium frequency
MF Middle French

mfd manufactured
mfg manufacturing
mfr manufacture, manufacturer
mg milligram
Mg magnesium
MG machine gun, military government
MGk Middle Greek
mgr manager, monseigneur, monsignor
mgt management
mi mile, mill
MI Michigan, military intelligence
MIA missing in action
Mic Micah
Mich Michigan
mid middle
mil military
min minimum, mining, minister, minor, minute
mineral mineralogy
Minn Minnesota
misc miscellaneous
Miss Mississippi
mixt mixture
mk mark
Mk Mark
ML Middle Latin
MLD minimum lethal dose
Mlle mademoiselle
mm millimeter
MM Maryknoll Missioners, messieurs

Mme madame
Mn manganese
MN Minnesota
mo month
Mo Missouri, molybdenum
MO mail order, medical officer, Missouri, money order
mod moderate, modern
modif modification
mol molecular, molecule
mol wt molecular weight
MOM middle of month
Mon Monday
Mont Montana
mos months
mp melting point
MP member of parliament, metropolitan police, military police, military policeman
mpg miles per gallon
mph miles per hour
Mr mister
Mrs mistress
MS manuscript, master of science, Mississippi, motor ship
msg message
msgr monseigneur, monsignor
MSgt master sergeant
msl mean sea level
MSS manuscripts

MST Mountain standard time
mt mount, mountain
Mt Matthew
MT metric ton, Montana, Mountain time
mtg, mtge mortgage
mtl metal
mtn mountain
mun, munic municipal
mus museum, music
MV mean variation, motor vessel
mythol mythology

n net, neuter, new, noon, note, noun, number
N knight, nitrogen, normal, north, northern
Na natrium (*Latin*, sodium)
NA no account
NAACP National Association for the Advancement of Colored People
Nah Nahum
NAS naval air station
nat national, native, natural
natl national
NATO North Atlantic Treaty Organization
naut nautical

nav naval, navigable, navigation

Nb niobium

NB Nebraska, nota bene (*Latin*, note well)

N.B. New Brunswick

NBC National Broadcasting Company

NBS National Bureau of Standards

NC no charge, North Carolina

N.C. North Carolina

NCE New Catholic Edition

NCO noncommissioned officer

Nd neodymium

ND no date, North Dakota

N.D. North Dakota

N.Dak. North Dakota

Ne neon

NE New England, northeast

Neb Nebraska

NEB New English Bible

Nebr Nebraska

NED New English Dictionary

neg negative

Neh Nehemiah

NEI not elsewhere included, not elsewhere indicated

NES not elsewhere specified

Neth Netherlands

neurol neurology

neut neuter

Nev Nevada

NF no funds

Nfld Newfoundland

NG National Guard, no good

NGk New Greek

NH New Hampshire

N.H. New Hampshire

NHG New High German

NHI national health insurance (*Brit.*)

Ni nickel

NJ New Jersey

N.J. New Jersey

nk neck

NL New Latin, night letter, non liquet (*Latin*, it is not clear)

NLT night letter

NM nautical mile, New Mexico, night message, no mark, not marked

N.M. New Mexico

N.Mex. New Mexico

NNE north-northeast

NNW north-northwest

no north, northern, nose, number

No nobelium

NOIBN not otherwise

indexed by name
nol pros nolle prosequi
(*Latin*, to be unwilling
to prosecute)
nom nominative
non seq non sequitur
Norw Norway,
Norwegian
NOS not otherwise
specified
Nov November
Np neptunium
NP no protest, notary
public
NPN nonprotein nitrogen
nr near, number
NS not specified
N.S. Nova Scotia
NSF not sufficient funds
N.S.W. New South Wales
NT New Testament
N.T. Northern Territory
NTP normal temperature
and pressure
nt wt net weight
NU name unknown
Num Numbers
numis numismatic,
numismatics
NV Nevada
NW northwest
NWT Northwest
Territories
NY New York
N.Y. New York
NYC New York City

N.Z. New Zealand

o ocean, ohm
O oxygen
o/a on account
OAS Organization of
American States
ob obiit (*Latin*, he [she]
died)
Obad Obadiah
obj object, objective
obl oblique, oblong
obs obsolete
obv obverse
OC overcharge
occas occasionally
OCS officer candidate
school
oct octavo
Oct October
o/d on demand
OD officer of the day,
olive drab, overdraft,
overdrawn
OE Old English
OED Oxford English
Dictionary
OES Order of the Eastern
Star
OF Old French
ofc office
off office, officer, official
OFM Order of Friars
Minor
O.F.S. Orange Free State
OG original gum

OH Ohio
OK Oklahoma
Okla Oklahoma
ON Old Norse
Ont Ontario
op opus, out of print
OP Order of Preachers
op cit opere citato (*Latin*, in the work cited)
opp opposite
opt optical, optician, optional
OR Oregon, owner's risk
orch orchestra
ord order, ordnance
Oreg, Ore Oregon
org organization, organized
orig original, originally
ornith ornithology
o/s out of stock
Os osmium
OS ordinary seaman
OS and D over, short, and damaged
OSB Order of St. Benedict
OT Old Testament, overtime
OTS officers' training school
oz ounce

p page, participle, past, penny, per, pint, purl

P pawn, phosphorus, pressure
pa per annum
Pa Pennsylvania
PA passenger agent, Pennsylvania, power of attorney, press agent, private account, public address, purchasing agent
Pac Pacific
paleon paleontology
pam pamphlet
Pan Panama
P and L profit and loss
par paragraph, parallel, parish
parl parliament, parliamentary
part participial, participle, particular
pass passenger, passive
pat patent
path, pathol pathology
payt payment
Pb plumbum (*Latin*, lead)
pc percent, percentage, piece, postcard, post cibum (*Latin*, after meals)
PC petty cash, privy council, privy councillor
pct percent
pd paid, pond
Pd palladium

PD per diem, potential difference

PE professional engineer, Protestant Episcopal

ped pedal

P.E.I. Prince Edward Island

pen peninsula

penin peninsula

Penn Pennsylvania

Penna Pennsylvania

per period

Per Persian

perf perfect, perforated

perh perhaps

perm permanent

perp perpendicular

pers person, personal

Pers Persia, Persian

pert pertaining

Pet Peter

pf preferred

pfc private first class

pfd preferred

pg page

PG postgraduate

pharm pharmaceutical, pharmacist, pharmacy

PhD doctor of philosophy

Phil Philippians

Phila Philadelphia

Philem Philemon

philos philosopher, philosophy

phon phonetics

photog photographic, photography

phr phrase

phys physical, physician, physics

physiol physiologist, physiology

P.I. Philippine Islands

pinx pinxit (*Latin*, he [she] painted it)

pk park, peak, peck

pkg package

pkt packet

pkwy parkway

pl place, plate, plural

pm premium

p.m. post meridiem (*Latin*, afternoon)

Pm promethium

PM paymaster, police magistrate, postmaster, postmortem, prime minister, provost marshal

pmk postmark

pmt payment

PN promissory note

pnxt pinxit (*Latin*, he [she] painted it)

Po polonium

PO petty officer, postal order, post office, putouts

POC port of call

POD pay on delivery

POE port of embarkation, port of entry

Pol Poland, Polish
polit political, politician
polytech polytechnic
pop popular, population
POR pay on return
Port Portugal,
  Portuguese
pos position, positive
poss possessive
POW prisoner of war
pp pages, past participle,
  pianissimo
PP parcel post, post
  position
PPC pour prendre congé
  (*French*, to take leave)
ppd postpaid, prepaid
PPS post postscriptum
  (*Latin*, an additional
  postscript)
ppt precipitate
pptn precipitation
PQ Province of Quebec
pr pair, price
Pr praseodymium
PR payroll, public
  relations, Puerto Rico
prec preceding
pred predicate
pref preface, preference,
  preferred, prefix
prelim preliminary
prem premium
prep preparatory,
  preposition
pres present, president

prev previous
prf proof
prim primary,
  primitive
prin principal
PRN pro re nata (*Latin*,
  for an occasion that has
  arisen) as occasion
  arises
PRO public relations
  officer
prob probable, probably,
  problem
proc proceedings
prod production
prof professor
pron pronoun,
  pronounced,
  pronunciation
prop propeller, property,
  proprietor, proposition
pros prosody
Prot Protestant
prov province, provincial,
  provisional
Prov Proverbs
prp present participle
Ps Psalms
PS postscriptum (*Latin*,
  postscript), public school
pseud pseudonym
psi pounds per square
  inch
PST Pacific standard
  time
psych psychology

psychol psychologist, psychology

pt part, payment, pint, point, port

Pt platinum

PT Pacific time, physical therapy, physical training

PTA Parent-Teacher Association

pte private (*Brit.*)

ptg printing

PTO please turn over

PTV public television

Pu plutonium

pub public, publication, published, publisher, publishing

publ publication, published

pvt private

PW prisoner of war

PX post exchange

q quart, quarto, query, question, quire

Q queen

QC Queen's Counsel

qd quaque die (*Latin*, daily)

qda quantity discount agreement

QED quod erat demonstrandum (*Latin*, which was to be demonstrated)

QEF quod erat faciendum (*Latin*, which was to be done)

QEI quod erat inveniendum (*Latin*, which was to be found out)

QID quater in die (*Latin*, four times a day)

Q'land Queensland

Qld Queensland

QM quartermaster

QMC quartermaster corps

QMG quartermaster general

qq v quae vide (*Latin*, which [pl] see)

qr quarter, quire

qt quart

q.t. quiet

qto quarto

qty quantity

quad quadrant

Que Quebec

quot quotation

q.v. quod vide (*Latin*, which see)

qy query

r rare, right, river, roentgen

R rabbi, radius, Republican, resistance, rook, runs

Ra radium

RA regular army, royal academy
RAAF Royal Australian Air Force
rad radical, radio, radius
RAdm rear admiral
RAF Royal Air Force
R and D research and development
Rb rubidium
RBC red blood cells, red blood count
RBI runs batted in
RC Red Cross, Roman Catholic
RCAF Royal Canadian Air Force
RCMP Royal Canadian Mounted Police
rd road, rod, round
RD rural delivery
re reference, regarding
Re rhenium
REA Railway Express Agency
rec receipt, record, recording, recreation
recd received
recip reciprocal, reciprocity
rec sec recording secretary
rect rectangle, rectangular, receipt, rectified
ref referee, reference, referred, reformed, refunding
refl reflex, reflexive
refr refraction
refrig refrigerating, refrigeration
reg region, register, registered, regular, regulation
regt regiment
rel relating, relative
relig religion
rep report, reporter, representative, republic
Rep Republican
repl replace, replacement
rept report
req require, required, requisition
res research, reserve, residence, resolution
resp respective, respectively
retd retained, retired, returned
rev revenue, reverend, reverse, review, reviewed, revised, revision, revolution
Rev Revelation
RF radio frequency
RFD rural free delivery
Rh rhodium
RH right hand
RI Rhode Island
R.I. Rhode Island

RIP requiescat in pace (*Latin*, may he [she] rest in peace)

riv river

rm ream, room

RMA Royal Military Academy (Sandhurst)

rms root mean square

Rn radon

RN registered nurse, Royal Navy

rnd round

RNZAF Royal New Zealand Air Force

ROG receipt of goods

Rom Roman, Romance, Romania, Romanian, Romans

ROTC Reserve Officers' Training Corps

rpm revolutions per minute

RPO railway post office

rps revolutions per second

rpt repeat, report

rr rear

RR railroad, rural route

RS recording secretary, revised statutes, right side, Royal Society

RSV Revised Standard Version

RSVP répondez s'il vous plaît (*French*, please reply)

RSWC right side up with care

rt right, route

RT radiotelephone

rte route

Ru ruthenium

Rum Rumania, Rumanian

Russ Russia, Russian

RW radiological warfare, right worshipful, right worthy

rwy railway

ry railway

s second, section, semi, series, shilling, singular, son, soprano

S sacrifice, saint, Saturday, senate, small, south, southern, sulfur, Sunday

Sa Saturday

SA Salvation Army, sex appeal, sine anno (*Latin*, without date), South Africa, subject to approval

S.A. South Australia

SAC Strategic Air Command

Sam Samuel

sanit sanitary, sanitation

SAR Sons of the American Revolution

Sask Saskatchewan

sat   saturate, saturated, saturation
Sat   Saturday
S. Aust   South Australia
sb   substantive
SB   bachelor of science, stolen base
sc   scale, scene, science, scilicet (*Latin*, that is to say), small capitals
Sc   scandium, Scots
SC   South Carolina
S.C.   South Carolina
Scand   Scandinavia, Scandinavian
ScD   doctor of science
ScGael   Scottish Gaelic
sch   school
sci   science, scientific
scil   scilicet (*Latin*, that is to say)
Scot   Scotland, Scottish
script   scripture
sctd   scattered
sculp, sculpt   sculpsit (*Latin*, he [she] carved it), sculptor, sculpture
SD   sea-damaged, sine die, South Dakota, special delivery
S.D.   South Dakota
S. Dak   South Dakota
Se   selenium
SE   southeast
SEATO   Southeast Asia Treaty Organization

sec   second, secondary, secretary, section, secundum (*Latin*, according to)
sect   section
secy   secretary
sel   select, selected, selection
sem   seminary
sen   senate, senator, senior
sep   separate
sepn   separation
Sept, Sep   September
seq   sequens (*Latin*, the following [singular])
seqq   sequentia (*Latin*, the following [plural])
ser   serial, series
serg   sergeant
sergt   sergeant
serv   service
sf   science fiction
SF   sacrifice fly
sfc   sergeant first class
sg   senior grade, singular, specific gravity
SG   solicitor general, surgeon general
sgd   signed
sgt   sergeant
sh   share, show
Shak   Shakespeare
shpt, shipt   shipment
shr   share
sht   sheet

shtg shortage
Si silicon
S.I. Sandwich Islands, Staten Island (N.Y.)
sig signal, signature
sigill sigillum (*Latin*, seal)
sing singular
SJ Society of Jesus
Skt Sanskrit
SL salvage loss
s.l.a.n. sine loco, anno, vel nomine (*Latin*, without place, year, or name)
sld sailed, sealed
sm small
Sm samarium
SM master of science, Society of Mary
Sn stannum (*Late Latin*, tin)
so south, southern
SO seller's option, strikeouts
soc social, society
sociol sociology
sol solicitor, soluble, solution
Sol Solomon
soln solution
sop soprano
SOP standard operating procedure
soph sophomore
sp special, species, specimen, spelling, spirit

Sp Spain, Spanish
SP shore patrol, sine prole (*Latin*, without issue)
Span Spanish
SPCA Society for the Prevention of Cruelty to Animals
SPCC Society for the Prevention of Cruelty to Children
spec special, specialist
specif specific, specifically
sp. gr. specific gravity
spp species (plural)
sq squadron, square
sr senior
Sr sister, strontium
SR shipping receipt
SRO standing room only
SS saints, steamship, Sunday school, sworn statement
SSE south-southeast
SSgt staff sergeant
ssp subspecies
SSR Soviet Socialist Republic
SSS Selective Service System
SSW south-southwest
st saint, stanza, start, state, stitch, stone, straight, strait, street
ST short ton

sta   station
stat   statute
stbd   starboard
std   standard
STOL   short takeoff and
   landing
STD   doctor of sacred
   theology
stg, ster   sterling
stk   stock
STP   standard
   temperature and
   pressure
str   stretch
stud   student
subj   subject, subjunctive
suff   sufficient, suffix
suffr   suffragan
Sun   Sunday
sup   superior,
   supplement,
   supplementary, supply,
   supra (*Latin*, above)
superl   superlative
supp, suppl   supplement,
   supplementary
supt   superintendent
surg   surgeon, surgery,
   surgical
surv   survey, surveying,
   surveyor
SV   sub verbo *or* sub voce
   (*Latin*, under the word)
SW   shipper's weight,
   shortwave, southwest
S.W.A.   South-West Africa

Switz   Switzerland
syll   syllable
sym   symbol, symmetrical
syn   synonym,
   synonymous, synonymy
syst   system

t   teaspoon, temperature,
   tenor, ton, troy
T   tablespoon, Thursday,
   true, Tuesday
Ta   tantalum
tan   tangent
Tas, Tasm   Tasmania
taxon   taxonomy
Tb   terbium
TB   trial balance,
   tuberculosis
tbs, tbsp   tablespoon
TC   teachers college
TD   touchdown
Te   tellurium
tech   technical,
   technically, technician,
   technological,
   technology
tel   telegram, telegraph,
   telephone
teleg   telegraphy
temp   temperature,
   temporary, tempore
   (*Latin*, in the time of)
ten   tenor
Tenn   Tennessee
ter   terrace, territory
terr   territory

Tex   Texas
Th   thorium, Thursday
ThD   doctor of theology
theat   theatrical
theol   theological,
   theology
therm   thermometer
Thess   Thessalonians
thou   thousand
Thu   Thursday
Thur   Thursday
Thurs   Thursday
Ti   titanium
TID   ter in die (*Latin*,
   three times a day)
Tim   Timothy
tinct   tincture
Tit   Titus
tk   tank, truck
TKO   technical knockout
tkt   ticket
Tl   thallium
TL   total loss
TLC   tender loving care
Tm   thulium
TM   trademark
TMO   telegraph money
   order
tn   ton, town
TN   Tennessee
tnpk   turnpike
TO   telegraph office, turn
   over
topog   topography
tot   total
tp   title page, township

tpk   turnpike
tr   translated, translation,
   translator, transpose
trans   transaction,
   transitive, translated,
   translation, translator,
   transportation,
   transverse
transl   translated,
   translation
transp   transportation
treas   treasurer, treasury
trib   tributary
trig   trigonometry
TSgt   technical sergeant
tsp   teaspoon
Tu   Tuesday
Tue   Tuesday
Tues   Tuesday
Turk   Turkey, Turkish
TV   television
TVA   Tennessee Valley
   Authority
TX   Texas

u   unit
U   university,
   uranium
UAR   United Arab
   Republic
UFO   unidentified flying
   object
UH   upper half
uhf   ultrahigh frequency
UK   United Kingdom
ult   ultimate

UMT Universal Military Training
UN United Nations
UNESCO United Nations Educational, Scientific, and Cultural Organization
univ universal, university
UNRWA United Nations Relief and Works Agency
UPI United Press International
u.s. ubi supra (*Latin*, where above [mentioned], ut supra (*Latin*, as above)
US United States
USA United States Army, United States of America
USAF United States Air Force
USCG United States Coast Guard
USES United States Employment Service
USIA United States Information Agency
USM United States mail, United States Marines
USMA United States Military Academy
USMC United States Marine Corps
USN United States Navy
USNA United States Naval Academy

USNG United States National Guard
USNR United States Naval Reserve
USO United Service Organizations
USP United States Pharmacopeia
USS United States Ship
USSR Union of Soviet Socialist Republics
usu usual, usually
UT Utah
UV ultraviolet
UW underwriter

v vector, velocity, verb, verse, versus, vide (*Latin*, see), voice, volume, vowel
V vanadium, victory, volt, voltage
Va Virginia
VA Veterans Administration, vice admiral, Virginia
VAdm vice admiral
val value
var variable, variant, variation, variety, various
vb verb
VC vice-chancellor, vice-consul
VD venereal disease
veg vegetable

vel   vellum, velocity
ven   venerable
vert   vertical
vet   veterinarian, veterinary
VF   video frequency, visual field
VFD   volunteer fire department
VFW   Veterans of Foreign Wars
VG   very good, vicar-general
vhf   very high frequency
vi   verb intransitive, vide infra (*Latin*, see below)
VI   Virgin Islands
vic   vicinity
Vic   Victoria
vil   village
VIP   very important person
vis   visibility, visual
viz   videlicet (*Latin*, namely)
VL   Vulgar Latin
vlf   very low frequency
VNA   Visiting Nurse Association
VOA   Voice of America
voc   vocative
vocab   vocabulary
vol   volume, volunteer
vou   voucher
VP   vice-president
vs   verse, versus, vide

supra (*Latin*, see above)
vss   verses, versions
V/STOL   vertical short takeoff and landing
vt   verb transitive
Vt   Vermont
VT   Vermont
VTOL   vertical takeoff and landing
Vulg   Vulgate
vv   verses, vice versa

w   water, watt, week, weight, wide, width, wife, with
W   Wednesday, Welsh, west, western, wolfram
WA   Washington
war   warrant
Wash   Washington
W. Aust.   Western Australia
WB   water ballast, waybill
WBC   white blood cells, white blood count
WC   water closet, west central, without charge
WCTU   Women's Christian Temperance Union
Wed   Wednesday
wf   wrong font
wh   which
whf   wharf
WHO   World Health Organization

whol   wholesale
whs, whse   warehouse
whsle   wholesale
WI   Wisconsin
W.I.   West Indies
wid   widow, widower
Wis   Wisconsin
Wisc   Wisconsin
wk   week, work
WL   wavelength
wmk   watermark
WNW   west-northwest
w/o   without
WO   warrant officer
wpm   words per minute
wrnt   warrant
WSW   west-southwest
wt   weight
WV   West Virginia
W. Va.   West Virginia
WW   World War
WY   Wyoming
Wyo   Wyoming

X   experimental
xd   without dividend
x div   without dividend
Xe   xenon
x in, x int   without interest
XL   extra large
Xn   Christian

Xnty   Christianity

y   yard, year
Y   YMCA, yttrium
Yb   ytterbium
yd   yard
yld   yield
YMCA   Young Men's
    Christian Association
YMHA   Young Men's
    Hebrew Association
YO   yarn over, year-old
yr   year, your
yrbk   yearbook
Yt   yttrium
YT   Yukon Territory
YW   Young Women's
    Christian Association
YWCA   Young Women's
    Christian Association
YWHA   Young Women's
    Hebrew Association

z   zero
Zech   Zechariah
Zeph   Zephaniah
ZIP   Zone Improvement
    Plan
Zn   zinc
zool   zoological, zoology
Zr   zirconium

PROOFREADERS' MARKS

ꝺ *or* ꝺ *or* ꝺ (L *dele*) dele *or* delete; take out or expunge

ꝺ̮ take out a letter and close up

⁀ print as a ligature; thus, a⁀e (i.e., print æ); also, close up

v *or* ‿ less space

◌͡◌ close up entirely; no space

9 turn a reversed letter

∧ *or* > caret; insert at this point the marginal addition

or # space or more space

Eq # space evenly—used in the margin

⌊ *or* ⌜ *or* [carry farther to the left

⌋ *or* ⌝ *or*] carry farther to the right

⊓ elevate a letter or word

⊔ sink or depress a letter or word

□ em quad space; or indent one em

$\frac{1}{m}$, |—|, $\frac{1}{em}$ *or* |$\frac{1}{}$| *or* $\frac{em}{}$ one-em dash

|| straighten ends of lines

═ *or* /// *or* \\\ straighten a crooked line or lines

⊥ *or* ⌣ push down a space which prints as a mark

× *or* + *or* ⊗ broken or imperfect type—used in the margin

¶ make a new paragraph

○ (a ring drawn around an abbreviation, figure, etc.) spell out—used in the text

(sp) spell out—used in the margin

⊙ period

,/ *or* ,/ comma

:/ *or* ⊙ colon

;/ semicolon

ᵛ apostrophe or single closing quotation mark

ꝟ double closing
quotation mark

ꝥ inverted comma
or single opening
quotation mark

ꝧ double opening
quotation mark

=/ *or* -/ hyphen

[/] brackets

(/) parentheses

wf wrong font—used
when a character is of a
wrong size or style

ital put in italic type—
used in the margin with
_____ under text matter

rom put in roman type—
used in the margin with
_____ under text matter

bf put in boldface type—
used in the margin with
_____ under text matter

⌐⌐⌐⌐ transpose

tr transpose—used in the
margin

lc lowercase—used in the
margin with a slanting
line drawn through the
letter in the text

= *or* sc *or* sm caps put
in small capitals—the
double lines drawn un-
der the letters or word

≡ *or caps* put in capitals
—the triple lines drawn
under the letters or word

ld insert a lead between
lines

stet restore words crossed
out—usually written in
the margin (with dots un-
der the words to be kept)

∨ set as a superscript;
thus, ꝫ̌ (i. e., print ³)—
used in the margin

∧ set as a subscript;
thus, ꝫ̂ (i. e., print ₃)—
used in the margin

? is this correct as set?—
used in the margin

PUNCTUATION

.	period	–	dash
?	question mark	( )	parentheses
!	exclamation point	[ ]	brackets
,	comma	-	hyphen
;	semicolon	" "	quotation marks
:	colon	'	apostrophe

PERIOD

- A period is used to mark the end of a sentence that is not a question and that is not an exclamation.
- A period may be used following an abbreviation. – U.S.A.; 7 a.m., Dr. John H. Doe.
- Periods usually follow common contractions formed by leaving out letters within a word. – secy.; mfg.; recd.
- A period is necessary before a decimal and between dollars and cents in figures. – .72 pounds; 16.6 feet; $12.95.

QUESTION MARK

- A question mark is used at the end of an interrogative sentence. – Will you be here on Thursday?
- A question mark, usually enclosed in parentheses, is often used after a word, phrase, or date to indicate uncertainty of its accuracy. – John Doe, the new secretary(?); James Doe began as an office boy in 1952(?); Richard Doe (1883–1918?).
- A question mark is *not* used after a sentence expressed as a question out of courtesy. – Will you kindly fill out the enclosed form and return it to this office.

EXCLAMATION POINT
- An exclamation point follows an expression or statement that is an exclamation. – Oh no! Not that! Hurry! We need help!

COMMA
- Commas are used to set off words, phrases, and other sentence elements that are parenthetical or independent. Items of this sort are contrasting expressions, prefatory exclamations, the names of persons directly addressed, and expressions like *he said* in direct quotations. – More work, not words, is what is needed. The monthly figures, though not entirely to our liking, are better than we expected. "Don't go to Chicago," he said. George, you must improve the efficiency of your department.
- A comma usually sets off appositional or modifying words, phrases, or clauses that do not limit or restrict the main idea of a sentence. – George, his own brother, turned against him. John, whom we saw yesterday, is away today. We leave at 3 p.m., when the bell rings, and return at 3:30. The formation is of great interest to geologists, although most of us would hardly notice it.
- Commas set off transitional words and expressions when they are subordinate. Such words and expressions include *on the contrary, on the other hand, consequently, furthermore, moreover, nevertheless, therefore*. – The question, however, remains unanswered. On the contrary, under the rules a report is due monthly.
- A comma usually separates words, phrases, or clauses that occur in a series. – The estate is to be divided among his wife, his son, and his daughters. He opened the carton, removed the contents, and replaced the lid.
- A comma is often used before *and* or *or* introducing the final item in a closed series. – Scientific, technical, and

academic periodicals are important sources. He ordered blue, yellow, green, and white cards.

- A comma separates statements or clauses joined by a coordinating conjunction. – He seemed unhappy, but he said nothing. We know very little about him, and he has volunteered no information.
- Commas are used without conjunctions to separate brief and closely related statements or clauses. – He delivered his report, then left the meeting. He will always remember, the experience is now part of him. Don't bother, it doesn't make any difference.
- A comma is used to separate items in dates and addresses. – She was born on January 16, 1937. Send your order directly to the Superintendent of Documents, Washington, D.C.
- A comma is used to separate expressions such as *namely, that is, i.e., e.g., viz.* from what follows. – There are two ways to do the job: namely, a right way and a wrong way. He forbade future forays; that is, there were to be no more raids.
- A comma usually indicates the place of an omitted word or group of words. – The yellow forms are for reporting sick days; the green, for vacation days.
- A comma usually separates a direct quote from the rest of a sentence. – He asked abruptly, "Where is the report?"
- In numbers, a comma is used to separate thousand, millions, and other groups of three digits except in dates, page numbers, street numbers, and in numbers of four digits. – More than 2,643,762 were registered. We received 67,413 replies.
- A comma is used to set off titles, degrees, etc., from names. – John Doe, M.D. Richard Doe, president. Henry Doe, M.A., Ph.D.
- A comma is customary after the salutation in personal letters and after the complimentary close in all letters. – Dear Joe, . . .   Sincerely yours, ...

- A comma may always be used to avoid ambiguity. – To Ruth, James was always a good worker. In 1972, 25% of the districts reported higher sales.

SEMICOLON
- A semicolon usually separates independent statements or clauses joined together in one sentence without a conjunction. Such statements are usually closely related. – Make no terms; insist on full restitution.
- A semicolon separates two statements or clauses when the second begins with a sentence connector or conjunctive adverb such as *accordingly, also, consequently, furthermore, hence, however, indeed, moreover, nevertheless, otherwise, so, still, then, therefore, thus, yet.* – His performance has been satisfactory; nevertheless he will not be promoted. You have recommended him highly; therefore we will give him a trial.
- A semicolon is used to separate phrases or clauses that are themselves broken up by punctuation. – The country's resources include large oil deposits; lumber, waterpower, and good soils; and a literate, active work force.
- A semicolon sometimes is used to separate items in lists of names with addresses, titles, or figures where a comma alone would not clearly separate the items. – Genesis 3:1–19; 4:1–16. John Doe, treasurer; Richard Doe, secretary.

COLON
- A colon is used to link two parts of a sentence. The second part, after the colon, usually balances, supplements, defines, restates, sums up, enumerates, or lists the idea expressed in the first part. – The same space appears on the statement: the buyer must express approval. His ambition must be stirred: his interest must be aroused. The following items are required: a valid passport, innoculation certificate, and visa. Representatives of four depart-

ments presented reports: advertising, customer service, sales, and shipping.

- Colons function as dividers in set formulas such as those expressing ratios, time, volume and page references, Biblical citations, and place and publisher. – We need a 3:5 ratio. It will be at 3:30. Check *Encyclopedia Britannica* 18:643. See Luke 2:12. Springfield: G. & C. Merriam Co.
- A colon is used after a formal salutation in a letter. – Dear Mr. Doe: . . . .
- A colon is used to introduce an extended quotation. – We quote from your letter: "The statement received on 23 May did not include all items."
- A colon is used to separate a title from a subtitle when the subtitle is not otherwise set off. – Monthly Report: June 1973.

DASH

- A dash usually marks an abrupt change or suspension in the thought or structure of a sentence. – He was – how shall I put it – unhappy with the results.
- A dash often makes parenthetic or explanatory matter stand out clearly or emphatically. – Two of our men – John and George – made a good showing. He is willing to discuss all operations – those that are efficient and the trouble spots.
- A dash often occurs before a summarizing statement. – Oil, steel, and transportation – these are the basis of development.
- A dash is used to precede the name of an author or source at the end of a quotation. – "In the beginning God created the heavens and the earth" – Genesis 1:1.
- A long dash often indicates the omission of a word or of letters in a word. – Mr. M– –, our department head. I don't really give a d– –.
- A dash is used to indicate extent or duration. – See pages

124–127. The New York–Chicago flight was late. The period 1962–1971 was exceptional.

PARENTHESES

• Parentheses set off supplementary material that is not part of the main statement or not a structural element of the sentence. – Our long-range goals (I think you have set them out clearly) are sound. The chart (Fig. 3) indicates the problem.
• Parentheses are used to set off parenthetic material when the interruption is more marked than that usually indicated by commas. – Three older lines (now all out of production) will be eliminated. He is hoping (as we all are) that it will succeed.
• Parentheses are used to enclose numbers in a series. – We must look at (1) advertising, (2) publicity, and (3) our customer relations.
• Parentheses enclose an arabic number confirming a number written out. – Delivery will be made in thirty (30) days.

BRACKETS

• Brackets serve as parentheses within parentheses. – Local regulations (City Ordinance 46 [sec. 5]) prohibit it.
• Brackets set off a word or phrase that is extraneous or incidental, or explanatory. – The department head [Richard Doe] must approve all requests.

HYPHEN

• A hyphen marks the separation of a word at the end of a line. – He will be here on Tues- [*end of line*] day, the 14th.
• A hyphen suspends the second part of a hyphenated compound when used with another hyphenated compound. – There will be ten- and twenty-year notes.
• A hyphen is used to link two or more words used as a sin-

gle modifying term. — We do not accept larger-than-life
material. Newly-produced items must be tested.

QUOTATION MARKS

- Quotation marks are used before and after a direct quote.
  In long quotations, repeat the double quotation marks
  at the beginning of each paragraph as well as at the beginning and end of the entire passage quoted. — He re-
  peated his instructions, "We cannot accept exchanges."
- Single quotation marks enclose a quotation within a
  quote. — The witness said, "I heard him say, 'I'll be back,'
  before he left."
- Quotation marks are used to enclose the title of a short
  poem, an article, or a chapter or part of a book. The title
  of a book or play is usually set in italics, or underlined in
  typing. — See his remarks in "Tomorrow's Goals," in
  Thirty Years of Progress.
- Quotation marks are sometimes used to emphasize a particular word or to set off a technical or unfamiliar word.
  — We will test your "unshrinkable" fabric. An "em" is a
  unit of measure used by printers.

APOSTROPHE

- An apostrophe is used to indicate possession. — John's;
  everyone's.
- An apostrophe may be used to indicate omission of letters
  within a word. — sec'y.

CAPITALIZATION

- A capital letter is used for the first letter of the first word
  of a sentence.
- A capital letter is used to begin a direct quote within a
  sentence. — He said, "Now is the time."
- A capital letter begins proper names and many of their
  derivatives. — All employees there must learn Spanish. A

new branch in New York will open soon. The style shows
a distinct French influence.

- A capital begins titles placed before the name of the hold-
  er. It is not usually used when the title follows the name.
  – Treasurer John Doe; John Doe, treasurer, ...
- Capitals begin all the words in a title, except for articles,
  conjunctions, and short prepositions. – United States of
  America; *Webster's Dictionary of Proper Names.*
- Capital letters are used throughout in the abbreviated
  form of the names of many organizations. – UNESCO;
  IBM.

WEIGHTS AND MEASURES

Unit	Equivalents in Other Units of Same System	Metric Equivalent
length		
mile	5280 feet 320 rods 1760 yards	1.609 kilometers
rod	5.50 yards 16.5 feet	5.029 meters
yard	3 feet 36 inches	0.914 meters
foot	12 inches 0.333 yards	30.480 centimeters
inch	0.083 feet 0.027 yards	2.540 centimeters
area		
square mile	640 acres 102,400 square rods	2.590 square kilometers
acre	4840 square yards 43,560 square feet	0.405 hectares 4047 square meters
square rod	30.25 square yards 0.006 acres	25.293 square meters
square yard	1296 square inches 9 square feet	0.836 square meters
square foot	144 square inches 0.111 square yards	0.093 square meters
square inch	0.007 square feet 0.00077 square yards	6.451 square centimeters
volume		
cubic yard	27 cubic feet 46,656 cubic inches	0.765 cubic meters
cubic foot	1728 cubic inches 0.0370 cubic yards	0.028 cubic meters
cubic inch	0.00058 cubic feet 0.000021 cubic yards	16.387 cubic centimeters
weight *avoirdupois*		
ton		
short ton	20 short hundredweight 2000 pounds	0.907 metric tons
long ton	20 long hundredweight 2240 pounds	1.016 metric tons

hundredweight		
short hundredweight	100 pounds	45.359 kilograms
	0.05 short tons	
long hundredweight	112 pounds	50.802 kilograms
	0.05 long tons	
pound	16 ounces	0.453 kilograms
	7000 grains	
ounce	16 drams	28.349 grams
	437.5 grains	
dram	27.343 grains	1.771 grams
	0.0625 ounces	
grain	0.036 drams	0.0648 grams
	0.002285 ounces	

troy

pound	12 ounces	0.373 kilograms
	240 pennyweight	
	5760 grains	
ounce	20 pennyweight	31.103 grams
	480 grains	
pennyweight	24 grains	1.555 grams
	0.05 ounces	
grain	0.042 pennyweight	0.0648 grams
	0.002083 ounces	

apothecaries'

pound	12 ounces	0.373 kilograms
	5760 grains	
ounce	8 drams	31.103 grams
	480 grains	
dram	3 scruples	3.887 grams
	60 grains	
scruple	20 grains	1.295 grams
	0.333 drams	
grain	0.05 scruples	0.0648 grams
	0.002083 ounces	
	0.0166 drams	

capacity
(U.S. liquid measure)

gallon	4 quarts	3.785 liters
	(231 cubic inches)	
quart	2 pints	0.946 liters
	(57.75 cubic inches)	
pint	4 gills	0.473 liters
	(28.875 cubic inches)	
gill	4 fluidounces	118.291 milliliters
	(7.218 cubic inches)	
fluidounce	8 fluidrams	29.573 milliliters
	(1.804 cubic inches)	

| fluidram | 60 minims
(0.225 cubic inches) | 3.696 milliliters |
| minim | 1/60 fluidram
(0.003759 cubic inch) | 0.061610 milliliters |

(U.S. dry measure)

bushel	4 pecks (2150.42 cubic inches)	35.238 liters
peck	8 quarts (537.605 cubic inches)	8.809 liters
quart	2 pints (67.200 cubic inches)	1.101 liters
pint	1/2 quart (33.600 cubic inches)	0.550 liters

**British imperial
liquid and
dry measure**

bushel	4 pecks (2219.36 cubic inches)	0.036 cubic meters
peck	2 gallons (554.84 cubic inches)	0.009 cubic meters
gallon	4 quarts (277.420 cubic inches)	4.545 liters
quart	2 pints (69.355 cubic inches)	1.136 liters
pint	4 gills (34.678 cubic inches)	568.26 cubic centimeters
gill	5 fluidounces (8,669 cubic inches)	142.066 cubic centimeters
fluidounce	8 fluidrams (1,7339 cubic inches)	28.416 cubic centimeters
fluidram	60 minims (0.216734 cubic inches)	3.5516 cubic centimeters
minim	1/60 fluidram (0.003612 cubic inches)	0.059194 cubic centimeters

NOTES